United Nations Conference on Trade and Development

Beyond Conventional Wisdom in Development Policy

An Intellectual History of UNCTAD 1964–2004

UNITED NATIONS
New York and Geneva, 2004

Note

- The views expressed in this volume are those of the authors and do not necessarily reflect the views of the United Nations Secretariat. The designations employed and the presentation of the material do not imply the expression of any opinion whatsoever on the part of the United Nations Secretariat concerning the legal status of any country, territory, city or area, or of its authorities, or concerning the delimitation of its frontiers or boundaries, or regarding its economic system or degree of development.

- The symbols of United Nations documents are composed of capital letters combined with figures. Mention of such a symbol indicates a reference to a United Nations document.

- Material in this publication may be freely quoted or reprinted, but acknowledgement is requested, together with a reference to the document number. A copy of the publication containing the quotation or reprint should be sent to the UNCTAD secretariat at: Palais des Nations, 1211 Geneva 10, Switzerland.

UN2

TD/UNCTAD/EDM/2004/4 UNCTAD/EDM/2004/4

ISBN: 92-1-112650-9

Sales No. E.04.II.D.39

Contents

Acknowledgments

This fortieth anniversary publication project was conceived by the Secretary-General of UNCTAD, Rubens Ricupero, in the fall of 2002. Shigehisa Kasahara and Charles Gore served as the editors for the book, authored articles and, as from December 2002, coordinated the project under the general supervision of the Deputy Secretary-General of UNCTAD, Carlos Fortin. The main contributors were the authors of the articles, namely Mehmet Arda, Awni Behnam, Philippe Brusick, Lucian Cernat, Pierre Encontre, Peter Faust, Torbjörn Fredricksson, Murray Gibbs, Lev Komlev, Victor Konde, Alexei Mojarov, Victor Ognivtsev, Assad Omer, Yehia Soubra and Zbigniew Zimny.

Ricardo Bielschowsky provided suggestions concerning the concept and structure of the book. Kanako Ishiyama served as the assistant to the project coordinators, Stephanie West provided secretarial and bibliographic support, Michael Gordy edited the text, Lori Hakulinen provided editorial assistance and carried out the desktop publishing, and Diego Oyarzun-Reyes designed the cover.

The editors are grateful to the Library of the United Nations Office at Geneva and the Dag Hammarskjold Library for their collaboration in ensuring the availability of essential documents for the CD-Rom project.

Abbreviations

ACIS	Advance Cargo Information System
ACP	African, Caribbean and Pacific countries
ACSTD	Advisory Committee on Science and Technology for Development
AGOA	United States African Growth and Opportunity Act
ANZCERTA	Australia New Zealand Closer Economic Relations Trade Agreement
APQLI	Augmented Physical Quality of Life Index
ASEAN	Association of South-East Asian Nations
ASYCUDA	Automatic System for Customs Data
BITs	bilateral investment treaties
BSFF	Buffer Stock Financing Facility
BWIs	Bretton Woods Institutions
CARICOM	Caribbean Common Market
CBTF	Capacity Building Task Fore
CCFF	Compensatory and Contingency Financing Facility
CDP	Committee for Development Planning (later Committee for Development Policy)
CIFT	Committee on Invisibles and Financing-related to Trade
CFF	Compensatory Financing Facility
CFC	Common Fund for Commodities
CI	Consumer International
COMESA	Common Market for Eastern and Southern Africa
CSTD	Commission on Science and Technology for Development
CTT	Committee on Transfer of Technology
DAC	Development Assistance Committee
DRF	Debt Resolution Facility
DTTs	double taxation treaties
DTIS	Diagnostic Trade Integration Studies
EBA	European Union Everything But Arms
EEC	European Economic Community
ECOSOC	United Nations Economic and Social Council
ECOWAS	Economic Community of West African States
EDI	Economic Diversification Index
EFF	Extended Fund Facility
EFTA	European Free Trade Association
EMPRETEC	Empresas Technologicas
EU	European Union
EVI	Economic Vulnerability Index
FAO	Food and Agriculture Organization of the United Nations
FDI	foreign direct investment

G-10	Group of Ten
G-77	Group of 77
GATS	General Agreement on Trade and Services
GATT	General Agreement on Tariffs and Trade
GDP	gross domestic product
GSP	Generalized System of Preferences
GSTP	Global System of Trade Preferences among Developing Countries
GNP	Gross National Product
HIPC initiative	heavily indebted poor countries initiative
IF	Integrated Framework for Trade-Related Technical Assistance, including for Human and Institutional Capacity-Building, to Support Least Developed Countries in their Trade and Trade-Related Activities
ICAs	international commodity agreements
ICAO	International Civil Aviation Organisation
ICCICA	Interim Coordination Committee for International Commodity Agreements
ICOs	International Commodity Organizations
ICTSD	International Centre for Trade and Sustainable Development
IDA	International Development Association
IDCs	island developing countries
IIAs	international investment agreements
IISD	Institute for Sustainable Development
IGE	Intergovernmental Expert Group
IGGTT	Intergovernmental Group on Transfer of Technology
IGCSTD	Intergovernmental Committee on Science and Technology for Development
IISD	International Institute for Sustainable Development
IMCO	Inter-Governmental Maritime Consultative Organization
IMF	International Monetary Fund
IMO	International Maritime Organization
IPC	Integrated Programme for Commodities
IPR	intellectual property rights
IRTMs	investment-related trade measures
ISAR	International Standards of Accounting and Reporting
ITC	International Trade Centre
ITCB	International Textiles and Clothing Bureau
ITT	International Telephone and Telegram
ITO	International Trade Organization
ITU	International Telecommunications Union
LDCs	Least Developed Countries
LDCRs	*Least Developed Countries Reports*

LLDCs	Landlocked Developing Countries
M&As	mergers and acquisitions
MAI	Multilateral Agreement on Investment
MERCSUR	Southern Common Market
MFA	Multi-Fibre Arrangement
MFN	most-favoured-nation
MTA	Multilateral Trade Agreement
MTNs	multilateral trade negotiations
NAFTA	North American Free Trade Agreement
NIEO	New International Economic Order
NIEs	Newly Industrialising Economies
NGOs	non-governmental organizations
NPV	net present value
ODA	official development assistance
OECD	Organization for Economic Cooperation and Development
OEM	original equipment manufacturing
OHRLLS	Office of High Representative on the Least Developed, Land-locked and Small Island Developing Countries
OPEC	Organization of the Petroleum Exporting Countries
POA	programme of action
PRSP	Poverty Reduction Strategy Paper
R&D	research and development
RBPs	restrictive business practices
RTA	regional trade arrangement
S&D	special and differential treatment of developing countries
SAPs	structural adjustment programmes
SCI	Sustainable Commodity Initiative
SDR	special drawing right
SIDS	Small Island Developing States
SME	small and medium-sized enterprise
SOE	state-owned enterprise
SPS	sanitary and phytosanitary measures
SNPA	Substantial New Programme of Action
STIP	science and technology policy reviews
STABEX	The European Community compensatory finance scheme to stabilize export earnings of the African, Caribbean and Pacific (ACP) countries
TBT	Technical barriers to Trade
TDB	Trade and Development Board
TDR	*Trade and Development Report*
TNC	transnational corporation
TRIMs	trade-related investment measures
TRIPs	trade-related (aspects of) intellectual property rights

vii

UEMOA	Union Economique et Monétaire Ouest Africaine
UN	United Nations
UNCED	United Nations Conference on Environment and Development
UNCSTD	United Nations Commission on Science and Technology for Development
UNCTAD	United Nations Conference on Trade and Development
UNCTC	United Nations Centre on Transnational Corporations
UNDP	United Nations Development Programme
UNEP	United Nations Environmental Programme
UNESCO	United Nations Educational, Scientific and Cultural Organisation
UNGA	United Nations General Assembly
UNIDO	United Nations Industrial Organization
UN-NADAF	United Nations Agenda for the Development of Africa in the 1990s
UPU	Universal Postal Union
VER	voluntary exports restraint
WAIPA	World Association of Investment Promotion Agencies
WID	World Investment Directories
WIPO	World Intellectual Property Organization
WIR	*World Investment Report*
WGISL	Working Group on International Shipping Legislation
WTO	World Trade Organization

Preface

Nine Years at UNCTAD: A Personal Testimony

Rubens Ricupero
Secretary-General of UNCTAD

I took over as UNCTAD's fifth Secretary-General in mid-September 1995, at the invitation of then United Nations (UN) Secretary-General Boutros Boutros-Ghali and after the approval of the UN General Assembly. I came on the scene at a time when UNCTAD, after thirty years of existence, found itself in the throes of a severe crisis that many saw as terminal. For over a year and a half it had been left without a Secretary-General, a clear indication that some influential people were plotting its extinction.

The year 1995 and the immediate following years also coincided with the broader crisis of the UN, of which the acute financial difficulties mainly created by the arrears on payment of the United States' contributions were one of the most damaging aspects. Thus UNCTAD's problems were a crisis inside a much bigger crisis involving the mother-organization. From the start it was made clear to me by the UN Secretary-General and the Under Secretary-General for Management that UNCTAD should undergo a drastic process of reform and downsizing. Together with my colleagues, I decided to face the challenge head-on. Without waiting for UNCTAD IX (May–June 1996), which took place only several months later in Midrand, South Africa, we went ahead with a radical restructuring of the organization. We adopted a new structure by regrouping the previously existing nine Divisions into four, based on their subject matters, namely: Globalization and Development Strategies (GDS); Investment, Technology and Enterprise Development (DITE); International Trade in Goods, Services and Commodities (DITC); and Services Infrastructure for Development and Trade Efficiency (SITE). Besides these 4 Divisions, a Special Coordinator would ensure the cross-sectoral cooperation of all the Divisions in favour of the Least Developed Countries (LDCs).

The reform was generally well-regarded and even received complimentary remarks in the report emanating from the Group of Seven (G-7) Summit in Lyon (June 1996). Having dealt in that way with immediate administrative problems, we then turned our attention to the ideological allegation that UNCTAD had become redundant after the establishment of the World Trade Organization (WTO) in 1995. It was argued that over the years UNCTAD had been the primary forum shared between the North and the South, i.e. between rich and poor countries, in the context of hostility typical of the bipolar world of the Cold War. Just as the East-West confrontation had collapsed with the fall of the Berlin Wall and the disappearance of the Soviet Union, the North-South confrontation should give way to a unified economy of planetary dimension through the globalization of trade, investment and financial flows. If the North–South antagonism was to be thrown into History's "dustbin", this should also be the fate of the institutions that had promoted or encouraged it.

* * *

It thus became necessary to rethink the very basis of UNCTAD's work. In the first phase of its life, UNCTAD had embodied the unique spirit of the turbulent 1960s, which had given birth to it. During one of the most intense moments of the Cold War, the decade opened with the construction of the Berlin Wall and the Cuban missile crisis while closing with the Thêt offensive and the escalation of the Viet Nam War. Just as important as these events in international relations was the inner convulsion of societies which broke out in the explosive uprising of Parisian youth in May 1968 and then spread to many countries and regions assuming different forms, as in the anti-Viet Nam War protests of Nixon's United States. In the aftermath of the turbulence in 1968 there was a rise in political violence that would herald the "leaden years" of terrorist actions in affluent countries such as then West Germany and Italy. The frustrated guerrilla outbursts in Congo or Bolivia, and the tragic death of Guevara in the latter; the military coups in Algeria, Brazil and Greece; the bloody succession of Sukarno in Indonesia and the Cultural Revolution in China, although independent of each other, are among the numerous examples of that tumultuous era.

External and internal episodes of violence reflected a deeper fermentation, a genuine crisis of this acute disenchantment with formerly accepted beliefs, including some of the values of consumer society. The craving for liberation came to a head in the guise of the sexual revolution in a broad sense, which implied above everything else the struggle for women's equality, i.e. the most important and far-reaching twentieth century contribution to the transformation in human relations. It also equally helped set off the reaction to the repression of homosexuality. Furthermore, changes were brought about by rock music, not only as a new form of artistic expression but almost as the manifestation of a new life style in the mammoth festivals, of which Woodstock became the symbol. These changes were also expressed in the hippie communes, intermixed with self-destructive developments such as the widespread consumption of drugs.

Those years also saw a heightened awareness of the problem of underdevelopment, an awareness that found its noblest expression in Pope Paul VI's statement: "Development is the new name of peace". A typical creature of the 1960s, UNCTAD shared this spirit, particularly as it gave impetus to a project with which it became indissolubly linked: the dynamic movement towards the creation of a New International Economic Order, in capital letters as the phrase was written then. It was believed to be possible for different countries to sit together and negotiate new rules that would reshape financial and trade relations in a fairer, more balanced manner and would propose codes of behaviour for private actors such as transnational corporations (TNCs). There was a utopian element (an echo of Illuminism?) in this concept, which posited – in a rational process, formalized in diplomatic agreements – the possibility for negotiating what in essence would be an international redistribution of power and wealth. This voluntarism, a highly idealistic approach, had a tendency to overlook the fact that power, as conventionally perceived by realists, remained the core reality of international relations in both the political and the economic fields. In the wake of the 1968 movement, when the surrealist slogan, "Be realistic, demand the impossible" was being written on Paris' walls, people tended to forget that power is expressed not only in nuclear devices, intercontinental missiles, and sophisticated electronic spying and surveillance systems, but also in the rule-making capacity to determine (if not dictate) financial and trade rules.

True, at that time the "international correlation of forces," to take up an expression dear to Marxist-Leninists, did not seem so untoward. The Socialist camp showed signs of vigour and a capacity for expansion around different, often clearly antagonistic poles such as Moscow and Beijing, or in symbolic and inspirational terms like the revolutionary examples of Havana and Hanoi. Not a few in the West feared the communist alternative's power of attraction to the point that by the early 1970s' – the Nixon and Brezhnev era – it came to be felt that the Soviets had achieved and perhaps even exceeded strategic parity with the Americans. Today all this sounds unbelievable and absurd, but one has only to peruse the papers and magazines of that time to realize what a different perception of the strength and durability of "real socialism" existed then.

In turn, the number of independent developing countries – not many more than twenty at the end of World War II, nearly all of them in Latin America – soon increased substantially, owing to decolonization particularly in Africa, Asia and the Caribbean. An indication of this continuous expansion is the fact that the Group of

77 (G-77) of developing countries, originally established in 1964 to act as the collective bargaining body within UNCTAD, has grown to number 132 members today! The work of strong personalities including India's Nehru, Egypt's Nasser, Indonesia's Sukarno, and Yugoslavia's Tito, had created the illusion of a Third World as a capable political mediator between the First World of capitalist Western countries and the Second World of Socialists of Soviet or Chinese persuasion. It was even believed for a short time in the 1970s that the configuration of forces had tilted in favour of the developing countries as a result of the two successive oil shocks, the American defeat in Viet Nam, followed by Nixon's resignation after Watergate and the relative disengagement of United States forces from many international conflict areas as a result of Congressional pressure.

It was thus not surprising that people came to accept the feasibility of negotiating the New International Economic Order because the disastrous economic impacts of the increase in fuel prices forced the West into a defensive position, inspiring Giscard d'Estaing to launch the North-South Dialogue at the Conference on International Economic Cooperation (CIEC) in Paris from 1975 to 1977 and eliciting conciliatory gestures even from a realist thinker and operator like Kissinger as witnessed at UNCTAD IV (1976). It was in this climate that negotiations took place at UNCTAD and other UN forums about the Charter of the Rights and Duties of States, the code of conduct for TNCs and for the Transfer of Technology; and the Common Fund for Commodities. (All of these matters are discussed in detail in different topical papers contained in this volume.)

These negotiations were not carried out by individual countries but by groupings of countries acting together with a common platform and a main spokesperson: the G-77 of developing countries – later named "G-77 and China" after Beijing replaced Taipei at the UN; Group B, formed by industrialized capitalist countries; and Group D, formed by socialist countries. A negotiating doctrine much in favour then, particularly among developing countries, held that at first each group should maximize its demand even at the risk of exacerbating contrasts and leading to greater tensions. It was thought that the face-off would thereafter lead to a stage of conciliatory negotiations where the identification of a common denominator and a possible compromise between confronting demands would be sorted out. In practice this "bloc system" proved to be excessively rigid and thus incapable of capturing the individual nuances within each group. The socialist countries felt that they were exempted from the G-77's claims as these demands were addressed, in their view, to the capitalists. Consequently the G-77, whose propositions enjoyed frequent support from Group D, became a sort of steamroller. Yet this parliamentary majority at UN and UNCTAD deliberations did not reflect the true distribution of power in the real world.

For this very reason the developed countries tended to regard the decisions made through this process as irrelevant to themselves (in contrast to the GATT negotiations) and possessing at best a declaratory value.

The developed countries tended to regard the UNCTAD forums as deliberative meetings where countries could exchange viewpoints and engage in general discussions. In contrast, the developing countries hoped that these forums would have some quasi-legislative traits and make at least certain decisions – however they might be called – that would commit the developed countries to a given course of action. Consequently the developed countries tend to shun any sort of "implementation" procedure (particularly in the Trade and Development Board (TDBs) for monitoring the follow-up actions of the decisions adopted at the Conferences), since they were adopted against their will or on a voluntary basis. The point is that because of the ambiguity of the legal status of the decisions, the implementation procedure has also been far from rigorous.

This situation was irreparably aggravated when to the disappearance of the Socialist alternative was added the dissolution of the relative unity that lent a certain consistency to the G-77's activity. One by one, the protagonists that stood out most prominently in this bloc began to break up or drastically change their position. The Latin Americans, weakened by the debt crisis of the 1980s, had to submit themselves to the International Monetary Fund (IMF) and World Bank's structural adjustment programmes, abandoning the economic theories that had inspired their former positions and stances, and often recreated themselves as ardent newly-converts to the triumphant neoliberalism. The clearest example was Mexico, the main promoter of the Charter of the Rights and Duties of States which, after entering the economic space created by the North America Free Trade Agreement (NAFTA), quit the G-77 to join the Organization for Economic Cooperation and Development (OECD), the developed countries' organization. Other Latin American nations – Argentina, Brazil and Chile – did not lag much behind as regards their conversion and subsequent adherence to the mainstream positions in economic philosophy.

Some other principal G-77 members went through much more radical transformations in their political and economic structures as well as in their position towards various international issues. Yugoslavia ceased to exist. For decades Algeria had struggled with an unending internal crisis. Egypt has become the second largest beneficiary of American aid after Israel. Indonesia stood out as a successful Asian "tiger" apprentice before the setback of the 1997 Asian crisis. The Africans have become victims of a disastrous combination of extreme political instability, often degenerating into civil wars, and unrelenting economic decline.

Much of what had happened to developing countries resulted from actions and decisions for which they were mainly responsible. They include: macroeconomic policy mistakes, such as baleful indulgence toward chronic inflation and budget deficits; prestige-driven projects that made no economic sense; widespread waste and corruption; incapacity to manage the legal and institutional framework required for the sound operation of a market economy; and ideological delusions about the role of the State as producer. It was thus inevitable that, when an acute crisis struck, some Governments would be forced to review their earlier position and correct them, often in a radical way.

Meanwhile it has been forgotten that the blame cannot be laid solely on the developing countries. UNCTAD had been pointing out since Raúl Prebisch's tenure that a considerable share of responsibility has to be ascribed to the imbalances and injustices of the world economy which perpetuated and intensified the inequality between rich and poor countries. While a new international economic order, perhaps, more appropriately "globalization order", did indeed begin to take shape in the late 1980s, it was not the fairest, most balanced order that had been envisaged by the reformers. In fact, the modality of the new order that emerged has shown the tendency to exacerbate the imbalances and inequalities of the old order, both among countries and within them, including in the most affluent ones.

The assertion of the globalized economy coincided with the rise of the administrations of Thatcher in England and Reagan in the United States, unleashing a hostile attack on numerous previous proposals for redressing past injustices and reforming the international economy so as to make it more friendly to genuine, equitable human development. That was the case when the Reagan administration, at the Cancun Summit in 1981, definitively buried the so-called "Global Negotiations" in the economic sphere encompassing finance, investment and trade under the auspices of the UN. Subsequently the field was laid open to the irrefutable rule of organizations more directly controlled by the developed countries: the IMF and the World Bank in matters related to money, finance and payments crisis in developing countries; and the GATT, superseded in 1995 by the WTO, in matters related to international trade. At the same time the developed countries' perspective has been actively promoted and coordinated by their own elite organizations, such as the OECD in matters related to development finance and the attempt to establish multilateral norms for international investment, as well as the G-7 or G-8 annual meetings in macroeconomic management and foreign exchange policy.

* * *

This was the prevailing environment when I arrived in Geneva in late 1995. For nearly four years, between 1987 and 1991, I had been the Permanent Representative of Brazil to the UN in Geneva. This period coincided with the first years of the GATT Uruguay Round, and intensive trade negotiations absorbed much of my time. During most of that period I had been the coordinator and spokesman for the so-called Informal Group of Developing Countries in the GATT, roughly the equivalent of the G-77 in the UN forums. I also occupied the functions of Chairman of the Committee on Trade and Development (1989), Chairman of the GATT Council of Representatives (1990) and Chairman of the Contracting Parties of GATT (1991). Thus when I was appointed to UNCTAD I became its first Secretary-General with a personal background in GATT and with practical experience in the reality of trade negotiations. Probably because of that particular background I tried to give emphasis to helping the developing countries adopt a more pro-active negotiating position in the WTO and lately to overcoming their supply-side constraints.

At the moment of my return to Geneva there were already clear symptoms of future complications on the path of the ascendant globalization, particularly the new cycle of financial and monetary crises set off by the Mexican problem in that year and the growing perception that savage globalization deepened disparities and asymmetries rather than narrowing the gap in growth and welfare levels.

Under these circumstances the UNCTAD secretariat had to show that on the basis of its impartial analyses the prevailing trends would require major corrections and reforms if one wanted to construct a better-balanced, stable economy. It would have been a mistake to go back to the old, worn-out approaches and failed visions, to the discredited methods of the past – negotiations by blocs in a rigid way. Even worse would have been to fail to recognize the reality of changes that had taken place in the member countries' attitudes, with an increasing diversification of concrete interests and positions as well as the emergence of new organizations such as the WTO. Instead of shutting itself up, UNCTAD had to reinvent itself so as to become an entity grounded on knowledge and at the service of developing countries – a laboratory of innovative ideas, ethically committed to the struggle for creating more equitable conditions for the least developed as well as the excluded or marginalized countries. Such an effort had to be conducted with the realistic awareness that we were starting from a minority position vis-à-vis the prevailing standard of a "single thinking". The task of reflection had to rest on an open attitude, ready to submit itself to its own and outside criticisms as well as to accept some of the undeniably positive contributions of the recent transformations occurring in the world at large.

Only by following this path could we hope to influence changes capable of positively contributing to international debates on development. It would be necessary to start with ideas whose force comes from their intrinsic qualities, particularly their capacity to provide effective solutions to contemporary problems – a key condition for building consensus among the positions of countries with different structures and at different stages of development. This would be achieved not only by enforcing and supplementing the traditional work among Governments but also by empowering the representatives of organized civil society: nongovernmental organizations (NGOs), churches, research centres and universities, social or cultural minorities, the press and other forms of communication. In other words, only through the mobilization of conscious sectors of civil society would it prove possible to effect changes in the current positions of Governments. In a sense, this method of work inverts the old assumption about the possibility of reforming the international economy first and foremost on the basis of placing all the initiative in the hands of Governments. In other words, change will come not from Governments attached to the prevailing and flawed development policies but from an alliance with different forces and movements that can act inside their own societies to change the perceptions and positions of Governments. It is a long-term strategy, but ultimately it is more realistic than the belief that developing countries' pressure would be able to force or persuade the developed countries to accept changes.

One possible objection to this approach, based on feasibility grounds, is the discrepancy between such ambitious objectives and the limited means available to achieve them. UNCTAD lacks the power to promote changes or to enhance international justice through the adoption of trade rules worldwide (as the WTO), or the power to finance development (as the World Bank), and to alleviate the debt burden, to prevent or to manage financial crisis (as the IMF). Those are the prerogatives of power, and they are usually expressed by continuous control of trade and financial decision-making installed in key organizations. This kind of objection should not surprise anyone. After all, as already mentioned, power is the core element in international relations. But not everything comes down to power. Just as in the sphere of social actions, relations among countries are characterized by a permanent dialectic tension between conflict and cooperation. Power always plays a decisive role whenever conflict of interests prevails over cooperation. This is particularly true in bilateral or plurilateral relations between countries, where there is no supranational authority.

The previous voluntarist notion – the one associated with the New International Economic Order – that the economic order could be changed through inter-Governmental deliberations not only underestimated the centrality of power but it discounted the possibility that the configuration of forces could very easily be tilted against the proponents of change. It also overlooked the fact that changes in the global economy depend not exclusively on Governments but on factors such as demographic trends and technological innovations (the computer and telecommunications revolution, for example). These factors can be subject to the influence of Government policies, but in turn can also influence Governments. The evolution in international economic relations therefore requires first, the sensitivity to recognize structural changes, and then time, patience, ideas and a sense of common interest to shape the reforms necessary to take advantage of the new conditions. In the last analysis, we should always return to the well-known passage by Keynes:

> "The ideas of economists and political philosophers, both when they are right and when they are wrong, are more powerful than is commonly understood. Indeed, the world is ruled by little else. Practical men, who believe themselves to be quite exempt from any intellectual influences, are usually the slaves of some defunct economist."

This is certainly true in the broadest sense but it should not misguide us into another type of delusion. This would be the case if we thought that reforming the global economy was a sort of Socratic process: a sincere search for the truth with the willingness to embrace it would in due course lead us to the light of reason. This would amount to ignoring what Machiavelli taught a long time ago: only the armed prophets are able to win. The unarmed prophets are doomed to failure and martyrdom. UNCTAD belongs more to the second category of prophets than the first. For that reason, if it does not want to follow the sad fate of so many prophets, it has to arm itself, through alliances with what the French call the "party of movement", i.e. those who favour not the *status quo* but change and reform: countries, individuals, civil society.

Alliances are built by two elements: a shared vision and common interests. In this particular case the common interests arise from the perception of interdependence, not conflict, between the North and the South. That was Prebisch's vision when the expression "interdependence" was not yet in general usage. He saw that the development of the South would only be possible if the economies in the North would grow fast enough to provide markets for Southern exports and to produce a surplus of capital and technological skills to be transferred to the South. Similarly, the North needed the development of the South in order to find an outlet for its exports of finance, advanced technology and capital goods. Is there any better illustration of this old and always renewed truth than what is now taking place with the emergence of China, its contribution to the growth of Japan's and other Asian countries' exports, to the recovery in commodity prices, as a major source of import demand growth for developed and developing countries alike?

* * *

The combination of ideas and work methods that constituted the renewed UNCTAD approach was first applied in UNCTAD IX (1996). Those days marked the climax, the peak, of globalization. With the benefit of hindsight it is now clear that the golden years of globalization coincided roughly with the first half of the 1990s, the phase between the crumbling of the Berlin Wall (1989) and the inauguration of a new cycle of financial crises starting in Mexico (1995). The atmosphere of triumphalism associated with globalization was still dominant in 1996. Accordingly, UNCTAD IX dealt mainly with the development of strategies for developing countries to cope with the challenges of a globalized economy. It also played a pioneering role in the UN system as seen in this Conference in Midrand by bringing together civil society organizations and the private sector as equal "Partners for Development", the subject of the Lyon Conference of 1998.

The second half of the 1990s witnessed the first major setbacks on the victorious path of globalization. The first and by far the most damaging of those setbacks was the growing frequency of monetary and financial crises. These crises were not the end of globalization but they undoubtedly acted as a sudden revelation of its mortality, its inherent vulnerability. In that sense their role reminds me of what Paul Valéry wrote about the First World War and how that European civil war had shown Europe its mortality: "Now we, civilizations, we know that we are mortals."

The UNCTAD secretariat played a non-negligible role in the necessary work of intellectual revelation and clarification regarding the frequency and destructive power of currency and financial crises. First, by saying as early as 1990, a few months after the fall of the Berlin Wall, that the 1990s would be characterized by a series of such crises. The secretariat was perhaps the only major international establishment that underlined, at that early stage and with such clarity, the extreme dangers of financial globalization. It continued to expose those dangers and to advance concrete proposals for a new financial architecture in its thoughtful and well-reasoned flagship annual reports – the *Trade and Development Reports* (the *TDRs*) – that, together with the extensive research on the debt crises of the 1980s, constitute one of the major intellectual contributions of the organization to the understanding of, if unfortunately not to the solution of, the threatening problems of international money and finance. In other words, UNCTAD was able to contribute to the understanding of the problems at stake but not to their solution because its proposals (i.e., those of an unarmed prophet) were not seriously considered.

At the same time and on another front, that of international negotiations, globalization was stumbling on the ambitious attempt to complete the legal regulatory framework so as to free global flows from the remnants of State control by imposing two major new sets of rules. The first was the ill-advised and untimely proposal by the IMF secretariat to amend its Articles of the Agreement, i.e. promoting the complete liberalization of the capital account in the balance of payments by banning any type of capital control. It is indeed hard to believe that this proposal was approved in a joint meeting of the IMF and the World Bank in the Autumn of 1997, in Hong Kong, when a financial crisis was already ravaging the East Asian region and was about to reach Hong Kong and Singapore. Obviously, the amendment has never been implemented. Subsequently, the IMF adopted the more realistic position that countries should abolish capital controls only in a gradual, cautious, progressive fashion.

The second stumbling block was the reaction that forced the OECD to suspend, as the euphemism goes, the negotiations of a Multilateral Agreement on Investment (MAI). The attempt to transfer the negotiations to the WTO met the same resistance and, at the current moment, the MAI initiative in Geneva undertaken by the European Union and Japan appears to be going nowhere.

Besides the recurrence of financial crises and normative setbacks, globalization was about to face a third disturbing challenge: the emergence worldwide of a powerful mass movement characteristically called the "anti-globalization movement". A loose coalition of environmental, human rights NGOs, trade unions and disaffected socialists have gradually become more determined and organized. Such a coalition has been supported by a growing literature of a popular or scientific nature and is fuelled by the anxieties generated by phenomena like the growth in unemployment in the European Union, the increasing precariousness of work contracts and the transfer of jobs to cheaper labour cost locations such as

South East Asia and China. Trade liberalization in general, and the WTO as well as the IMF (the central *bêtes noires* as the institutional embodiments of the former) in particular, have been the main targets of the street protests. After a series of episodes of violent confrontations, the backlash against globalization has managed to push Governments of major industrialized countries and those that are seen as proponents of *la pensée unique* into a defensive position. Gatherings of the IMF, the WTO, the G-7/G-8 and even those of a private character like the Davos Forum, were converted into battlegrounds, and as a result they had to be convened in far-away and highly protected places, if not cancelled altogether. The most symbolic events defining and marking the boundaries of the radical changes in the public atmosphere were, at one extreme, the Marrakech Ministerial Declaration of 1994 (including the announcement of the creation of the WTO), the highest point of globalization and, at the opposite end, the unexpected and humiliating debacle of the 1999 Ministerial Meeting in Seattle, a city known worldwide as the headquarters of some of the most important TNCs.

Against the background of growing resistance to the predominant modality of globalization, the UNCTAD secretariat has pursued its analytical and research work along three major directions. First, it has attempted to bring into light the financial, investment, technological and trade trends that were behind the unification of the economic space on a planetary scale, underscoring both the strengths and weaknesses of the process, its positive impacts together with its numerous flaws and shortcomings. One of the most original outcomes of that effort was, besides the work on the financial architecture already mentioned, the remarkable body of research on the operations of TNCs and world FDI flows.

Second, the secretariat has undertaken a rigorous critique of the simplistic, one-sided approach to development embodied in formulations such as the Washington Consensus. Alongside economists like Joseph Stiglitz and the new perspectives brought by the concept of Human Development (propagated by the United Nations Development Programme (UNDP)), the secretariat has consistently emphasized the need for a pluralistic approach that would value the diversity of development strategies according to national and regional specificities. Within that framework, particular attention has been given to the lessons of the East Asian experience and the need to create development strategies appropriate to cope with the specific and challenging difficulties faced by predominantly rural and low-productivity economies such as the least developed countries (LDCs) and some other similarly vulnerable low-income countries.

Finally, a traditional area of the secretariat's work has been the analysis of the imbalances and asymmetries embodied in a multilateral trading system which has been almost exclusively oriented towards industrial countries' priorities. Since the Uruguay Round, the UNCTAD secretariat has been assisting developing countries in improving their bargaining capacity in trade negotiations. That effort found expression in the negotiations of the General Agreement on Trade in Services (GATS) when some of the most serious problems could only be overcome thanks to technically sound proposals originating in the secretariat. Building upon that past experience the secretariat also inaugurated in 1997 the *Positive Agenda for Trade Negotiations*, a title where "positive" is to be interpreted not as a judgement of value but as a synonym for pro-active. The departure point of the programme was the realization that during the Uruguay Round and afterwards most of the developing countries had maintained a largely defensive and reactive attitude. With some exaggeration it was possible to say that they knew what they did not want but they did not know what they should want, or how they should ask for it. In an organization like GATT–WTO, whose culture was trade liberalization, this kind of predominantly "negative" strategy would have to be replaced by a more open and forthcoming position if developing countries really wanted to change the *status quo*.

The purpose of the *Positive Agenda* was not so much to explain trade agreements or simply to train and produce competent negotiators. Its ultimate goal was, in effect, to help create in each developing country an autonomous capability of formulating negotiating positions inspired by its own economic specificities on a sound technical and legal basis. It was not up to the UNCTAD secretariat to tell national negotiators what those particular negotiation positions should be. Instead it provided them with analytical tools and training indispensable to defining their own agenda. At least in part as a result of the programme, developing nations were for the first time the source of nearly 50 per cent of the total number of proposals submitted to the Seattle meeting. As happened with other initiatives of UNCTAD, this one inspired different international organizations, NGOs or countries to launch their own similar projects in the area of trade-oriented capacity-building.

Thanks to the work carried out in the second half of the 1990s, UNCTAD X, held in Bangkok in February 2000, was able to make a constructive contribution to the post-Seattle healing process and to the re-establishment of developing countries' trust in the multilateral trading system. This, in turn, eventually helped pave the way for the launching in Doha, in 2001, of a new round of negotiations, this time with the specific goal of addressing developing countries' grievances in a so-called "Development Agenda for Trade Negotiations".

The flexibility shown by the major trading countries in the declaration about trade-related intellectual property rights (TRIPS) and public health in the somewhat more comprehensive and balanced character of the Doha Agenda and combined with the exaggerated denomination of the round to spur the interest and the engagement of developing countries. At the same time this combination generated high expectations of the outcome of the negotiations. Meeting these expectations has so far proven to be an elusive goal. The failure to agree in Cancún on negotiating modalities to allow the Doha Round to conclude its work by the chosen deadline (31 December 2004) has dashed many of the initial hopes.

* * *

The current trade round has been taking place against a worrying international background. First, the sudden increase in violence and conflict after the terrorist attacks of 11 September 2001 immediately found an expression in the predominance of strategic and security considerations over economic interests as well as in the affirmation of the power of the State and political concerns over the forces of the market and the economy in general.

Second, the overwhelming concern with security has undoubtedly stopped, and to some extent even reversed, the previous trend towards the erosion of border controls and in favour of freer trans-border flow of persons, goods, services and money. Two basic forces behind globalization – namely the technological revolution in information and communications technologies, and the internationalization of production through TNCs – remain as strong as ever before. However, these forces can no longer rely on the supportive help of the political developments of the recent past, which were also working in favour of convergence and unification.

In effect, during the period between the crumbling of the Berlin Wall of November 1989 and the terrorist attacks of September 2001, politics and economics were reinforcing each other; the end of communism leading to the fall of barriers everywhere: in Berlin, across Germany, Europe, and including the racial fence of Apartheid. Nowadays barriers are being re-erected and reinforced. For instance, a simple act such as entering the United States is a cumbersome and often unpleasant experience. Ports, airports, containers and the electronic transfer of money are being scrutinized to make sure that they are not being used in terrorist operations. The best illustration of these dramatic changes is the contrast between the visual symbols of two phases of history: the demolition of the Berlin Wall (as the departure point of a 10-year period of convergence) and the erection of the Separation Wall in Israel as well as the restrictive entry requirements in the United States (as the expression of the restrictive spirit of this new age).

Assuredly, the war against terrorism has not put an end to globalization in the way the First World War marked the demise of a similar phenomenon, the globalization of the Victorian Age. In the long run, however, it is hard to believe that an almost permanent state of mobilization and war against States and organizations suspected of terrorism will allow the continuation and deepening of a process of unification that depends on the dilution and weakening of national frontiers and other types of barriers to the free flow of persons, goods, services, money and investment.

Third, in the short period of three years since 11 September 2001, we have already witnessed two international wars, against Afghanistan and Iraq; several dangerous confrontations vis-à-vis the Democratic People's Republic of Korea, the Islamic Republic of Iran and the Syrian Arab Republic; an unprecedented level of deterioration in the Israeli-Palestinian conflict; and an unmistakable aggravation and even split between the United States and its closest allies on the one hand and various Western countries or nations of different persuasions on the other. The return in force of divergence and heterogeneity among States renders much more difficult the task of building international consensus, an adverse tendency that culminated in one of the most serious breaks with the cornerstone principle of collective security and the pre-eminence of the UN Charter as the source of legitimacy in international relations: the decision to attack Iraq despite the Security Council's refusal to grant its authorization. In other words, unilateralism on the part of major countries, particularly the United States, has been thriving to the detriment of multilateralism. This is by no means confined to the political-strategic sphere, for it equally finds expression in trade protectionism with the proliferation of regional and bilateral trade arrangements at the expense of the Most Favoured Nation principle. Economic nationalism is becoming fashionable again as a popular way of protecting local industries and jobs against the delocalization in manufacturing and outsourcing in services.

Never before has it been so crucial to return to the concept of interdependence as the missing element in the current one-dimensional incarnation of globalization. Its absence is indeed the main reason why a phenomenon of such historical significance and promise ended up as being perceived as the mother-of-all-threats. Rather than a mere unification of markets worldwide for the sake of competition and profits, genuine globalization should be seen as the desirable outcome of a long historical process that started with the maritime voyages of Vasco da Gama and Colombo in the late fifteenth century. That process brought about gradual increase in contacts, reciprocal influence, cultural exchanges, among the hitherto separate branches of civilizations and cultures. The radical facilitation of communications, particularly through increase in rapidity and reduction of costs, has created the possibility of accelerating the process of human understanding. However, in order for this promise to be fulfilled, it will be indispensable to promote the economic modernization and technological progress in societies that have not yet been adequately integrated in that movement. Globalization and marginalization should be seen as mutually incompatible concepts. There can be no true globalization if the process contains exclusion instead of inclusion: it would be a contradiction in terms of the very concept, the very meaning of the word "globalization".

Thus it makes no sense to be against or in favour of globalization, to promote or to oppose the integration of developing countries in the globalization process, without specifying what kind of globalization and integration we are talking about. What really counts here is not the mere quantity of integration with a flawed variety of globalization such as the prevalent one, characterized by an increase in exclusion and inequality. Instead, the goal to be sought is quality integration of the many excluded and marginalized developing countries into a more balanced and more development-friendly kind of globalization. This requires an external economic environment that favours a much larger dissemination of successful development experiences similar to the few examples of "success stories" so far, almost all of which are concentrated in Asia. In other words, the *status quo* of globalization should not be accepted as a given, an unchangeable consequence of uncontrollable forces as in the case of physical phenomena. Globalization is a product of culture and history, that is, of societal choices, which can and ought to be transformed and perfected.

UNCTAD's efforts are geared precisely towards the creation of a better kind of globalization through regulations and negotiations that will help countries lift themselves out of poverty. This development-friendly framework, if accepted, would make possible the adoption of more appropriate public policies to foster capital accumulation and technological innovation. The objective of these efforts would be to bring forth a productive system that allows developing countries to climb the value-added chain and integrate themselves into a globally unified economic space in such a way that they will be able to narrow the productive and technological gap that separates them from fully-developed countries. Quality integration in the globalization process means, among other things, not only high-value exports but a type of development which is environmentally friendly and socially balanced. In the 1960s, development was usually expressed in purely, sometimes crude, economic terms and was often presented as dependent on an initial phase of authoritarian rule, indifference to environmental destruction as well as to wealth and income concentration.

Since those days, the disastrous experience of many countries has taught us that in development, as in all other areas, the end cannot justify indefensible means. A sound development strategy has to be built on the solid foundations of participatory democracy, environmentally-sustainable practices and redistributive policies, all of which are aimed at fighting inequality in all aspects, from gender to race or minority discrimination. And it has to conform to the best and most concise definition of development, the one proposed by the French philosopher Jacques Maritain: "the promotion of all men and of man as a whole" (in French *la promotion de tous les hommes et de tout l'homme*).

It is obvious that an organization like UNCTAD, committed to these philosophical and ethical objectives, cannot be reduced to an institution devoted exclusively to trade matters. Indeed, as repeatedly defined in many documents and confirmed by the UN General Assembly, UNCTAD is the focal point in the UN for the integrated treatment of finance, currency, investment, trade and technology from the developmental perspective. Two major aspects should be highlighted. First, obviously, whenever we speak about these sectoral issues the perspective of development, i.e. the need to bring development into the picture, stands out. This is what makes UNCTAD, above all, an agency devoted to development. After all, its primary goal is to propose the most adequate public policies and the best tested strategies to promote development. Second, UNCTAD is not so much focused on individual, separate studies of trade, investment, technology or finance, but on their interactions (or reciprocal influence) as well as on the way they create a system that is bigger than the sum of its parts. By the way, this is one of the reasons why UNCTAD sees the world not as a theatre of confrontation between the North and the South but as a human and social system based on the essential interdependence of each and all its elements.

Anyone who shares this belief will easily understand that, contrary to views expressed in the mid-1990s, the WTO and UNCTAD are two perfectly distinct organizations that could and should join forces for the common goal of creating a multilateral trading system free from the inherited imbalances of the past and better able to facilitate development.

* * *

In order fully to grasp the difference in the nature of the two organizations it is useful to remember how both gradually evolved over the past several decades. A helpful guide in that endeavour is the excellent historical analysis *Also Present at the Creation – Dana Wilgress and the United Nations Conference on Trade and Employment at Havana,* of a half century of efforts to build an effective trading system, written in 1995 by the Canadian economist Michael Hart. His thoughtful account is admittedly much more concerned with the mainstream approach of developed economies – how to create a mechanism to promote and regulate free trade – rather than how to deal with development questions. In spite of this particular angle, or rather should we say because of its distinct motivation, the book provides us with invaluable insights for our purpose. It clearly indicates that there were differences in approach between advanced and developing countries in matters related to trade, development and, more generally, to the desirable characteristics of the international system since the very beginning of the post-World War II period, i.e. "at the creation" as Hart puts it. In other words, the "North-South divide" had existed long before it would come to be known as such.

In effect, it is curious how he describes the surprise of the "veterans of Geneva", the small group of like-minded individuals who had been involved in the negotiation of the General Agreement on Tariffs and Trade (GATT) and had also tried their hand in preparing a draft charter for the future trade organization to be negotiated in Havana, when they arrived in Cuba and found out that the "underdeveloped or poor countries" had a very different way of approaching the subject. He says:

> "Once in Havana, it came as a major disappointment to the 'veterans of Geneva' to discover that the 33 delegations which now joined them for the United Nations Conference on Trade and Employment did not share their assessment that the Charter needed little more than polishing. Instead, it came under wholesale attack by the underdeveloped or poor countries, particularly the Latins led by Argentina, who had not participated in the preparatory meetings but, nevertheless, had both general and particular views on the Charter. They concluded that the Charter was too one-sided and served the rich at the expense of the poor. They took up the same theme that India, Lebanon and others had unsuccessfully pursued in the preparatory work. As a result, they made more than 800 proposals for improvements, many of which would have emasculated the carefully developed compromises worked out in Geneva." (Hart, 1995: 44).

Reading this passage, anyone familiar with Seattle or Cancún will have an eerie feeling that history is repeating itself, as there are many similarities between the distant 1947 and either 1999 or 2003. But what is striking here is not so much the similar reaction of those who had not participated in the original preparations and demanded the right to be included, as was the case in those two failed WTO meetings. Above all, the significant aspect is the recognition that there was from the start a "gap in understanding" between the "veterans of Geneva" – we will see in due course that they were basically five industrial powers – and the others, defined as the underdeveloped or poor countries, particularly the Latins led by Argentina, that took up the same theme that India, Lebanon and others had unsuccessfully pursued in the preparatory work. Needless to say, there was no G-77 at the time and no one spoke about a North–South divide.

The text continues by saying that the Geneva veterans accepted various changes that, to me at least, appear rich in meaning: "For example, they adjusted the more objectionable aspects of the investment provisions; they accepted the principle of one country-one vote; they clarified the relationship of the Charter to the IMF; they spelled out members' obligations to non-members; and they once again tackled the thorny issue of the criteria for discriminatory BOPs [balance of payments] measures and economic development measures" (Ibid.: 44). It will not escape the attention of any reader that many if not all of those "thorny" issues are still with us to this day. Not only that, most are what we call to this day "the development issues" discussed at the Monterrey Conference on Financing for Development, among other meetings. "The result", says the book, "was an increasingly complex and increasingly compromised document" (Ibid.: 44–45).

That complexity can be illustrated by the example of commodities. Indeed, Hart reminds us that Chapter VI of the Havana Charter set out an elaborate series of principles relating to commodity agreements and that it recognized "that problems connected with primary commodities are of a special nature which do not apply to manufactured goods. It provides a systematic approach to the solution of such problems. There is to be careful examination of all aspects of a commodity problem and such examination is to be conducted on a wide basis with adequate representation of both producing and consuming interests" (Report, Part. II: 125, as cited in Hart, p. 48). Chapter VI, as the author further states, "was not carried into the General Agreement, which remains largely silent on the subject of commodity agreements" (Ibid.: 48). This again is meaningful, as the problems in the field of commodities had already been present (and side-lined) at the Bretton Woods meeting, where they were the central interest and concern of some developing countries, such as Brazil and others.

It was because of the inclusion of commodities and other subjects that the ITO came to be rejected by the United States and other developed countries: "The additional functions that would have been assigned to the ITO in such areas as employment policy, restrictive business practices and international commodity agreements could have overburdened the ITO and detracted from more central trade policy issues that are the main focus of GATT" (Ibid.: 52). This statement confirms the narrow trade approach of the "veterans of Geneva". According to Hart's book, "the negotiation of this limited agreement succeeded because it reflected careful, step-by-step preparation .... Identification of the basic issues flowed from shared analysis ... of the problems generated by the economic crisis of the 1920s and 1930s", a point worth retaining as it shows that the motivation of the process was basically the *problématique* of developed economies, with little or no reference to questions affecting developing nations. This is confirmed by another passage of the book that asserts:

> "It was largely the work of the five delegations: the US, the UK, France, Canada and the Benelux countries, together the five most important economic powers of the day. These five delegations were not unhappy with the way GATT obligations differed from those in ITO, and they resisted all efforts by the smaller countries to dilute the GATT with some of the gains they had made in the ITO Charter" (Ibid.: 53).

This is perhaps the passage where the author states most explicitly that the founders of the post-Second World War economic order were not prepared or willing to work together for broader development objectives, which would be the case had there been an institution like the ITO. They were simply interested in pursuing national interests and objectives, and the better instrument for achieving that goal proved to be the GATT rather than the ITO.

Such was then the prevailing situation in the late 1940s. After several decades and the upheavals brought by globalization, Hart indicates that the atmosphere had changed:

> "By the early 1980s, these changing circumstances and priorities disposed GATT members to determine whether the time had come to shed this conservatism and try once again to develop a more comprehensive code on commercial policy that would have universal appeal. The Uruguay Round of GATT negotiations ... became the vehicle for harnessing a new set of conflicting approaches to international trade policy. In the end, it succeeded not only in developing a far-reaching set of rules, but also in establishing a multilateral trade organization, the World Trade Organization"(Ibid.: 56-57).

He concludes on a somewhat questioning note: "We will see over the next few years the extent to which the world has changed to make possible today what was impossible nearly five decades ago" (Ibid.: 57). The "today" of the sentence was written in 1995 when there was still a mood of unqualified hope in the WTO, which produced, at its early stage, several significant agreements such as the ITA during its First Ministerial Meeting in Singapore and the two agreements on Basic Telecommunications Services and Financial Services in Geneva. Those were the golden years before the setbacks in Seattle (1999) and Cancún (2003). One wonders what Hart would write nowadays? Has the world really changed enough "to make possible today what was impossible nearly five decades ago"?

Be that as it may, this is beyond my point. My central interest lies elsewhere, in the passage where the Canadian economist speaks about differences between two types of international organizations:

"There was a fundamental difference between creating a *supranational* organization to address trade issues and establishing *international* institutions to address diplomatic relations, civil aviation, health, culture and science. The latter, in many cases, involved the establishment of mechanisms to promote cooperation and did not threaten deeply entrenched domestic economic interests .... A trade organization involved legal obligations requiring changes in domestic law and thus cut much closer to the sensitive bone of national sovereignty.... The intellectual appeal of an international trade organization had to stand up to the varied special interests in each country and their ability to appeal to concerns about sovereignty, if it was to survive" (Ibid.: 55).

The distinction established in the book between *supranational* and *international* organizations is made on the grounds that the former involves "legal obligations (that) cut much closer to the sensitive bone of national sovereignty", while the latter only promotes cooperation without having a justification in international law. In reality, both types of organizations do limit sovereignty, albeit not always in ways affecting economic interests. It is sufficient to think about treaties limiting armaments to see the point. What Hart really means is that GATT (today the WTO) obligations are not more "legal" than other commitments or more limitative of sovereignty but that they are enforceable because they have at their disposal a dispute-settlement mechanism capable of imposing sanctions, that is, with teeth. In that sense, one may say that GATT/WTO is not entirely unique but belongs in the very rarefied category of the "happy few". UNCTAD, on the contrary, clearly falls into the second category, namely that of organizations better defined by Celso Lafer, former Minister of External Relations of Brazil, in a recent article published in the Brazilian newspaper *O Estado de São Paulo* (A Conferência da UNCTAD) 30 June 2004: A2.)

In that article, Lafer, currently Professor of International Law at the University of São Paulo, clarifies: "UNCTAD, it is useful to stress, is not a specialized international organization created by a specific treaty, as in the case of the IMF or the World Bank, with their own competences and resources in the area of finance and which are part of the UN system... UNCTAD is a subsidiary body with a permanent character that emanated from the UN General Assembly. Precisely because it emanated from the UN General Assembly, it operates through the logic of parliamentary diplomacy. It is not a permanent negotiating forum, like the WTO, an international organization independent from the UN system, created in 1994, when those former functions of GATT were broadened and consolidated... It is not easy to negotiate trade agreements through parliamentary diplomacy...." Professor Lafer's distinction is extremely useful for understanding the differences between the WTO and UNCTAD, including the role of blocs in the latter.

I have no problem in concurring with a view that reaffirms the need for a strong institution embodying multilateral trade rules and dispute-settlement mechanism, as described historically by Hart in relation to GATT and the WTO. Even if developing countries did not exist or were located in a separate planet such an institution would have been indispensable in order to negotiate new rules and to solve problems that continue to exist in the international trade between fully-developed countries, for instance between Japan and the United States or between the European Union and Switzerland. After all, despite the recent enthusiasm that industrial countries have been showing in promoting so-called "free trade agreements" with developing countries, the fact is that no such thing as free trade or free trade agreements exists between the three main industrial countries or group of countries that are members of OECD, namely between the United States, the European Union and Japan, for example, and that no one is even seriously considering starting negotiations for reaching that kind of agreement between those three. There is no denying, therefore, that developed countries do need the WTO and this in total abstraction from the development *problématique.* As Hart demonstrated, it was that obvious necessity and the unhappy past experience of developed countries in the 1920s, and 1930s, when the system of trade rules had collapsed, that were the primary factors behind the creation of GATT and the WTO.

In the same way as the neo-classical economists never bothered to create a development theory because it was not their own problem, the developed countries were not interested in a trade-cum-development organization. Hart recognizes that: "Efforts by the United Nations through its Conference on Trade and Development (UNCTAD) to address issues 'lost' when the ITO failed to come into being were never embraced by the major trading countries" (op.cit.: 56). The "lost issues" were, among others, commodities, chronic balance-of-payments disequilibria (the "trade gap"), non-reciprocal treatment to foster economic growth, access to technology, restrictive business practices and "development issues" in general. It is very suggestive that such matters were never considered by the major trading powers as "objectives that were widely shared". They never qualified to be included among the matters that deserved to become elements of "a pragmatic but limited instrument that successfully imposed discipline where governments were prepared for discipline". They belonged, on the contrary, to the category that the author describes as "extraneous issues", where other delegations tried to divert the five leading countries but which "were successfully resisted or contained within a set of special rules, e.g., those that dealt with economic development, or that were addressed in the ITO Charter", which of course never came into being.

On the basis of the assumptions implied in Hart's text, one would easily be led to believe that the reason for such rejection was the fact that the "extraneous issues" were outside the limits carefully chosen by the five so as to deal only with one set of policy issues: "trade in goods". That was not the case, however, because as the article explicitly recognizes, politically sensitive issues within trade in goods such as agriculture and textile products were isolated by means of special rules. As nothing could be more central to trade in goods than these two most ancient goods in the history of civilization and trade, one is forced to conclude that the choice was not the result of principle and sound economic doctrine but simply of expediency and national interests or, as the text puts it, that some issues were excluded because they were "politically sensitive". In other words they belonged to the area where power rather than economic logic plays a prevalent part. So much then for the ideological argument that issues like commodities were "extraneous" and would "overburden" an organization devoted to the pure ideal of liberalization of trade in goods.

The reason why I went to such lengths in following Hart's text is not exclusively because it contains discussions of high analytical quality, but also because it strongly represents the predominant approach of the so-called "world trade community" consisting of the major trading partners, the secretariats of GATT–WTO, the IMF, the World Bank, and the OECD as well as mainstream liberal economists, developed countries' journalists, etc. In the same way as Marxists-Leninists liked to call themselves "scientific", this is equally a doctrine that purports to be entirely objective and scientific despite its undeniable ideological elements in Karl Mannheim's sense of a set of beliefs and values, apparently factual but fitting or disguising class or national interests. Therefore it is necessary to undertake a sort of "deconstruction" of the study in order to identify better the points that illustrate an ideological choice as regards attitudes towards the ITO in the past and the WTO in the present.

The draft charter for the ITO was condemned and rejected because it had been overburdened by extraneous issues like commodities, restrictive business practices and development provisions. Those matters were beyond the limits of the few "areas pragmatically chosen on account of their capacity to inspire a widely-shared consensus, one that makes possible painful changes in national law challenging entrenched economic interests". The argument sounds reasonable and moderate, finding an elegant expression in the following words: "This conservatism and caution allowed the more limited GATT to mature gradually and to gain the momentum and respect required to make it work". (Ibid.: 56.)

Nonetheless a few lines later we learn that the changes and priorities of globalization disposed GATT members to shed this conservatism, succeeding "not only in developing a far-reaching set of rules, but also in establishing a multilateral trade organization, the World Trade Organization" (Ibid.: 56–57). The paragraph says nothing of the incongruity of the fact that the Uruguay Round set of rules did include "extraneous" issues such as the TRIPS agreement on intellectual property, whose relations to trade are doubtful at best, but failed in liberalizing trade in agricultural goods and in outlawing agricultural subsidies, which should be at the very heart of trade liberalization from the start. Was this a consequence of the changes and priorities of globalization or simply the expression of the most powerful trading partners' priorities, that is, a matter of power? Of course when the writer states that the cause was globalization, the assumption is that the inclusion of intellectual property rules was as much in the interest of Argentina and Brazil as it clearly was in the interest of the US pharmaceutical industry, which is patently false. The only reason the Uruguay Round went much further in intellectual property than in agriculture liberalization was naturally the fact that the United States and the European Union held much more power in GATT/WTO deliberations than Brazil and Argentina.

It seems to me that the expansion of the frontiers of the trade system to cover areas like intellectual property – an expansion criticized by people of unimpeachable liberal credentials such as Jagdish Bhagwati, Martin Wolf, J. Michael Finger – at the time when that very same system has not yet been able to liquidate the outstanding debt of agriculture, is a deeply disturbing trend. It is disturbing because it smacks more and more of power politics and less and less of a movement guided by the principles of sound economic doctrine and the need to address the legitimate grievances of underdeveloped economies. It is this feeling of injustice that is driving growing negative reactions inside and outside the trade system. Having been personally present at almost all the ministerial meetings of GATT and the WTO since the mid-1980s, that is for nearly two decades, I find striking the contrast between the predictable, uneventful nature of such meetings in the past and their growing unpredictability and volatility in recent years. Since December 1988 four ministerial meetings, two of GATT and two of the WTO, ended without agreement and in different degrees of disarray: Montreal, the Midterm Review of the Uruguay Round (December 1988), Brussels, when the Uruguay Round was supposed to end (December 1990), Seattle (November 1999) and Cancun (September 2003). In all those episodes, disagreement over development issues was at the centre of the storm. Even in the case of the abolition of subsidies and the liberalization of agricultural trade, the ultimate confrontation never took place with developed members of the Cairns Group – Australia, Canada, New Zealand – or with the United States, which also shared for a time the goal of liberalizing trade in agriculture: when the moment of truth finally arrived, it always took the form of a stalemate between most, if not all, developed countries on the one hand, and developing countries on the other – Argentina, Brazil, Chile, Colombia, Uruguay, in the Uruguay Round and the G-20 in Cancún.

In the former example the United States was still a proponent of farm trade liberalization, although it chose not to actively support the five Latin American countries that refused to go along with the Uruguay Round unless there were progress on agriculture. In the latter case the situation had become more polarized. On the road to Cancún, on 13 August 2003, the European Union and the United States submitted a joint proposal that in effect amounted to a minimalist approach to the goal of agriculture trade liberalization set out at Doha. In reaction, a core group of developing countries – Argentina, Brazil, China, India and South Africa – advanced a counter-proposal that clearly constituted a more ambitious modality of dealing with farm trade reform. The resulting impasse over agriculture was the real and hidden cause of the failure in Cancún and not the disagreement over starting negotiations on the so-called Singapore issues – investment, competition, government procurement and trade facilitation – as it was technically arranged to appear.

All those facts seem to suggest that neither the old system (GATT) nor the new (the WTO) have been able to build a successful link between trade and development. The need for such a link and the willingness to try the challenging adoption of a fresh approach to forge it were at the heart of UNCTAD's creation in 1964. As Celso Lafer reminds us in his article, UNCTAD devoted itself from the start to the elaboration of an autonomous reflection on development with emphasis on a new commercial policy that would be sensitive to the South's problems. From that choice, he affirms, "a conflictive but fertile interaction with the GATT originated, for the latter was concentrated on the functioning of the multilateral trading system, whereas UNCTAD wished to change it". Part IV of the GATT, as he says, was born of this interaction and represented a new opening in the [GATT] trade–development relationship.

Forty years later the international community is still struggling with the same need and challenge. In the future, if we are to avoid the repetition of failures as the ones in Seattle or Cancún, asymmetric approaches and unfair imbalances such as those behind the collapse of those two meetings will have to be replaced with thoughtful and balanced solutions. The role of UNCTAD is to act as a moderate and constructive forum where such solutions may be developed and matured for eventual adoption in negotiations by the WTO members. It is by no means impossible, as we can see in the examples listed in Professor Lafer's article: the Generalized System of Preferences and special and differentiated treatment together with the Enabling Clause, first initiated in UNCTAD and later adopted by GATT. At the moment that trade issues have again become politically explosive subjects, UNCTAD and the WTO have no other choice than to closely cooperate in order to integrate development and poverty reduction in trade negotiations for the benefit of an interdependent world and for the consolidation of a fair and balanced multilateral trading system.

Editors' Introduction

Shigehisa Kasahara and Charles Gore*

Since its historic Conference in 1964, the United Nations Conference on Trade and Development (UNCTAD) has pursued its mandate of promoting the international trade and economic development of developing countries with a view to creating a more efficient, more stable and more equitable global economy that serves the interests of all people. It has pursued this goal through three types of work: first, analytical research and the elaboration of policy proposals by the UNCTAD secretariat; second, negotiations and consensus-building within the UNCTAD inter-governmental machinery – the Conference (which meets every four years), the Trade and Development Board (TDB), and various technical subsidiary bodies; and third, technical cooperation with developing countries to support their efforts to integrate into the global economy in a way which supports their development needs. Over the last 40 years, UNCTAD's work has evolved considerably. This book commemorating the fortieth anniversary of the establishment of UNCTAD shows how UNCTAD's work has evolved and identifies some of the major intellectual contributions that the organization has made in terms of both analytical views and policy proposals.[1]

Undertaking any intellectual history is a complex task, and it should be stressed at the outset that this book is not intended as a comprehensive official history of the organization. Such a history was created for the first 20 years of the organization (UNCTAD, 1985). Since then, however, there has been no serious historical stockpiling of any kind until now,[2] and this publication is something closest to its follow-up. We have not intended to produce this book as a substitute for the intense historical research which is on-going within the United Nations Intellectual History Project (see Emmerij, Jolly and Weiss, 2001). In fact, this

---

* Shigehisa Kasahara is an Economic Affairs Officer in the Macroeconomic and Development Policies Branch, Division of Globalization and Development Strategies (GDS). Charles Gore is a Senior Economic Affairs Officer in the Special Programme for Least Developed, Land-locked and Island Developing Countries.
[1] In a broader sense, the intellectual history can be taken to mean the history of conceptual evolutions not only in the analyses of general international economic trends (particularly their development-related implications) but also as very concrete programmes and projects under the general heading of technical cooperation emanating from these analyses and inter-governmental deliberations.
[2] Nevertheless recent short analyses of UNCTAD's evolving work include Kasahara (2001) and Köhler (2001).

project already includes a volume on international trade, finance and development based on close study of both the UN archives and personal papers of key contributors to the post-1945 debate on trade and development (Toye and Toye, 2004).

The present book is a collection of case studies prepared by experienced staff members of the UNCTAD secretariat, each describing how a particular intellectual topic in UNCTAD's analytical work has evolved. While the substantive elements of each paper are basically personal reflections, they are supported by the official documents listed in the "references" section at the end of each paper. These documents represent some of important research or policy contributions accomplished by the organization. Many of these key documents (together with some additional ones) are also reproduced on a CD-ROM attached to the inside back-cover of the book.

By reproducing these key official documents on the CD-ROM, we intend to give readers who are interested in UNCTAD easy access to its most important texts, texts that are currently spread about in a very fragmented way throughout countless publications, many of which are extremely hard to find. Of course, since the selection of these documents for reproduction also involved the personal judgments of individual authors, some readers may find some significant omissions. It is our hope that each topical paper (together with the selected documents for that topic) will still enable readers to construct a verifiable recapitulation of the intellectual history of UNCTAD over the last 40 years. We also intend to enable readers to judge for themselves what the contents of UNCTAD's thinking have been and how the general principles underlying UNCTAD's intellectual work have found practical expression. It would satisfy our overriding purpose if the book would help those who may in the future prepare a more comprehensive history of UNCTAD.

I.   A Brief History of the Project

The project of this fortieth anniversary publication was conceived by the Secretary-General of UNCTAD, Rubens Ricupero, in the fall of 2002 when he invited from the secretariat of the Economic Commission of Latin America and Caribbean (ECLAC) Ricardo Bielschowsky, who had previously prepared a two-volume historical survey of the history of economic research and analysis in Latin America. An initial roundtable meeting was held in October 2002, where some twenty senior staff members were invited from a wide range of areas in the UNCTAD secretariat. Many participants in the initial meetings became project members, although the participation of additional members was also solicited at the later stages. At that occasion Bielschowsky presented his initial project outline for this book (Bielschowsky, 2002). The participants intensely discussed his postulation of three broad phases of UNCTAD's work.

The first phase of intellectual contribution (1964–1980) was mainly focused on elaborating practical policy proposals, particularly at the international level as part of the North-South dialogue. There was then a close harmony between UNCTAD's research and analytical output and its policy proposals. UNCTAD also acted as a forum for negotiations. This phase reached a climax in the mid-1970s with the UN General Assembly resolution to establish a New International Economic Order. UNCTAD's intellectual activity then reflected the "Southern" development initiative in multilateral diplomacy, roughly corresponding to a mature or late period of post-war Keynesian macroeconomic management.

The second phase (the 1980s) was a transitional decade during which there occurred the rise of neo-liberalism and the decline of the North–South dialogue. The cycle of intellectual production aiming at policy proposals for negotiating purposes continued, but with what Bielschowsky's calls "declining intensity". As a matter of fact, there was a rising cycle of intellectual contributions that has focused on research and analysis, particularly on critically assessing the new conventional wisdom and seeking to reconstruct an alternative approach to development. However, the link between research and analysis on the one hand and policy proposals for negotiations on the other progressively weakened. In particular the topics that used to be important in the early years of UNCTAD – notably commodities, shipping and technology – were downsized. But new subjects started to flourish, notably work on foreign direct investment (FDI), least developed countries (LDCs) and services in development.

The third and current phase (since the early 1990s) has witnessed the climax and moderation of neo-liberalism. The relevance and importance of UNCTAD's research work has become increasingly clear. This is particularly notable in the work on globalization and financial crises as well as in its contributions to understanding what is happening in the global economy in terms of FDI flows and the activities of TNCs. This phase has also reflected UNCTAD's initiatives in favour of developing countries in multilateral trade negotiations.

At the occasion of the initial meeting, it was stipulated that the principal elements at the core of the present publication should be official documents carefully selected and compiled. The general understanding was that UNCTAD's intellectual activity could be divided among the seven topics:[3](1) Money, Finance and Development; (2) Trade and Restrictive Business Practice (RBP); (3) Commodities; (4) Shipping; (5) Technology; 6) Least Developed Countries (LDCs); and (7) Foreign Direct Investment (FDI). Each of the seven sets of official documents would be accompanied by a brief analytical introduction (5–10 pages) to underline the importance of these official documents in the history of UNCTAD's analyses and policy proposals. Furthermore, it was thought that while the seven topics as identified above have had different weight in the intellectual production of UNCTAD over the period, they could be combined into three major groupings. The first grouping consisted of the "core topics", namely (1) Money, Finance and Development and (2) Trade and RBP; which have consistently remained principal areas of work throughout the history of UNCTAD. The second grouping consisted of those topics that were much more prominent in the earlier periods (say, the first and second periods) than in the later ones, such as (3) Commodities, (4) Shipping, and (5) Technology. The third grouping consisted of two topics, namely (6) LDCs and (7) FDI, of which the significance has become increasingly recognized in the recent period.

After the departure of Mr. Bielschowsky at the end of 2002, Kasahara and Gore jointly took over the task of project coordination and management under the guidance of the Deputy Secretary-General of UNCTAD, Carlos Fortin. In January 2003 the first brainstorming session among potential project members (authors of the topical papers) were held so as to enhance the understanding of the project. In March 2003 the project team held the second roundtable meeting where the designated authors of the topical papers presented the preliminary outlines of their writing. It was then decided that the topics of "Trade and RBP" should be dealt with separately, with the second element, RBP, being renamed as "Competition Law and Policy." Meanwhile, it became clear that the plan of writing a brief "reader's guide" as suggested by Bielschowsky would be rather difficult. Subsequently, both the topical papers and the list of official documents were lengthened. In June 2003 the project team had the third roundtable meeting where the first drafts were presented and discussed. During the second half of 2003 all topical papers were submitted to and commented on by the Project Coordinators who, through discussions with their authors, fine-tuned their paper's contents so as to enhance the consistency of the presentational framework as well as to fill gaps and eliminate duplications in presentation. At the end of 2003 and beginning of 2004, through discussions between the project coordinators and Ricupero, two

---

[3] These topics, which are far from mutually exclusive, are not exactly based on "sectoral" distinctions in functional terms. Furthermore, all of these topics are commonly linked to the development perspective, the traditional conceptual mainstay of UNCTAD.

topical papers, "Services in Development", and "Development Strategies" were added.

Each topical paper carries explicit authorship. However, each author was encouraged to seek reviews of his writing from his peers, where the project coordinators provided a hard copy of all topical papers to the project members for that purpose. Furthermore, the head of each Division of the secretariat was requested to undertake a quality check of all the papers relevant to his or her Division.

II. Continuity and Changes in the Work of UNCTAD

While each topical paper in this book describes major changes in both the scope and content of UNCTAD's work over the past 40 years, it is still possible to see continuity in it. This continuity is rooted in the basic philosophy that informs all of UNCTAD's work. The foundations for this philosophy were originally set out in 1964 in the Final Act of UNCTAD I in the form of a list of 15 general principles and 13 special principles which, it was recommended, should govern "international trade relations and trade policies conducive to development". Looking back from the vantage point of 2004 we can identify several fundamental ideas that, with varying levels of intensity, run through the work on all the different topics covered in this book, namely

- The need for greater global equity, which can be achieved through accelerating inclusive national development within developing countries and giving their needs and interest a greater voice in international decision-making;
- Interdependence of economic well-being in developed countries with economic well-being in developing countries;
- The importance of international trade for economic development;
- The need to analyse development processes and formulate development policies within a global framework;
- The responsibility of developing countries for their own development and the need to protect their policy autonomy, coupled with the importance of international economic cooperation to speed up, and reduce the social costs of, national development;
- The need for coherence between trade and development policies at the national, regional and international levels;

- The interdependence of trade, finance, investment and technology in the development processes and the consequent need to take account of the ways in which policies in each of these sphere mutually reinforce each other;
- Dissatisfaction with the status quo and scepticism about purely free market solutions in developing countries and in international economic relations;
- The need to take account of differences between developing countries.

The topical papers identify three major sources of changes. They are: changes in the world economy (such as globalization), new institutional configurations (such as the establishment of the WTO) and ideological shifts in development thinking (such as the emergence of the Washington Consensus).

It is difficult to summarize the evolution of UNCTAD's intellectual work. But many of the topical papers share the view that there was a general pattern of change across topics over the period. In the early years UNCTAD's work was mainly geared to conceptualizing and developing international policy proposals, and UNCTAD acted as an important forum for negotiations in the North–South dialogue. There was then a tight link between research, analysis, policy proposals and negotiations. In the later phase of UNCTAD's work (i.e. since the late 1970s), there has been a major intellectual contribution in terms of research and analysis to make a critical assessment of the evolving conventional wisdom which has dominated development thinking. This work has also identified the development implications of new forms of global interdependence associated with globalization and liberalization. And as for the more recent past, many of the topical papers also make clear that UNCTAD VIII, held in Cartegena in 1992, was a critical watershed for the organization's work.

What has happened to UNCTAD's work in various analytical areas is a much more complex story than one of "declining intensity", however. The papers on International Trade and on Commodities make it abundantly clear that UNCTAD is still making important contributions to international policy-making and negotiations. Indeed, UNCTAD's work on LDCs, for instance, has in many ways become more, rather than less, central to international policy discussions of the development problems of LDCs, and this work has become increasingly important as the international community has turned to address the issue of extreme poverty. Moreover, the work on technology, competition law and policy, and shipping (according to the authors of these topics) has continued to evolve in different ways, reflecting new demands and a changing global context. In the 1990s in particular, as the personal reflections of Ricupero in the Preface to this book make clear, the organization has been seeking to re-invent itself, while retaining its underlying philosophy so as to become more relevant to contemporary challenges.

III. Organization of the Book

This book is organized in three parts. Part One includes papers on what may be called "core issues" that have always occupied the broad and basic concern of the secretariat, while Part Two includes other papers whose significance, as the topic of intellectual work, has evolved over time. Specifically, Part One includes three topical papers: (1) International Trade (2) Money, Finance and Debt; and (3) Development Strategies. These core subjects reflect the central idea of interdependence – both global interdependence between developed and developing countries and inter-sectoral interdependence between trade and finance – which is so important to UNCTAD's work. Moreover, the paper on international trade examines the changing interrelationships between UNCTAD and GATT, and then between UNCTAD and the WTO.

Part Two focuses on specific topics that have been important in UNCTAD's work: (4) Commodities; (5) Shipping; (6) Technology; (7) Competition Law and Policy; (8) Least Developed, Land-locked and Island Developing Countries; (9) Services in Development and (10) Foreign Direct Investment and Transnational Corporations (FDI/TNC). More specifically, commodities, shipping, technology and competition policy and law were all topics in the debates of the 1970s on establishing a New International Economic Order which would be more in favour of developing countries. The papers on these subjects indicate how this work has evolved from the early phase of UNCTAD activities in the 1960s to the late phase. The paper on LDCs shows how UNCTAD has handled differentiation among developing countries according to their levels of development and geographical handicaps. The papers on services in development, FDI and TNCs cover those topics that became more important to UNCTAD in the 1980s and 1990s. This last group of papers highlights the effects on UNCTAD work that occurred after the transfer of the UN Division on Transnational Corporations (formerly the UN Centre on Transnational Corporations (UNCTC)) to UNCTAD in 1993.

Part Three of the book contains a list of the principal official documents that are considered to be most relevant to the individual papers. These are reproduced in an electronic format on the CD-ROM that comes with this book.

References

Bielschowsky R (2002). The UNCTAD system of political economy: Preliminary outline for the selection of representative documents (mimeo).

Emmerij L, Jolly R and Weiss TG (2001). *Ahead of the Curve? UN Ideas and Global Challenges.* Bloomington and Indianapolis: Indiana University Press.

Kasahara S (2001). United Nations Conference on Trade and Development: The review of its past activities and the future prospect (in Japanese). In: Yamazawa I, ed. *New Development Strategies of UNCTAD.* Chiba, Japan: The Institute of Developing Economies.

Köhler G (2001). La UNCTAD: Aportación a las politicas de desarrollo. *Commercio exterior*, 51(1): 66–83.

Toye J and Toye R (2004). *The UN and Global Economy: Trade, Finance, and Development.* Bloomington and Indianapolis: Indiana University Press.

UNCTAD (1985). *The History of UNCTAD 1964-1984.* New York: United Nations.

Part One

International Trade, Finance and Development

International Trade

Murray Gibbs and Victor Ognivtsev*

Introduction

Throughout its history the UNCTAD secretariat has injected ideas and analysis into the international trade debate with the goal of constructing an international trading system more consistent with the needs and aspirations of developing countries. This paper traces this intellectual role against the background of the changing realities of international trade relations, focusing on those ideas that have had the greatest influence on the international trade agenda as well as the most positive impact on the efforts of developing countries to regain the initiative in trade negotiations.

As early as the 1947–1948 Havana Conference, the Latin American countries, many of which were original contracting parties to the General Agreement on Tariffs and Trade (GATT), had been advocating setting up a system of multilateral trading rules that would be more consistent with their development goals. The independence of the former colonies in Asia and Africa gave momentum to this cause. In this context, UNCTAD was viewed by many as an alternative to the GATT system that was considered by developing countries to have been drawn up without their effective participation and thus not reflecting their interests. While UNCTAD has addressed a wider spectrum of issues in international economic relations, in the area of international trade its primary goal was to modify the most-favoured-nation (MFN) clause with an exemption in favour of developing countries, i.e. their preferential treatment based on the principle of "non-reciprocity", on the assumption "that treating unequals equally simply exacerbated inequalities". Thus, the first major accomplishment of UNCTAD in the area of trade was the approval of the Generalized System of Preferences (GSP) in 1968, by which the preferential treatment of developing countries was accepted as a normal practice.

---

* Murray Gibbs was the Senior Advisor to the Secretary-General of UNCTAD on Trade Negotiations. Victor Ognivtsev, is a Senior Economic Affairs Officer, Trade Negotiations and Commercial Diplomacy Branch, Division on International Trade in Goods and Services, and Commodities (DITC). It is derived from their deep personal involvement in UNCTAD's work on trade over several decades.

This paper identifies four periods in the intellectual history of UNCTAD and is structured accordingly. During these periods UNCTAD has assumed somewhat different roles in the international trading system both reflecting and influencing the realities and developments in trade relations, including the outcome of multilateral trade negotiations. During the first period, from 1964 to 1979 – UNCTAD I through UNCTAD V – UNCTAD was clearly viewed by many Member States as an alternative to the GATT. At that time UNCTAD was acting as a negotiating forum, and considerable effort was invested in adopting numerous recommendations and resolutions at the Conferences. The work of the secretariat focused on preparing studies and reports for a variety of UNCTAD's intergovernmental bodies including the Conference every four years, the Trade and Development Board (TDB) and its subsidiary bodies such as the Committee on Manufactures and the Special Committee on Preferences.

The second period began around 1980 in association with UNCTAD VI in 1983, and lasted until the early 1990s. Over this period the primary aim of UNCTAD's bodies and the secretariat shifted to attempting to influence the evolution of the GATT system so as to make it better serve the interests of the developing countries. This took place in a situation where the developing countries became aware that, as a result of the so-called "erosion and fragmentation" of the GATT system, they were becoming clear victims of increasing trade discrimination. The period witnessed a new strategy on the part of the major industrialized countries to expand the scope of the multilateral trading system in such a way as to provide greater, more liberalized and secure access for the operations of transnational corporations (TNCs).[1] This process resulted in the beginning of the Uruguay Round of multilateral trade negotiations (MTNs), in which the UNCTAD secretariat continuously supported developing countries' participation therein. This period also culminated in the proposals for a new trade organization submitted initially in 1990.

The third period ran from 1990 to 1995 during which UNCTAD was obliged to react to the establishment of the World Trade Organization (WTO) and to the claims that it was no longer relevant. The struggle to survive by re-defining its role in the post-Uruguay Round multilateral trading system preoccupied the minds of the secretariat. The fourth period, following the establishment of the World Trade Organization (WTO), began with UNCTAD IX in 1996, which re-legitimized the overall role of UNCTAD in the area of international trade and focused its work, in a more precise and continuous manner, to assist developing countries to participate effectively in the multilateral trading system. It set the stage

---

[1] See, topical paper on FDI/TNCs in this volume.

for the *Positive Agenda*, a partnership between UNCTAD and developing country trade negotiators, that enabled the developing countries to regain the initiative in multilateral trade relations through the 1999 Ministerial Conference in Seattle up to the 2001 Ministerial Conference in Doha and afterwards.

I. Pre–1964

When it became evident by 1950 that the Havana Charter for an International Trade Organisation (ITO) would not enter into force, the idea of establishing a comprehensive international trade organisation within the United Nations was revived in the Economic and Social Council (ECOSOC). In 1955, at the twentieth session of ECOSOC, a draft resolution to that effect was submitted by the Soviet Union,[2] which proposed "setting up within the framework of the United Nations an international organisation which would facilitate the development of international trade relations and thereby raise the level of living of the peoples and mitigate the tension in international relations". This initiative subsequently received support from developing countries, particularly in the Cairo Declaration adopted at the Conference on Problems of Economic Development (9–18 July 1962), which in turn led to a recommendation by ECOSOC in 1962 that a UN Conference on Trade and Development be convened.

During this period, although GATT was based on a shaky foundation as only a provisional agreement without an institutional basis and comprising very limited membership (in 1955, there were only 34 GATT contracting parties,[3] 14 among them were developing countries), it was nevertheless designed to provide an overall institutional framework for international trade. This system failed to ensure a suitable institutional framework for addressing the development concerns of a growing number of newly independent countries in the post-colonial period as well as of existing ones (such as in Latin America) that had reached only substantially lower levels of development. Despite the wider political ambitions on reforming the existing trade and economic order, the dissatisfaction with GATT finally led to the establishment of UNCTAD in 1964 as an organ of the UN General Assembly, but not as a comprehensive trade organization in terms of coverage and institutional basis as had been envisaged in the Havana Charter in the 1940s. Developing countries and the then-socialist countries of Eastern Europe

---

[2] *International trade relations*, draft resolution, E/L.677, 14 July 1955. This draft resolution was not approved by ECOSOC.
[3] As GATT was not an international organization as such, but a provisional legal instrument, its participants were called *contracting parties*. On the other hand, the participants to the WTO, which is a fully fledged international organization, are called *members*.

clearly viewed UNCTAD at that time as a new institution capable of addressing their interests and concerns in an alternative way as compared to GATT. However, they also recognized that the establishment of UNCTAD was a compromise that was far from their original ambitions.

II.   1964–1979[4]

The 1964 Conference (UNCTAD I, Geneva) adopted The Final Act (UN, 1964), which contained 15 General and 13 Special Principles designed to govern international trade relations and trade policies conducive to development.[5] These principles were based on the development concepts put forward by Raúl Prebisch, the first Secretary-General of UNCTAD. These Principles, which would have a substantial impact on the approaches to trade and development issues in subsequent years, were adopted by roll call votes. Some of the developed countries cast negative votes and others abstained, while developing countries as a rule voted in favour as a bloc. UNCTAD I also marked the formation of the Group of 77 (G-77).

At UNCTAD II (New Delhi, 1968), the Conference adopted resolution 21 (II) calling for tariff preferences in favour of developing countries in line with the

---

[4] One of the areas, in which UNCTAD endeavoured to provide substantive intellectual contributions, was trade relations between countries with different social and economic systems. This direction of UNCTAD's work was actively exploited (although without meaningful success) by the former socialist countries of Eastern Europe to fight against their discriminatory treatment in East-West trade. Also, for more than two decades (from the mid-1960s to the end of the 1980s), UNCTAD was a pioneer in exploring and designing new forms of trade and economic cooperation between developing countries and the socialist countries of Eastern Europe based on the realities of a centrally-planned system in the latter. These activities ceased at the end of 1980s when fundamental political and economic systemic transformation occurred in Eastern Europe and will not be discussed in this paper.

[5] The General Principles included, *inter alia,* the sovereign right of countries to dispose freely of their natural resources; non-discrimination on the basis of differences in socio-economic systems; recognition that international trade was one of the most important factors in development; emphasis placed on international trade being conducted to mutual advantage on the basis of the MFN treatment with the proviso that developed countries should grant both tariff and non-tariff preferences in trade to developing countries; and a requirement that developed countries participating in regional economic groupings should do their utmost to ensure that their economic integration did not cause injury to developing countries. The Special Principles included, in particular, the provision that developed countries should cooperate with developing countries in setting targets for the expansion of trade of the latter; the right of developing countries to protect their infant industries; universal commitment to refrain from all forms of dumping; and arrangements to correct and compensate for the deterioration in terms of trade of developing countries.

proposal made earlier by Prebisch, although the endorsement by the TDB[6] of the specifics as spelled out in the "Agreed conclusions" on the Generalized System of Preferences (GSP) had to wait until 1970. In 1971 the GATT Council adopted the decision on the "Enabling Clause", which gave the GSP a 10-year temporary legal status as the allowed exception from the MFN treatment under the GATT Article I (later, in 1979, the Enabling Clause was incorporated in the outcomes of the Tokyo Round with a permanent GATT legal status). Subsequently the GSP schemes were introduced in many developed countries: by the mid-1990s developing countries received trade preferences for their exports to developed countries amounting annually to approximately $80 billion. However, individual GSP schemes failed to give full effect to the principles and objectives of the preferences as originally conceived. Many products of export interest to developing countries (such as textiles and clothing, footwear) were often subject to exemptions and restrictive qualifications, some of which were also based on the concept of "graduation" of developing countries from the preference-receiving status.

UNCTAD III (Santiago, 1972) could be characterized by two major initiatives. First was the proposal by Mexico to draft a Charter of the Economic Rights and Duties of States. Second was the proposal by Brazil to prepare a Charter of an International Trade and Development Organization. The latter proposal, which stipulated a possible merger of UNCTAD and GATT, was later debated without success in the TDB (in 1973–1975). On the other hand, Mexico's proposal was discussed by an UNCTAD Working Group of governmental representatives, which submitted the draft Charter to the UN General Assembly in 1974 (UNCTAD, 1974). The Charter was subsequently adopted as the UN General Assembly resolution by vote at its Twenty-ninth regular session.[7] The Charter was deemed by the developing countries to constitute an effective instrument towards the establishment of a new international economic order. These developments marked a new departure in the North–South dialogue by shifting the emphasis from the improvement of the existing international trade and economic system (those were mainly the objectives of UNCTAD I and II) to the establishment of a new order aimed, *inter alia*, at achieving economic and social progress of developing countries, and more equal world trade. The underlying ideas were: the emphasis on the significant role played by governments in the development process; and the conclusion that heavy reliance on the free play of market forces tends to increase rather than reduce the existing inequalities among countries. In the area of

---

[6] Generalized System of Preferences, Decision 75(IV) adopted by the TDB at its fourth special session, 12-13 October 1970.
[7] *Charter of Economic Rights and Duties of States,* UN General Assembly resolution 3281(XXIX), 12 December 1974.

international trade, special emphasis was placed on a wider application of the principle of non-reciprocity in trade relations between developing and developed countries.

At UNCTAD III, UNCTAD was also given the mandate (Conference resolution 82(III) entitled *Multilateral Trade Negotiations*) to assist developing countries to negotiate in the new round of MTNs in GATT which was to be launched in Tokyo later in 1972.

UNCTAD IV (Nairobi, 1976) and UNCTAD V (Manila, 1979) brought relatively few new ideas with regard to trade issues. The main sector-specific emphasis at these Conferences was on commodities. However, one of the systemic concerns that drew much attention was the issue of structural adjustment in the developed countries, i.e. the need for structural changes in their economies that could accommodate comparative advantages enjoyed by developing countries so as to enable them to increase their exports to developed countries' markets. The concept of structural adjustment was closely related to the policy requirement to avoid protectionist tendencies emerging despite the conclusion of the Tokyo Round of MTNs in 1979. Eventually, in 1981–1992, the TDB held regular annual meetings in which issues of protectionism and structural adjustment were debated.

The UNCTAD secretariat worked closely with developing country delegations during the five years of the Tokyo Round, preparing studies and reports for their use as well as organizing seminars and servicing meetings of the Group of 77. This work provided the secretariat with a new insight into the functioning of the GATT system. At the end of the Tokyo Round the secretariat came up with its evaluation of the outcome, which set the stage for a major shift in UNCTAD's approach to trade issues. It should be noted that the main developing country achievement in the Tokyo Round was to legitimize on a permanent basis, in GATT, the GSP and the concept of Differential and More Favourable Treatment for Developing Countries (which has come to be abbreviated as Special and Differential Treatment: S&D).

III. 1980–1995

This period witnessed several important emerging issues, and the presentation in the following pages specifically focuses on the three most prominent among them: the erosion of the multilateral trading system; the development of the South–South trade cooperation through the Global System of

Trade Preferences among Developing Countries (GSTP); and the decision to establish the World Trade Organization (WTO).

A.   Erosion of the Multilateral Trading System

The preliminary elements of the analysis of the post-Tokyo Round trading system were set out in a statement to the TDB by the Director of the Manufactures Division (UNCTAD, 1981). This statement noted that while the Tokyo Round of MTNs had resulted in a decline in "conventional barriers to trade", notably customs duties, "there is now greater reliance upon mechanisms of flexible protection, under which restrictions or other measures can be applied when specific conditions exist". In fact, "the interpretation of the various terms used to describe the conditions justifying the introduction of these measures has become an issue of fundamental importance in international trade relations" This provided governments with mechanisms to "manage" trade as well as to control the quantities and prices of imports sold on their domestic market. This situation was exacerbated by the decline of the unconditional MFN principle as the "cornerstone" of the multilateral trading system. This fact was seen by the secretariat as an implicit recognition on the part of major developed countries that the original GATT system could not be applied effectively in a universal context. The conclusion made by the secretariat was that different regimes for trade between different categories of countries and within different product sectors were being established, and that the basic rules and disciplines of the system were becoming increasingly irrelevant.

This statement was received with considerable interest and led to a new standing item on the agenda of the TDB, entitled "Developments in the International Trading System". Under this item a background note on MTNs was prepared for the Twenty-fifth session of the TDB (UNCTAD, 1982). This note extended analysis to different areas of international trade relations, including the principles and mechanisms for MTNs, the growing discrimination targeted mostly against developing countries represented by such measures as anti-dumping duties, agricultural protectionism, the so-called "grey area measures", such as voluntary export restraints and the Multi-Fibre Arrangement (MFA), and its extensions.[8] The note went so far as to set out a series of recommendations including the need for

---

[8] The MFA, formally the Agreement Regarding International Trade in Textiles, an agreement which was first concluded in 1973 within GATT between textile-exporting and importing countries to manage trade in textile products through a web of quotas imposed on imports. The MFA was aimed at mostly developing countries and violated the GATT non-discrimination provisions, including the unconditional MFN treatment.

rules for the negotiations of concessions and commitments and for their application. These rules should be clearly understood, precise and non-discriminatory, with the object of reversing the dangerous trend towards the so-called "conditional application" of the MFN treatment. Another recommendation was to set up adequate mechanisms for ensuring predictable and equitable adjustments to shifts in international comparative advantage, including the establishment of an effective, non-discriminatory safeguard clause (i.e. applied to all sources of imports without selectivity) and for determining the economic criteria which determined what constitutes "injury" to domestic industry. It was also recommended that action be taken to ensure that commitments at the international level were effectively translated into domestic laws and regulations.

In the negotiations on textiles, the developing countries were confronted with some developed countries that aggressively negotiated cut backs in quotas under the principle of "reasonable departures". Furthermore, the European Economic Community (EEC) and the United States attempted to extend the MFA-style export restraints to other sectors. These experiences led many developing countries to realize that they stood to be victims of discrimination rather than its beneficiaries following the implementation of the GSP. In the early 1980s the UNCTAD secretariat set up a project to assist developing countries in negotiating the planned extension of the MFA. This eventually evolved into a new international organisation, the International Textiles and Clothing Bureau (ITCB),[9] which was ultimately successful in securing the elimination of the discriminatory trade regime in this sector as the result of the Uruguay Round.

At UNCTAD VI (Belgrade, 1983), the secretariat, in its report to the Conference entitled *Protectionism, trade relations and structural adjustment* (UNCTAD, 1983), advanced its ideas in a comprehensive manner, including an historical account of the process of erosion of the multilateral trading system. The report observed: "It is thus possible to trace a consistent pattern within the multilateral trading system towards increased trade liberalization, including through special measures in favour of the developing countries. On the other hand, it is possible to detect a contrary trend, the net result of which has been to alter considerably the character of the multilateral system. The main factors contributing to this trend have been (i) ad hoc solutions in particular sectors, outside, and in

---

[9] A body located in Geneva with two principal objectives of achieving the elimination of discrimination and protectionism directed against its members' exports of textiles and clothing, and promoting the full application of GATT principles to trade in these products. The present members are Argentina, Bangladesh, Brazil, China, Colombia Costa Rica, El Salvador, Egypt, Hong Kong (China), India, Indonesia, Jamaica, Macao (China), Maldives, Mexico, Pakistan, Peru, Republic of Korea, Sri Lanka, Thailand, Turkey and Uruguay.

direct conflict with the rules, (ii) the introduction and often unilateral application of new concepts, and (iii) the new structure of commitments arising from the Tokyo Round". Among a long list of proposals for action presented by the secretariat was that of "identifying the content and scope of future multilateral trade negotiations".

Conference resolution 159(VI), "International Trade in Goods and Services: Protectionism, Structural Adjustment and the International Trading System", embodied this new perception of the role of developing countries in the international trading system. It implied that the preferential and differential treatment in their favour, mostly of an "autonomous" nature (i.e. given by developed countries on a voluntary basis) was nullified by other policy actions legitimized by the system that effectively discriminated against the developing countries. Thus, it also implied that in the new context developing countries should take a much more active role in GATT and in the new multilateral round which was emerging from the results of the 1982 GATT Ministerial meeting. This resolution identified a series of issues for studies and actions, urging improvement of the GSP and other commitments to provide differential and more favourable treatment for developing countries on the one hand while on the other, targeting issues which had been identified in the secretariat's documentation as contributing to the erosion of the multilateral trading system such as the misuse of anti-dumping and countervailing duties, the elimination of quantitative restrictions and "measures having similar effect", as well as the need for "an improved and more efficient safeguard system". The resolution assigned to the TDB the task of making proposals that would strengthen the trading system with a view to giving it a more universal and dynamic character while fully respecting the principles of most-favoured-nation treatment and non-discrimination. This in effect set out the core agenda for developing countries in the forthcoming Uruguay Round of MTNs. The message was clear in that the developing countries should not concentrate solely on obtaining preferential treatment but take an active role in seeking major improvements in the GATT system that would make its provisions more pro-development and reflect trade interests of developing countries.

B.   The Uruguay Round of MTNs

UNCTAD provided major inputs to the evolution of the Uruguay Round negotiations both in the documents presented to intergovernmental bodies, notably the Trade and Development Board, the Trade and Development Report, and most intensively in the context of the UNDP financed technical assistance projects established to support developing countries in the Uruguay Round. These projects were the catalyst for a mobilization of thinking on the part of the secretariat on the development aspects of the issues set out in the Punta del Este Declaration (UNCTAD 1989a; 1990).

C. The Global System of Trade Preferences among Developing Countries (GSTP)

In parallel with the GATT negotiations, developing countries, with UNCTAD's substantive and technical assistance, launched an initiative to establish a framework for the exchange of trade preferences among themselves with a view to promote mutual trade.[10] Developing countries considered that the GSTP Agreement constituted an historic achievement of long-lasting political and economic significance and a milestone in South–South cooperation. Its ultimate objective was to help integrate all developing countries into the world economy in a manner that enhanced their development process. In the words of Rubens Ricupero, the Secretary-General of UNCTAD, "developing countries have become the most dynamic force in the growth of the world economy and trade. There is no doubt that the new locomotive of the international economy and the gate for a new push in world trade will be the developing countries. This is an additional reason for giving a new lease of life and greater prestige to the GSTP" (UNCTAD, 2000a).

D. Trade in Services and Development

The 1982 GATT Ministerial meeting had decided to include a new issue on its agenda: Trade in Services. Drawing from the mandate provided by Conference resolution 119(V) entitled "Protectionism in trade in the services sector", the secretariat began to work in this area beginning in the late 1970s. Later, Conference resolution 159(VI) mandated a major study on the role of services in the development process. The ensuing study entitled *Services and the Development Process* (UNCTAD, 1985), attracted considerable international attention. For example, the secretariat was asked to present it at a GATT Council meeting on services in 1985, an extraordinary occurrence for that period. This study opened the way for a whole new area of intellectual activities in the UNCTAD secretariat,

---

[10] The GSTP came into being after a long process of negotiations during the Ministerial Meetings of the G-77, notably at Mexico City in 1976, Arusha in 1979, and Caracas in 1981. The Ministers of Foreign Affairs of the G-77 in New York set up the GSTP Negotiating Committee in 1982. The New Delhi Ministerial Meeting held in July 1985 gave further impetus to the GSTP negotiation process. The Brasilia Ministerial Meeting held in May 1986 launched the First Round in April 1988. In Belgrade the GSTP Agreement was signed on 13 April 1988. The Agreement entered into force on 19 April 1989. Forty-three countries have ratified the Agreement and have become participants.

where it would exert a major influence on the Uruguay Round negotiations in terms of advancing concepts and objectives of the future General Agreement on Trade in Service (GATS).

In the above-mentioned study the secretariat concluded that services played a far more important role in the development process than was suggested by their direct contribution to GDP. Because of their inter-linkages with other activities, services could dramatically affect the over-all development performance of countries. It challenged conventional economic theories that viewed the role of services in the economy as a consequence of the development process and observed that in many cases development of tertiary production may be not a result of growth but rather one of its preconditions. The study noted that attempts to introduce services conceptually into a trade policy framework had encountered difficulties in differentiating trade from foreign investment issues. Efforts to equate trade concepts such as "access to markets", with investment concepts such as "establishment" have further obscured the debate. It noted that the definition of trade in services used by the International Monetary Fund (IMF) only included services traded between residents and non-residents.

The study also pointed out that developing countries were faced with a dilemma: on the one hand, identifying the required inputs – domestic and foreign – of certain services sectors would raise their competitive position in the production of manufactures and agricultural products, but on the other hand acquiring efficient service sectors from abroad might make their position more dependent on foreign services providers. The secretariat called for a more complete understanding of the role of services in the development of the national economy and an improved awareness of the effects of technology and other factors on the rapidly changing world market for services. It therefore called for a greater understanding of how these effects might best be reconciled with the development needs of developing countries.

The UNCTAD secretariat was requested by TDB Decision 309 (XXX), entitled "Services" (Thirtieth session, 1985), to follow up with work on (a) definitional aspects of services (this stimulated the thinking that led to the idea of "the mode of supply"); (b) strengthening and refining the data base; (c) further in-depth studies of the role of services in the development process; and (d) assisting member states in their analysis of the role of services in their economies. This decision enabled the secretariat to go into the field and glean ideas from its participation in studies and seminars (UNCTAD, 1989b) at the national level in developing countries.

This led to a series of national studies, particularly in Latin America. The national study on Mexico (UNCTAD, 1991a) clearly had an impact on policy making in that country, which found itself shortly afterward actively engaged simultaneously in negotiations on services in NAFTA and the Uruguay Round. Subsequently Mexico negotiated a series of FTAs with other Latin American countries, including those on services for the first time in the framework of Latin American integration. Furthermore, the secretariat maintained intensive contacts with those academic and private sector groups in developed countries which were attempting to convince their governments to give higher priority to services in domestic policy and in international negotiations, particularly in the Uruguay Round of MTNs.

During the early period of the Uruguay Round, the period leading up to the 1988 Montreal Ministerial meeting for the mid-term review, the UNCTAD secretariat presented its comprehensive analysis on trade in services in the *Trade and Development Report, 1988*. The Report examined services in the developed market economies, the then-socialist countries of Eastern Europe and the developing countries. It analysed trade in services in the world economy and the strategic role of services, and suggested a set of service strategies for development. Among the most innovative ideas emerging from it were the importance of the "externalization" of services and the significance of knowledge-intensive services emanating from externalization in the development process. It noted: "the key to the maintenance of a competitive position in world markets has been the maintenance feedback links between downstream, upstream and on-stream services". It also proposed the crucial idea of "modes of delivery" (eventually termed the "modes of supply" in the GATS), by identifying what actually crosses national frontiers when services were sold to foreign clients, to which multilateral rules and national implementing regulations would thus have to be addressed, and discussing issues relating to the mobility of capital, trans-border data flows, the mobility of labour and services requiring the mobility of the consumer. It recommended that developing countries devise overall services policies and set out elements of possible export and import strategies for trade in services. The acceptance that conditions, such as access to technology, could be attached to these commitments also emerged from this analysis. Thus *TDR 1988* set out much of the intellectual basis for the GATS negotiations in the Uruguay Round.

The secretariat put its ideas into practice within the framework of the UNDP-financed technical assistance projects in the Uruguay Round. It assumed a major role in providing developing countries with ideas relating to the overall concept of the GATS, its provisions on definitions, the positive list, the separation of market access and national treatment commitments and the telecommunications Annex. The secretariat was also responsible for the initial drafting of the text (1990, Mexico), which later became the Annex on Movement of Natural Persons. A series of additional studies on trade in services was prepared by the secretariat during the Uruguay Round, notably the book entitled *Trade in Services: Sectoral Issues*, which examined the development implications of trade in a number of key service sectors (UNCTAD, 1989c). The major thrust of the findings of this analytical work by the secretariat was that developing countries could gain from the liberalization of trade in services, from improved access to producer services, improved service infrastructures and from more open markets for their service exports (which often involve the movement of persons). On the other hand, the service sector is crucial for adapting to new technologies and constitutes a major employer; thus any liberalization should be undertaken cautiously, in parallel with measures to ensure the development of a strong indigenous services sector. It should be noted that the agreed structure of the GATS, in the negotiation of which UNCTAD ideas had a major influence, permits and even encourages this approach.

E. A New Trade Organization

In parallel to the work on services, the UNCTAD secretariat continued its analysis on developments in the international trading system and prepared a background document for UNCTAD VII (1987). Throughout the period of the Uruguay Round UNCTAD intergovernmental bodies, particularly the TDB, regularly addressed, on the basis of specific mandates by the General Assembly, developments and issues in the Uruguay Round that were of particular concern to developing countries. The secretariat provided regular analytical reports and studies as well as carrying out a wide-range of technical cooperation programmes which, it was internationally recognized, substantially facilitated the participation of developing countries in the negotiations.

The secretariat's work, however, took on dramatic new importance in the beginning of the 1990s when it became evident that the Uruguay Round was likely to result in the establishment of a new institution to replace the GATT. Proposals submitted by the EEC and Canada advocated a new "Multilateral Trade Organization" (as named in the EEC proposal of 1990). The logic behind these proposals was that the modifications to the GATT resulting from the Uruguay Round and its many new multilateral trade agreements could not be absorbed through the amendment procedure on an individual basis (as was done in the

Tokyo Round),[11] since it would result in a further and more dangerous fragmentation of the multilateral trading system by assigning different sets of rights and obligations to individual contracting parties. The idea was to establish a new institution that, as stated in the Canadian proposal, would provide an institutional framework and a formal legal status for the overall multilateral trading system. The modality proposed was that the GATT contracting parties would accept the new institution as part of their approval of the Uruguay Round agreements in a "single undertaking".[12]

These proposals, put forward only a few months before the Brussels Ministerial meeting of GATT (December 1990) which was intended to conclude the Uruguay Round, caused considerable consternation among developing countries who were not sure how to react, as well as within the UN system. The fact that the new institution was being portrayed as constituting the missing "third pillar" of the international economic system, absent since the failure of the Havana Charter, had obvious implications for UNCTAD. However, the Brussels Ministerial meeting broke down in disarray and the negotiation on the institutional issues continued.

Meanwhile the UNCTAD secretariat organized a high-level roundtable on 10 November 1990, i.e. only weeks before the Brussels Ministerial meeting. In its background note prepared for this roundtable,[13] the secretariat argued that the idea of a new trade organization was largely prompted by the pragmatic need to find an appropriate institutional and administrative mechanism that would incorporate and implement the Uruguay Round agreements. The scope of such an organization would also be determined by the agreements, which could be reached within the context of the relative power relationships prevailing at that time. As argued by the UNCTAD secretariat, the implementation of the Uruguay Round agreements presented the GATT contracting parties with challenging legal questions: how to incorporate results in new areas which were totally outside the scope and competence of GATT such as new agreements on services and trade-related aspects of intellectual property rights (TRIPS); how to define new rules on agriculture as well as the extensive interpretations of GATT Articles embodied in the Multilateral Trade Agreements (e.g. subsides, anti-dumping, customs

---

[11] In the Tokyo Round of MTNs (1973-1979), all negotiated agreements were optional for participants. This resulted in a situation where many participants, particularly developing countries, decided to stay away from these agreements, thus creating a phenomenon of "fragmentation" of rights and obligations under the GATT system.
[12] The concept became the legal requirement of the WTO in that all members must join all the agreements administered except for very limited plurilateral or optional agreements.
[13] Later the note was circulated under the UNCTAD/UNDP Project RAF/87/157 as doc. UNCTAD/MTN/RAF/CB.7, January 1991.

valuation); and, finally, how to bring all the results under the concept of the "single undertaking". Based on the above arguments the secretariat concluded that the proposal to establish a new organization would not constitute an attempt to create the comprehensive trade organization foreseen in the Havana Charter.

It was also clear from the beginning that the proponents intended that the new trade institution would be placed completely outside the UN system. ECOSOC reacted with a resolution requesting that the UN Secretary-General report to the UN General Assembly at its Forty-sixth session (1991) on these institutional developments, taking into account all relevant proposals related to strengthening international organizations in the area of multilateral trade. The UNCTAD secretariat was assigned to prepare such a report. The draft report was prepared and circulated to governments and relevant international organizations, including GATT, for their comments (UNCTAD, 1991b). The secretariat then prepared the final report by the UN Secretary-General for that session (UN, 1991).

The report emphasized that all efforts to strengthen international organizations in the area of multilateral trade should be adapted to modern realities and avoid the inadequacies of the existing institutional structures by addressing issues such as (a) setting objectives by the international community with respect to international trade and development within a framework designed to facilitate consideration of interrelated issues including trade, finance, investment, technology, anti-competitive practices, information, services, access to networks and distribution as well as labour migration; (b) ensuring maximum transparency and full participation of all countries in international decision-making, and contributing to greater coherence in global economic policy-making through the formulation of broad guidelines and effective coordination among relevant international organizations; (c) providing a source of intellectual support and a forum for international consensus building; (d) providing an improved mechanism for the administration of contractual multilateral trade agreements, particularly in new areas such as services and intellectual property rights along with future agreements which may be negotiated (competition, investment, TNCs, technology, etc.); (e) strengthening secretariat support capacities, including capacities for independent research and policy analysis, for initiatives and for the provision of technical assistance and expertise to enable smaller and more vulnerable countries effectively to take part in and advance their interests in consensus building and negotiating processes; and (f) streamlining mechanisms for mutual support, collaboration and coordination between programmes and agencies within the UN system (UN, 1991, 15–17).

The report provided innovative ideas that were later incorporated in the decisions agreed to at the conclusion of the Uruguay Round at Marrakech in April 1994 (e.g. on greater coherence in global economic policy-making),[14] and also served to find a new international consensus with regard to relations between various international organizations, particularly to secure and re-emphasize the relevance of UNCTAD, after the decision to establish the WTO was taken.

Nonetheless, the actual establishment of the WTO in 1995 brought the issue of UNCTAD's overall relevance to the forefront rather dramatically. Views, opinions and even proposals were aired which, in various degrees, highlighted the possibility that the creation of the WTO made UNCTAD irrelevant. For example, the independent Commission on Global Governance identified UNCTAD as one of agencies that could be abolished in order to streamline the UN system (Commission on Global Governance, 1995).[15]

The UN General Assembly, by adopting resolution 49/99 entitled "International Trade and Development", at its Forty-ninth session in 1994, reaffirmed UNCTAD's role as the most appropriate focal point within the UN proper for the integrated treatment of development and interrelated issues in the areas of trade, finance, technology, investment, services and sustainable development. It was also agreed that UNCTAD, even after the establishment of the WTO, would remain an important international instrument in the area of international trade particularly as a source of policy analysis, consensus building and technical assistance in the context of the Uruguay Round Agreements and their implementation, notably in the new areas of services, intellectual property and investment. The UN General Assembly also recognized that there was a considerable scope for complementarity between the WTO and UNCTAD. More specifically the policy analysis and consensus-building roles of UNCTAD could make essential contributions to the negotiating processes in the WTO. Obviously, complementarity also existed in the field of technical cooperation, where one of UNCTAD's main focuses was on assisting countries in

---

[14] The Marrakech Ministerial Declaration on the *Contribution of the WTO to Achieving Greater Coherence in Global Economic Policymaking* recognized that the globalization of the world economy had led to ever-growing interactions between economic policies pursued by individual countries, including those in the spheres of macroeconomics, trade, finance and development. The coherence of these policies at the international level was viewed as an important and valuable element in increasing their effectiveness at the national level. Therefore, the Declaration requested the WTO to pursue and develop cooperation with international organizations responsible for monetary and financial matters.

[15] The Commission's views apparently coincided with that of Mr. K.T. Paschke, head of the newly created UN Office of Internal Oversight Services, who was quoted by the German magazine *Stern* as saying that UNCTAD had been made obsolete by the creation of the WTO (See, article entitled "G-77 upset over inspector Paschke's remarks", *SUNS*, 16 February 1995, Geneva).

their efforts to participate effectively in the WTO processes and integrate themselves fully into the multilateral trading system.

F. New and Emerging Trade Issues

Immediately after the conclusion of the Uruguay Round the UNCTAD secretariat initiated a series of analytical studies and reports to focus on new and emerging issues on the international trade agenda underlying the question of whether and how the international trading system could adapt to the forces of globalization (UNCTAD, 1994; 1995). In particular, on the basis of its analysis of the specific emerging trade-related issues, the secretariat introduced three broad categories:

(1)   Issues which gave rise to demands for domestic policy harmonization, greater degree of uniformity of standards, (e.g. labour rights and environmental standards). Developing countries, as was argued, were unable to meet the norms established by developed countries, while negotiations on specific multilateral rules related to such policy harmonization would open the door to a whole new generation of trade remedies with protectionist intent.

(2)   Issues which reflected concern over the lack of coherence among global policy objectives. For example, in view of the secretariat the stringent constraints on national trade policies written into the Uruguay Round Agreements contrasted sharply with the absence of effective similar disciplines over national monetary and foreign exchange policies. Developing countries and economies in transition which have substantially liberalized their economies in the 1980s–1990s were particularly vulnerable to the effects of interest rate and exchange rate instability resulting from the absence of effective international macroeconomic coordination and surveillance arrangements. The predicament of these countries was compounded by commodity dependence and external debt problems. Another issue concerned the international movement of factors of production, notably the fact that, while the movement of capital and information was becoming freer, there was a tendency for the other factor, labour, to be ever more restricted. Capital could move to countries where returns were greatest while labour could not, thus creating the perception that there was a significant imbalance in the benefits which labour-rich and capital-rich countries derived from the trading system.

(3)   Issues related to the impact of trade, investment and technology-flow liberalization as well as intensified multilateral trade disciplines on the ability

of countries, especially the least developed countries (LDCs)16 and small economies, to pursue national goals effectively, i.e. there was often a conflict between multilateral disciplines and domestic policy objectives in developing countries.

IV. 1996–Present

During the period covering from 1996 to the present the UNCTAD secretariat has been occupied with, among others, the following major issues: institutional survival in light of the establishment of the WTO; a new initiative of *Positive Agenda* in future trade negotiations; interaction between trade and the environment; relationships between trade and energy; and intellectual and technical support of developing countries in the new MTNs known as the Doha Work Programme.

A.   Survival Assured

UNCTAD IX (Midrand, South Africa, 1996) reconfirmed the survival of UNCTAD and defined its role in the international trading system. UNCTAD's fundamental mandate on trade as stipulated in its two principal documents, the *Midrand Declaration and A Partnership for Growth and Development* (UNCTAD, 1996a) was to assist developing countries in their effective integration into the international trading system so as to promote their development. The key provision was to enable them "to respond to the opportunities arising from the Uruguay Round Agreements so as to derive maximum available benefits by...facilitating the understanding of the multilateral trading system, by analysing, from a development perspective, issues on the international trade agenda, including new and emerging issues" (Ibid., paragraph 91(i)).

For UNCTAD IX the secretariat, jointly with the WTO secretariat, prepared a detailed conceptual paper entitled *Strengthening the Participation of Developing Countries in World Trade and the Multilateral Trading System* (UNCTAD, 1996b), which effectively defined the role of UNCTAD in the post-Uruguay Round trading system. This report reviewed the outcome of the Uruguay Round primarily from the perspective of identifying areas for future actions by the international community to support developing countries in deriving benefits from the post-Uruguay Round trading environment. For example, in its assessment of market access opportunities for developing countries the report highlighted that the

---

[16] See topical paper on LDCs in this volume.

post-Uruguay Round protection in industrialized countries was characterized by the existence of "tariff peaks"[17] for some products of critical interest to developing countries, including textiles, clothing, agricultural products, fish and fish products, etc. It singled out areas in the built-in agenda,[18] a term coined by UNCTAD, where attention should be focused.

The report pointed out that in addition to agriculture and trade in services, where new negotiations were foreseen, many WTO Agreements provided for improved rules under the auspices of administering committees (e.g. provisions on safeguards, subsidies and government procurement in GATS, anti-circumvention measures on anti-dumping duties, rules of origin). In addition the operation of the WTO Multilateral Trade Agreements (MTAs)[19] was to be reviewed, which implied possible renegotiations of these Agreements. Therefore, even without the addition of new issues, the WTO would be a forum for continuous negotiations in which the developing countries would need to prepare themselves to participate effectively. The analysis set out in the report, and subsequent UNCTAD studies focusing on some of the issues identified (e.g. tariff peaks), provided the basic elements for the *Positive Agenda* (see below) and "Implementation Issues", both of which became a unifying rallying point for the developing countries in the WTO Doha Work Programme.

The report also discussed the problems facing those countries in the process of accession to the WTO. These countries often lacked the institutional and human capacities required to negotiate effectively, as well as the capacity to "live up" to WTO rules and obligations. It also noted that many of the applicant governments, particularly those in transition to a market economy, were still experimenting with various policy options and had not yet formulated precise trade policy objectives or established the necessary mechanisms to implement such polices with regard to "WTO consistency". As mentioned earlier, UNCTAD IX provided the secretariat with a clear mandate to assist developing countries and countries in transition in the process of accession to the WTO. With considerable outside donor support, the

---

[17] As a result of the Uruguay Round and national tariff reforms, average tariff levels of many countries have now been reduced to relatively low levels. This has led to a widespread belief that tariffs are no longer a major problem for international trade as substantial barriers, particularly for trade by developing countries. However, even after the full implementation of all Uruguay Round tariff concessions a substantial number of high tariffs or tariff peaks have remained, particularly affecting exports from developing countries.

[18] Some of the WTO Agreements, in particular the Agreement on Agriculture and the GATS, provided for the continuation of negotiations and defined their respective scope and starting times. Such provisions were called the "built-in agenda".

[19] The MTAs are defined as those WTO agreements that are obligatory for each WTO member under the concept of the "single undertaking" (see above).

UNCTAD secretariat subsequently became directly involved in assisting the negotiating teams of a wide variety of developing countries and countries in transition including China, Russia, Viet Nam, LDCs, and petroleum exporting countries. These activities, intending to help these countries achieve balanced and pro-development terms of accession, provided UNCTAD staff members with an intimate insight into the functioning of the trade regimes of a variety of countries. In 2002 the secretariat released an original publication containing a comprehensive analysis of issues related to the WTO accessions (UNCTAD, 2002).

The secretariat's work on WTO accessions led to important policy developments at the Third United Nations Conference on the Least Developed Countries (Brussels, May 2001) which adopted in its Programme of Action a set of substantive commitments by the development partners of LDCs with the aim of facilitating and accelerating the WTO accessions of LDCs. Subsequently, WTO member countries in the Doha Declaration (WTO, 2001) agreed "to work to facilitate and accelerate negotiations with acceding LDCs" and reaffirmed the commitments undertaken at the Third LDC Conference. In pursuance of the Doha mandate, on 10 December 2002, the WTO General Council adopted the Decision on the accession of LDCs (WT/L/508). This Decision was expected to substantially facilitate accessions of LDCs, particularly by exercising restraint of WTO members in seeking concessions and commitments on trade in goods and services from acceding LDCs, and by allowing acceding LDCs to benefit from the S&D provisions under the WTO Agreements. Finally, the Fifth WTO Ministerial Conference (Cancún, September 2003) approved terms of accession for Cambodia and Nepal, the first LDCs to accede to the WTO after its establishment in 1995. Needless to say, the UNCTAD secretariat provided comprehensive technical support to these LDCs throughout their long accession process.

B.   Initiative Regained: the Positive Agenda

From his participation at the First WTO Ministerial Conference (Singapore, 1996) and his observation of some earlier developments in the WTO,[20] the Secretary-General of UNCTAD recalled his experiences in the Uruguay Round, drawing the conclusion that the developing countries needed to refrain from assuming defensive and reactive positions but rather formulate a *Positive Agenda*. In setting their *Positive Agenda* they would systematically identify their interests and set realistic objectives with respect to all issues, not only those where they were "demandeurs", and pursue these objectives by submitting concrete, technically sound proposals in alliances with like-minded countries. In his view, negotiating proposals acquired much more "weight" when they were in consonance with the culture of an organization founded on the belief that all countries should strive for freer trade.[21]

The intergovernmental mandate of UNCTAD IX, particularly with respect to the international trade agenda, provided UNCTAD with a base for launching the *Positive Agenda* programme with a view to assisting developing countries in building their capacity to identify their interests, formulate trade objectives and pursue those objectives in international trade negotiations. The new mechanism of expert meetings permitted a discussion in UNCTAD bodies on specific issues to be negotiated in the WTO. Such meetings, which focused on issues identified by Member States, served to increase understanding of the development aspects of trade in many service sectors as well as agriculture, anti-dumping, etc., thus

---

[20] At the GATT Marrakech Ministerial Meeting (Canberra, 1994) some countries pressed for the introduction of a future work programme for the WTO containing new issues that had not been dealt with in the Uruguay Round as a component of the final package. A compromise had been reached in the form of a statement by the Chairman of the Trade Negotiations Committee listing possible issues for inclusion in the work programme which included the items proposed by developed countries such as labour standards, investment, competition policy, but also some of interest to developing countries such as compensation for the erosion of preferences, commodities and immigration. Many developing countries opposed the inclusion of investment in any WTO work programme and even more firmly opposed any mention of labour rights. They also resisted further work on environment and competition policy. During the period of negotiation of what was to become the Singapore Ministerial Declaration, developing countries focused attention on keeping these issues off the agenda. Thus it came a surprise when, from the opening statements at the First WTO Ministerial Conference, it became apparent that a major goal of the developed countries was the adoption of the Information Technology Product Agreement (ITA) and the rapid completion of the negotiations on financial services and basic telecommunications. Together these were seen as enhancing the legal foundation of the globalization process, which was presented as bringing benefits to all. The developing countries, by contrast,
had not formulated new initiatives of their own nor had they yet fully recognised the extent to which the WTO had become a forum for a continuous negotiating process.

[21] See, foreword by the Secretary-General of UNCTAD in *A Positive Agenda and Future Trade Negotiations*, (UNCTAD, 2000b: vi-vii).

providing the elements for future positions taken by developing countries on most of the subjects studied.

For the Second WTO Ministerial Conference (Geneva, 1998) the UNCTAD secretariat had prepared a discussion paper for the Group of 77 entitled *Building a Positive Agenda for Developing Countries in View of Future Multilateral Trade Negotiations: The Scope and Timing of Future Multilateral Trade Negotiations* (March 1998) which examined the issues involved in the "built-in agenda" in the WTO Agreements and the "New Issues" which had been proposed for inclusion in future multilateral rounds. Although the Ministerial Conference, marking the fiftieth anniversary of the GATT system, with the participation of heads of State and Government, was ceremonial, it did put into play a preparation process for the Third WTO Ministerial Conference (Seattle, 1999) where it was evident that the major trading powers would be pressing for the launch of a new round of negotiations. While negotiations in certain key areas such as agriculture and services were already foreseen in the "built-in agenda", pressure was mounting for much more comprehensive coverage. This preparation process was to be "proposal driven", thus placing every WTO member country under pressure to submit proposals to ensure that the trade issues of its specific interest would not be omitted in future negotiations.

The UNCTAD secretariat was thus called upon by developing countries to prepare short papers on a wide series of subjects, going so far as to envisage the final wording that an agreement might take. Its intellectual effort was focused on defining possible outcomes of negotiations on a wide range of issues. This work was carried out with the active participation of developing country delegations which met at least once a week with the secretariat. These delegations reflected the whole spectrum of ideologies, united in the common concern that developing countries must regain the initiative for the Third WTO Ministerial Conference. As stressed by one delegate at the meeting on the *Positive Agenda* (Boca Chica, Dominican Republic, August 1999, in which the Secretary-General of UNCTAD participated), "we don't need more studies, we need intelligence".

Almost 250 proposals were submitted to the WTO General Council in the preparatory process for the Seattle Ministerial Conference. Developing countries assumed an active role by submitting over one half of those. Their proposals focused largely on two aspects: (1) how to ensure that the "built-in agenda" negotiations on services and agriculture would focus on their particular interests, and (2) how to cope with specific actions related to the MTAs (including the mandated reviews) under the broad title of "implementation". Within the category of implementation issues, proposals addressed the issue of S&D with the principal objective of elaborating more binding commitment language for "best endeavours" type undertakings.[22] The implementation proposals also aimed at reaching agreement on interpretations of the MTAs to deal with specific problems which had arisen in practice, particularly those which did not take account of the special characteristics of developing country economies, administrations and enterprises. The difficulties they faced in meeting the administrative and procedural costs of implementation were also the subject of proposals, notably with regard to extending the transitional periods for the agreements on Trade-Related Aspects of Intellectual Property Rights (TRIPS), Trade-Related Investment Measures (TRIMs) and Customs Valuation. Another important element in their proposals was to introduce the concept of "imbalance" of rights and obligations. Thus the TRIPS Agreement was the subject of particular attention, where developing countries wished to ensure that this Agreement actually promoted the transfer of technology as stated in its provisions.[23]

However, the main concern of the implementation proposals focussed on achieving better market access rather than increased policy space. The proposals sought specific actions to reduce adverse impacts on exports by anti-dumping and countervailing duties and of sanitary and phytosanitary (SPS) regulations, to accelerate the stages of quota elimination under the agreement on Textiles and Clothing, and to ensure that negotiations under the "built-in agenda", such as on rules of origin, were concluded.

At the Third WTO Ministerial Conference, WTO Members were not able to change these proposals. More specifically, the developed countries had not prepared themselves for a scenario in which the developing countries would assume the initiative within the multilateral trading system. The position of the majority of developing countries that the implementation issues had to be resolved before the Fourth WTO Ministerial Conference (Doha, 2001) provided a rallying point for their coordinated efforts to ensure that the issues of concern to them would be on the agenda in any future multilateral round. To a large extent they succeeded in this endeavour in Doha. The Doha Work Programme ensured that the issues emerging from the *Positive Agenda* remained not only on the table but positioned in the timetable so that agreement on them would have to be reached before proceeding to action in areas where the developed countries were

---

[22] They are those undertakings expressed in "general" policy terms lacking "precise" operational meaning.
[23] See, topical paper on Technology in this volume.

"demandeurs", such as investment.[24] It also brought about a "resurrection" of the principle of S&D as an "integral part" of the WTO Agreements.

In retrospect, the *Positive Agenda* exercise represented a major intellectual effort on the part of the UNCTAD secretariat in that a large number of staff members contributed to the development and refinement of thinking on a wide variety of issues. The publication entitled *A Positive Agenda and Future Trade Negotiations* (UNCTAD, 2000b), compiling the key background papers presented during the pre-Seattle process, contained a few articles by prominent international experts but the large majority had been prepared by UNCTAD staff members. This work was commended in the Bangkok Plan of Action at UNCTAD X in 2000.

C. Trade and Environment[25]

UNCTAD's work on trade and environment has had a very significant impact on the international debate since the early 1990s. In July, 1991 UNCTAD submitted a report on "Environment and International Trade" to the third session of Preparatory Committee of the United Nations Conference on Environment and Development (UNCED). UNCTAD's work, in particular the outcome of UNCTAD VIII in Cartagena, provided the basis for the Agenda 21 Chapter 2 on "International Co-operation to Accelerate Sustainable Development in Developing Countries and Related Domestic Policies" as well as Principle 12 of the Rio Declaration. Some conclusions of UNCTAD's early work reflected in Agenda 21 and setting the tone for the trade and environment debate since then are (UNCTAD, 1993):

- Sustainable development requires a dynamic international economy and an open, equitable, secure, non-discriminatory and predictable multilateral trading system to support sound domestic economic and environmental policies in both developed and developing countries.

- Future growth of developing countries and countries in transition, which is critical to their ability to mobilize resources needed for improved environmental protection, depends among other things on access to developed-country markets.

- Trade liberalization, including the removal of existing distortions in international trade, must be pursued to support sustainable development policies in developing countries.

---

[24] See, topical paper on FDI/TNCs in this volume.
[25] This section has been prepared by René Vossenaar, Chief of Trade, Environment and Development Branch, Division on International Trade in Goods and Services, and Commodities (DITC).

- Trade and environment should be mutually supportive in the pursuit of sustainable development.

UNCTAD was the first institution to initiate empirical work on trade and environment linkages. Through the pioneering effort of the UNCTAD/UNDP joint project on *Reconciliation of Environment and Trade Policies*, a series of country case studies were carried out (1993–1996) by local research institutes in the following developing countries: Brazil, China, Colombia, Costa Rica, India, Malaysia, Philippines, Poland, Thailand, Turkey and Zimbabwe (Jha, Markandya and Vossenaar, 1999). These studies were the first attempts to analyse trade and environment linkages in developing countries. The studies concentrated on the effects of environmental requirements on market access and competitiveness. The studies also examined the environmental effects of changes in production patterns associated with trade liberalization and globalization, highlighting the importance of introducing appropriate environmental and macroeconomic policies to strengthen positive and mitigate negative pressures on the environment resulting from freer trade.

Over the years UNCTAD has taken numerous actions to assist developing countries in the area of trade, environment and development through intergovernmental work, studies, seminars, workshops and training covering a large number of issues highlighted in Agenda 21 and subsequent discussions in the Commission on Sustainable Development. In doing so, UNCTAD has been cooperating closely with other intergovernmental organizations and major groups including serving as UN system-wide task manager on trade, environment and sustainable development. In 2000 UNCTAD and UNEP launched a joint Capacity Building Task Fore (CBTF) on Trade, Environment and Development.

The first mandate on trade and environment dates from UNCTAD VIII (1992). It was strengthened in UNCTAD IX in 1996 and again broadened in UNCTAD X in 2000. Trade and Environment has been an issue for intergovernmental deliberations since 1993. It was selected as a priority issue for the first part of the TDB at its Forty-first session (1993) and Forty-second session (1994). Given the complexity of the issue, the TDB decided to establish an ad hoc working group on trade and environment which met 4 times in 1994 and 1995. Since 1996 UNCTAD Member States convened a large number of expert meetings on a range of issues such as environmental management standards, multilateral environmental agreements, traditional knowledge, environment-friendly products, environmental requirements, market access along with environmental goods and services. These expert meetings have been followed up by concrete actions. In

2003 UNCTAD launched a new annual publication: the *Trade and Environment Review.*

D.   Trade and Energy

Major petroleum-producing developing countries did not have any interest in becoming contracting parties to the GATT; those that did accede achieved this as GATT de facto contracting parties under Article XXVI by simple declaration (i.e. without accession negotiations).[26] Petroleum and energy issues were not discussed in the GATT as a "gentlemen's agreement" supposedly existed among the major trading countries not to discuss such issues because of the fear that the strategic nature of petroleum trade and the importance of security concerns in petroleum products would "politicize" the GATT debates. Security considerations greatly influenced trade policy in the energy sector as seen in the decision of the United States to leave its tariff on crude petroleum unbound in its GATT tariff schedule. In any case it was only immediately before and during the Uruguay Round that petroleum-exporting developing countries began to accede to the GATT. At the end of the Round certain petroleum exporting countries in the Arab world asked the UNCTAD secretariat to study their possible benefits in acceding to the WTO given that they only exported one product, petroleum, which they claimed had never been covered by the multilateral trade rules and disciplines.

This prompted an in-depth analysis by the UNCTAD secretariat on what may be described as the trade/energy interface. It examined the history of attempts to include energy issues in the GATT negotiations and the implications of multilateral and regional agreements for energy policies. The UNCTAD secretariat articulated its ideas on the trade/energy interface in the publication entitled *Trade Agreements, Petroleum and Energy Policies* (UNCTAD, 2000c). It noted, for example, that energy services constituted the value-added chain of energy production and were central to the energy policies of all countries, both exporters and importers.

The issues at stake in the energy services negotiations were also subject to greater scrutiny in an UNCTAD expert meeting on energy services in July 2001. This meeting presented an opportune occasion to discuss the impacts of liberalization, privatization and new technologies in the energy sector as well as the dramatic need for investment to ensure that production would keep up with

---

[26] The GATT had a special *de facto* status for countries formerly colonies and dependent territories. These countries had an opportunity to become GATT contracting parties without entering into a laborious process of accession negotiations through a simple declaration made on their behalf by the former metropolitan territory. This status does not exist in the WTO.

demand. The papers presented at the Expert Meeting, accompanied by additional contributions from the UNCTAD secretariat and political analysts, were published in *Energy and Environmental Services: Negotiating Objectives and Development Implications* (UNCTAD, 2003a). It was stressed in this publication that energy issues were now being fully dealt with within the framework of trade agreements and the WTO, and that developing countries should be prepared to address this reality. As around half of petroleum production and a greater percentage of oil and gas reserves were accounted for by countries that were not Members of the WTO, energy issues were moving to the forefront in accession negotiations. UNCTAD entered into arrangements with UNDP and OPEC to carry out studies on trade and energy issues.

E.   Doha Work Programme

In the new MTNs, the UNCTAD secretariat felt that its central mission was to continue to help developing countries increase development gains from international trade and trade negotiations. In particular, in line with the Doha Ministerial Declaration, the secretariat proposed that its vision of a modernized, strengthened and development-oriented set of S&D should be based on the following principles: strengthening MFN and non-discrimination while maintaining development flexibility by upholding the principles of non-reciprocity in Part IV of the GATT, and non-full-reciprocity as called for in the Doha Declaration; equitable treatment of developing countries through calibration of disciplines in a manner commensurate with their trade, financial and developmental needs and capacities; adequate flexibility and policy space for developing countries in regard to inside-border issues and trade-related agreements with significant implications for resources and domestic policy space; greater stability, security and predictability of S&D; preferential market access; special consideration by developed countries to refrain from using trade defence measures against developing countries; and full consideration of development dimensions in new and emerging issues (UNCTAD, 2003b).

The secretariat also argued that a more comprehensive understanding of the interconnections between trade and development gains needs to be established, including the identification of existing positive synergies between national and international trade policies and negotiations on the one hand and development strategies on the other. In this context identification of common standards or benchmarks to measure development gains is a particularly important and challenging task. The secretariat has been working on trade-related development benchmarks and presented its first vision of such benchmarks at the Fiftieth regular session of the TDB in October 2003 following the failure of the Fifth WTO Ministerial Conference at Cancún. Thus eight development benchmarks have been identified, i.e. openness and liberalization; harvesting gains; equal opportunity for unequal partners; striving for a better balance; the public interest; the importance of commodities; coherence; and technical assistance and capacity building (UNCTAD, 2003c).

V. Concluding Observations

UNCTAD's ideas and perceptions were taken up by the academic community *ex post*. Throughout its history, the UNCTAD secretariat maintained an intellectual advance on trade issues. For example, in the early 1980s it was the first to identify the changes in the international trading system and how its erosion was seriously affecting developing countries. The secretariat was also the first to address in a comprehensive manner the issue of services and the development process, and to speak of the modes of delivery (later referred to as the modes of supply in trade in services). In the early 1990s it prepared the first Annex on Movement of Natural Persons and put forth a suggestion for the structure of the future GATS as well as substantively contributed to the debate on a new international trade organization. In the mid-1990s it was one of the first to publish an assessment on the outcome of the Uruguay Round (UNCTAD, 1994), complemented by the pioneer policy research on trade in various service sectors such as health, energy and environmental services. Finally and more recently, the secretariat was also one of the first to address in a comprehensive manner the problems and issues concerning the process of accession to the WTO, particularly of LDCs, and brought international attention to the trade/energy interface in the modern context.

UNCTAD's intellectual contributions have resulted from closer working relations with developing-country governments, which have continually called upon the secretariat for new approaches and ideas. In other cases, notably on trade in services, it has benefited from close relations with the business community in both developed and developing countries. The Positive Agenda Initiative, which helped developing countries to strengthen their participation in the multilateral trading system, was the culmination of over three decades of partnership with those countries in pursuit of an international trading system more suited to their particular needs and aspirations.

References

Commission on Global Governance (1995). *Our Global Neighbourhood.* New York: Oxford University Press.

Jha V, Markandya A and Vossenaar R (1999). *Reconciling Trade and the Environment: Lessons from Case Studies in Developing Countries.* Edward Elgar: Cheltenham, United Kingdom, Northampton, United States.

UN (1964). *Proceedings of the United Nations Conference on Trade and Development,* Geneva, 23 March – 16 June 1964. Vol. I. Final Act and Report, E/CONF.46/14.

_____ (1991). Strengthening International Organizations in the Areas of Multilateral Trade, Note by the Secretary-General of the United Nations. A/46/565, 16 October.

UNCTAD (1974). Report of the Working Group on the Charter of Economic Rights and Duties of States. TD/B/AC.12/4 and Corr.1.

_____ (1981). Statement by R. Figueredo, Director of the Manufactures Division, at the fourth meeting TDB Sessional Committee I. TD/B(XXIII)/SC.1/Misc.1, 1 October.

_____ (1982). Specific matters arising from the resolutions, recommendations and other decisions adopted by the Conference at its fifth session requiring attention or action by the Board at its Twenty-fifth session. TD/B/913, 20 July.

_____ (1983). Protectionism, trade relations and structural adjustment. TD/274, June.

_____ (1985). Services and the Development Process. TD/B/1008/Rev.1.

_____ (1988).

_____ (1989a). Uruguay Round: Papers on Selected Issues. UNCTAD/ITP/10.

_____ (1989b). Services and Development Potential: The Indian Context. UNCTAD/ITP/22.

_____ (1989c). Trade in Services: Sectoral Issues. UNCTAD/ITP/26.

_____ (1990). Uruguay Round: Further Papers on Selected Issues. UNCTAD/ITP/42.

_____ (1991a). Mexico: Una Economía de Servicios. UNCTAD/ITP/58.

_____ (1991b). Note-verbale, TD/420/11, 27 September.

_____ (1993). UNCTAD's contribution, within its mandate, to sustainable development: Trade and environment – Trends in the field of trade and environment in the framework of international cooperation. TD/B/40(1)/6, 6 August.

_____ (1994). *Trade and Development Report, 1994*, UNCTAD/TDR/14, and the Outcome of the Uruguay Round: An Initial Assessment. UNCTAD/TDR/14(Supplement), August.

_____ (1995). New and Emerging Issues on the International Trade Agenda, Note by the secretariat to the tenth executive session of the TDB. TD/B/EX(10)/CRP.1, 2 March.

_____ (1996a). Midrand Declaration and a Partnership for Growth and Development. TD/377.

_____ (1996b). Strengthening the Participation of Developing Countries in World Trade and the Multilateral Trading System. TD/375/Rev.1.

_____ (2000a). The Global System of Trade Preferences among Developing Countries. UNCTAD/DITC/MISC.57.

_____ (2000b). A Positive Agenda and Future Trade Negotiations. UNCTAD/ITCD/TSB/10.

_____ (2000c). Trade Agreements, Petroleum and Energy Policies. UNCTAD/ITCD/TSB/9.

_____ (2002). WTO Accessions and Development Policies. UNCTAD/DITC/TNCD/11.

_____ (2003a). Energy and Environmental Services: Negotiating Objectives and Development Implications. UNCTAD/DITC/TNCD/2003/3.

_____ (2003b). Preparations for UNCTAD XI: Submission by the Secretary-General of UNCTAD. TD(XI)/PC/1: 37, 6 August.

_____ (2003c). Review of Developments and Issues in the post-Doha Work Programme of Particular Concern to Developing Countries: The Outcome of the Fifth WTO Ministerial Conference, Note by the UNCTAD secretariat. TD/B/50/8, 29 September.

WTO (2001). Doha Declaration, WTO Ministerial Conference, Fourth Session. WT/MIN(01)/DEC/1, 20 November.

Money, Finance and Debt

Shigehisa Kasahara*

Introduction

Throughout the past 40 years UNCTAD's role in the wide field of money, finance and debt has consisted of two specific processes: identifying and securing a broad appreciation of the major issues, mainly through the research activities of the secretariat,[1] and seeking to exert influence, mainly through the deliberations at its intergovernmental machinery (deliberative forums).[2] Between these processes the UNCTAD secretariat has provided substantive and logistic backup to the efforts of developing countries in formulating their common positions. Indeed, the UNCTAD secretariat's concern has been reflected in intensive research activities covering the refinement and formulation of concrete proposals for the resolution of outstanding problems and the pursuit of international agreements.

Interdependence, a regular item on the agenda of UNCTAD forums, is understood as a general conceptual framework depicting the interrelation between money, finance and debt along with their respective and collective effects on trade and development in developing countries on the other hand. It is understood that *money* is a shorthand expression for issues related to *the international monetary system* whereby international liquidity is denominated and exchanged as well as created and stored. Furthermore, the international monetary system also involves the issue of adjustment obligations covering government policies regarding how external payments disequilibria should be rectified. *Finance* is a shorthand expression for issues related to *the international financial system* which affect financial flows, i.e. transfers of savings and investment between countries. As for

* The author is an Economic Affairs Officer in the Macroeconomic and Development Policies Branch, Division of Globalization and Development Strategies (GDS). He wishes to acknowledge helpful comments from his colleagues, including Samuel Gayi, Mehdi Shaffaedin and Stefanie West.
[1] Various *ad hoc* international expert groups to consider specific monetary and financial issues have occasionally strengthened technical analyses undertaken by the UNCTAD secretariat.
[2] The principal forums include the Conference as well as its subsidiary bodies such as the Trade and Development Board (TDB) and the Committee on Invisibles and Financing-related to Trade (CIFT). CIFT, which was established in 1965 following the agreed institutional arrangements at UNCTAD I (1964), ceased to exist as a result of the reform agreed at UNCTAD XIII (1992). Since then issues of money, finance and debt have been discussed under the agenda item of "interdependence" at the TDB.

debt, UNCTAD concentrates principally on issues related to the external debt held by developing countries. Let us note that financial flows (particularly private flows) to developing countries have been considerably affected by their stock of debt, as it exerts influence on perceptions of their creditworthiness. These perceptions depend on the concept of debt-service capacity of countries in question that hinges on, most importantly, their export performance. Again, money, finance and debt are clearly linked to trade and development.

Intergovernmental deliberations within UNCTAD on various aspects of money, finance and debt boil down to the question of finding both ways and means to shape existing international economic relations in a direction that is supportive not only of creating a more equitable trading system but also of facilitating the development of developing countries. In this regard UNCTAD has also insisted that the nature of the international monetary system should be supportive of trade and development, arguing that a healthy and equitable trading system can reduce the burden placed on the intentional monetary system by reducing the need for financing payments disequilibria among trading countries. Equally, international financial flows (public and private) should play the role for not only resolving debt issues but also lubricating (and compensating for the inadequacy of) the existing trading system.

While monetary, financial and debt issues might not have appeared to occupy a prominent place in UNCTAD during its very early years, many of these issues were already identified at the first session, UNCTAD I (1964), and have since become prominent in its intergovernmental deliberations.[3] In fact the first session adopted a series of recommendations, many of which were aimed at improving the international monetary system in a broad sense and promoting further financial flows to developing countries. Within UNCTAD the idea of interdependence has evolved within the whole complex of policy issues of interest to the world economy, particularly to the developing countries. Whereas there has been a general persistence of the "development-oriented perspective" in its dealing with a wide range of issues, the specific emphasis of UNCTAD among these issues has been subject to certain swings. In examining proposed policy measures addressed to particular issues it is necessary to bear in mind possible harmful repercussions that they may induce elsewhere. Similarly, when it is too formidable

---

[3] The background documents for the agenda item "Finance and Invisibles" at UNCTAD I (1964) were prepared for and submitted to the Conference by either international organizations, experts or member Governments. One among them entitled "Finance in International Trade" was prepared by the United Nations secretariat (the Bureau of General Economic Research and Policies, the Department of Economic and Social Affairs, New York).

to directly tackle particular issues, realistic solutions for them may entail some roundabout actions for implementing policy measures elsewhere.

For expositional purposes this paper is divided into four broad parts; (I) Overview of UNCTAD's activities in the field of money, finance and debt; (II) UNCTAD's activities concerning issues related to the international monetary system; (III) UNCTAD's activities concerning issues related to financial resources for developing countries; and (IV) UNCTAD's activities concerning issues related to debt problems of developing countries.

I.   An Overview of UNCTAD's Activities on Money, Finance and Debt

A broad brushstroke review of UNCTAD's activities in the field of money, finance and debt may be summarized as follows: In the 1960s the principal concern of UNCTAD was focused on financial flows in light of the notion of "trade gap" articulated by Raul Prebisch, the first Secretary-General of UNCTAD, in his Report to UNCTAD I. According the Report, a satisfactory rate of economic growth (i.e. the minimum goal of 5 per cent growth as indicated in the United Nations (UN) Development Decade of the 1960s) in developing countries would require greater amounts of foreign exchange (for importing capital goods) than they could normally earn through "free trade".[4] Based on Prebisch's argument, developing countries stressed that their capacity to earn foreign exchange should be primarily raised to the maximum possible through institutionalizing the practice of preferential treatments of their exports, and that the remaining foreign exchange shortage should be filled by external finance. The various shortcomings of the existing international monetary system linked to the external debt of developing countries were also identified and solutions were suggested.[5]

While UNCTAD in its early years actively pursued the objective of a fundamental reform of the international monetary system, the relative emphasis

---

[4] Following Recommendation A.IV.2, "Growth and aid" adopted at UNCTAD I, the UNCTAD secretariat undertook extensive technical case studies of individual developing countries to determine the feasibility of rates of growth higher than those experienced in the past and to indicate measures to achieve them. For more details, see UNCTAD, 1968.

[5] One of the first topics identified was the problem posed by fluctuations in export earnings of developing countries. Consequently various compensatory credit schemes, something in the spirit of social insurance schemes, were suggested within the UN and outside. The pre-UNCTAD studies undertaken by the UN secretariat include UN, 1961; 1962a; and 1962b.

was more on proposing various countermeasures to systemic disturbances that had deleterious effects on the growth process of developing countries. Specifically, the UNCTAD secretariat gave a prominent place in its general analysis to the question of compensation for fluctuations in the export earnings of developing countries. Partly due to the promptings of the UN, particularly its Commission on International Commodity Trade (CICT), the International Monetary Fund (IMF) established the compensatory financing facility (CFF) in 1963. The CFF, a permanent part of the financing machinery of the IMF, was designed to extend support to member countries experiencing external deficits due to temporary export shortfalls (especially exports of primary commodities). Subsequently, discussions in UNCTAD forums focused on improvements of the facility's operation, particularly on: (1) the method of measuring export shortfalls to isolate the short-term portion of a change in the balance-of-payments position of a country; (2) the procedures for drawing and repayments; and (3) the size of the facility.

Furthermore, UNCTAD's early concern was also the issue of the creation (and the expansion of availability) of international reserve assets for developing countries. Since the late 1960s UNCTAD analysed and proposed solutions to current problems of the then existing international monetary system (often referred to as the Bretton Woods system). When the initial systemic crisis struck in 1971 UNCTAD became even more vocal, stressing that trade and payments systems should not depend on the payments deficit of a reserve currency country, the United States, and that they should be made more capable of fostering assistance and balanced growth in the world economy. In all cases UNCTAD (the secretariat in particular) consistently featured the growth and development of developing countries as the central goal of its debates.

UNCTAD III (1972) coincided with an uncertain period of transition of the international monetary system accompanied by growing currency turbulence. The UNCTAD secretariat perceived that the move to a "managed floating" regime (i.e. the departure from the Bretton Woods system) would bring forth a less stable environment (thus, introducing an element of uncertainty into import costs and export revenues) which the developing countries would be unable to influence due to their lack of resources for intervening in foreign exchange markets. Contrary to the monetarist expectation (or promise) of greater policy autonomy for Governments, as they would be free from the policy of achieving the external payments equilibrium, the floating exchange regime that came to exist in the early 1970s failed to make this materialize. In fact, the new regime did not relieve countries from payments deficits, and instead entailed the maintenance of even larger foreign reserves against external shocks than before.

The oil shocks in the 1970s brought forth intensive discussions of financing mechanisms for developing countries' import bills. The emergence of surplus in some developing countries (particularly the oil producers) together with the worsening position of external payments in many developed countries induced a new turn in monetary discussions, where developing countries were now no longer uniquely deficit countries (thus perpetual borrowers).

At the Sixth Special Session of the UN General Assembly in 1974 many ideas of the Group of 77 (G-77) developing countries, which had been nurtured in various UNCTAD forums, were formulated into a package and negotiated in the context of a New International Economic Order. Subsequently, General Assembly resolutions 3201 and 3202 (S-VI) were adopted and spelled out "objectives" and "measures" related to money, finance and debt along with a host of other issues. (In fact, almost all issues involved in these resolutions had been extensively discussed at UNCTAD forums.[6]) At the 29th regular session of the same year the General Assembly also adopted the "Charter of Economic Rights and Duties of States" (resolution 3281 (XXIX)), which sought to establish "generally accepted norms to govern international economic relations systematically" and to promote the establishment of the New International Economic Order. Originally proposed by the President of Mexico, the Charter was drafted over a 17-month period by a working group of 40 UN member countries under UNCTAD's auspices (Singh, 1977: 13).

It seems that after the above-mentioned Sixth Special Session in 1974, many of the discussions on monetary, financial and debt issues were shifted from the UNCTAD forums to the UN General Assembly. Nevertheless, the UNCTAD secretariat continued to engage itself actively in various analyses and submitted its findings to the General Assembly. (One notable exception was foreign direct investment (FDI) which was dealt with more or less exclusively by the UN Centre on Transnational Corporations (UNCTC) in New York. The UNCTC, which provided the administrative and technical support to the UN Commission on Transnational Corporation, existed from the mid 1970s to the very early 1990s.)

During the 1970s the secretariat became firmly established as a focal agency within the UN, undertaking analyses on the ways and means to enhance the volume of development assistance flows to the developing countries and to ensure

---

[6] One of the principal G-77 negotiators of these resolutions was Manuel Perez-Guerreo from Venezuela who had been the second Secretary-General of UNCTAD until just before the Special Session.

that such assistance was predictable and continuous.[7] The sharp rise of bank lending, particularly through the Euro-currency markets (petrodollar recycling) in the 1970s, greatly altered the composition of international financial flows, resulting in private bank lending taking an overwhelming share within the total financial flows to the developing countries. Thus UNCTAD IV (1976) and V (1979)[8] drew attention, among other things, to the increasing tendency towards the creation of international liquidity being assumed by the private sector (particularly commercial banks) instead of the IMF. Consequently, the prevailing situation brought about the shift of UNCTAD's concern towards measures for improving the access of developing countries to international financial markets.

Toward the very end of the 1970s there was a decisive shift in the emphasis of macroeconomic policies in some of the major developed countries where they now focused on the task of combating inflation to the virtual exclusion of other policy objectives, assuming that the decisive defeat of inflation was a necessary prerequisite to the restoration of a viable growth process in their economies. At the same time a number of major countries adopted monetary policies that placed exclusive reliance on the control of the monetary variables rather than giving weight to both interest and monetary growth objectives as had previously been the practice. (This seemed to many the death knell for post-war Keynesianism.) These two shifts combined produced a contraction in aggregate demand in major creditor countries that was accompanied by extremely high rates of interest. Consequently, the impact on the external payments of developing countries was immediate and severe.

The surfacing of the debt crisis in the early 1980s resulting from the situation in major creditor countries induced extensive discussions on the ways and means of coping with the crisis in order to protect the development process of developing countries and give greater security to the international monetary system. In the midst of the global recession in the early 1980s, the UNCTAD secretariat attempted to address the immediate financial problems of developing countries in the context of efforts to improve the performance of the world economy as a whole. The secretariat put forward a proposal package comprised of more expansionary fiscal and monetary policies in developed countries to be undertaken in a prudent fashion so as to ensure that previous gains from anti-

---

[7] One of the earliest studies undertaken by the UNCTAD secretariat and submitted as a Report of the Secretary-General to the UN General Assembly was UNCTAD, 1976.

[8] It seems, however, that at UNCTAD IV (1976) and V (1979) monetary and financial issues (perhaps with the exception of the issues related to the IMF CFF) were somewhat overshadowed by the overwhelming concern of that period, i.e. commodity issues.

inflationary measures were not jeopardized. (Thus the secretariat's position was still Keynesian, although it was a "prudent" kind.)

At the same time the structural adjustment programmes popularized and prescribed in the 1980s by the Bretton Woods institutions (the IMF and the World Bank) were also placed under scrutiny, and the market-based principle of what would be later called "the Washington Consensus" was seriously questioned. The IMF's role became much more important as a facilitator of lending and rescheduling of private and other official sources than as a source of funds. This was because the structural adjustment programmes became a catalyst for financial flows, both private and official, to borrowing countries and consequently the endorsement of their policies and commitments became known as "a seal of good housekeeping". Upholding the development-oriented perspective, the UNCTAD secretariat, on the other hand, felt that the most pertinent shortcoming of the existing international monetary system was the lack of the capacity to deliver expanding access to low conditionality credit to debtor countries, particularly developing countries, in the face of growing trade and international payments as well as growing economic turbulence.

A serious concern of the international community during the decade of the 1980s was that the role of international financial flows involving developing countries had changed radically. In the past, positive net transfer to developing countries permitted investment to take place at a level higher than would have been allowed by the domestic savings effort alone. In the 1980s, however, a number of developing countries, particularly those in Latin America, and the developing world as a whole, were faced with a situation of negative net transfer, i.e. an excess of interest and debt repayments over current financial receipt (grants and loans).[9] The decline in international bank lending also coincided with the growth of the Euro-bond market as a source of financing for corporations and governments of countries belonging to the Organization for Economic Cooperation and Development (OECD). FDI was the dominant channel for net private capital flows to the developing countries as a whole, although the increasing portion of FDI flows was directed to a relative few Newly Industrialized Economies (alternatively known as "emerging market economies"), particularly those in Asia.

Let us also note one new development in the modality of decision-making in the Conferences in the 1980s. UNCTAD VI (1983) was the last session where

---

[9] This was because many of the loans to developing countries were contracted in the crisis years of the early 1980s and were short-term in maturity; they fell due later in the decade. The slowdown in financial flows to developing countries in the 1980s coincided with the increasing flows directed to developed countries, particularly the United States.

numerous resolutions (including those in money, finance and debt) were introduced by the G-77 and adopted by a vote. From UNCTAD VII (1987) onward, substantive elements of past resolutions that had been problematic to developed countries have been either softened or eliminated in the process of preparing a consensus text, the Final Act of the Conference.[10] Therefore, in the name of consensus-building, all radical proposals that were deemed unacceptable to developed countries would not appear in the Final Acts of subsequent Conferences. The intergovernmental machinery of UNCTAD has therefore been politically tamed. On the other hand, the secretariat has managed to retain the discretion of putting forth provocative analyses in its reports to the Conferences as well as other periodic publications.[11]

Until the Mexican financial crisis in 1994 the growth in net foreign portfolio investment was extraordinary, although as mentioned above the investment flows (including FDI) were directed to those emerging market economies. Therefore, foreign portfolio investment practically excluded the majority of developing countries (not to mention the least developed ones) that had failed to develop local capital markets.

The disintegration of the Eastern bloc (socialist countries) in the early 1990s and their subsequent shift towards market-oriented management raised concerns among the developing countries regarding the diversion of international financial flows (public and private) from them to these "economies in transition". Therefore during the 1990s, the first post-Cold War decade, developing countries put forward the concept of "additionality", meaning that financial flows to the economies in transition should be made *in addition to, rather than by diverting from,* existing financial conditions.

Furthermore, the proliferation of political elements in conditionality attached to official development assistance (ODA) became a worrying concern as an increasing number of developing countries felt that the trend implied the further erosion of their policy autonomy. Although specific monetary issues relevant to developing countries remained crucial, vocal critics toward the international monetary system became considerably subdued within the intergovernmental machinery of UNCTAD. This was partly due to an agreement of UNCTAD VIII

---

[10] The drafting of the Final Act of the Conference usually begins in Geneva long before the Conference itself.
[11] Toye and Toye (2004: 273) explain: "The UNCTAD management's control of the content of its ... flagship publications is light, as is evident from the contradictory positions the different reports sometimes take on issues such as the benefits of foreign investment".

(1992) by which CIFT, the principal technical forum within UNCTAD dealing with international monetary issues, ceased to exist.[12]

Meanwhile, at the insistence of some OECD countries (particularly the United States) and despite the strong opposition of developing countries, the General Agreement on Tariffs and Trade (GATT) decided to include the item of "trade in services" in the Uruguay Round multilateral trade negotiations (1985–1993). There then arose a greater recognition of financial services as tradable activities in the international community. (For further discussions see topical papers on International Trade and Services in Development in this volume.) In this regard a great deal of discussion ensued concerning the merits and disadvantages of financial liberalization. (As will be mentioned later, the critical position of the UNCTAD secretariat on rapid financial liberalization in developing countries became much stronger after the outbreak of the East Asian Crisis of 1997–1998.)

In 1994 the Group of Twenty-Four (Group of 24) developing countries[13] sponsored an important conference in Cartagena, Colombia, on the occasion of the fiftieth anniversary of the Bretton Woods Conference. On this memorable occasion participants took stock of issues of economic policy substance and many

---

[12] It was agreed at UNCTAD XIII (1992) that the existing Committees should be suspended and replaced by four Standing Committees. The Standing Committees were on: (1) commodities; (2) poverty alleviation; (3) economic co-operation among developing countries; and (4) developing services sectors: fostering competitive services sectors in developing countries. While the existing terms of reference of CIFT were included in the fourth Committee listed above, the critical fact of matter was that UNCTAD lost the forum of historical importance. For details on changes in the intergovernmental machinery of UNCTAD agreed at UNCTAD III, see UNCTAD, 1993. As noted in footnote 2, many issues related to money, finance and debt have been discussed in a lukewarm fashion at the TDB (formally more intensively at CIFT). One notable exception that has actually received an increasing attention is FDI, particularly after the UNCTAD secretariat absorbed the UN Programme of Transnational Corporations (formerly the UNTNC) from New York in 1993.

[13] The Group of 24, with eight members from each of the three regional groups, was established following a decision at the Second Ministerial meeting of the G-77 in Lima in 1971. Its principal objective has been to co-ordinate the position of developing countries on international monetary and financial issues, in particular those issues under consideration in the Bretton Woods institutions. Developing countries felt that they should play a meaningful role in negotiations on international monetary and financial issues and that the effectiveness of this role would be enhanced if they were to meet regularly as a group, as the developed countries had been doing for some time in the Group of Ten (G-10).

suggestions that were raised at the conference are still of present concern to developing countries.[14]

The financial crises of the 1990s in the emerging market economies, for example Mexico (1994), East Asia (1997) and Brazil (1998), and ongoing financial difficulties in virtually all "economies in transition" brought about serious policy discussions on what came to be known as the reconstruction of the "international financial architecture" i.e. an appropriate governance structure for managing international financial flows. Particularly after the East Asian crisis, the secretariat has increasingly stressed the importance of the stabilizing role of regional and subregional reserve funds, swap arrangements and similar mechanisms to complement the efforts of international financial institutions.

During the 1980s and 1990s the UNCTAD secretariat paid special attention to two groups of developing countries, namely the least developed countries (LDCs) (since the early 1980s) and the Sub-Saharan African countries (since the mid-1980s). For each of these groups, which overlap in membership, the secretariat has periodically undertaken research on economic performances, prospects and policy issues, and the TDB has considered its substantive reports. (Note: The LDCs are treated separately in another topical paper in this volume.) As for sub-Saharan Africa, the TDB's considerations in the 1980s were in the context of implementing the United Nations New Agenda for the development of Africa in the 1990s (UN-NADAF). Towards the end of the decade the secretariat, upon the request of the UN General Assembly, prepared a comprehensive research paper as its contribution to the preparatory process for the final review and appraisal of the implementation of the UN-NADAF. More recently the UNCTAD secretariat began another annual development report with the geographical focuses on sub-Saharan Africa, including finance and debt.[15]

One of the noteworthy proposals of the secretariat in the recent past was the possible application of domestic bankruptcy procedures to the developing countries

---

[14] The report, entitled: *The International Monetary and Financial System: Developing Country Perspective - Proceedings of a conference sponsored by the Group of Twenty-Four on the occasion of the Fiftieth Anniversary of the Bretton Woods Conference, Cartagena, Colombia, 18-20 April 1994*, was published by UNCTAD in 1994 as Vol. IV of the series called *International Monetary and Financial Issues for the 1990s: Research papers for the Group of Twenty-Four.*

[15] The first issue of the report in 2000 had the title *Capital Flows and Growth in Africa.* The subsequent issues have the common title *Economic Development in Africa,* together with subtitles reflecting their specific research focus. For instance the most recent issue, UNCTAD (2004), focuses on the question of "debt sustainability" in the highly indebted poor countries (HIPCs) in Africa.

in order to resolve the compounding debt problem of those countries. (For further discussions, see Section IV of this paper.)

As mentioned above, the abolition of the CIFT after UNCTAD XIII (1992) was a critical blow as far as the intergovernmental machinery of UNCTAD to deal with the secretariat's research of monetary, financial and debt issues were concerned. Nevertheless, the research of the secretariat continues to enjoy a wider audience beyond that of diplomats attending UNCTAD's intergovernmental meetings as well as seminars and training courses in Geneva, through publications such as *The Trade and Development Reports* (*TDRs*), *The World Investment Reports* (*WIRs*), *the Least Developed Countries Reports* (*LDCRs*), and others.

II. Money: Issues Related to the International Monetary System

UNCTAD's central monetary issue about the international monetary system may be understood in the context of "adjustment-vs.-financing" debates. UNCTAD has consistently advocated that the existing system (in the Bretton Woods period (1944–1973) as well as the post-Bretton Wood period) be improved so as to become able to provide more adequate finance to deficit countries (particularly developing countries) without compelling them to undertake excessively contractionary adjustments. Specific issues are related to, among others, reforming the international monetary system, particularly in its payments adjustment mechanism, financing facilities of export shortfalls, the creation (and expansion of availability) of international reserve assets and the like.

Typically, the IMF's analysis of the causes of payments problems has put heavy emphasis on a programme of adjustment, in particular on contraction of domestic demand in deficit countries. The IMF's response has been, therefore, based on adjustment through deflation rather than through growth and development. The UNCTAD secretariat has underlined that payments problems of developing countries have often been associated with changes in global economic conditions or factors beyond their control as in the case of the imposition of protectionist measures affecting their exports, world recessions and inflation, etc. In these circumstances the stress laid by the IMF on domestic contraction is not appropriate.

Instead the financing of externally induced difficulties should be carried out in a framework that would make proper allowance for the global dimension of the problem. More specifically, the framework should also take into account the financing requirements for world trade as well as economic development and maintenance of high employment levels with respect to debtor countries. Furthermore, regarding its financing method, the secretariat critically argued that "stand-by" arrangements offered the IMF the possibility of enforcing implementation of the prescribed domestic polices in its member countries.[16]

A.   The 1960s

As mentioned earlier, partly due to the promptings of the UN, the IMF CFF[17] was created in 1963. This facility was intended to provide quickly disbursable, short-term loans to commodity-producing developing countries in order to help offset a temporary and presumably self-correcting shortfall in their export-earnings due to fluctuations in commodity prices.[18] The strategy of activating the CFF was to isolate those components of the current account whose fluctuations were most clearly outside the country's control so as to maintain the criterion of conditionality. It was highly valued by developing countries for its suitability to their use and for the relatively low conditionality attached for drawing under it. The UNCTAD secretariat persistently urged easier access to the CFF for developing countries.[19]

Meanwhile, in attempting to rectify what was known as the "Triffin Dilemma" – the problem the US dollar (the central key currency) had been faced with as a result of the simultaneous need for both extra liquidity and confidence – of the existing international monetary system, Professors Hart, Kaldor, and Tinbergen presented to UNCTAD I (1964) a scheme for an international

---

[16] Originally, the stand-by arrangements were supposed to give the member countries the right to engage in transactions to the amount of the total credit granted without further review by the IMF. But the continuously increasing inclusion of terms, the "trigger" clauses, along with the gradually emerging technique of "phasing" (meaning that the full extent of the stand-by could be withdrawn not in a lump sum but only instalments, the continuity of which was linked to fulfilment of the performance clauses) gave the IMF, in effect, the right to cancel these arrangements.

[17] As will be discussed later, the transformation of the CFF into the Compensatory and Contingency Financing Facility (CCFF) in 1988 suddenly reduced its accessibility.

[18] From the viewpoint of individual commodity-producing developing countries, this facility seemed to have some advantages over schemes that were designed for compensating price falls, because it would operate when quantities of exports fell as well as when price fell.

[19] According to Toye and Toye (2004: 222), the IMF CFF could be faulted on two grounds. First, the facility was intended to compensate for temporary price downturns (if they were not offset by quantity increases) rather than to reduce actual price fluctuations. Thus it did nothing about the problem of underinvestment and overinvestment induced by erroneous future expectations. This pointed back to schemes such as the installation of buffer stocks that could actually moderate price cycles. Second, the facility of strictly short-term loans limited its usefulness as export earnings of developing countries could undergo protracted declines, disrupting their development plan.

commodity reserve currency. Their scheme suggested that the IMF create internationally acceptable commodity-based reserves not linked to gold or key currencies. It was thought that by monetizing primary commodities the backing required to make the new asset acceptable would be provided.[20]

A number of recommendations adopted at UNCTAD I were directly concerned with the working and future structure of the international monetary system. One of the earliest contributions of UNCTAD on compensatory financing schemes was the adoption of a recommendation, entitled "Study of measures related to the compensatory credit system of the International Monetary Fund" (A.IV.17),[21] which suggested that the IMF consider measures, among others: "to increase, as soon as possible, the amount allocated to the Fund to compensatory financing, over and above its current transactions, from 25 per cent to 50 per cent of a member country's quota". In another recommendation, "Supplementary financing measures" (A.IV.18), UNCTAD itself was instructed to examine this matter with a view to ensuring that any future organization of international monetary relationships be consistent with the needs of developing countries. A further study of payments arrangements was also recommended by recommendation entitled "International monetary system" (A.IV.19).

In order to accomplish these ends the Secretary-General of UNCTAD convened a group of experts – chaired by Gamani Corea who would become the third Secretary-General of UNCTAD in the 1970s – on international monetary issues, focusing particularly on those relating to problems of trade and development. In this regard, the central purpose of convening this group was to consider how the developing countries would be affected by the nascent plan of the Group of Ten (G-10) industrial countries to create additional reserve assets that could be used as international liquidity.

The 1965 Report of the Expert Group entitled *International Monetary Issues and Developing Countries* (UNCTAD, 1965) was one early milestone publication that set the tone of the North-South debate on the reform of the international monetary system for the purpose of making it more responsive to the needs for growth of the world economy, particularly those of developing countries. Therefore, the report established first of all that the developing countries did have a need for additional unconditional liquidity, not merely a need for additional aid. In

---

[20] Other secondary features of the scheme were first, that by acquiring commodities from reserve currency countries as well as from primary products, these currencies could be amortized over time. And second, by buying commodities in times of falling prices and selling in time of rising prices, the overall price of commodities would be stabilized.
[21] Third Part - Annexes of UN (1964) lists all of the recommendations that were adopted at UNCTAD I.

this regard, the G-10 countries should not simply seek changes in the international monetary system on their own when such changes would have consequences on others. As for the existing IMF CFF, the report envisaged that the possibility of its use could be made entirely outside the structure of gold and credit tranches so that drawings of such credits would not prejudice a member's ability to make an ordinary drawing. The report also proposed the concept of "link", i.e. the idea of linking two different objectives, that of the creation and allocation of internationally created and managed reserve assets to satisfy reserve accumulation objectives and that of securing a transfer of real resources to developing countries to the levels of need for development finance.[22] Although there were many variations, all link schemes involved the *lesser* use of national wealth (or some proxy for wealth) as a criterion for determining the level of allotment of special drawing rights (SDRs).[23]

For various reasons, however, IMF CFF drawings failed to grow.[24] Subsequently the CFF underwent improvements with respect to drawing rights and shortfall definitions in 1966 (and 1975) in the general direction of enlargement of its operational scope. According to the UNCTAD secretariat, one of the most critical shortcomings of the facility was due to the IMF's formula for defining the shortfall, i.e. the deviation of export values from a moving average corrected for trends. Linking the traditional terms-of-trade framework, the secretariat argued:

> "It [the IMF's formula to define the export shortfall] does not distinguish between price and volume movements and does not take into account fluctuations in import prices. These lacunae are of crucial importance in today's world of rapidly changing and widely fluctuating export and import prices. It is thus clear that the IMF CFF could be significantly improved in this area (UNCTAD 1979a: 9)."

---

[22] For an informative historical review of various link proposals, see UNCTAD (1971), which was submitted to UNCTAD III (1972).

[23] The report was discussed in 1965 and 1966 at CIFT. While agreeing that the interest of developing countries in international monetary reform should be taken into account, the Group of B developed countries insisted that UNCTAD was not the proper forum for a discussion of international monetary issues. They further argued that as monetary reforms had already been taking place in the G-10 and in the IMF, it was not possible for them to participate in substantive discussions elsewhere. This position has been maintained up to the present.

[24] The infrequent use of the facility between 1963 and 1966 was partly due to the fact that export earnings of developing countries showed a general upward trend. Less favourable trends after 1966 promoted the greater utilization of the facility, but again fell towards the end of the 1970s. For further discussions see, for example, UNCTAD, 1967; 1968.

After intensive negotiations, mainly among the G-10 countries, the IMF Board of Governors agreed in 1967 to establish the SDR facility.[25] However, there was a clear and unresolved conflict of opinion among advocates of SDR creation, specifically between those who were concerned about a global reserve shortage, and those who were chiefly interested in transferring resources to developing countries. Thus, negotiations continued.

By adopting Conference resolution 32(II), UNCTAD II (1968) decided to consider the implementation of the "link" concept. Subsequently the concept was elaborated by another UNCTAD group of experts in 1969, which proposed two main types: (a) an "organic" link involving the allocation of SDRs to the International Development Association (IDA) or the regional development banks either directly by the IMF or by developed countries receiving SDRs; and (b) a "non-organic" link involving the contribution in national currencies to IDA or the regional development banks by developed countries, upon receipt of their SDR allocation. In each case the volume and timing of SDR creation/allocation would be determined by the level of need for development finance of the world economy, particularly of the developing countries. It was thought that the link would meet the problems of donor countries that felt unable to appropriate public funds for more aid because of budgetary reasons.[26]

The Development Strategy for the Second UN Development Decade (for the 1970s) also proposed that the possibility of establishing a link should be considered. The concept received wider endorsements, including that of the UN General Assembly in 1971 and was studied by the IMF, giving rise to an active and long-lasting debate.

As mentioned earlier, while the United States maintained its opposition toward the link proposal of any kind and its negative view dominated the G-10 discussions, an agreement was finally reached at the IMF on the amount of the SDR allocation of 9.3 billion SDRs between 1970 and 1974. The proposal was not taken up in the actual distribution of the SDR: in the end, 7.0 billion SDRs were

---

[25] SDRs were not only unconditional and automatic as distinguished from credit tranche drawing rights, but also free to the drawers, as they did not involve any transfer of real resources to the IMF. According to the agreed Outline on the SDR facility in 1967, the decisions regarding timing, volume and distribution of SDRs would be under the firm control of the developed countries, which presented extremely controversial institutional elements.

[26] Critics of the link proposals argued that their implementation would impair the development of the use of the SDR and that the high likelihood of over-allocation of SDRs beyond the true liquidity need would lead to undue delays in the process of payments adjustment (thus causing persistent imbalance) in deficit countries, as well as to global inflation.

distributed to the developed countries whereas only 2.3 billion SDRs were allocated to developing countries.

The continuous examination in UNCTAD forums of the adequacy of the international monetary system that had become apparent during the 1960s contributed to many reforms. By adopting resolution 18(II), UNCTAD II (1968) also called on the Bretton Woods institutions to concentrate on the problem of financing buffer stocks. As a result, the IMF established in 1969 the Buffer Stock Financing Facility (BSFF) where member countries could draw on IMF resources to finance their contributions to international buffer stock arrangements. The early UNCTAD works on the commodity-based currency system and the Supplementary Financing Facility (envisaged to be established in the World Bank) did not lead to any concrete results.

B.   The 1970s up to 1982

Immediately after the first debacle of the international monetary system in 1971, the UNCTAD secretariat highlighted in UNCTAD (1971a) various negative effects (such as depreciation of foreign reserves, the rise of debt burden, worsening of terms of trade, etc.) on developing countries induced by foreign exchange rate, realignments of major countries. According to an estimate contained in the report the total loss in foreign reserves from the US dollar depreciation would amount to some $950 million. As a remedial measure the report proposed a special issue of SDRs. (The advocacy by the UNCTAD secretariat of additional SDR allocations has continued up to the present. For instance, in *The Trade and Development Report (TDR) 1995* the secretariat called for a new SDR allocation, a portion of which could be used to alleviate multilateral debt, i.e. debt owed to multilateral financial institutions, of developing countries.)

UNCTAD III (1972) was held during a transitional period of growing turbulence and uncertainty in the international monetary system.[27] Naturally, various concerns about the system were extensively discussed during the session. For instance, attention was drawn to the adverse effects on developing countries with respect to terms of trade, reserves and debt-servicing payments owing to the

---

[27] During the period of 1972-1974 the IMF's Committee on Reform of the International Monetary System and Related Issues (known as the Committee of Twenty) attempted (and failed) to reach agreement on the reform. It was a straight North-South confrontation throughout, unyielding on either side of the confrontation. Toye and Toye (2004: 238) states: "When the industrial world gradually discovered, after May 1973, that floatation of the major currencies was a tolerable alternative to a system that was established in a multilateral agreement, further efforts to negotiate such a system faded away. With them the idea of the SDR-aid link effectively disappeared from the international agenda."

changes in exchange rates between major currencies. By adopting resolution 58(III), therefore, UNCTAD recommended that donor countries and multilateral financial institutions take measures to compensate for these losses and that an additional allocation of SDRs be made to developing countries that had suffered losses in the value of reserves because of such exchange rate realignments.

Meanwhile, the Declaration on the Establishment of a New International Economic Order (resolution 3201 (S-VI)) and the Programme of Action (3202 (S-VI)) adopted at the Sixth Special Session of the UN General Assembly in 1974 were very emphatic about the link proposal.[28] Nevertheless, from the time of the first allocation in 1974 to the second half of 1978, no additional issues of SDRs were authorized since the developed countries argued that greater liquidity was unnecessary and even inflationary (thus harmful) to the world economy.

At UNCTAD IV (1976) where the overwhelming concern was on commodity questions, the financial implications of price stabilization in the overall framework of the Integrated Programme for Commodities (IPC) were intensively discussed. The essence of the secretariat's scheme of the IPC was that all price stabilizing operations for a group of specifically designated commodities should be done through buffer stocks. During the negotiations some developing countries were adamant about the point of making the setting of what was termed as the Common Fund for Commodities (CFC) a precondition for negotiations on other part of the IPC. Many among them also announced their readiness to make contributions to the fund. The negotiations on the CFC were extremely difficult, reaching the "point of collapse" (Toye and Toye, 2004: 248) towards the very end of UNCTAD IV. Finally under the forceful leadership of Gamani Corea, the Secretary-General of UNCAD, delegations agreed to the secretariat's compromise proposal to the effect that the Secretary-General should convene a negotiation conference open to all members of UNCTAD on the CFC no later than 1977.[29]

---

[28] The Programme of Action contained, in the field of the international monetary system, the following objectives:

II (d): "Adequate and orderly creation of additional liquidity with particular regard to the needs of the developing countries through the additional allocation of special drawing rights based on the concept of world liquidity needs to be appropriately revised in the light of the new international economic environment: any creation of international liquidity should be made through international multilateral mechanism,"

II (e) "Early establishment of a link between special drawing rights and additional development financing in the interest of developing countries, consistent with the monetary characteristics of special drawing rights."

[29] This provision was incorporated into Conference resolution 93(IV), entitled "The Integrated Programme of Commodities".

Over the four years (1976–1980) following UNCTAD IV a vast international effort under the auspices of UNCTAD was devoted to forming individual commodity agreements through difficult negotiations concerning the CFC. Out of the post-1976 activities, however, only one new commodity agreement emerged i.e. for natural rubber (in 1979), and it was only in 1980 that intergovernmental agreement on the construction of the CFC was reached. The secretariat argued that the paucity of new commodity agreements was attributable to the slow progress on the CFC during the period.[30]

A major monetary trend observed in international monetary relations since 1973 (i.e. in the post-Bretton Woods period) was the increasing instability in exchange rates among major currencies, where daily fluctuations were extremely large in spite of substantial interventions by central banks. These fluctuations, associated with massive short-term financial movements induced by arbitrage or speculative factors, undermined the usefulness of changes in exchange rates as meaningful signals for external account adjustment. The economic costs of deviations in short-run exchange-rate movements from the path dictated by long-term factors tended to reduce effective investment planning and possibly diverted financing into activities of low priority. Foreign exchange instability could also adversely affect trade. The UNCTAD secretariat claimed, in one of the background documents submitted to UNCTAD V (1979), that the general climate of uncertainty, which such instability introduced into international economic relations, might have become one of the most significant trade barriers in practice, tending to induce protectionist responses (UNCTAD, 1979c).

The secretariat also expressed concern for the floating interest rate system and viability over time of maturities on new lending that it felt greatly enhanced the potential debt problems of developing countries. When the link proposal was first considered, the interest rate on the SDR was very low; however, during the course of the 1970s, the SDR interest rate was increased for the purpose of promoting its status. Paradoxically, countries found the benefit of new SDR allocations would be reduced, as the trend was that the advantage of borrowing at the SDR interest rate rather than at the higher rate in the capital markets diminished.

Various concerns voiced in UNCTAD (the intergovernmental machinery and the secretariat) were also taken up by the aforementioned Committee of Twenty in which the Secretary-General of UNCTAD was also invited; however,

---

[30] Toye and Toye (2004: 249) argue that the reverse reasoning is also plausible, i.e. that the absence of new commodity agreements made the CFC negotiations less urgent.

the Report of the Committee fell short of the developing countries' expectations.[31] The work of the Committee of Twenty culminated in agreement in the IMF Interim Committee on Monetary Affairs in Kingston, Jamaica in 1976, principally on the exchange rate system and the role of gold. More specifically the Kingston meeting agreed on, among other things, the legitimization of the currency system of floating exchange rates, the gradual replacement of gold by the SDR as an international reserve asset, the liberalization of access to the IMF's compensatory facilities, and the establishment of the Trust Fund to be financed principally from the sale of one sixth of the IMF's gold with the remainder coming from voluntary contributions. Yet many proposals that the UNCTAD secretariat considered essential for improving the system failed to be adopted.

Meanwhile, in 1975 the secretariat also became the executing agency for an UNDP project designed to assist the Intergovernmental Group of Twenty-Four on International Monetary Issues (the Group of 24) of developing countries in elucidating technical issues under negotiations in the international monetary field. This was to take the form, principally, of analytical papers prepared by competent experts (including some UNCTAD staff members) on issues currently under discussion. This project, to which the UNCTAD secretariat provides both substantive and administrative backstopping, has continued to operate up to the present.

Since the mid-1970s there has emerged renewed interest in the issue of compensatory financing. This interest was reflected in the establishment of STABEX in the context of economic relations between the European Economic Community (EEC) and certain African, Caribbean and Pacific (ACP) countries. Recognizing that instability in commodity trade was the major cause of instability in the export revenue of developing countries, the developing countries urged further liberalization in the IMF CFF. Several governments put forward proposals for additional compensatory financing schemes. Compensatory finance was included in the Integrated Programme for Commodities (IPC) (Conference resolution 93(IV)) adopted at UNCTAD IV (1976) as one of many measures

---

[31] According to UNCTAD (1985: 85), the Report of the Committee fell short in several aspects: problems of commodity trade and trade barriers restricting the exports of developing countries, which exert a profound influence on their external payments, were largely ignored. The Committee's concern with swift adjustment of imbalance led it to overlook the inequality in the ability of developed and developing countries to finance deficits; the oil price increases at the first oil shock and the resultant unprecedented imbalances in international payments caused the focus of attention from "adjustment" to "financing"; this led to the denial of preferential access to it, although developing countries did benefit from a scheme designed to reduce the interest burden of borrowing under the facility. Efforts to achieve symmetry of responsibility between surplus and deficit countries met with little success.

designed to impart strength and stability to commodity markets. The Group B developed countries were generally supportive of the idea of strengthening the IMF CFF, as it was likely to reduce the size of financial resources envisaged to be required in the CFC.

UNCTAD V (1979) adopted resolution 128 (V) entitled "International monetary reform" which again called on the IMF Interim Committee to consider the establishment of a development link in the context of allocating SDRs based on long-term global liquidity needs. The resolution also stressed the need to apply conditionality in IMF loans flexibly, taking into account domestic social and political objectives and priorities of borrowers, so as to encourage them to make full use of its facilities. The resolution also invited the IMF to examine the overall size of its quotas in relations to levels of international trade and balance-of-payments deficits and the need to finance them in the context of the adjustment process.

Subsequent to UNCTAD V in September 1979 the Development Committee of the World Bank and the IMF agreed that the subject of export earning stabilization should be viewed by the Committee in light of experience in the recently improved CFF (second revision in 1977), the ongoing negotiation on the CFC, and a further study being undertaken by the UNCTAD secretariat in cooperation with the Fund staff.

With the heavy emphasis on commodity issues in the 1970s, UNCTAD continued to stress the importance of the CFF and the BSFF of the IMF. In 1974 the IMF also established the Extended Fund Facility (EFF) designed to provide conditional assistance (up to three years) to member countries in implementing comprehensive programmes to correct imbalances. In light of the first oil shock the IMF began to activate the Oil Facility,[32] financed by borrowing from oil exporting countries where the new facility had the same or similar characteristics as the EFF in terms of eligibility and repayment period. The Oil Facility, however, carried higher interest rates than the EFF although it intended to meet an acute payments crisis beyond the control of the borrowing countries. The concerns about commodity prices in the 1970s also induced interesting discussions on linking the SDR with commodity prices with the aim of preventing large and essentially short-term variation in the market prices of certain major primary products. (Again, as in

---

[32] The Oil Facility was available to both developed and developing countries. As its name indicates, the facility did not seek to provide assistance to offset the rising costs of imports other than oil, even though many developing countries were faced with the rising costs of intermediate imports and capital goods as a result of the higher rate of inflation in developed countries. Needless to say, the oil facility did not compensate for a deterioration in terms of trade.

the case of the link proposal, this indexation proposal failed to lead to any concrete actions.)

Despite the rapid increase in international bank lending in the 1970s only a relatively limited creditworthy number of developing countries could effectively utilize private funds for financing deficits. Thus the UNCTAD secretariat argued that the financing of externally induced deficits should be carried out in a framework that would make proper allowance for the global dimension of the problem. In this regard the secretariat's proposal was for the establishment of a "multilateral facility to deal with externally induced deficits" which would collect funds from private and public sources and recycle them on terms appropriate to the debt-serving capacity of all countries. The secretariat spelled out the principal functions of the proposed facility as follows:

> "The facility would make resources available on terms which recognized the long-term structural character of many payments problems. It would assist countries in the financing of imbalances during the period required for the implementation of an agreed programme which took due account of the global aspects of the adjustment process. In this way it would meet an important institutional need. It would help to fill the gap between the largely short-term financing geared to programmes of national adjustment which is provided by [the] IMF on the one hand and the long-term project financing available from the development institutions on the other. It would also provide a forum in which the adjustment process is treated in a manner that full cognizance of the interrelationship of problems in the areas of trade, development, money and finance. At the same time it would reduce dependence on private mechanisms of recycling for countries facing structural problems associated with externally induced deficits, whilst providing surplus countries with a safe outlet for their excess savings (UNCTAD 1979: 188)."

Conference resolution 125(V), entitled "Complementary facility for commodity-related shortage in export earnings" adopted at UNCTAD V (1979), requested the Secretary-General of UNCTAD to prepare, in consultation with the IMF, a detailed study on the operations of a complementary facility to compensate for shortfalls in export earnings of individual commodities. The facility in the study was an institutional possibility in addition to the improvement of the IMF CFF and other existing facilities which should play an important financial role in the operation of the IPC.

By the end of the 1970s the Group B developed countries became increasingly more vocal against UNCTAD's involvement in issues relating to the international monetary system, repeating their traditional position that an appropriate forum for international monetary issues had already existed at the IMF. As a result they even refused to participate in some inter-governmental meetings on international monetary issues held by UNCTAD. A case in point is the 1980 meeting of the ad hoc Intergovernmental High-Level Group of Experts on the evolution of the International Monetary System, in pursuance to Conference resolution 128 (V) entitled "International monetary system" adopted at UNCTAD V (1979). The Group B countries decided not to be represented at the meeting (UNCTAD, 1982).

C.   The 1980s

In retrospect, the decade of the 1980s was the "lost decade" for development in most developing countries and was a decade of struggle with the Washington Consensus for UNCTAD. At the heart of the problem was the belief held by the Bretton Woods institutions (particularly the IMF) that countries should implement policies to deflate or contract their economies to whatever level of resources was available to them. These financial institutions stressed their belief in a minimum of interference with the price mechanism no matter how inadequate such adjustment policies would be from the point of view of development and social objectives.

In September 1981 the United Nations Conference on the Least Developed Countries (LDCs) in Paris adopted the Substantial New Programme of Action (SNPA) for LDCs in the 1980s which provided for substantially strengthened international measures of support for the development efforts of these countries. It was then agreed that developed countries trading primary commodities with LDCs should provide ways and means to help these countries offset the damaging effects of the loss of foreign exchange earnings arising from price fluctuations of their exports of primary commodities. The SNPA specifically entrusted UNCTAD with the focal role in global monitoring of its implementation. Subsequently the first publication of the *Least Developed Countries Report* (*LDCR*) in 1983 presented the very first assessment of financial needs of this group for development. (For further discussion on analyses presented in various *LDCRs*, see the topical paper on the LDCs and other countries in this volume.)

Meanwhile, in response to the abovementioned Conference resolution 125 (V) of UNCTAD V (1979), the Secretary-General of UNCTAD presented a series of reports containing proposals for a compensatory financing facility for commodity-related earning shortfalls.[33] Many of these proposals were made in support of an additional facility which could be designed so that a country's access to commodity financing would be linked to the measures intended to address the causes of commodity earnings instability of individual countries as well as global commodity market instability generated through fluctuations in supply.

The early period of the 1980s witnessed a worldwide recession affecting virtually all the economies in the world. The UNCTAD secretariat put forth three sets of mutually supportive measures in its report to UNCTAD VI (1983) namely, a substantial enlargement of the liquidity and financing available to developing countries; greater efforts by developing countries to increase the inflow of foreign investment and foreign exchange earnings; and increased emphasis on the part of the developed countries to bring down unemployment, interest rates and protectionist barriers.

Particularly for increasing liquidity the secretariat continued to call for a new SDR allocation, the advantages of which were that it would neither impose budgetary burden on the IMF members nor require equivalent contributions of national currencies. The secretariat underlined the fact that the level of reserve assets (including SDRs) available to the international community represented a lower proportion of world trade than in any earlier period and argued that there was considerable room for increasing them without risking global inflationary pressures. According to the secretariat, returning to the use of SDR would represent a decisive step towards a goal that had been accepted by the international community.[34]

Following Conference resolution 157 (VI), entitled "Compensatory financing of export earnings shortfalls" adopted at UNCTAD VI (1983), the Secretary-General of UNCTAD convened an expert group on the compensatory financing for export earnings shortfalls to consider the following questions: (1) the need for an additional complementary facility to compensate for export earning shortfalls, (2) the nature of an additional complementary facility, (3) the sources of finance for an additional complementary facility, and (4) the relationship of an

---

[33] These proposals were discussed at the ninth session of the UNCTAD Committee on Commodities (September 1980), at its first special session (November 1981) and its tenth session (December 1982).

[34] In the report of the Secretary-General of UNCTAD to Conference VI (1983) contained in UNCTAD (1983), the secretariat proposed an allocation of SDRs of $30 billion over the next two years. Pointing out furthermore that the share of the developing countries in any SDR allocation was only 30 per cent, the secretariat argued that different patterns of distributions would be required if an SDR issue were to serve the purpose of meeting the critical requirement of developing countries.

additional complementary facility to existing facilities and inter-governmental organizations.[35]

The 1980s witnessed the increasing trend of the Bretton Woods institutions to link short-term balance-of-payments adjustment to long-term structural reforms. The UNCTAD secretariat admitted that structural adaptation and growth in developing countries were integral parts of growth and adjustment on a global scale. Nevertheless it pointed out that while the prevailing international adjustment process provided for pressures on debtor developing countries to adjust, no comparable pressure could yet be exerted on creditor countries either to expand their rates of economic growth and structural change in their own economies or to recycle their surpluses to deficit countries. (This was a rebirth of the argument of deflationary bias in external adjustment made by Keynes at the Bretton Woods Conference in 1944.) This asymmetric burden sharing (i.e. disproportionate burdens of adjustment being placed on deficit countries rather than surplus countries), together with increased protectionism, high interest rates and depressed commodities prices, were major reasons for the disproportionate burden of global adjustment of developing countries in the 1980s. Thus UNCTAD promoted the concept of "adjustment through growth" rather than "adjustment through austerity".

In 1988 the IMF CFF, after the liberalization steps of 1966 and 1975, was transformed into the Compensatory and Contingency Facility (CCFF), now equipped with full-fledged conditionality. By making access to the CCFF strictly conditional (like access to ordinary drawings), the IMF made the facility redundant. Needless to say, such an institutional transformation was particularly harmful to the poorest countries that tend to depend most heavily on commodity exports and can least afford to cope with fluctuations in their export prices by holding large reserves.

D. The 1990s

The overriding concern of the international financial system at the commencement of the new decade was the provision of finance to the "transition countries" of central and eastern Europe given the collapse of the Eastern bloc as well as that of the Soviet Union. The void in economic ideology was quickly filled by a single market blueprint – that of globalization. This refers to the increasing flows of goods and resources across borders and the emergence of new institutional set-ups (private and public) to cope with them.

---

[35] The report of the expert was published as UNCTAD (1985).

The question of modality (i.e. appropriate pace and extent) of the integration of the financial system of developing countries into the global financial system was one of the most intensively discussed issues in UNCTAD in the 1990s. With the growing integration of international financial markets and the increased contagion risk, the issue of who would play the role of the international lender of last resort acquired greater importance. This problem became obvious from devastating experiences – most notably, Mexico (1994), East Asia (1997), and Brazil (1998) – where liquidity crises led to the collapse of the currencies of many developing countries before an international lender-of-last-resort agreement could be put together. The subsequent multilateral support operation in each crisis situation was mounted on an ad hoc basis. Thus it was recognized that an examination of ingredients of successful development strategies must be pursued so that each developing country could have at its disposal a full understanding of the options available on the basis of which its own strategy could be constructed or revised.

In retrospect there has gradually occurred the general shift in emphasis in the UNCTAD's intergovernmental machinery away from monetary issues towards financial flows (Section III) and debt problems in developing countries (Section IV).

III. Finance:
Issues Related to Financial Flows
for Developing Countries

As mentioned earlier, international monetary issues are mainly linked to the IMF. On the other hand, international financial issues encompass a much wider range of institutional actors including of course the Bretton Woods institutions, but also regional development banks, donor governments and private financial institutions. Principal issues here include those related to (a) volume, terms and conditions of financial flows, (b) usefulness of private financial flows, (c) mobilization of domestic and international resources, and (d) policies on managing financial resource flows. (Note: The debt problem of developing countries is treated separately in Section IV of this paper.)

As for development finance, the focus of UNCTAD has remained broadly consistent in emphasizing the need for an adequate volume of transfers along with appropriate terms and conditions. UNCTAD, along with others, played an important role in laying the foundations for international consensus on targets for the volume and terms of financial flows (public and private). Intergovernmental deliberations within UNCTAD in the 1960s focused on quantitative targets for financial flows and the quality of flows, especially of bilateral official development assistance (ODA), and emphasis was also placed on the key roles played by multilateral public financial institutions.

In the later period (the 1970s and beyond) private financial flows became an increasingly important issue as a crucial factor for promoting the local development of developing countries. In the recent past (particularly in the 1990s) analytical works of international financial flows to developing countries (as a whole as well as to specific groups such as LDCs and Africa) over an extended period of time were undertaken by the secretariat through its major publications such as *TDR*, *The World Investment Reports* (*WIRs*), and *The Least Developed Countries Reports* (*LDCRs*).

A. The 1960s

During this period the emphasis of the UNCTAD analysis was on private finance to developing countries, principally in the form of FDI and guaranteed export credits. The period of the 1960s and early 1970s was devoted to refining the idea and to objective measures of international financial flows (both private and public).

UNCTAD II (1968) adopted resolution 27(II) entitled "Growth, Development Finance and Aid (synchronization of international and national policies)" which considered the possibility of a supplementary target for net ODA of 0.75 per cent of the GNP of developed countries, in addition to the overall target of "financial resource transfer of a minimum net amount of 1 per cent of the GNP". This sub-target for official flows was considered useful insofar as these flows were more responsive to government policies and were, therefore, more amendable to meaningful international agreement. This sub-target, combined with the total flow target, could also be seen as the desirable balance between private and public flows.

By adopting resolution 29 (II) entitled "Improving the terms and conditions of aid alleviating the problems of external indebtedness", UNCTAD II recommended that further efforts be made by donor countries to soften the terms of aid beyond the norms set out by the OECD's Development Assistance Committee (DAC) and the UN General Assembly, and that the terms be harmonized among donor countries. It was proposed that the terms of aid should be softened by increasing the amount of aid given in the form of grant or by improving interest rates, maturities or grace periods for the ODA loans.

After UNCTAD II the international community paid increased attention to the question of the terms of development finance. The Commission on International Development (known as the Pearson Commission)[36] and the UN General Assembly – through its work on the elaboration of the International Development Strategy for the Second UN Development Decade (of the 1970s) – contributed to the further clarification of targets, particularly the 0.7 per cent ODA target.

In the 1960s the UNCTAD secretariat also undertook the first substantial attempt to quantify capital requirements of developing countries (see, for example, UNCTAD (1968b), prepared for UNCTAD II). Along with quantitative estimates of the volume of flows, the secretariat examined in detail the terms and conditions of flows that would be suitable to the needs of developing countries.

The history of multilateral finance reflects to some extent the changing fashions and ideas among major donors. Multilateral finance was seen as a superior form to bilateral finance in that it provided greater objectivity in assessment of needs and was thought probably to lead to more equitable distribution. At UNCTAD I for instance, reference was made to the possible role of a multilateral investment scheme then under study in the World Bank as a means of promoting FDI in developing countries. UNCTAD II considered the question of a multilateral interest equalization fund. The proposal, known as the Horoweitz proposal, would allow an international institution to borrow funds in financial markets on commercial terms and re-lend these funds to developing countries at lower rates of interest and with longer maturities where interest rates subsidies were to be covered by contributions from developed countries and from the World Bank.

B. The 1970s up to 1982

Whether due to severe shocks to the international economy or for other reasons, the fact remained that there was a growing tendency towards bilateral settlement of issues and a general emphasis on bilateral relations. With respect to aid, multilateral financial institutions saw their previously recognized central role in supporting development under increasing attack from a few major donors.

---

[36] The Pearson Commission was established in 1968 upon a request from the President of the World Bank to consider all aspects of problems and policies related to the development of developing countries and to make relevant recommendations.

The aforementioned International Strategy for the Second United Nations Development Decade (of the 1970s) provided the basic framework for financial co-operation between developed and developing countries. UNCTAD contributed a great deal to giving greater precision and operational content to the framework.

Through Conference resolution 60(III), "Terms and conditions of official development assistance", UNCTAD III (1972) again called for qualitative and quantitative improvements of public financial flows to developing countries. Specifically it was urged that developed countries should reach an international agreement on the general untying of their external assistance to developing countries at the earliest possible date and to soften further the terms of their external assistance. Other recommendations contained in the resolution included a request for developed countries to take into consideration the view that interest rates for official development loans should not exceed 2 per cent per annum, maturity periods should be at least 25 to 40 years with a grace period of no less than 7 to 10 years, and that the proportion of grant in the total assistance of each developed country should be progressively increased.

By adopting resolution 61(III) entitled "Financial resources for development: total flow of public and private resources", UNCTAD III now firmly endorsed the 0.7 per cent-of-GNP ODA target in addition to the 1 per cent target for total net flow. Specifically, the developed countries were asked to increase ODA to reach a minimum net amount of 0.7 per cent of GNP by 1975. Furthermore, these donor countries were urged to take measures to ensure continuity of ODA flow· through multi-year programming or other means compatible with budgetary or parliamentary procedures. The resolution also requested the TDB to examine further the concept of aid and flow targets in order to prepare for discussions to take place at the mid-term review of the implementation of the Development Strategy. In the mid-1970s member countries and national and multilateral institutions of OECD began a substantial aid programme for the benefit of other developing countries. The UNCTAD secretariat undertook the task of compiling data on these activities, and the first report of complied data appeared in 1977 (see UNCTAD, 1977).

Meanwhile the Group of Experts on the Concepts of the Present Aid and Flow Targets was established by the TDB and met in 1973, 1974 and 1977. The Group examined the question of definition and means of flows, including the question of netting out reverse flows.

Since the adoption of the Development Strategy (for the second UN Development Decade of the 1970s), increasing recognition has been given to the

LDCs. In view of the fact that LDCs would require larger amounts of external finance at highly concessional terms over an extended period, particular attention was given to the terms of assistance to these countries. Therefore in Conference resolution 62(III) entitled "Special measures in favour of the least developed countries", UNCTAD III recommended that bilateral ODA to LDCs "should be extended on highly concessional or International Development Association terms and preferably in the form of grants." (For further discussions, see the topical paper on the LDCs and other countries in this volume.)

The role and contribution of private finance in supporting development has always been a concern of UNCTAD. As mentioned earlier, private financial flows to developing countries in the 1960s were primarily in the form of FDI and export credit. From the 1970s onwards attention was given to questions of the direct access of developing countries to the rapidly expanding Euro-Currency markets as well as proposals for an export credit finance or guarantee facility. UNCTAD III (1973) adopted Conference resolution 56(III) on FDI, entitled "Foreign private investment in its relationship to development" which was broadly critical of it and authorized the Secretary-General of UNCTAD to continue studies on it "with a view to determining with the greatest possible accuracy the effects of foreign private investment on the development process of the developing countries."

In its report submitted to the Sixth Special Session of the UN General Assembly (1974), where two resolutions, 3201 and 3202 (S-VI) of a New International Economic Order[37] were adopted, the UNCTAD secretariat expressed concern about the ongoing operations of bank lending of petrodollar recycling.

"The growth of external debt of developed countries could be offset, to some extent, by additional exports to developing countries, which would occur if some proportion of ... [petrodollar was] directed to investment in developing countries through the operation of market forces. While this process would alleviate the overall deficit position of developed countries, as well as supporting the economic development of developing countries, it is likely to have its drawbacks, in so far as it would tend to strengthen

---

[37] UN General Assembly resolution 3202 (S-VI) spelled out a series of urgent measures to finance the development of developing countries and to meet the balance-of-payments crises in these countries. They included, among others:
(a) Implementation at an accelerated pace by developed countries of the time-bound programmes, as already laid down in the International Development Strategy for the Second United Nations Development Decade, for the net amount of financial resources transfers to developing countries so as to meet and even to exceed the target of the Strategy;
(b) International financing institutions should effectively play their role as development financing banks without discrimination on account of the political or economic system of any member country, assistance being untied; etc.

the position of multinational or transnational corporations in the international economy in general, and in the non-oil exporting developing countries in particular (UNCTAD 1974: 14)."

Immediately after the adoption of the above-mentioned UN General Assembly resolutions on the New International Economic Order in 1974 we witnessed the arrival of the heyday of various proposals on international financial transfer. These proposals included the establishment of a type of world tributary system which would apply international rates in the use of the universal common heritage (such as sea and outer space resources), taxes on non-renewable resources and the assets of the transnational corporations, and devolution to the country of origin of the tax collected on incomes of experts and professionals from developing countries. While they were intellectually stimulating to many observers, none of these "automatic" systems of financial transfer could convince developed countries to accept them.

In line with the spirit of the establishment of the New International Development Order, UNCTAD IV (1976) adopted resolution 97 (IV) on TNCs entitled "Transnational corporations and expansion of trade in manufactures and semi-manufactures", by which action was recommended to be taken at the national, regional and international levels to achieve a reorientation of the activities of TNCs and thus to safeguard the interests of developing countries. The Conference resolution also recommended that measures be designed and implemented to strengthen the participation of developing countries' national enterprises in the activities of TNCs. In retrospect the contents of these resolutions reflected the overall critical sentiment of many developing countries pushing the establishment of a New International Economic Order, particularly on formulating an international code of conduct for TNCs.[38] (For further discussions, see the topical paper on FDI/TNCs in this volume.)

---

[38] In section V, "Regulation and control over the activities of transnational corporations", the Programme of Action of the Establishment of a New International Economic Order, contained in UN General Assembly resolution 2202 (S-VI) stated:
"All efforts should be made to formulate, adopt and implement an international code of conduct for transnational corporations:
(a) To prevent interference in the internal affairs of the countries where they operate and their collaboration with racist regimes and colonial administrations;
(b) To regulate their activities in host countries, to eliminate restrictive business practices and to conform to the national development plans, and in this context facilitate, as necessary, the review and revision of previously concluded agreements;
(c) To bring about assistance, transfer of technology and management skills to developing countries on equitable and favourable terms;
(d) To regulate the repatriation of the profits accruing from their operations, taking into account the legitimate interests of all parties concerned;

Conference resolution 98 (IV) also adopted at UNCTAD IV (1976), recommended that bilateral ODA to the two categories of handicapped developed countries, namely Island and Land-locked developing countries, in addition to the LDCs, be provided essentially in the form of grants.

The UNCTAD secretariat undertook various analyses of newly perceived problems of developing countries particularly those related to access to international capital markets. It focused on hardening of the terms of such finance (i.e. increases in interest rates and margins as well as shortening maturities). The secretariat specifically examined several methods for enlarging the access of developing countries to the Euro-market (private bank lending and bond markets) and for ensuring stability in the supply of this type of finance. With respect to export credit the original focus had been on the case of export credits extended by developed countries as a source of finance for developing countries. Continued concern over various issues of export credits became subsumed under the discussion of problems of the external debt of developing countries. Thus discussion of export credits *per se* shifted in the mid-1970s to the consideration of proposals for an export credit refinancing or guarantee facility that would assist developing countries by offering credit on their non-traditional exports. Nevertheless the secretariat after all insisted on the indispensable importance of public finance, particularly ODA, for many poorer developing countries that were unable effectively to tap private financial markets.

As a follow-up to a General Assembly Resolution of 1977 entitled "Finance and development" (32/177), UNCTAD convened a meeting of high-level experts in August 1978. The objective of this meeting was to enhance the access of developing countries to international capital markets, in particular to markets extending long-term portfolio finance. One of the principal issues discussed by the group was the desirability and feasibility of establishing a multilateral insurance and reinsurance agency.[39]

In one of the reports it submitted to UNCTAD V (1979b), the UNCTAD secretariat discussed current issues related to international financial cooperation for development including the rules and regulations that restricted developing countries' access to international capital markets. One noteworthy proposal contained in the report was that of the "international pooling of ODA funds". The report proposed:

(e) To promote reinvestment of their profits in developing countries."
[39] The report of the high-level group (UNCTAD, 1978) was reproduced and submitted to the UN General Assembly by the Secretary-General of the UN in his report (A/33/230).

"Consideration...might be given to the possibility of making use of the committed but undisbursed funds for general development purposes. For example, as soon as funds of ODA programmes are approved by national legislature, they might be placed in an international fund. Each donor country would draw down the monies which it had previously paid into the fund at the rate required for the financing of programmes for which the funds were originally approved. Given that ODA commitments would continue to increase, total resources if the fund are most unlikely to decrease; in fact, they might be expected to increase over time."

C. The 1980s

The 1980s was a decade of debt crisis for developing countries. As mentioned earlier, attention had already been drawn at UNCTAD III (1972) to the dangerous worsening of debt-servicing problems of developing countries and to the urgent need of adopting measures for debt relief. After several years of difficult deliberation, a set of agreed guidelines for debt operations was finally adopted by the TDB (in resolution 222(XXI)) in 1980.[40] In pursuance of the commitment to implement this Board resolution, UNCTAD VI (1983) adopted resolution 162(VI) whereby UNCTAD stressed that debt restructuring should contribute to debtor countries' efforts to re-establish their creditworthiness and regain access to financial resources on appropriate terms, thereby restoring their development momentum. The resolution also stressed the need for continued collaboration between all parties involved in dealing with debt-servicing problems, and invited bilateral and multilateral donors to ensure that their actions were based on an adequate assessment of the economic situation and medium-term development objectives of the countries concerned.

In real terms net external financial flows to developing countries in 1989 were about half the level of 1981. This decline was accompanied by an unprecedented reversal of net financial transfer to developing countries suffering from rising interest rate payments. The level of official financial flows to developing countries was virtually stagnant in real terms over the decade, and

---

[40] These guidelines set out the following general objectives of international action in the event of debt problems, specifying that such action may vary according to the nature of the problems dealt with: "[it] (a) should be expeditious and timely; (b) should enhance the development prospects of the debtor country, bearing in mind its socio-economic priorities and the internationally agreed objectives for the development of developing counties; (c) should aim at restoring the debtor country's capacity to service its debt in both the short term and long term, and should reinforce the developing country's own efforts to strengthen its underlying balance-of-payments situation; [and] (d) should protect the interest of debtors and creditors equitably in the context of international economic co-operation."

financial flows from multilateral financial institutions were very small. The secretariat's report to UNCTAD VII (1987) documented that, for instance, non-concessional lending by the World Bank made a marginal contribution to net financial flows to developing countries in fiscal year (FY) 1986, following a declining trend which emerged in FY 1984. Net flows from the IMF to developing countries, which had risen from SDR 1.6 billion in FY 1981 to a peak of SDR 7 billion in FY 1983, had since fallen and turned into a net flow to the institution from developing countries as a whole of SDR 341 million in FY 1986.

Whereas the importance of FDI as a source of "non-debt-creating" financial flows was increasingly recognized, the share of developing countries as a whole as the recipients of total FDI fell from more than one quarter in the early 1980s to less than one fifth towards the end of the decade. The secretariat reasoned that the debt crisis in the 1980s continued to stifle FDI flows to developing countries by feeding the general perception of their high risks, diminished profitability and poor prospects for growth.

The emergence of the Washington Consensus in the 1980s was in a way a sign of retreat from multilateralism. This retreat reflected the view that the existing economic difficulties in developing countries resulted primarily from inappropriate policies at the national level. Therefore, the prescribed solutions to these difficulties would include primarily the reduction or elimination of fiscal deficits together with the adoption of sound monetary policies, followed by structural adjustments designed to increase the flexibility of economies and improve the efficiency of resource use. In short, the emphasis was to "put one's house in order". Consequently, the development issue was viewed less in terms of improving the external financial and trading environment, and more in terms of improving allocative efficiency through structural reforms designed to provide incentives for the private sector to be a driving force for development.

In the 1980s the debates in UNCTAD forums on international financial flows were increasingly concentrated on concrete policy issues of non-debt-creating financial flows, particularly FDI flows. However, the lingering debt crisis in many developing countries continued to stifle FDI by feeding the general perception of high risk, diminished profitability and poor prospects for growth. In fact, despite the use of debt-equity swap, the volume of net FDI inflows in real terms to developing countries at the end of the decade was still lower than it had been before the outbreak of the crisis. Furthermore, the share of developing countries in total FDI fell from more than one quarter in the early 1980s to less than one fifth in the late 1980s.

The rapid growth of foreign portfolio investment in the 1980s was initiated by the Thatcher government (UK) at the beginning of the decade and culminated later in the restructuring of many developing countries along the lines of the Washington Consensus. Privatization of state enterprises in a growing number of developing countries greatly expanded the menu and volume of financial instruments available in their capital market for purchase by foreign portfolio investors. Needless to say, this financial development would further accelerate in the 1990s due to massive privatization policies in transition economies.

D.   The 1990s

The drastic changes in international relations emanating from the disintegration of the Eastern bloc, which slowly progressed in the 1980s and began to accelerate at the very end of the decade, gave rise to various concerns in developing countries. Most obviously, Central and Eastern European countries drastically reduced their financial assistance to developing countries, and most of them became recipients of finance by substantial amounts from official sources. There were also many uncertainties about the content and pace of the reform process of these countries, and most importantly about the extent to which financial support would be needed and offered. As a result many developing countries were fearful of the diversion of traditional North-South financial flows to these economies in transition. Another concern was the proliferation of conditionality associated with multilateral and bilateral financial assistance. Furthermore, the gradual convergence among conditionality elements effectively narrowed the scope of choice regarding sources of public financial resources from which developing countries can obtain necessary development finance.

Perhaps UNCTAD XIII (1987) was the last session of the Conference where the question of public financial flows was extensively debated. Since then the issue of the volume and terms of ODA began to disappear gradually from UNCTAD documents. As pointed out earlier, after the "suspension" of CIFT was agreed to at UNCTAD VIII (1992), UNCTAD has been missing the most relevant intergovernmental forum in which to discuss the question.

The decade of the 1990s witnessed a phenomenal increase in the level of financial flows to developing countries and a shift in the composition of the flows (with a remarkable increase of the FDI subcomponent).[41] *TDR 1999* critically argued that the strong growth of FDI flows to developing countries in the 1990s had largely reflected mergers and acquisition (rather than greenfield investment), which accounted for well over half of the total FDI flows in 1992-1997 and for almost three quarters if China was excluded. The report further argued that much of this merger activity was in services sectors and had the potential to add to payment difficulties.

One of the noteworthy new developments in the UNCTAD secretariat's research on finance in the 1990s was the increased recognition of its unique publication: *The Least Developed Countries Report (LDCR). LDCR 2000* was prepared specifically as a comprehensive background document for the Third UN Conference on the LDCs held in May 2001. It provided information on economic growth and social trends in the 1990s, with particular focus on the question of financing development in LDCs. More specifically the Report discussed the scale of the development finance challenge in LDCs, the scope for meeting this challenge through domestic resource mobilization, and the constraints which are limiting the LDCs' access to international capital markets and attractiveness for FDI.

According to *LDCR 2000,* the two key features of the developing financing patterns of LDCs had emerged in the 1990s. First, the central accumulation and budgetary process of the LDCs has been dominated by external rather than domestically generated resources. Second, almost all the external finance for most LDCs has come from official rather than private sources. The development prospects of most LDCs, therefore, have depended critically on aid relationships and associated external debt dynamics. Among the highly aid-dependent countries have been the island LDCs. According to the Report, this is due to their small size and extreme limitations as regard to agricultural land and other resources. Thus these countries, being highly dependent on imports for a major part of consumption and production requirements, must find high-value export niches – high value

---

[41] In 1990, of the net long-term flows of just over $ 100 billion, official flows accounted for about 57 per cent. By 1996, before the onset of the East Asian crisis, net flows had rocketed to $338 billion, $299 billion of which came from the private sector. The most remarkable increase was in the subcomponent of FDI flows to developing countries, which increased from a mere $24.5 billion in 1990 to over $163 billion in 1996 (Botchwey, 2003: 133-135). In fact, from a peak in 1991 when they reached about $63 billion, net official long-term flows declined in both absolute terms and as a percentage of total flows to developing countries (Ibid. 136). As discussed in the text, however, private financial flows - whether FDI or other flows - to developing countries have been directed to a relatively small number of them, and the vast majority (particularly the sub-Saharan African countries, with a few exceptions) has continued to rely heavily on public finance.

relative to transport costs and to domestic labour requirements for production. Otherwise they are bound to remain dependent on external resources to bridge their balance-of-payments gap even with low standards of living. (See *LDCR 2000*: 41–47)

LDCR 2002 further developed the analysis on financial flows to LDCs in the 1990s in the development context. It warned against the optimism based on the trend of increase in private capital flows, particularly FDI, to these countries by pointing out a few reasons. First, long-term net capital flows to the LDCs continued to decline during the decade in per capita and real terms (deflated against the index of manufactured exports from industrial countries). Second, although LDCs as a whole have received more FDI, they remained excluded from international bank finance and bond; therefore, with few exceptions, private debt flows to them were negative for every year. In other words, repayments of existing debt to private creditors were in excess of new loans. Third, the increase in capital flows to the LDCs has been highly concentrated, where a few among them received a large share. Fourth, the LDCs continued attract a relatively low share of the aggregate net flows going to all developing countries despite high levels of aid (see *LDCR 2002*: 7–12).

Meanwhile the absorption by the UNCTAD secretariat of the UN Programme on Transnational Corporations (formerly the UNCTC) from New York in 1993 was an added factor in expanding the secretariat's involvement in the research and analysis of international financial flows. As a result the major concern of the secretariat regarding international financial flows has been predominantly on FDI flows. One of the principal roles that UNCTAD is likely to play more in the foreseeable future is to help developing countries, and LDCs in particular, by attracting and using FDI in the process of improving their competitiveness. Needless to say, if FDI is to be a vital contributory factor to long-term development the effective establishment of linkages between TNCs' local subsidiaries and the rest of the local economy is absolutely essential. (For further discussions, see the topical paper on FDI/TNCs in this volume.)

IV. Debt:
Issues related to External Debt
of Developing Countries

The issue of the external debt of developing countries was already considered at UNCTAD I when the amount of debt was still relatively small. The

UNCTAD secretariat then drew attention to the debt-servicing burden imposed on the development process of many developing countries and called for its alleviation. Adequate balance-of-payments financing mechanisms, appropriate terms and conditions of finance flows and effective debt management have been seen as forward-looking and inter-related measures to reduce the likelihood of debt crises.

The concern for the external debt of developing countries grew with the increase in size of their debt burden in the 1970s and onward, particularly in the 1980s with the outbreak of the debt crisis. As far as UNCTAD (its intergovernmental machinery and secretariat) is concerned, what have been prominent in the area of external debt are its efforts to work out proposals on debt relief measures and guidelines for debt rescheduling as well as in providing technical assistance on debt management to developing countries. More specifically, the perspective of the secretariat is that debt should be seen within the overall framework for the terms and volumes of transfer of resources for development, and that the need for debt-relief for debtor countries should be considered positively in light of debt sustainability.

UNCTAD has also focused on the question of establishing appropriate rules and multilateral machinery for future operations relating to the debt problems of developing countries. The essential feature of such a multilateral framework has been the increasing awareness that debt reorganization should be a "development-oriented" operation rather than short-term financial stabilization exercises so as to enable the debtor countries to overcome underlying problems and resume their development path.

A.   The 1960s–1982

At UNCTAD I (1964) the report of the Secretary-General of UNCTAD pointed out that, while capacity of developing countries to repay their debt had been reduced by the slow growth of exports and deterioration in terms of trade, the burden of servicing debt had increased as a result of hardening the terms of lending due to a shortening of maturities and increase in interest rates. Consequently the Conference recommended (via recommendation entitled "Problem of debt service in developing countries" (A.IV.5)), among other things, that competent UN bodies and/or other international financial institutions stand ready, at the request of any developing countries, to review the external indebtedness of developing countries in co-operation with the creditor concerned and where appropriate with a view to securing agreement or consolidation of debt with appropriate periods of grace and amortization as well as reasonable rates of interest.

At UNCTAD II (1968), the UNCTAD secretariat placed additional emphasis on the institutional aspect of debt rescheduling. Shortcomings of the then prevailing *ad hoc* process of rescheduling for public and private debt were highlighted. Rescheduling techniques were informal and resulted in a general agreement between the debtor and the creditor country but required for its application further complicated bilateral arrangements between the debtor and its numerous creditors. This process – largely creditor-dominated and insufficiently development-oriented – seemed time-consuming, giving rise to a good deal of uncertainty, and tended to disrupt not only trade and payments but also the inflows of capital and the entire development process. The secretariat suggested the adoption of an early warning system within an appropriate institutional framework in order to avoid a debt crisis that would compel debtor countries to take drastic measures. Moreover, rescheduling criteria and procedures should not disrupt the development process of debtor countries and should be tailored to the special characteristics of each case, particularly in situations where the imbalance was more structural than short-term in nature.

At UNCTAD III (1972), attention was drawn to the dangerous worsening of debt servicing problems of developing countries and to the urgent necessity of adopting measures for debt relief. It was stressed that debt relief should not be a limited response to a crisis situation and should be examined within the context of broad development goals. A multilateral framework was needed to examine the debt problems of a country in the context of its overall development plan and the requisite net transfer of resources. Other proposals were produced by the secretariat such as the inclusion of a "bisque clause" whereby, under certain conditions, the debtor would be accorded some pre-agreed measures of relief in the form of postponement of standards and procedures to be applied in debt renegotiation so as to assure equal treatment of countries in similar situations.

With the rapid expansion of commercial lending in the 1970s, the trend of accumulating external debt in developing countries became an international concern. As a result an ad hoc Group of Government Experts on the Debt Problem of Developing Countries was established in 1974 and held three sessions. The final report[42] of the Group in 1975 contained in UNCTAD (1975) presented a set of

---

[42] The annex of this report contained the numerous documents the UNCTAD secretariat had prepared for the Group's three sessions.

agreed common elements[43] for consideration in future debt renegotiations which could provide guidelines and contribute to securing equal treatment of debtor countries in similar situations.

Furthermore, upon recommendation of the Group the TDB in 1975 by resolution 132 (XI) authorized the Secretary-General of UNCTAD to provide appropriate assistance to debtor countries in relation to the holding of *ad hoc* meetings where creditors would examine the debtor developing countries and a number of developing countries would examine the debtors' situation in a broad development context prior to debt renegotiations in the usual form. The UNCTAD secretariat was also authorized to participate in debt renegotiation meetings organized by the Paris Club on the same basis as other international organizations.[44] Socialist countries, however, refused to participate in debt-renegotiations, claiming that since credits granted by them to developing countries shared many specific features of a bilateral character, the re-negotiations of these credits would have to be carried out within a bilateral framework, i.e. through direct arrangements between debtor and creditors. It was hoped by many developing countries that the presence of the secretariat at these meetings would

---

[43] The common elements enlisted in the report are as follows:
(i) Debt re-organization would take into account the development prospects of a debtor country, thereby enabling it to continue debt servicing payments and restore its creditworthiness;
(ii) Such re-organization would be conducted in the customary multilateral framework with the intent to conclude agreements as speedily as possible in order to avoid prolonged uncertainties regarding foreign exchange availabilities;
(iii) Equality and non-discrimination among creditors is an essential principle underlying the operation of debt renegotiation. Creditor countries with minor debts due, which frequently include developing countries, would generally, however, be excluded from the multilateral debt renegotiation;
(iv) The terms of debt relief, such as consolidation, repayment and grace periods as well as the interest rate, would take into account the anticipated long-term debt servicing capacity of the debtor country and the legitimate interest of creditors; and
(v) Debt-reorganization arrangements would provide for flexibility to review the situation at the end of the consolidation period in the light of unforeseen circumstances. They would also provide for accelerated repayments in an agreed manner if the debtor's economic situation improves more rapidly than anticipated. (UNCTAD, 1975: 14-15).
[44] In 1978 the UNCTAD secretariat began to participate in Paris Club meetings. In these meetings its representatives presented a broad analysis of the debtor country in question, emphasizing in particular the trade-related causes of the problem (e.g. decline in terms of trade or protectionist measures affecting the country's exports, etc.). The analysis has also set out various scenarios for the country's economic perspective under different assumptions of the amount and terms of debt relief. Prior to each meeting, upon the request of the debtor country, the UNCTAD secretariat provides assistance in preparing its case. Furthermore, the secretariat also provides requesting countries with technical assistance on debt management, including a computerized debt recording and management software. This software, management and financial Analysis System (DMFAS) developed in the early 1980s, has been upgraded and is now installed in 50 users (including 19 HIPCs) (Jolly, et al. 2004: 144-145).

strengthen the long-term development dimension of the discussion therein, which would otherwise be less prominent.

At UNCTAD IV (1976) the debt problem of the most seriously affected as well as LDCs was given prominence. The Conference adopted resolution 94 (IV), entitled "Debt problems of developing countries", whereby the governments of developed countries pledged themselves to respond quickly within a multilateral framework to requests arising from these countries for relief of their debt-services payments. This resolution also called upon international forums to work out features that could provide guidance in future operations relating to the debt problems of developing countries.

Subsequently, the TDB ministerial session in March 1978 adopted resolution 165(S-IX). In section A, developed donor countries committed themselves to providing debt relief to low-income developing countries, particularly LDCs, by means of an adjustment of the terms of past bilateral ODA loans to the then prevailing terms (interest rates, grace and maturity periods, etc.), as a means of improving net ODA flows.[45] In effect donor countries agreed to soften the terms of ODA debt, including the option of converting loans to grants where applicable so as to apply retroactively to outstanding ODA loans the benefits of the significant softening of ODA terms that had occurred during the 1970s.[46] The basic principles regarding operations relating to debt problems contained in section B were refined and elaborated in the detailed features contained in TDB resolution 222 (XXI) of 1980.

Section A of resolution 222 (XXI) reiterated the commitment made by developed countries to proceed with the retroactive term adjustment of the ODA debt of poorer countries and introduced a dynamic element whereby developed donor countries agreed "to seek to continue to adopt retroactive adjustment of

---

[45] Eighteen developed donor countries adopted such relief measures for developing countries. Since the relief was accorded principally to LDCs, whose outstanding indebtedness was largely composed of ODA lending, it represented a substantial reduction in their total debt-service burden. According to an estimate of the UNCTAD secretariat the relief provided by these creditors amounted to approximately $6 billion to the benefit of 45 developing countries. However, some donors, including the United States (the largest donor) as well as socialist countries, did not apply measures in line with this resolution (UNCTAD, 1984: 96).

[46] The logic was that developing countries should not have to continue servicing past ODA debt on hard terms if they were currently recipients of much softer ODA from the same sources. The snag is that the amount of debt relief that can be granted in this way is constrained by the amount of softening in new ODA that has actually taken place and is limited to those donor countries that have softened their ODA. Arguably, this debt relief formula could discourage donor countries from further softening of ODA terms on account of the cost of applying the new terms to old debt. Nevertheless the political appeal of this technique to several donors is undeniable. (Haji, 1985: 155).

terms or equivalent measures in accordance with section A of resolution 165 (S-IX), so that the improvement in current terms can be applied to outstanding official development assistance", and requested the TDB to keep this matter under review. Section B of the resolution contained detailed features for future debt-relief operations. The objectives of such guidelines were: to assure expeditious and timely action; to enhance the development prospects of the debtor country; to restore the debtor country's capacity to service its debt in both the short term and the long term; and to protect the interests of debtors and creditors equitably. In this regard the UNCTAD secretariat argued that the prevailing arrangements had by and large failed to achieve the desirable objectives and were in need of improvement if the detailed features were to be implemented more effectively:

> "International action has not been sufficiently expeditious and timely. Efforts to restore the debtor country's capacity to service debt and to reinforce its own efforts to strengthen its underlying balance-of-payments situation have been primarily short-term in nature. The interest of debtors have not been protected equitably in the context of international economic co-operation (UNCTAD 1983b: 15)."

B. 1982–1996

While developing countries warned repeatedly of the inherent danger in debt accumulation in many international forums – for instance at UNCTAD IV (1976) and UNCTAD V (1979) – as well as during the failed negotiations of the Conference on International Economic Co-operation (1975–1977), no concrete solutions beyond TDB resolution 165 (S-IX) were agreed upon.

When the 1982 debt crisis broke out with the Mexican declaration of default[47] the initial policy stance of creditor countries was based on the so-called "illiquidity theory", the assumption that there was no fundamental crisis but only a temporary inability to service debt. It was optimistically perceived that debt-service ratios of developing countries would return to levels previously associated with creditworthiness. Despite the initial optimism, however, the Mexican shock led to a sudden halt in new lending by commercial banks. As a result a growing number of heavily indebted countries found themselves in the state of insolvency. The virtual cessation of private lending combined with continued stagnation in indebted countries intensified social problems in a growing number of countries.

---

[47] Earlier in the year Argentina had suspended payment on its $37 billion debt following the Falkland Islands war with the United Kingdom. However, the debt crisis is usually said to have begun in August 1982 when Mexico declared its inability to service the debt and shook the financial world.

Subsequently the creditor countries came under increasing pressure to modify their debt policy. In 1984, therefore, the commercial banks were obliged to agree to multiyear rescheduling (Jolly et al., 2004: 142).

During the 1985 World Bank/IMF meeting, US Treasury Secretary Baker proposed a plan (thus, the Baker Plan), calling in international financial institutions (private and public) to support macroeconomic and structural policies undertaken in developing countries. The plan specifically demanded a continued central role of the IMF together with multilateral development banks as well as more intensive collaboration between the IMF and the World Bank. Financial assistance was proposed in the form of an additional net lending of $29 billion over three years, where commercial banks were supposed to lend $20 million while public institutions were to lend $9 billion (Raffer and Singer, 2001: 166). Supported by all creditor countries, Baker firmly rejected any general solution, insisting on solving debt problems in developing countries on a case-by-case basis. The instrument "on the menu" of the Baker Plan that received most attention was debt-equity swaps. They allowed investors to buy from banks at secondary market discounts and to finance direct investment worth the face value of acquired claims. When commercial banks failed to participate substantially in the Baker Plan, it became clear that multilateral funds poured into developing countries was basically a bail-out exercise for private banks.

Meanwhile, the secretariat undertook comprehensive historical research on the debt of developing countries and included its findings in Part II of *TDR 1985*. It was argued that in the absence of timely provision of adequate liquidity to counter currency attacks, initial liquidity crises could lead to widespread default and bankruptcies. *TDR 1996* suggested that the most effective way to prevent such an outcome would be by the extension and application to developing countries of insolvency principles such as those in chapter 11 of the United States Bankruptcy Code. The increasingly private character of external debt in developing countries (perhaps excepting LDCs) not only raised the likelihood of harmful debt runs and asset-grab races by international creditors and investors but also gave greater pertinence to those bankruptcy principles in the management and resolution of their external debt. Since then the issue has become a recurrent theme of the *Reports.* For instance, *TDR 1998* presented detailed technical discussions on the application of the above-mentioned Bankruptcy Code.

By the time of UNCTAD VII (1987) developing countries had been in an unprecedented debt crisis for almost five years. In UNCTAD's perspective the prevailing international strategy for dealing with the debt problems had contributed little to a durable solution. Noting that a solution to any case could be sought either by raising the country's capacity to service debt, reducing its obligation by an appropriate amount or by some combination of the two, the secretariat stressed that the debt strategy had so far depended only on the first of these options.

At the Toronto G-7 Summit in 1988 the major industrial countries accepted the principle of debt rescheduling for the first time. In 1989 new US Treasury Secretary Brady proposed a plan, of which two main elements were voluntary debt reduction by commercial banks and public guarantee via international public financial institutions (such as the Bretton Woods institutions). While it was of limited financial importance, the Brady Plan opened the door for debt reduction. In the UNCTAD secretariat's view the Brady Plan needed to be strengthened in several ways. The Report of the Secretary-General to UNCTAD VIII (1992) put forward three specific points: (1) the negotiation process between debtor countries and commercial banks should be anchored in authoritative estimates of the country's debt-reduction and cash-flow needs rather than determined by the balance of payments strength; (2) national laws and regulations in creditor countries could be directed more effectively towards achieving adequate levels of debt and debt-service reduction; (3) any increase in the financial support for debt reduction provided by multilateral financial institutions and the regional development banks should be accompanied by measures to put additional funds at the disposal of these institutions (see UNCTAD 1991a: 49). In the year the Brady Plan was announced, IDA also introduced a Debt Resolution Facility (DRF) for the purpose of reducing commercial debt for what the Bretton Woods institutional call the "low-income developing countries". In 1990 US President Bush declared debt reduction as an option under the *Enterprise for the Americas* initiatives.

During the first half of the 1990s a noteworthy step in the evolution of the debt strategy on the part of major creditor countries was the adoption by the Paris Club in December 1994 of the Naples terms of debt reduction (a roughly 67 per cent reduction in the net present value (NPV) of eligible debt). Provided the Paris Club creditors applied the country eligibility criteria flexibly, it was hoped that these terms would significantly alleviate the debt burden of low-income countries. As for multilateral public debt, the secretariat proposed the following ideas: (1) the sales of a portion of IMF gold reserves; (2) a new SDR allocation, a portion of which would be used to provide multilateral debt relief; and (3) drawing on the reserves and loan loss provisions of multilateral financial institutions.

C. 1996–Present

The launch of the HIPC Initiative, a "two-stage process" of debt reduction,[48] in September 1996 by the Bretton Woods institutions was instigated in response to the increasing perception that many developing countries, particularly "heavily indebted poor countries" (HIPCs), would continue to face unsustainable external debt even after receiving debt relief. It has since become the standardized framework for all debt negotiations for low-income developing countries, and the UNCTAD secretariat has closely monitored its operations. It soon became evident that the original Initiative was not sufficient in providing HIPCs with a permanent exit from repeated debt rescheduling, nor did it provide enough resources to deal with the pressing challenge of poverty reduction.

The change in the HIPC arrangements – thus the enhanced HIPC framework – agreed at the G-7 meeting in Cologne in 1999 (the Cologne Initiative) made important modifications to the original initiative as it would provide "deeper, broader and faster" debt relief by softening eligibility criteria based on changes in the sustainability thresholds. For instance, it lowered the minimum ratio of debt (NVP) to exports to 150 per cent replacing the previous ranges of 200 to 250 per cent. It also lowered the minimum thresholds for the export-to-GDP to 30 per cent (previously 40 per cent) and for the revenue-to GDP ratio to 15 per cent (previously 20 per cent). It was estimated that the enhanced HIPC initiative would make seven additional countries eligible for HIC debt relief (UNCTAD, 2004). Another main innovation under the enhanced HIPC framework was the explicit link to poverty reduction. HIPCs were now required to present Poverty Reduction Strategy Papers (PRSPs) as part of the debt-relief process.

LDCR 2000, which served as a principal background document for the Third UN Conference on LDCs (May 2001), made a cogent analysis of the development and debt situation in these countries. It considered even the enhanced HIPC Initiative inadequate to meet the growth requirement of these countries. It

---

[48] Under the "original" HIPC Initiative, eligible countries qualified for debt relief once they went through two stages (three years each stage). In the first three years a country would establish a track record of good performance in its implementation of the ESAF of the IMF. In return its Paris Club creditors would commit themselves to rescheduling debt service payments so as to achieve a roughly 67 per cent reduction in the NPV of eligible debt comparable to relief which non-Paris members would also provide. At the end of the first three-year period the country would reach a "decision point" when it would be decided whether it would be given HIPC debt relief (to the point of the level of sustainability, say, 200-250 per cent in the debt (NPV)-to-export ratio). The country would then begin a second three-year period, also requiring an ESAF-supported programme, during which time the Paris Club creditors would provide debt relief up to 80 per cent in NPV terms. A so-called "completion point" would be reached at the end of the second three-year stage when the creditor would reduce the country's debt burden to a sustainable level.

argued that there was a danger of debt relief being substituted for development assistance. In a situation of stagnant or even declining flows of ODA, not only would debt reduction fail to induce overall increases in resources flows for them but it would even deflect such increases from countries that have managed to avoid debt crisis. In sum the report argued that the additional of the PRSP, a new element of conditionality, to the already formidable list of policy tasks would further complicate the local political situation by reducing the degree of policy autonomy of the eligible HIPCs.

The most recent African report (UNCTAD, 2004) constituted one substantive element in the recent contributions by the UNCTAD secretariat to the analysis of the HIPC Initiative. It provided a full technical analysis of the issues of debt sustainability in African countries. It also addressed the debt problem of African countries in the context of achieving the Millennium Development Goals by 2015.

References

Bhagwati, JN, ed.. *The New International Economic Order: The North–South Debate*. Cambridge, Massachusetts: MIT Press.

Botchwey K (2003). Financing for development: Current trends and issues for the future. In: Toye J, ed.: 131–150.

Bird G (1976). The role of SDRs in financing commodity stabilization, *Journal of World Trade Law* 10(4): 371–379.

Cumby, RE (1983), Special Drawing Rights and plans for reform of the international monetary system: A survey. In: von Furstenberg, GM, ed., 1983, *International Money and Credit: The Policy Roles*. Washington: IMF: 435–473.

Griffith-Jones S (1998). Regulatory challenges for source countries of surges in capital flows. In: Teunissen JJ, ed.: 34–55.

Haji I (1985). Finance, money, developing countries and UNCTAD. In: Zammit Cutajar M, ed.: 145–174.

Helleiner G K (1994). Introduction, In: The *International Monetary and Financial System: Developing Country Perspectives.* Proceedings of a Conference sponsored by the Group of Twenty-four on the occasion of the fiftieth anniversary of the Bretton Woods Conference. Published as Volume IV, *Special Issue of International Monetary and Financial Issues for the 1990s*, New York: United Nations: 1–7.

Islam N (1996). New mechanisms for the transfer of resources to developing countries, *Journal of Development Planning*. 10: 59–103.

Jolly R, Emmerij L, Ghai D and Lapeyre F (2004). *UN Contributions to Development Thinking and Practice*. Bloomington and Indianapolis: Indiana University Press.

Kenen P B (1993). Reforming the international monetary system: An agenda for the developing countries. In: Teunissen JJ, ed.: 19–41.

Lawrence R (1984). Money, finance and global macroeconomics: UNCTAD in the 1970s and 1980s. *IDS Bulletin*, 15(3): 51–56, July.

Raffer K and Singer H W (2001). *Economic North-South Divide: Six Decades of Unequal Development*. Cheltenham, United Kingdom: Edward Elgar.

Singh J S (1977). *A New International Economic Order: Towards a Fair Redistribution of the World's Resources,* New York: Praeger Publisher.

Teunissen JJ, ed. (1992). *Fragile Finance: Rethinking the International Monetary System.* The Hague: Forum on Debt and Development (FONDAD).

_____ (1993). *The Pursuit of Reform: Global Finance and Developing Countries.* The Hague: Forum on Debt and Development (FONDAD).

_____ (1998). *The Policy Challenges of Global Financial Integration.* The Hague: Forum on Debt and Development (FONDAD).

Toye J, ed. (2003). *Trade and Development: Directions for the 21st Century.* Cheltenham, United Kingdom: Edward Elgar.

Toye J and Toye R (2004). *The UN and Global Economy: Trade, Finance, and Development.* Bloomington and Indianapolis: Indiana University Press.

UN (1961). International Compensation for Fluctuations in the Export Income of Primary Producing Countries. New York: United Nations.

_____ (1962a). Consideration of compensatory financing measures to offset fluctuations in the export income of primary producing countries: Stabilization of export proceedings through a development insurance fund, A study by the Secretariat. E/CN.13/43.

_____ (1962b). A development insurance fund for single commodities, Report by the United Nations secretariat. E/CN.13/45.

_____ (1964). *Proceedings of the United Nations Conference on Trade and Development,* Geneva, 23 March – 16 June 1964. Vol. I: Final Act and Report, E/CONF.46/141.

UNCTAD (various years). *The Least Developed Countries Reports* (Due to its analytical importance and frequent references in the text, individual reports of this UNCTAD flagship publication are specially referred to as: *LDCR2000, LDCR2002, LDCR2004* for *The Least Developed Countries Reports, 2000, 2002 and 2004*)

_____ (various years). *The Trade and Development Report* (Due to its analytical importance and frequent references in the text, individual annual reports of this UNCTAD flagship publication are specially referred to as: *TDR1981, TDR1982 ... TDR2004,* for *The Trade and Reports, 1981, 1982 ... 2004*)

_____ (1965). International monetary issues and developing countries. TD/B/32.

_____ (1967). Progress report on compensatory financing of export fluctuations, Note by the UNCTAD secretariat.TD/7/Supp.6.

_____ (1968a). Economic growth and development financing: Issues, policies and proposals, Report by the UNCTAD secretariat. TD/118.

_____ (1968b). Trade prospects and capital needs of developing countries, Study prepared by the UNCTAD secretariat. TD/34/Rev.1.

_____ (1971a). The International Monetary Situation: Impact on World Trade and Development, Preliminary report by the UNCTAD secretariat. TD/B/C.3/98.

_____ (1971b). The Link, Report by the UNCTAD secretariat. TD/118/Supp.4.

_____ (1974). Problems of Raw Materials and Development, Report of the Secretary-General of UNCTAD prepared for the sixth special session of the General Assembly. TD/B/488.

_____ (1975). Report of the Ad Hoc Group of Government Experts on the Debt Problem on its third session. TD/B/545.

_____ (1976). Ways and Means of Accelerating the Transfer of Real Resources to the Developing Countries on a Predictable, Assured and Continuous Basis, Report of the Secretary-General. A/31/186.

_____ (1977). Compliance of Donors with UNCTAD and United Nations resolutions, Report by the UNCTAD secretariat. TD/B/C.3/AC.7/7.

_____ (1978). Finance for development, Report of the High-level Group. TD/B/722, 8 September.

_____ (1979a). Compensatory Financing for Export Fluctuations, Note by the UNCTAD secretariat. TD/B/C.3/152/Rev.1.

_____ (1979b). International Financial Co-operation for Development – Current Policy Issues, Report of the UNCTAD secretariat. TD/234.

_____ (1979c). International monetary issues, Report by the UNCTAD secretariat. TD/233.

_____ (1982). Report of the Ad Hoc Intergovernmental High-level Group of Experts on the evolution of the international monetary system. TD/B/823/Rev.1.

_____ (1983a). Report by the Secretary-General of the United Nations Conference on Trade and Development to the Conference at its sixth session – Development and recovery: Realities of the new interdependence. TD/271.

_____ (1983b). Review of the implementation of Trade and Development Board resolution 222 (XXI), section B, Report of the UNCTAD secretariat.

_____ (1985a). Compensatory financing of export earnings, Report of the Expert Group. TD/B/1029/Rev.1.

_____ (1985b). *The History of UNCTAD 1964–1984.* UNCTAD/OSG/286, New York: United Nations.

____ (1993). *Proceedings of the United Nations Conference on Trade and Development,* eighth session, Cartagena de Indias, Colombia, 8–25 February, Report and Annexes. TD/364/Rev.1.

____ (1994). The international monetary and financial system: Developing country perspectives – Proceedings of a Conference sponsored by the Group of Twenty-four on the occasion of the fiftieth anniversary of the Bretton Woods Conference, Cartagena, Colombia, 18–20 April 1994. New York: UN. (This publication was also published as Vol. IV of the series called, *International Monetary and Financial Issues for the 1990s: Research papers for the Group of Twenty-four.*)

____ (2000). Capital Flows and Growth in Africa. UNCTAD/GDS/MDPB/7.

____ (2002). Economic Development in Africa – From adjustment to poverty reduction: What is new? UNCTAD/GDS/AFRICA/2.

____ (2004). Economic development in Africa – Debt sustainability: Oasis or mirage? UNCTAD/GDS/AFRICA/2004/1.

Weiss TG, Forsythe DP and Coate RA (2004). *The United Nations and Changing World Politics* (4th ed.). Boulder, Colorado: Westview Press.

Williamson J (1992). International monetary reform and the prospects for economic development. In: Teunissen JJ, ed.: 86–100.

____ (1993). Economic reform and debt relief in Eastern Europe: Lessons from the 1980s debt crisis. In: Teunissen JJ, ed.: 113–129.

Zammit Cutajar M, ed. (1985). *UNCTAD and the South–North Dialogue: The First Twenty Years.* Oxford: Pergamon Press.

Global Interdependence
and National Development Strategies

Charles Gore*

Introduction

This paper describes UNCTAD thinking on national development strategies during two periods: first, the 1960s when the initial UNCTAD development paradigm was articulated; and second, the post-1980 period during which globalization and liberalization have increasingly influenced development thinking. The paper summarizes some of the major intellectual contributions of UNCTAD in each of the periods, identifies commonalities and differences in UNCTAD thinking on development strategies between them and suggests some reasons for continuity and change.

For both periods the hallmark of UNCTAD's approach to national development strategies, and also the source of its originality, has been that national strategies are discussed in the context of global interdependence. What this means in practice is that strategic options have been assessed in a global context. That is to say, the desirability and feasibility of different development strategies does not simply depend on national factors, though these necessarily are important, but also on international relationships and the global environment in which national development takes place. From this perspective, national action has always been considered by UNCTAD as part of a global development strategy, or in the language which is now popular, as part of a development partnership between national and international action.

Because such partnership has been central to UNCTAD thinking from the outset, there is a danger that focussing solely on the national element of UNCTAD's proposals could distort their fundamental nature. However, this paper is founded on the view that it is possible to isolate the UNCTAD understanding of national development, and on top of this, that it is necessary to isolate this understanding of national development in order to evaluate proposals for international action from a development perspective.

* The author is a Senior Economic Affairs Officer in the Special Programme for Least Developed, Land-locked and Island Developing Countries.

The paper is founded on two types of documentary sources. The discussion of the first period draws on the Secretary-General's reports to UNCTAD I and UNCTAD II (UN, 1964; UNCTAD, 1968). The discussion of the latter period is mainly based on the analyses contained within successive *Trade and Development Reports* (*TDR*) which UNCTAD started publishing in 1981, and also within *The Least Development Countries Reports* (*LDCR*) published since 2000. These documentary sources do not provide a comprehensive picture of UNCTAD work on development strategies, which encompasses, for example, issues of diversification in commodity-dependent economies and service development strategies (see Service paper in this volume). But they are sufficient to reconstruct how UNCTAD ideas have changed over the last 40 years along with ideological shifts in the development thinking and also with changes in the forms of global interdependence.

I.   UNCTAD's Initial Development Paradigm of the 1960s and 1970s

A.   The Need for an Outward-looking Industrialization Strategy

UNCTAD's initial development paradigm is set out in the Report of the Secretary-General to UNCTAD I, "Towards a new trade policy for development" (UN, 1964). At that time, the development goal of the international community, which had been set for the first United Nations Development Decade, was to attain a minimum annual growth rate of 5 per cent in the income of the developing countries by 1970. The Report, which is often referred to as the Prebisch Report, is an analysis of the implications for trade policy, at both national and international levels, for achieving this objective. The fundamental insight of the Report, and also the basic axiom of the UNCTAD approach to development, is that trade issues must be integrated within both national development strategies and international development cooperation (Ibid.: 5–23). As the Report puts it: "One cannot posit a 5 per cent rate of development without accepting also all the consequences that implies for the rate of growth of imports and exports" (Ibid.: 6).

The proposals of the Prebisch Report begin from the fact that in the 1950s, even with some degree of import substitution and a rate of economic growth of 4.4 per cent per annum, export growth of developing countries was not fast enough to meet import needs, and external financial liabilities were being built up. The acceleration of economic growth required by the 5 per cent growth target was expected to widen the trade gap unless new trade policies were adopted. The basic reason for this is that additional investment is needed to accelerate economic growth and in developing countries the import content of investment is generally higher than the import content of income. The 5 per cent annual growth target implied import growth of 6 per cent per annum. Thus exports would have to rise at a rate of 6 per cent per annum in order to maintain balance-of-payments equilibrium, or even higher if, as in the 1950s, the terms of trade moved against developing countries. If the means of bridging the potential trade gap were not found, the Report noted, "the developing countries will be forced to reduce their rate of growth unless they are prepared to achieve higher rates at an excessive economic and social cost involving serious political consequences" (Ibid.: 6). The emergence of a debt crisis was also a possible outcome and this implied that the trade issue could not be addressed in isolation from external financial flows.[1]

The Report identifies various alternative ways in which the persistent trend towards a widening trade gap could be reversed and external resources could be increased: through additional exports of primary products; through more exports of manufactures; and through greater external aid. The best solution entails a combination of these interdependent elements. But the Report argues that the first and the last are basically "palliatives". The central proposal of the Report is that there is an absolute necessity for developing countries to end what it called "inward-looking industrialization" and to promote exports of manufactures. Although the Report does not use the term, the basic strategic proposal of the Report is that developing countries should pursue outward-looking industrialization.

Underlying this radical proposal there are three basic arguments: first, the need for industrialization; second, the limits of inward-looking industrialization; and third, limits to national development based on exports of primary commodities.

The basic argument for industrialization is a social one. Agriculture cannot provide sufficient employment for the economically active population, particularly when new techniques are introduced which increase productivity and reduce the demand for labour (Ibid.:15). But the argument against inward-looking industrialization is an economic one, founded on a critique of the inefficiency of import substitution industrialization undertaken in developing countries. This process is described as proceeding "piecemeal in large number of water tight

---

[1] Work was requested from the International Bank for Reconstruction and Development on the methods of relating the terms and conditions of aid to long-term needs of developing countries as an input to UNCTAD I and this provided the basis for important analysis on the parameters which could lead to a debt crisis in developing countries - see D Avramovic (1964: 3).

compartments with little communication" (UN, 1964: 14). Focusing in particular on the Latin American experience, the Report argues that "The relative smallness of national markets...has often made the cost of industries excessive and necessitated recourse to very high protective tariffs; the latter in turn has had unfavourable effect on the industrial structure because it has encouraged the establishment of small uneconomical plants, weakened the incentive to introduce modern techniques, and slowed the rise in productivity. Thus a real vicious circle has been created as regards exports of manufactured goods. These exports encounter great difficulties because internal costs are high, and internal costs are high because, among other reasons, the exports which would enlarge the markets are lacking" (Ibid: 14). In addition, "excessive protectionism has generally insulated national markets from external competition, weakening and even destroying the incentive for improving the quality of output and lowering costs under the private-enterprise system. It has thus tended to stifle the initiative of enterprises as regards both the internal market and exports" (Ibid.: 15). Moreover, excessive protectionism has exacerbated the problem of the concentration of income in the hands of a privileged few (Ibid.: 59).

The Report stresses that the abandonment of inward-looking industrialization does not mean the abandonment of import substitution. Nor does it mean a rejection of the need for protectionism to support the development of infant industries – "It is not a matter of controversy among economists that national protection of infant industries is justifiable wherever such industries have a long-run prospect of reaching a high level of efficiency" (Ibid.: 35). But what it does entail is the rejection of inefficient forms of import substitution. There is still a margin for import substitution in some countries that have not made much headway in industrialization and in which opportunities for raising income and employment through the simple early phases of import substitution exist. Moreover, this margin could be increased if import substitution were to be carried out, "not within each individual country's domestic market, but within groupings of countries so as to reap more easily the benefits of competition, specialization and economies of scale" (Ibid.: 16). But the "rational policy", the report argues, is one "judiciously combining import substitution with industrial exports" (Ibid.: 14). The promotion of exports of manufactures should be pursued both in those developing countries which already achieved a measure of industrialization and also those which are just starting to industrialize following national independence.

Promoting exports of manufactures is also necessary because of the limited ability to achieve sufficiently fast export growth, and thus sufficiently dynamic economic growth, through primary commodity exports. This is related to the tendency for terms of trade to decline, which "should not be regarded as an immutable law" as it "can be slowed down or halted when the demand for primary commodities in the major centres expands very rapidly" (Ibid.:11). But it is argued that it is a "spontaneous feature of economic development" that primary exports of developing countries tend to grow slowly whilst industrial imports tend to accelerate.

B.   The Promotion of Exports of Manufactures

The Report makes various proposals for national and international trade policies which will help developing countries achieve accelerated economic development (UN, 1964: 24–54). It realistically recognizes that it will take time for developing countries to become exporters of manufactures and it is for this reason that the Report makes various international policy proposals to improve international trade in primary commodities, notably to ensure higher prices for producing countries and to reduce instability. The report also argues for compensatory financing to transfer additional resources to developing countries to offset the losses in their purchasing power that arise from declining terms of trade. Most significantly it introduces the idea of helping industries grow in developing countries through the introduction of general preferences for selected manufactures exports of developing countries into developed country markets. Such preferential treatment is seen as "a logical extension of the infant industry argument" (Ibid.: 35). However, national policies within developing countries to promote exports of manufactures are also important (Ibid.: 40–42).

In this regard the Report argues that "first and foremost it is necessary to induce export-mindedness" (UN, 1964: 41). Where import substitution industries exist, these industries can be encouraged, "as they gain experience and efficiency, to branch out into export markets" (Ibid.: 41). Thus there is no conflict between import substitution and export promotion. But the Report also advocated promoting industries "in areas of more dynamic demand" which go beyond these old import substitution industries. The policy measures are all geared to animating the private sector towards export activity and amongst policy those which are seen as important are:

- Governments undertake investigation of foreign market possibilities, introduce inspection and quality control programmes to export industries and foster better design through institutes and research centres
- Governments share risks involved in breaking into markets abroad by underwriting feasibility studies, providing information, risk insurance and export credit facilities

- Fiscal and other incentives such as tax advantages, special treatment in allocation of import licences and export bonuses, and favourable transport rates
- Avoidance of an overvalued exchange rate
- Removal of administrative obstacles to exporting.

The Report identifies the role of trade liberalization in the approach. It makes clear that "protectionism has been carried too far by many developing countries" (UN, 1964: 19) and thus the correction of "excessive protectionism" is also an important element of the policy. However, this does not mean that all protectionism should be abandoned but that there should be "a rational concept of protectionism" (Ibid.: 20). This is different from the unilateral removal of all trade restrictions. Thus in the initial UNCTAD development paradigm the converse of inward-looking industrialization is not trade liberalization, a conceptual error which has confounded the design of creative trade policies in the 1980s and 1990s. Significantly as well, the rational concept of protectionism was not the same as the reciprocal reduction of tariffs in industrial and developing countries. Application of the principle of reciprocity in trade liberalization would not result in maximum expansion of trade in view of structural differences between countries in the centre and the periphery, and equal treatment between structurally unequal partners would lead to unequal outcomes. Industrialization in peripheral countries is a necessary precondition for worldwide trade liberalization.

The problem of "excessive protectionism" is that "tariffs are much higher than is needed to compensate for differences in costs". Re-adjustment is justified "by the desirability of progressively encouraging competition and vitalizing the industry of developing countries thus helping to accelerate their rate of growth". But it cannot be undertaken unless targets for increasing exports are reached. "No such readjustment would be possible unless exports expand and the external bottle-neck hampering development was reduced until it ceased to exist, for if foreign competition is to have this effect, it is essential for a country to have sufficient external resources to cope with the possible impact of tariff reduction on its imports and to avoid new elements of imbalance in trade" (Ibid.: 19–20).

The Report also notes, with great prescience given current debates, the importance of using international financial and technical assistance to develop export capacities. It indicates that it may be feasible to promote international sub-contracting and argues that "there is scope for private foreign capital to play an invaluable role in promoting exports of manufactures from developing countries", particularly as they have the most up-to-date knowledge. A particular problem has been that FDI has frequently focused on import substitution, "avoiding exports which would compete with the output of their home-based plants". To reduce this tendency, "governments of developing countries should study the possibility of making cooperation of private foreign capital conditional upon adequate export performance, and certainly any special incentives provided to private foreign capital should be linked to such performance" (Ibid.: 42).

C.   Some Refinements of the Development Approach at UNCTAD II

The Report of the Secretary-General to UNCTAD II, "Towards a Global Strategy of Development", re-affirmed the main lines of the development approach outlined in 1964. In its first sentence, it asserts that the meagre results of the first United Nations Development Decade are the inevitable consequence of "a development decade without a development policy" (UNCTAD, 1968: 1). The Report argues that insufficient dynamism in peripheral countries is related to the persistent trend to external disequilibrium associated with imports growing faster than exports, the savings gap and external economic vulnerability, which arises owing to continuous fluctuations of export earnings that are largely the result of the instability of international prices. Outward-oriented industrialization is the way to overcome this problem, and this required trade policy, international financial cooperation and domestic development policy. The international trade measures which are advocated are seen as transitional measures that would support outward-oriented industrialization in developing countries and thus create a new international division of labour which would pave the way for a mutually-beneficial worldwide trade liberalization.

The Report lays greater emphasis on the importance of technological progress than the Prebisch report (UNCTAD, 1968: 1–13). It also focuses more fully on the social consequences of inadequate economic dynamism. The urgency of the development problem is related to the inability of peripheral countries to generate sufficient employment for their population and, with rural-urban migration, the emergence of outright unemployment or "redundant manpower" gravitating "to personal services or minor and very poorly paid activities, or forced to live from hand to mouth with no stable employment" (Ibid.: 8). Slow growth rates are also associated with obstacles to social mobility which, in conjunction with "the frequent spectacle of gross social differences, and the mushrooming of the marginal and redundant labour force" (Ibid.: 12), creates the basic conditions for civil conflict.

With regard to development strategies there is an elaboration of how trade expansion amongst developing countries can be encouraged (UNCTAD, 1968: 24–27). This includes the need for international financial cooperation provided through regional or sub-regional banks, the institution of regional payments arrangements, and gradual trade liberalization within regional and sub-regional groups. Moreover, the Report makes important remarks on conditionality and ownership in relation to international financial cooperation (Ibid.: 62–67).

It does not proceed under the illusion that peripheral countries had an automatic right to expect external financial resources and does not minimize the problem of wastage of these resources. For this reason it argues that finance should be provided to those peripheral countries which show the willingness and discipline to promote their own development. As the report puts it, "With regard to financial cooperation, the action of the centres consists essentially in making international finance fully accessible to those peripheral countries which are prepared, under a well-concerted development plan, to take the steps just mentioned to halt the trend towards external disequilibrium, which propose to mobilize their own resources progressively in order gradually to close the savings gap and which show their determination to lessen their external economic vulnerability and its internal effects. The granting of international finance should thus be closely linked to the way in which a development plan proposed to achieve these aims" (Ibid.: 60). In effect, "the plan is the expression of the primary responsibility of the peripheral countries to solve their own problems" (Ibid.: 66).

This raises difficult issues about how such development policies should be examined (Ibid.: 62–67). The Report argues that the critical criterion should not be policy but rather domestic savings mobilization and productive investment. The Report also cautions against too intrusive conditionality and floats the idea of a body of independent experts as undertaking this task.

II. The Breakdown of the Initial Development Paradigm in the Early 1980s

In the 1960s, when UNCTAD's initial development paradigm was first articulated, the issue of development strategy was placed within the context of a centre-periphery view of the world in which there were rich, technologically advanced industrial countries and poor, technologically backward developing countries. The basic pattern of international trade was the exchange of manufactures produced in the former for primary commodities produced in the latter. Steady economic growth was assumed to be inevitable in the advanced industrial countries and the problem of development in the peripheral countries was seen as a question of how to integrate them into the growth dynamic of the centre in a way in which there were mutual benefits for both the centre and the periphery. It was believed that the dynamism of the centre would not be automatically transmitted to the periphery and that the free play of market forces could not guarantee fast enough economic growth rates in developing countries to address the pressing social problems of poverty, malnutrition and accelerating jobless urbanization. There was therefore a need for development planning to help developing countries to accelerate the process of development and such disciplined effort should be supported by international cooperation. The content of development policies and international cooperation was derived from the analysis of constraints arising from the centre-periphery pattern of global interdependence.

In the early 1980s it was recognized that this initial conceptualisation of the development problem was becoming obsolete. There was a need to search for what the first TDR called "a new development paradigm" (*TDR 1981*:5).

The recognition of the need for a new development paradigm coincided with a fundamental swing in mainstream development thinking away from the idea that development was a process which should be planned by Governments towards the idea that development was best promoted by freeing market forces both nationally and internationally. However, the need to search for a new paradigm was influenced as much by three real changes in the world economy as by the swing in the pendulum in development ideologies.

The first change was the need to address the consequences of economic recession in developed countries and the de-railing of development strategies by the balance of payments adjustment problems associated the oil shocks of the 1970s and then the debt crisis that struck in 1982. The economic recession brought to the fore the need for a strategy which integrated short-term stabilization and adjustment measures with long-term development. But it was also recognized by the Secretariat that the recession was a manifestation of increased instability in the world economy that was associated with the breakdown of the Bretton Woods system. The deeper emerging problem was how to promote development in a more unstable global environment.

The second change was the breakdown of the fundamental grounds on which UNCTAD had been promoting a "development consensus" between developed and developing countries. The basic argument of the Secretariat had been that accelerated economic development in developing countries would increase their purchasing power, and if their import capacity increased this would also promote economic growth in developed countries. But with the abandonment of full employment as the basic objective of economic policy in developed countries, the old basis for a development consensus broke down. It was believed that controlling inflation, the new basic objective, was best supported by restrictive monetary policies and low commodity prices also mattered. But both of these would inevitably have negative effects on developing countries. *TDR 1984* emphasized that a viable international system needed "to reaffirm the emphasis on employment and growth that underlay the design of post-war systems" and called for "a development consensus that would recognize that rapid development in developing countries is an imperative both for developing countries and for the proper functioning of the world economy" (*TDR 1984*: 127). But the objective bases for building such a "development consensus" were fundamentally weakened at the start of the 1980s and it has been difficult to rebuild them ever since.

The third change was the discovery by the Secretariat of a set of processes which later came to be called "globalization". The term "globalization" was not used by UNCTAD at the time and, of course, UNCTAD was not the first to discover these processes. But the first TDRs in the early 1980s make clear that a new form of global interdependence was emerging which was rendering obsolete the centre-periphery pattern which had underpinned UNCTAD's development paradigm of the 1960s.

The first TDR identifies and discusses three of the important components of the new form of global interdependence (*TDR 1981*, Part III, Chapters 1, 2 and 4). These are: (i) "internationalization of output and trade" through the rise of transnational corporations"; (ii) the emergence of a new international division of labour as industrialization progressed in a few developing countries, particularly, as the report notes, those which moved from policies based on import substitution to policies placing greater emphasis on export promotion; and (iii) the increasing role of private financial institutions in the world economy, a phenomenon which was labelled "the growing privatization of the international monetary system" (Ibid.: 75).

TDR 1982 develops a conceptualization of the long-term changes which were occurring in the global economy under the rubric of "structural change". This is presented as a multidimensional concept which encompasses three basic aspects (see *TDR 1982*, Part III, Chapter 1). The first is global trends in production, consumption, trade and relative prices, including the relative importance of national economies. The second is change in the pattern of effective control of resources, where the key trend is the increase in effective control by transnational corporations and their ability to capture a disproportionate share of the benefits of trade owing to their dominant market power. The third is the emergence of international regimes, i.e. systems of principles and rules which govern international economic and financial relations. It is clear from *TDR 1982* that the emergence of the new international division of labour with the industrialization of the periphery and the expansion of manufactures exports is a rather halting and uneven process. But the composition of developing countries' exports are shifting from primary commodities to labour-intensive manufactures (*TDR 1982*, Part III, Chapters 4 and 5; Part IV, Chapter 1). *TDR 1982* also identifies the increasing role of services within the world economy and increasing international trade in services (see topical paper on International Trade in this volume).

TDR 1984 builds on both these Reports. It adds a further component to those set out in *TDR 1981* – the increasing openness of national economies in terms of both trade and finance and as a consequence the increased interdependence of the performance of national economies (*TDR 1984*, Part II, Chapter I). The stark fact it highlights is that "Over the last three decades the ratio of exports to GDP has doubled for the world, for develop market-economy countries and for developing countries, each taken as a whole" (Ibid.: 3). Important consequences of this increased international economic integration are the increased influence of effective demand abroad on the level of home output. As the Report put it, "the income multiplier" has been increasingly internationalized", and "the competitiveness of a country in foreign trade, its access to foreign markets and the access of others to its home market have become increasingly important influences on the level of economic activity" . In addition, "national money and capital markets have increasingly become integrated into a world money and capital market" (Ibid.: 54). As a result, "real economic variables in the world economy have come increasingly under the influence of monetary and financial variables" and "the ability of the regimes governing international monetary, financial and trading relations to blunt the transmission of negative impulses and to propagate positive impulses has thus become a key feature in determining the degree of stability of the world economy and the rhythm of international trade and development" (Ibid.: 55). *TDR 1984* also sets out a series of question through which it is possible to judge the extent to which international trade and payments regimes were supporting development (Ibid.: 127–129), and points to various inconsistencies between the regimes governing trade, money and finance, which it argues, should be treated as interdependent (Ibid.: 112–115).

III. The UNCTAD Critique of Structural Adjustment Policies and the Washington Consensus

UNCTAD's work on development strategies since 1985 can be understood as part of a search for a new development paradigm in the light of these new features of the global environment in which national development takes place. This transformation is still in progress as the processes of globalization evolve and the understanding of them in UNCTAD increases. But the body main intellectual contribution of UNCTAD exists in two basic strands of work.

The first strand is a critical assessment of structural adjustment policies and the set of policy reforms that are commonly labelled the Washington Consensus.[2] This critique has evolved considerably over time as the meaning of "structural adjustment" has changed. But, taken altogether, this body of work is one of the most sustained and balanced assessments of the *economic underpinnings* of the Washington Consensus. The UNCTAD approach contrasts with the other major critique of the Washington Consensus, stemming from UNICEF's publication *Adjustment with a Human Face*, which focuses mainly on the adverse social implications of these policies (Cornia, Jolly and Stewart, 1987). The second strand is the construction of a credible development alternative based on analysis of the East Asian development experience.

Arguably these two strands of work constitute UNCTAD's major intellectual contribution to thinking on national development strategies. The initial development paradigm is of course important. It guided UNCTAD's work on international economic cooperation until the end of the 1970s, underpinning the demands for a New International Economic Order made in the UN General Assembly in 1974, and its proposals on national development strategy remain surprisingly fresh. However the major elements of the initial paradigm were identified in ECLAC. When Raúl Prebisch moved from ECLAC to UNCTAD, ECLAC's seminal ideas on development of the early 1960s were injected into UNCTAD's work and projected on an world scale through UNCTAD (Rosenthal 2004). It will require more detailed research than that undertaken here to sort out precisely where UNCTAD added value in this process. It is clear from other essays in this book that important additions were made by UNCTAD in its early years in the areas of commodities, shipping, technology and money and finance. But

---

[2] The best summary of the policies of the Washington Consensus is Williamson (1993).

whatever the respective contributions, the post-1985 UNCTAD work on development strategies is a distinctive and original contribution in its own right.

The rest of this section and section 5 identify key contributions in the critical and constructive strands of work respectively.

A.   The Initial Analysis of the Balance-of-Payments Adjustment Policies

The foundation of UNCTAD's analysis of adjustment policies is a multi-country comparative study of the process of adjustment to balance of payments disequilibrium in 13 developing countries after the 1973 oil shock (UNDP/UNCTAD, 1979). The report, which was prepared for the Group of 24 in a joint UNDP/UNCTAD project, argued that "many of the developing countries were faced with a burden of adjustment out of all proportion to their degree of responsibility for the imbalances arising in the payments system" (Ibid., paras. 3) and in the balance of payments adjustment process, "avoidable costs were incurred by many developing countries, particularly by the poorest among them" (Ibid., para. 11). Much of the analysis is concerned with the required changes in international environment for adjustment policies in developing countries. However, the Report also makes a number of key observations on adjustment policies within developing countries.[3]

First and most basically, it argues that adjustment policies should be designed in such a way that they are compatible with long-run development. "A period of adjustment should be nothing more than an episode in a long-run process, and it is indispensable that the categorical imperatives of the short run should not be allowed to dominate and perhaps even overwhelm the requirements of the long run" (Ibid., para. 33). It states that "one of the most disturbing features of the experience of adjustment reviewed…is the large number of cases in which there were major declines in investment growth" (Ibid.: 36). Adjustment will be illusory if it is simply based on suppression of domestic demand as the balance of payments pressures will re-emerge once development processes recommence. There is thus "a need for measures to tackle the basic causes of disequilibrium and the long-run obstacles to growth along with the proximate phenomena of inflation and balance of payments pressure that accompany them" (Ibid., para. 25).

---

[3] For further analysis of adjustment and conditionality by the director of the multi-country research project on which the report is based, see Dell (1991), especially the chapters on "The Adjustment Process" and "Stabilization, Conditionality and Cross-conditionality".

Second, the type of adjustment policies should vary according to the nature of the causes of balance of payments disequilibrium. The Report argues that adjustment policies have been based mainly on the view that their cause is the excessive pressure of domestic demand, yet in fact they have generally arisen owing to external factors, in particular, sharp changes in the terms of trade as well as the slow-down in demand in industrial countries. The design of adjustment policies and their financing must take account of whether the developing country is itself responsible for the balance of payments deficit or whether this deficit is due to factors beyond its control.

Third, different developing countries also have different capacities to adjust in terms of expanding exports on the one hand and compressing imports without suffering adverse effects on the other hand. In general "the elasticity of an economy, especially of its foreign trade sector, and the mobility of its resources, and hence its capability for withstanding external shocks, depends on its level of development" (Ibid., para. 13). The type of adjustment policies should vary according to the capacity of developing countries to adjust. In general, "the package of measures proposed for adoption should be sensitive to the particular situation of each country, including the political and social philosophy underlying its development programme, the level of development and degree of flexibility and diversification of its economy, the extent to which its balance of payments difficulties are of internal or external origin, and the impact of the package on long-run development prospects" (Ibid., para. 81(c)).

Fourth, the Report argues for a slower pace of adjustment, particularly in cases where the deficit is due to external factors. The costs of adjustment can be reduced and its compatibility with development increased if the rate of adjustment is slower. Such a slower rate of adjustment will require new extended financing facilities to address the "medium-term adjustment-cum-development problems" (Ibid., para. 111).

Fifth, the principle of conditionality should be applied "in as flexible and responsive a manner as possible" (Ibid., para. 35(i)). Performance criteria should be limited to macroeconomic variables and should pay attention to growth considerations and also differences in point of view on broad questions of political and economic philosophy. Discussing the case where an effort was made to persuade a country to dismantle its price controls, it notes that this was controversial in terms of economic logic "in view of the limited effectiveness of market forces in providing unequivocal signals in a world remote from the neo-classical assumption of a fully employed and competitive economy" (Ibid., para. 71). But it argues that this kind of choice is beyond economic logic and is not simply a technical question. The choice of such priorities is a political one "and only the government can take responsibility for that kind of decision" (Ibid., para. 72). "It is important that international agencies should not directly or indirectly substitute their own political judgement for that of their member governments" (Ibid., para. 98). The Report argues that trade liberalization should not be an aspect of conditionality but a matter for governments. As it puts it, "in some countries foreign exchange budgeting and import controls are regarded as indispensable tools for economic planning. As in the case of price controls, liberalization would imply abandonment of fundamental aims of the government, and cannot therefore be viewed solely in terms of the usual technical criteria" (Ibid., para. 91).

Finally, it argues that it is necessary "to balance considerations of monetary and payments stability with those of equity. Explicit attention to the distribution of the burden of adjustment among various segments of the population is needed" (Ibid., para. 70).

The Report pays particular attention to the role of trade and exchange rate policies as part of the adjustment package. It is clear that increasing export earnings and increasing the flexibility of the export sector are regarded as central to the adjustment process – this is why the wave of protectionism in industrial countries is so disturbing. But the Report argues that the usefulness of devaluation depends on circumstances and in some cases should be a last resort. Moreover, perhaps most controversially, it argues that "Under current world trade conditions, especially as they affect developing countries, traditional approaches to the question of trade restrictions [which argue that they should not be adopted to deal with balance of payments disequilibrium] would appear to require some revision. The case of direct trade controls is particularly strong where a country is forced into substantial deflation and unemployment as a means of reducing imports, and where the requisite import reduction could be achieved with a lesser decline in real income and employment if such controls were sanctioned" (Ibid., para. 89).

B. Structural Adjustment as a Strategy to Deal with the Debt Crisis

In the early 1980s the meaning of "adjustment" changed from referring to the process of adaptation to ensure external viability in the new external environment in which developing countries found themselves to referring to a set of policy reforms which developing countries should undertake to correct the errors of their past development policies. This inverted the respective roles of internal and external factors in the origins of the balance of payments disequilibria identified in the earlier UNCTAD study. The shift in meaning was doubly ironic in terms of UNCTAD's work, as in the 1970s as UNCTAD had used the term "structural adjustment" as an important policy for *developed countries* to enable faster industrialization in developing countries.[4]

The type of policy reforms being advocated sought to link short-term stabilization measures with supply-side improvements, which was a change in the direction that UNCTAD had been advocating in UNDP/UNCTAD (1979). But the policy reforms entailed shifting the balance between markets and States so that free market forces could play a greater role in resource allocation and removing border restrictions so that price incentives for domestic resource allocation were in line with international opportunity costs. This approach went right against the grain of UNCTAD's (and also almost other developmentalist organizations') advocacy of development planning.[5] In effect, a new international economic order was being constructed on a country-by-country basis from the bottom-up. But this international order was completely different in content from the Programme of Action on the Establishment of a New International Economic Order agreed in the UN General Assembly in 1974, which in retrospect can be seen as a climax in the elaboration of UNCTAD's initial development paradigm in terms of international policy proposals.

In the early 1980s, the weaknesses of the balance-of-payments adjustment process of the 1970s, the economic recession in the developed countries, rising interest rates and falling commodity prices all combined to precipitate a major debt crisis. In dealing with the debt crisis and attempting to restore external viability, developing countries were recommended to adopt the new structural adjustment policies, a recommendation which was reinforced with policy conditionality which regulated access to both official and private finance. The next important contributions to UNCTAD's assessment of adjustment policies thus focus on their efficacy as part of a strategy to resolve the debt crisis (see also the topical paper on Money, Finance and Debt in this volume).

TDR 1985 (Part Two, Chapter II) and *TDR 1988* (Part One, Chapter IV) are the key contributions. *TDR 1985* includes an analysis of "the conditions necessary for correcting the twin disequilibria of excessive indebtedness and inadequate development by examining the dynamic relationships among debt accumulation,

---

[4] UNCTAD (1985: 118-122) summarizes the secretariat's work in the 1970s on the importance of structural adjustment policies in developed countries. Such policies were designed to facilitate the transfer of capital and labour out of those industries where the developed countries were losing competitiveness to make room for exports of manufactures from the developing countries. This, it was argued would reduce protectionist pressures.
[5] For a discussion of this shift as a "counter-revolution", see Toye (1993.)

capital accumulation and the penetration of foreign markets" (*TDR 1985:* 75). It argues that this cannot be achieved efficiently through import substitution, and thus there is a need to expand exports. Export growth cannot be sustained without stepping up investment. However, investment has been cut as part of the adjustment process and increased investment also requires imports to increase. In short, "when adjustment designed to maintain debt-servicing checks investment, it can become "self-defeating". The analysis goes on to show how protectionist measures in developed countries can aggravate the task of resolving the debt problem. *TDR 1988* provides a description of the debt strategy that had emerged in the 1980s and more evidence of how structural adjustment policies are working as part of a strategy to resolve the debt crisis. The analysis notes that there have been national policy failures, with policy advice not always being followed. But the overall verdict is that "the adjustment achieved has amounted to little more than an accommodation to external constraints at the expense of stability and growth, and external debt has been serviced either at the cost of accumulating internal debt or by drastically reducing productive investment, or by a combination of the two" (TDR 1988: 108). In short, the basic critique is that short-term adjustment policies designed to deal with the debt crisis actually worked against long-term development prospects.

C. The Critique of the Washington Consensus

The spectre raised in *TDR 1985* of development strategies being replaced by perpetual self-defeating adjustment policies can arguably be said to have come to pass (see, for example, IMF Internal Evaluation Office, 2003). But this has occurred after a further twist in the tale of adjustment.

In 1989, the Washington Consensus was born. This term referred to a set of policy reforms that were said to be "common sense" economic policies for Latin America. These policies actually conformed to *national* elements of the *international* debt strategy identified in *TDR 1988* (see pp. 94–97). But at the same time as these policy reforms came to be named the Washington Consensus they were separated from the international elements of the debt strategy of which they were a part. Moreover, as they became generalized as the list of policy reforms which were appropriate for all developing countries, and not simply Latin America, they were also dis-embedded from the problem which they were intended to address, namely how to resolve the debt problem of middle-income countries.

With the birth of the Washington Consensus, the criticism that short-term adjustment policies could undermine long-term development processes was effectively absorbed. Re-labelled as policy reforms, structural adjustment policies *became* the development strategy. The absence of an approach to deal with "medium-term adjustment-cum-development problems" identified in UNDP/UNCTAD (1979) was now being rectified with a vengeance in a form that entailed propagation of particular policy model and also extensive policy conditionality. An outward-oriented strategy was also advocated. Catching up with the Prebisch Report, inward-oriented development strategies were described as very inefficient.[6] But in this new context, outward-orientation was equated with trade liberalization and laissez-faire in the domestic economy and the idea that it was possible to be both outward-looking and to have an active role for the state in economic policy, which animated earlier UNCTAD work, was effectively marginalized. The link between outward-orientation and industrialization was also completely broken in the Washington Consensus, which was propagated as a strategy suitable for all countries.

From 1989, successive TDRs add elements to a comprehensive critical assessment of Washington Consensus policies which, throughout the 1990s, were the dominant national economic strategy being recommended to developing countries. It is difficult to summarize briefly this major corpus of work, which includes both assessments of particular policies within the Washington Consensus and how they operate in different regional contexts.[7] However, the following paragraphs highlight some key findings in relation to the three main pillars of the Washington Consensus approach namely that developing countries should: (a) pursue macroeconomic stability by controlling inflation and reducing fiscal deficits, (b) liberalize their domestic product and factor markets through privatization and deregulation and (c) open their economies to the rest of the world through trade and capital account liberalization.

1.   *Macroeconomic stabilization*

TDR 1989 argues that the implementation of adjustment policies has increased macroeconomic instability. This is because measures taken to deal with external shocks have aggravated fiscal imbalances (for example, through reduced

---

[6] This idea gathered strength in the late 1970s and early 1980s. An important statement of the relative effectiveness of inward-oriented and outward-oriented industrialization is World Bank (1987), which is concerned with different strategies of industrialization.
[7] The major assessments of the Washington Consensus in different regions of the world or different groups of countries are: Least developed countries: *TDR 1989*, Part Two, Chapters III and IV; Sub-Saharan Africa - *TDR 1993*, Part Two, Chapter II; *TDR 1998* Part Two, Chapter I: D, Latin America - *TDR 1993*, Part Two, Chapter III; *TDR 1995*, Part Two, Chapter II; *TDR 2003*, Part Two, Chapter VI; East Asia - *TDR 1998*, Part One, Chapter III; and Central and Eastern Europe - *TDR 1993*, Part Two, Chapter V.

tariff revenues and the effects of currency devaluations on the domestic currency value of debt servicing and costs of imports for public investment). Moreover, austerity and the adjustment process have led to social conflicts over the distribution of income which have intensified inflationary pressures. Public sector deficits have also been swollen by the effects of slower economic growth and accelerated inflation. A major policy implication of the analysis is that it is necessary to include the reconciliation of income claims of different social groups in the design of stabilization policies.

2. *Liberalization of domestic markets and privatization*

TDR 1992 argues that "public enterprises have performed poorly, and need to be radically overhauled in order to accelerate economic growth" (Ibid.: 117). But privatization is only one solution – it is desirable in some circumstances but not in others. There is also a need to address the underlying social and distributional problems which public enterprises were often designed to address. *TDR 1998* shows that attempts to improve real producer prices at the farm-gate level through agricultural marketing reform in sub-Saharan Africa have been offset by falling international commodity prices. There has been a positive short-term supply response, particularly in areas with high population density and good rural infrastructure. This has been associated with expansion in output through a vent for surplus mechanism, along with efficiency gains resulting from reallocation of resources, changes in output mix and intensification of production. But the critical problem of African agriculture is its undercapitalization and policy has not removed technical and financial constraints to the capacity and willingness to invest. In effect the policy has sought to improve profitability on one side of the equation, through higher output prices, but farmers have been squeezed through increases in production and marketing costs, while the dismantling of marketing boards has increased risks and reduced access to credit and inputs for many farmers owing to the inadequacy of private sector replacement. Public expenditure in agriculture has also been far too low, partly because of a marked decline in official development assistance to agriculture.

3. *Openness: (1) Trade policy reform*

This issue is addressed in *TDR 1989* and *TDR 1992*. These do not dispute the evidence that export growth is important for economic growth but question the link between import liberalization and export growth on the basis of evidence of export success and also on theoretical argumentation. In particular, the Reports emphasize the facts that exports develop through learning and there are economies of scale (see *TDR 1992*: 108). The analysis is also deepened in *TDR 1999* where the balance of payments consequences of trade liberalization are examined. This was a particularly innovative contribution to the literature as most focused on the micro-economic effects of liberalization on firm-level competitiveness and on the efficiency of inter-sectoral resource allocation. *TDR 1999* shows that trade liberalization was associated with increasing trade deficits. Thus even if positive effects occurred in terms of improved supply-side efficiency, the worsening trade deficit could, in the absence of capital inflows, constrain the level of economic activity and resource utilization. Econometric analysis in the Report also shows that whilst trade liberalization has had an adverse impact on the current account of developing countries, the higher the growth rate of industrial countries, the lesser the adverse impact.

The overall UNCTAD analysis does not lead to blanket condemnation of trade liberalization but rather to a nuanced view regarding its timing and speed, as well as a rejection of reductionist analyses which simply limit policy decisions to either/or choices. It is argued that "import protection and export promotion are not incompatible strategies" (*TDR 1992*: 108), and that export promotion should also include active industrial policies. A "big bang" approach to liberalization, which seeks to undertake stabilization and structural reforms all together and very rapidly, is likely not to work since export capacities take time to develop. Echoing the original Prebisch Report, it is said that "import liberalization should be adopted only when substantial export success has been guaranteed" (*TDR 1992*: 115).

4.   Openness (2): Financial liberalization

TDR 1991 argues that financial openness can have significant negative consequences in developing countries. First, there is a loss of policy autonomy, i.e. reduced ability of Governments to achieve national objectives by using the policy instruments at their disposal. The ability of governments to influence capital flows and exchange rates through monetary policy actions becomes much more limited. This is related to the fact that "external capital flows make it very difficult to delink domestic interest rates from those prevailing in world markets and to decouple interest rates and exchange rates" (*TDR 1991:* 130). Second, there is increased instability as countries are exposed to speculative capital flows. This increases the probability of financial crises which occur when there is a loss of confidence that triggers capital outflows. The typical form of such a crisis includes a first phase, when interest rates are much higher than abroad and the country has a relatively high credit standing because of its export performance. Short-term capital inflows are thus attracted, but this leads to currency appreciation. There is then a deterioration of the trade balance, a crisis of confidence arises and this triggers capital outflows. *TDR 1993* warns of the vulnerability of Latin America to the reversal of capital inflows, a prediction which was realized the next year by the Mexican financial crisis. *TDR 1995* looks back on this, including a summary of its repeated warnings of a financial crisis in Latin America (*TDR 1995: 76–77*). The East Asian financial crisis is also explained as a result of this process in *TDR 1998* (Part One, Chapter III), an analysis which sets out in more detail the anatomy of crises in the post-Bretton Woods period after the adoption of financial liberalization policies.

UNCTAD's analysis of financial openness is more critical than its analysis of trade liberalization. However, as with trade liberalization there is not blanket condemnation but rather a critique of the crude application of the policy without attention to the necessary preconditions for success. Financial crises have been avoided where "financial liberalization was adopted after – not before – a considerable degree of industrialization had been achieved, and from a position of economic strength, not as a response to weakness. The presence of strong institutions and markets, and of competitive industries, proved to be essential preconditions for successful liberalization…and [where] "liberalization was undertaken gradually and without making it impossible to continue to pursue active industrial policy. In successful cases governments continued to intervene directly in capital markets, financial intermediaries and corporate finance in order to preserve financial stability, and acted to strengthen existing market institutions and build new ones; they did not leave financial development to emerge spontaneously" (*TDR 1991*: 113).

D. Globalization and the Critique of the Washington Consensus

During the 1990s, the mainstream rationale for the Washington Consensus evolved[8]. It became increasingly common to link the case for liberalization with the process of globalization. The basic argument was that: (a) globalization is a process which brought both opportunities and risks for developing countries; (b) it is possible to maximize the opportunities and minimize the risks through good national policies; and (c) the best national policies are macroeconomic stabilization, domestic liberalization and trade and financial openness.

---

[8] World Bank (1991) is a particularly important statement of the market-friendly approach to development which relaxes somewhat the laissez-faire stance of the 1980s.

It was at this time that the TDRs began to look at the benefits and costs of globalization.[9] Globalization was understood as referring "both to an increasing flow of goods and resources across national borders and to the emergence of a complementary set of organizational structures to manage the expanding network of international economic activity and transactions" (*TDR 1997:* 70). It was not considered to be an inevitable process but rather one which is due to policy choices including, in particular, liberalization. It was also not considered to be simply a post-1989 phenomenon but one with historical antecedents that held important lessons for understanding the consequences of the contemporary phase of globalization. Finally, an important feature of the UNCTAD approach to globalization was that it did not valorize the process positively or negatively.

UNCTAD's analysis was sceptical with regard to the argument that globalization was strengthening the case for economic liberalization. *TDR 1997* argues that globalization has not been associated with economic convergence (*TDR 1997,* Part Two, Chapter II). Only a few developing countries were catching-up with the developed countries and most were experiencing slower growth and greater instability following the "unleashing of market forces" in the early 1980s. Within developing countries there has also been a recurrent pattern of distributional change since about 1980 in which there was an increase in the income shares of the rich, which was almost invariably associated with a fall in income shares of the middle class. For many countries this was a reversal of trends before the 1980s, which involved middle class gaining income shares whilst the rich lost shares (Ibid., Part Two, Chapter III). It is argued that rapid liberalization has strengthened forces making for greater income inequality and also a hollowing out of the middle class. There is growing wage inequality between skilled and unskilled workers. Capital has gained at the expense of labour and profit shares have risen everywhere. Financial liberalization has given rise to a rapid expansion of public and private debt while a new rentier class has emerged worldwide. Agricultural price liberalization has benefited traders more than farmers (Ibid., Part Two, Chapter IV).

TDR 1999 deepens the overall analysis by examining what was happening to the trade gap and balance of payments constraint – the pivotal issues in the Prebisch Report of 1964 – during the period of globalization and liberalization. This document can be read as a succinct synthesis of the new international context facing developing countries. It is a statement which, like the Prebisch Report,

---

[9] Apart from the TDRs of the early 1980s referred to earlier, *TDR 1987* (Part Two, Chapter II) adds a further element to the UNCTAD discussion of globalization in the 1980s. It focuses on the increasing diversification in channels of technology transfer.

identifies the key constraints on development within developing countries in the new global context. In essence, the Report (*TDR 1999*) argues that trade liberalization has resulted in a fundamental transformation in the relationship between the balance of payments and economic growth such that a given level of trade deficit is associated with a lower growth rate than before the policy reform process. The need to finance growing external deficits has encouraged financial liberalization. But this has led to currency appreciations and instability, which have undermined trade performance. There is increasing dependence of national economies on external capital. But with the current international financial architecture this is exposing countries to speculative flows and inevitable financial crises. The international trade regime is also confounding development prospects owing to continuing tariff peaks and other market access barriers in rich industrial countries as well as increasing restrictions on the policy space of developing countries to build up the international competitiveness of their domestic enterprise.[10] Finally trends in international finance are coming to dominate what was happening in international trade in this new global environment.

IV. The UNCTAD Alternative to the Washington Consensus

Although most developing countries have been unable to create and sustain the level of economic dynamism necessary to address their grave social problems of poverty and joblessness, a few countries, particularly in East Asia, have been able to do so. UNCTAD's alternative to the Washington Consensus has been founded on close analysis of successful East Asian experience, the identification of its key ingredients, and the generalization of these ingredients into a number of key strategic orientations which might be applicable for all developing countries.

This work was mainly completed after the publication of *The East Asian Miracle* study (World Bank, 1993). Two multi-country research projects financed by the Japanese government were important in enabling the basic research: *East Asian Development: Lessons for a New Global Environment* launched in 1995 and *Economic Development and Regional Dynamics in Africa: Lessons from the East Asian Experience*, launched in 1996. The results of this work were distilled in the TDRs. But spinning off it, an increasing body of research has been published in academic journals. The most significant examples are the special issue of the *Journal of Development Studies* on "East Asian Development" published in 1998,

---

[10] The report estimates an annual export gain of $700 billion by 2005 if developed countries remove barriers to labour-intensive and resource-based manufactures (*TDR 1999:* 143).

and the special issue of the *Cambridge Journal of Economics* on "African Economic Development in a Comparative Perspective" published in 2001. There were also two special research paper series on East Asian development and on its lesson for economic development and regional dynamics in Africa based on multi-country research projects financed by the Japanese government. Gore (2000) situates UNCTAD thinking in relation to emerging trends in development policy analysis including the Washington Consensus, UNDP's human development approach and the neo-structuralist approach to development elaborated by ECLAC in the 1990s. Kozul-Wright and Rayment (2004) also situate UNCTAD thinking within the context of debates on globalization. *TDR 2003* (Part Two, Chapters IV and V) provides an overall synthesis of key empirical findings with regard to two key elements of the UNCTAD approach – economic growth and capital accumulation, and industrialization, trade and structural change. Finally, UNCTAD 2003 provides a summary of the approach, including many of the important underlying working papers that inform it.

A. The Nature of East Asian Development Strategies

The basic ingredients of East Asian development strategies were originally set out in *TDR 1994* (Part Two, Chapter I) and *TDR 1996* (Part Two).[11] In these works East Asian development is understood as a process of late industrialization. Rising incomes and reduced poverty have been associated with rising productivity and a dramatic shift in the structure of production and employment in which agriculture has become relatively less important and industry, particularly manufacturing, has become relatively more important. The engine of this process of structural change and productivity growth has been rapid and sustained capital accumulation and technological progress. The development of productive capabilities has enabled domestic producers to compete in ever-more sophisticated international markets. At the same time the generation of employment opportunities has enabled the working age population to become progressively more fully and productively employed, and as this has occurred extreme poverty has fallen rapidly.

According to the UNCTAD view there is no single East Asian model. However, in successful cases the development process has been animated and guided by a developmental state. Private enterprise and the profit motive have been the driving forces behind the development process. But the pursuit of private

---

[11] Part II of *TDR 1994* is entitled "Re-thinking Economic Policies" and Part II of *TDR 1996* "Rethinking Development Strategies".

interests has been harnessed for the achievement of national development objectives through national policies. A key ingredient has been the establishment of an independent and highly competent economic bureaucracy. There have also been strong government-business networks. Through these ties, the economic bureaucracy has developed a common vision with business concerning development objectives and targets along with a common understanding of how these can best be achieved.

The basic components of the development strategies stimulating and guiding this process have been:

- Policies to create and sustain a dynamic process of capital accumulation, structural change and technological upgrading
- Policies to manage integration with the global economy
- Policies to manage the distribution of the benefits of development

In each of these areas, policies change over time as late industrialization strengthens and the major locus of capital accumulation, productivity growth and export expansion shifts from agriculture to industry. The respective roles of markets and States also change over time. Economic liberalization proceeds as economic development strengthens and to the extent that the basic conditions for the proper working of a market economy are established within the country and that domestic enterprises develop sufficient production capabilities to compete internationally. As in Prebisch's original paradigm, it is economic development that enables successful liberalization.

In the initial stages of the development process, the major strategic focus of efforts to accelerate capital accumulation is on measures to increase agricultural productivity. But as industrialization increases, the central locus for capital accumulation switches from agriculture to industry while domestic resource mobilization and the growth of savings increasingly depend on corporate profits and their use. (*TDR 1994:* 71) identifies the existence of a strong investment-profits nexus as the essential hallmark of successful East Asian policies and argues that the underlying logic of East Asian development strategies is to animate and sustain that nexus.

The second key component of the strategy is management of the integration of the domestic economy with the global economy. This process is analysed in depth in *TDR 1996*. It finds that in the early stages of the development process, when investment demand exceeded domestic savings, official financing plays a key role in filling the financing gap. Later on, private capital inflows became more important, but their form varied. FDI was critical in some countries, whilst others relied on bank lending. In either case, government played a role in ensuring that capital inflows supported national development objectives and complemented rather than substituted for the process of accumulation by domestic enterprises. In all cases international trade was central to the development process. But rather than being simply "export-led" or "export-oriented" as the conventional wisdom has it, policies were directed to create mutually supportive links between expansion of exports and investment. The growth process in most successful East Asian countries has thus entailed the animation of an export-investment nexus (*TDR 1996*: 108) together with an investment-profits nexus. This could entail direct links between investment and exports within particular sectors. But the process of export development involved a dynamic sequence from natural-resource based products (particularly agricultural products) to labour-intensive manufactures to more skill-intensive and capital-intensive manufactures. In this process, exports at earlier phases earned the external finance required to support investment in industries which became export activities in later phases. The trade policies used to animate this complex process were a mix of import substitution through protection and export promotion. Regional trade and investment dynamics were also important, and government policy has played a key role in facilitating a sequentially developing regional division of labour in which follower countries progressively take over less advanced export activities as leading countries lose competitiveness in them.

The last component of the development strategy is management of the distribution of the benefits of development. This is examined in *TDR 1997* which includes discussion of the forces making for greater and lesser inequality during a process of industrialization as surplus labour gets absorbed (*TDR 1997, Part Two, Chapter II: D*), the compatibility of capital accumulation with a not-too-unequal income distribution (Ibid., Part Two, Chapter V), and also the East Asian policies which have enabled a rapid pace of economic growth, accumulation and industrialization without severely widening inequality (Ibid., Part Two, Chapter VI). This analysis shows that the basis for more inclusive growth was: agrarian reform measures undertaken at an early stage, which ensured a more equal distribution of assets; broad-based human resource development, with the expansion of the educated labour force not out of line with the pace of industrial growth; and the expansion of productive employment opportunities. The reconciliation of the objectives of rapid capital accumulation and a reasonable income distribution was also achieved though fiscal policies which discouraged the distribution of profits in the form of personal income and luxury consumption. Profit-related payment systems were also introduced.

B. Lessons for Other Developing Countries

Some may argue that the financial crisis in 1997 has rendered the East Asian development experience irrelevant. *TDR 1998* (Part One, Chapter III) and *TDR 2000* (Chapter IV) rebut this view. The former argues that the crisis was due to a too-hasty break with past developmentalist practices, i.e. "the problem was not so much with [excessive corporate] leverage as with liberalization" (*TDR 1998*: 76). The latter shows that the rapid recovery afterwards was not due to austerity measures recommended as the orthodox (but mistaken) response to the crisis, but rather due to the abandonment of these policies as the severity of their negative social effects became apparent. Nevertheless in deriving lessons from East Asian development success, UNCTAD has been careful not to propagate simple formulae or recipes. One basic feature of its overall approach has been scepticism against a one-size-fits-all approach and sensitivity to the variety of development contexts. It is nevertheless possible to highlight some key lessons for the design of effective development strategies.

First, UNCTAD's approach highlights the paramount importance of a stable macroeconomic environment as the necessary basic condition for capital accumulation and growth. Fiscal and monetary discipline is thus essential. But macroeconomic policies should not simply be concerned with achieving financial targets, which dominate orthodox stabilization approaches. They must also be sensitive to the need to expand productive capacity and productivity. They must also manage the inevitable cyclical ups-and-downs of the accumulation process.

Second, responsible macroeconomic management in and of itself is insufficient to create the dynamic process of accumulation, structural change and technological upgrading that underpins sustained growth in a successful development strategy. Macroeconomic policies need to be complemented with productive development policies which develop productive capacities. Such policies should encompass both economy-wide "functional" measures (such as SME development) together with sectorally-focused and enterprise-level measures. These measures should address specific market failures which impede the achievement of national development objectives including: missing markets and the lack of an entrepreneurial base, imperfections in technology and capital markets, risks of starting-up new activities and exporting, and linkages and externalities which make investment amongst sectors highly complementary. The measures should be market-creating and market-stimulating rather than market-replacing, the aim being to catalyse, stimulate and guide private enterprise in support of national development.

Third, it is absolutely necessary for developing countries to integrate with the world economy and adopt an "outward-looking" development strategy. De-linking from the rest of the world is not a viable policy option. But rather than openness based on rapid across-the-board trade and financial liberalization, it is necessary to follow a policy of strategic integration. This means that the timing, speed and sequencing of opening, in relation to different types of international flows, should be decided on the basis of the national interest in terms of promoting development. Import liberalization should be gradual (to enable national enterprises to build up production capabilities and thus face external competition), sectorally selective, and should follow rather than precede rapid export growth. Capital account liberalization should also be gradual and managed, in coordination with domestic financial development, to ensure that capital flows are, as much as possible, additional to, rather than a substitute for, domestic resources, that they support increased investment rather than consumption, and that they do not undermine macroeconomic stability. Domestic policies should ensure that inward FDI supports the build-up of domestic production capacities and exports, and that there are positive linkages between FDI and the domestic economy. National policy should also seek to develop sub-regional and regional trade and investment flows, which are an important part of strategic integration.[12]

Fourth, the successful formulation and implementation of all these development policies requires government-business cooperation within the framework of a pragmatic development State. The policies should be implemented as far as possible through private initiative rather than public ownership and through the market mechanism rather than administrative controls. But the government should play a key role in animating the animal spirits of the private sector and harnessing the aggressive pursuit of profits, which is the motor of the system, to the realization of national development goals. This requires the enhancement of State capacities rather than state minimalism.

Fifth, development strategies need to treat poverty, human development, distributional and environmental concerns as integral aspects of macroeconomic and productive development policies. Social goals should not be seen as a secondary issue to be achieved through fiscal transfers but rather should be achieved through the productive process which determines the pre-tax and pre-transfer income distribution and also the generation of employment. Development

---

[12] Regional financial arrangements can also play an important role in buffering developing countries from the vagaries of international financial markets (see *TDR 2001*, Chapter V).

cannot be sustained if it is not inclusive. But what is required is a distribution of income that is considered legitimate in the national society. Widening inequality may not be a problem if it is associated with rising incomes and if it also remains within the bounds of legitimacy.

V.   Emerging Trends in the New Millennium

UNCTAD's work on development strategies has continued to evolve since 2000. Two main lines of work are: firstly, continued analysis of globalization and its relationship with development strategies (which has also been done in the context of WIRs, (see topical paper on FDI/TNCs); and secondly, analysis of the implications of the new Millennium Development Goals for the design of development strategies, including assessment of the new conventional wisdom which has emerged following the alleged "death" of the Washington Consensus.

A.   Globalization, Liberalization and Industrialization

A significant further advance in UNCTAD thinking on development strategies in relation to global interdependence was made in *TDR 2002* which analysed the development of the international production networks and also some of the consequences of the increasingly widespread adoption of export-oriented growth strategies.

TDR 2002 shows the extent of change in the international division of labour which has occurred through industrialization and the expansion of manufactures exports since the 1960s. Between 1970 and end of the 1990s, the share of developing countries in merchandise exports increased from about one-quarter to about one third. Moreover, the share of manufactures in the total merchandise exports of developing countries increased from around 20 per cent in the 1970 to 70 per cent at the end of the 1990s (*TDR 2002*: 51 and 52). However, the process of industrialization in the old periphery has been very uneven with some countries being left out and others actually experiencing de-industrialization. Moreover, contrary to initial expectations, the form of integration which has developed with globalization and liberalization over the last 20 years in those countries which have actually managed to sustain a process of industrialization has not usually resulted in as positive a relationship between international trade and development as expected.

An important feature of the process of industrialization in developing countries and the new international division of labour that has emerged since 1980 is that it is associated with the development of international production networks either through large TNCs or through international subcontracting relations between groups of small and medium-sized enterprises located in different countries. Such networks, which fragment the production process between different countries, have developed in three major product groups – parts and components for electrical and electronic goods, labour intensive products such as clothing and finished goods with a high (research and development content. Developing countries have been able to shift their export composition from primary commodities to manufactures by hooking into such networks. But in general they have done so by focussing on labour-intensive products or assembly activities. A problem is that these products are generally not dynamic in terms of growth of world demand and they also tend to have a relatively low potential for productivity growth and learning. Moreover, as these manufactures exports depend on large quantities of imported inputs, there has been a tendency for many developing countries to experience significant increases in manufactures exports without significant increases in manufacturing value-added. It is the latter which is critical for rising incomes.

Thus just as in the 1960s it became apparent that there were limits to inward-looking industrialization, it is starting to become clear that there may also be limits to outward-looking industrialization, or at least to the type of industrialization which is emerging with globalization and liberalization. The problem is that economic progress falters as developing countries get stuck in the easy stages of export of manufactures and are unable to upgrade into more skill-intensive and technologically-sophisticated exports. This is not an inherent feature of outward-oriented industrialization, as the experience of the East Asian NIEs shows. But with globalization of production networks, trade liberalization and the abandonment of industrial policy, it is becoming a very likely outcome.

TDR 2002 also argues that the development potential of outward-looking industrialization under liberalization may be undermined by "a risk of excessive competition among developing countries in world markets for labour-intensive products and for FDI through participation in labour-intensive segments of international production networks" (*TDR 2002*: 136). The Report finds that: "The countries with the lowest proportion of technology-intensive manufactures and the greatest proportion of low-skill, labour-intensive products in their manufactured exports have faced declining terms of trade in manufactures"; and that this tendency coincides with the shift in the mid-1980s of several highly populated, low-income economies towards more export-oriented strategies. Whether this tendency for declining terms of trade for simple manufactures will continue or not is uncertain. It depends, according to the Report, on (i) faster growth of markets of labour-intensive goods in advanced economies – both industrialized economies and first tier NIEs – which depends on income growth and market access in these countries; (ii) economic growth and structural transformation in middle income countries which can create space for low-income countries and also expand global demand; and (iii) emphasis on expansion of developing countries' domestic markets as part of a process of overcoming deep-seated problems of unemployment and poverty.

The development strategy implications of all these developments have not yet been worked out. However, one implication is that more attention needs to be paid to expansion of the domestic markets of developing countries. A second is that there is a need for greater diversity in development strategies amongst developing countries at different levels of development. Finally it is clear that the export of manufactures should not be considered a panacea. Industrialization through networks can be as much a dead-end as what the Prebisch Report called industrialization in water tight compartments. The policy challenge is to increase the value-added component of exports and to link manufactures exports to the overall process of industrialization.

B. Millennium Development Goals and Beyond the Washington Consensus

A second area of new work on development strategies arises from the global development goals which stem from the Millennium Declaration adopted by the UN General Assembly in 2000. These goals are very different from the 5 per cent economic growth goal set out in the first United Nations Development Decade. They focus on individual well-being and seek to establish progress towards minimally acceptable standards of living, in terms of income poverty, human development and the local environment. But just as the economic growth goal of the first Development Decade was central to UNCTAD's policy recommendations of the 1960s, so the new Millennium goals are becoming central to UNCTAD's work now. Paraphrasing the Prebisch Report, "one cannot posit a halving of the incidence of extreme poverty between 1990 and 2015 without accepting also all the consequences that implies for imports and exports".

This strand of work is not only significant because of the new Millennium development goals but also because of the evolving conventional wisdom on development strategies. Since Joseph Stiglitz started to call for a "post-Washington consensus" – the main elements of which he outlined in the Prebisch Lecture organized and hosted by UNCTAD in 1999 (Stiglitz, 1999) – there has been a tendency to argue that the Washington Consensus is now dead. But the new orthodoxy on development strategies is like an onion with layers. Firstly, social concerns, including greater attention to poverty reduction, health, education, governance and corruption, have been added to the core Washington Consensus policy reform package (what some observers have called "Washington Plus"). Secondly, there has been increased recognition of the importance of the external environment for national development and thus of the need for a development partnership between international and national action to support countries in implementing this package (which together with "Washington Plus" essentially constitutes the so-called Monterrey Consensus).[13] In this process, the radical critique of the adverse social implications of the Washington Consensus has been incorporated into a new conventional wisdom which is synthesis of the package of policy reforms with the policy proposals stemming from UNICEF's Adjustment with a Human Face and most forcefully articulated in UNDP's Human Development Report.

But this approach has a basic problem. As UNCTAD's work on the Washington Consensus shows, the economic core of the onion will not deliver as expected. The challenge now, therefore, is to integrate poverty, human development and social concerns with the insights of UNCTAD's critique of the Washington Consensus and its constructive alternative. Along with the identification of new forms of globalization and interdependence and their implications for development strategies, forging this new synthesis is another emerging frontier of UNCTAD work on development strategies.

Work in this area has mainly focused on the Millennium poverty reduction goal and has been carried out in the context The Least Developed Countries Report. The *LDCR 2000* (Part Two, Chapters 4 and 5) provides an initial assessment of the new Poverty Reduction Strategy Paper (PRSP) approach as an evolution out of the old structural adjustment programmes. It is argued that the PRSPs are seeking to make the quality of growth more pro-poor whilst the problem of structural adjustment programmes, which many LDCs intensively implemented in the 1990s, is that they cannot deliver a sufficiently high rate of economic growth to make a dent in poverty. This argument is taken further in *LDCR 2002* (Part Two, Chapter 5) which also proposes a way to improve the PRSP approach. The proposal for a "development-oriented poverty reduction strategy" rather than an "adjustment-oriented poverty reduction" builds on accumulated knowledge about

---

[13] The Monterrey Consensus refers to the outcome of the UN International Conference on Financing for Development, held in Monterrey, Mexico, 18-23 March 2002.

development strategies within UNCTAD work and applies it to the context of the LDCs. The *LDCR 2004* extends the analysis further. It includes analysis of the relationship between trade liberalization and poverty reduction in the LDCs (*LDCR 2004* Part Two, Chapter 5) as well as proposals for improving the trade-poverty relationship through national development strategies (Ibid, Part Two, Chapter 7). As most of the LDCs have already undertaken extensive trade liberalization, it argues that it is necessary to undertake post-liberal development strategies. Export-led growth with a human face is one option. But the Report argues that this is unlikely to be sustainable or sufficiently inclusive. There are a number of alternative development strategies which pay more attention to the development of domestic markets and seek to achieve export expansion adequate for national development rather than export-led growth. These strategies include: balanced growth based on agricultural productivity growth and export-accelerated industrialization; agricultural-led industrialization with increased value-added in agricultural exports; development and diversification through the management of mineral or oil revenues; a development strategy founded on natural-resource-based production clusters; and an employment-led growth strategy which is founded on the development of international competitiveness in tradables, employment expansion in non-tradables and technological change in subsistence activities.

The *LDCR 2002* conceptualizes the poverty reduction problem in the LDCs as a problem of escaping an international poverty trap. This trap arises when international trade and financial relations reinforce domestic vicious circles of pervasive extreme poverty. Commodity-dependent LDCs are particularly prone to be caught in such a trap. Slow and unstable export growth which follows from specialization on a narrow range of low-productivity, low-value-added and weakly competitive primary commodities serving declining or sluggish international markets is associated with the build-up of an unsustainable external debt owed to official creditors and the emergence of an aid/debt service system which has undermined the effectiveness of development aid.

This is precisely the old development problem which was identified in UNCTAD (1964). It now applies to a smaller group of countries, those where the poverty problem is most intractable. But the *LDCR 2002* also argues that the situation in these countries is also related to the problems which more advanced developing countries face. As it puts it, "Various asymmetries in the international system, together with global financial instability, are currently making it difficult for the more advanced developing countries to deepen industrialization and move up the technological ladder and out of simpler products being exported by poorer countries. As the more advanced developing countries which have achieved a small measure of prosperity meet a "glass ceiling" which blocks their development, LDCs find it increasingly difficult to mover up the ladder of development" (*LDCR 2002*: Overview: VIII). The centre-periphery structure of the world has broken down. But development is still constrained within new forms of global interdependence in which relationships between more advanced and less advanced developing countries are increasingly important and are structured by relationships between both groups of developing countries and developed countries.

For the LDCs, escaping the poverty trap certainly requires export expansion. But the LDCR 2004 also examines the relationship between export expansion and poverty reduction in the LDCs and finds that in countries where the majority of the population is living at a bare subsistence level export-led growth tends to be associated with an exclusionary growth trajectory. The strategic challenge for LDCs is to escape the poverty trap while promoting inclusive development.

VI.   Conclusion

Over the last 40 years, the centre-periphery view of the world – in which, on the one side, there were rich, technologically advanced industrial countries and, on the other side, there were poor, technologically backward developing countries, and the basic pattern of international trade was the exchange of manufactures produced in the former for primary commodities produced in the latter – has broken down. Industrialization of the periphery and the expansion of manufacturing exports have created a new international division of labour. But the process of industrialization of the old periphery has been highly uneven. The poorest countries at the bottom of the world economy continue to specialize in primary commodities and continue to face development problems identified by UNCTAD 40 years ago. A number of more advanced developing countries have also experienced de-industrialization. Those more advanced countries which have increased their manufacturing exports have often done so through integration in international production networks, a process which has not yielded as great benefits in terms of growth of manufactures value-added as expected. Private capital inflows have become highly important for most middle-income developing countries. But globalization and liberalization has been associated with slower growth and increasing economic instability in developing countries. There are now also signs that the problem of declining terms of trade for commodities is also being repeated for labour-intensive manufactures. Thus the new pattern of global interdependence has not eradicated earlier asymmetries in the world economy between developed and developing countries but rather has transformed them.

Against this background, and greatly facilitated by a few multi-country research projects, UNCTAD has evolved an alternative approach to development strategies. The essence of this strategy is "manage accumulation, manage integration, manage distribution". This is a much more detailed view of the national development strategies than that set out in the 1960s. But there is a strong continuity between the 1960s and post-1985 UNCTAD work in terms of its understanding of how development can be started, accelerated and sustained. In particular:

- The paramount need for industrialization in order to ensure accelerated and sustained development
- The importance of capital accumulation and technological progress as underlying forces which drive the development process
- The necessity of linking international trade with economic development, and the central significance of the balance of payments, particularly the trade gap, as a constraint on accelerated development
- Interdependence between trade and finance in the external economic relationships of developing countries
- The important role of regional cooperation as an extension of national development strategies
- Scepticism about the ability of free market forces to achieve national development goals given market failures, structural bottlenecks and sectoral interdependence
- Recognition that the underlying purpose of development is to reduce poverty and to provide meaningful and productive employment for the rapidly growing working-age population.

Perhaps the most notable change in the UNCTAD approach to development strategies is the shift from an emphasis on development planning to one that argues the need for a developmental state to animate and guide the private sector in order to achieve national development objectives. The need for such a developmental state is based on recognition of the importance of profits as the motor of change, but at the same time knowledge that this process is characterized by creative destruction, instability and social conflict where there are winners and losers. Harnessing the transforming potential of capitalist production for national development is not likely to be successful when based on idealist views of the working of free markets.

Finally, the most notable continuity in the UNCTAD approach to development strategies is its advocacy of an effective development partnership between national and international action. This has now become a commonplace. But UNCTAD's analysis shows that the types of partnership envisaged by the current conventional wisdom will not enable developing countries to promote economic development effectively and thus substantially reduce poverty and increase productive employment. The struggle to identify pragmatic alternatives and re-build a development consensus continues.

References

Akyuz Y and Gore CG, eds. (2001). Special Issue on African Development in a Comparative Perspective. *Cambridge Journal of Economics*. 25(3) May.

Avramovic D et al. (1964). *Economic Growth and External Debt.* Baltimore: John Hopkins University Press.

Cornia A Jolly R and Stewart F, eds. (1987). *Adjustment with a Human Face: Vol. 1 – Protecting the Vulnerable and Promoting Growth.* Oxford: Clarendon Press.

Dell S (1991). *International Development Policies: Perspectives for Developing Countries.* Durham and London: Duke University Press.

Gore CG (2000). The rise and fall of the Washington Consensus as a paradigm for developing countries. *World Development*, 28 (5): 789–804.

IMF Internal Evaluation Office (2003). *Evaluation of Prolonged Use of IMF Resources.* Washington DC.

Journal of Development Studies (1998). *Special Issue on East Asian Development: New Perspectives.* Y Akyuz, ed.

Kozul-Wright R and Rayment P (2004). Globalization reloaded: An UNCTAD perspective. *UNCTAD Discussion Paper*, No. 167, Geneva.

Rosenthal G (2004). ECLAC: A commitment to a Latin American way toward development. Chapter 4. In: Y. Berthelot, ed. *Unity and Diversity in Development Ideas: perspectives from the UN Regional Commissions.* Bloomington and Indianapolis: Indiana University Press (published as part of the United Nations Intellectual History Project).

Stiglitz J (1998) Towards a new paradigm for development: Strategies, policies and processes. Prebisch Lecture delivered at UNCTAD, Geneva.

Toye J (1993). *Dilemmas of Development: Reflections on the Counter-Revolution in Development Theory and Policy.* Second Edition. Oxford, United Kingdom and Cambridge, United States: Blackwell.

UN (1964). Towards a New Trade Policy for Development, Report of the Secretary-General to UNCTAD I (often known as the "Prebisch Report"). In: *Proceedings of the United Nations Conference on Trade and Development.* Vol. II: Policy Statements. E/CONF.46/141.

UNCTAD (1968). Towards a Global Strategy of Development, Report of the Secretary-General to UNCTAD II. TD/3/Rev.1.

____ (1985). *The History of UNCTAD, 1964–1984*, UNCTAD/OSG/286, New York: United Nations.

____ (2003). Development strategies in a globalizing world, UNCTAD/GDS/MDPB/Misc.15.

____ (various years). *The Least Developed Countries Reports* (Due to its frequent reference in the text, individual reports of this UNCTAD flagship publication are specially referred to as: *LDCR2000, LDCR2002, LDCR2004* for *The Least Developed Countries Reports, 2000, 2002 and 2004*)

____ (various years). *The Trade and Development Report* (Due to its frequent reference in the text, individual annual reports of this UNCTAD flagship publication are specially referred to as: *TDR1981, TDR1982 ... TDR2003*, for *The Trade and Reports, 1981, 1982 ... 2003*)

UNDP/UNCTAD (1979). The Balance of Payments Adjustment Process in Developing Countries: Report to the Group of Twenty-four. UNDP/UNCTAD project INT/75/105, United Nations.

Williamson J (1993). Democracy and the "Washington Consensus". *World Development*, 21 (8): 1329–1336.

World Bank (1987). *World Development Report 1987*. New York: Oxford University Press.

____ (1991). *World Development Report 1991*. New York: Oxford University Press.

____ (1993). *The East Asian Miracle: Public Policy and Economic Growth*. New York: Oxford University Press.

Part Two

Selected Topics

Commodities

Alexei Mojarov and Mehmet Arda*

Introduction

The subject of commodities has been at the heart of UNCTAD's trade and development agenda since its inception. For many developing countries, particularly the least developed countries (LDCs), commodities have long been the main generator of employment, income and foreign exchange, linking their national economies with the global economy. Even for those countries that have recently succeeded in diversifying their economies and have achieved a significant degree of industrialization, commodities have remained vitally important for certain geographical areas and considerable portions of their populations. In fact, the role of commodities in developing countries' economies was one of the principal concerns that led to the decision of the General Assembly to create UNCTAD in 1964.

UNCTAD has endeavoured to analyse commodity problems and search for solutions to them at the national and international levels, with a view to transforming the commodity sector from being a poverty trap to an engine of growth, development and structural change. More specifically, UNCTAD's activities in commodities have ranged from taking a leading role in multilateral negotiations through its intergovernmental machinery to providing information and assistance in relevant areas. In this context, major inputs were provided for national and international policies affecting the commodity sector.

This paper begins with some background information on the treatment of the commodity problem in multilateral fora before the founding of UNCTAD. This is followed by a discussion of UNCTAD's intellectual contributions during the period of the late 1960s and 1970s when solutions to commodity problems were sought in the context of the North–South dialogue (particularly by establishing international commodity organizations and agreements). The next section covers UNCTAD's contributions to the debate during 1980s when there was a strong shift from regulatory to market based approaches in the mode of thinking on

* Alexei Mojarov is an Economic Affairs Officer, Commodities Branch, Division on International Trade in Goods and Services, and Commodities (DITC). Mehmet Arda is Head of the Commodities Branch, DITC.

development issues and when UNCTAD specifically advanced on approach stressing the balanced roles of governments and the markets. It is followed by a section dealing with the 1990s when UNCTAD stressed the importance of several key issues that tended to be overlooked in the commodities debate. In next section, UNCTAD's recent intellectual contributions to understanding the commodities-development interface and its pioneering approach to partnerships are covered. The paper ends by summing-up the evolution of the international commodity *problématique* during the period under review.

I.   Pre–1964: A Brief Overview

International trade in primary commodities has been a subject of concern to governments since colonial times, but efforts to evolve an international policy among governments based on mutual cooperation only began in the early decades of the 20th century. A first attempt at international cooperation in trade in commodities dates back to the World Economic Conference in Geneva in 1927 which recommended, among other things, the establishment of international commodity agreements (ICAs)[1] whose objectives were limited to rationalization of production, reduction of costs and the more efficient use of existing equipment (Gordon–Ashworth, 1984).

In 1932 and 1933 the League of Nations addressed the question of ICAs as a potential solution to the commodity price crisis. However, only a few ICAs were established during the inter-war period (for tin, wheat, tea, sugar and rubber). In the early 1940s two important developments in international commodity policy emerged. The first was the concept of a unified approach to international commodity price stabilization advocated by Keynes (Keynes, 1974) in 1942, who proposed a comprehensive plan for international actions over a range of commodities to be administered by a general council for commodity controls. One important feature of this proposal was that in order to avoid collusion among producers or consumers, both sides had to be equally represented in the council.

The second development was the recognition by the 1943 Conference on Food and Agriculture that ICAs were one of means of promoting world economic

---

[1] ICAs are the agreements among Governments of commodity producing/exporting and commodity consuming/importing countries which can be either "stabilization (or economic) agreements" or "administrative agreements". The former involve economic mechanisms (or "commodity control schemes" along the principles of Havana Charter) for regulation of production, exports and consumption. The latter, on the other hand, do not involve such mechanisms, being only fora for discussion, development programmes and source of information and statistics.

growth. This was the first official recognition by a group of countries that clearly linked international actions in the area of commodity trade with development. In 1947 the UN Economic and Social Council (ECOSOC) established an Interim Coordination Committee for International Commodity Agreements (ICCICA) to coordinate international efforts towards establishing commodity control schemes with participation of both producers and consumers. Four commodity stabilization agreements – on coffee, sugar, tin and wheat – were concluded under the aegis of the ICCICA. The Havana Charter adopted in 1948, although disapproving restrictive business practices and cartels of any kind, recognized that ICAs could be employed to stabilize prices around trend, to ensure reasonable and stable incomes for producers and to correct adverse situations resulting from "burdensome surpluses" of commodities.

However, by the early 1960s the agreements had failed to cover as many commodities as would be effective for providing a solution to the commodity problem in general, and the mechanisms of ICAs concluded under the ICCICA proved to be generally inadequate except for tin. In 1964 the UN General Assembly adopted resolution 1995 (XIX) by which UNCTAD took over the mandate of the ICCICA as the organ within the United Nations system responsible for formulating principles and policies on international trade along with related problems. It would not be an exaggeration to say that a major reason for setting up UNCTAD as a UN body dealing with trade and development was the concern of developing countries and of the international community in general with the problem of instability in commodity markets. While only one product, namely coffee, among those covered by agreements concluded under the ICCICA was produced exclusively by developing countries, UNCTAD's attention was to turn to generalizing the agreements to cover commodities exported by developing countries (Megzari, 2000).

II. 1964–the 1970s:
Rise and Climax of UNCTAD's Negotiating Role

An important milestone in the development of internationally coordinated commodity policy was Secretary-General Prebisch's report to UNCTAD I (UN, 1964: 9–13). This report not only established the links between trade in primary commodities and development but also provided a theoretical framework for international commodity policy. The Prebisch argument, based on the historically deteriorating tendency in developing countries' terms of trade, particularly for commodity exports measured against manufacture imports, provided a solid basis for proposals for diversification of productive capacities. These included increased processing of primary products in developing countries and enhanced access for these products to the markets of the developed countries as well as pure stabilization measures. After UNCTAD I the link between international commodity policy and the development needs of the developing countries became a common feature of both developed and developing countries' approach to dealings with commodity problems.

Though the Final Act of UNCTAD I outlined a set of new principles and a global framework for development, sharp divergences in the views and attitudes of governments in the area of commodity analysis and in proposals for remedial actions were clearly evident. Developed market economy countries expressed reservations on a number of critical issues: for instance, twelve countries opposed the recommendation on price stabilization agreements for primary commodities while most others abstained. A large number of developed countries abstained from a recommendation to modify their price support policies for primary production and the United States opposed recommendations on disposal of stocks of primary commodities held by developed countries.

In April 1965 UNCTAD's Trade and Development Board (TDB) established the Committee on Commodities (resolution 7 (1) of 29 April 1965). The major task of the Committee was to "promote general and integrated policies in the commodity field to follow and facilitate inter-governmental consultations and action on the problems of particular commodities and to promote and encourage the conclusion of international stabilization agreements or other commodity arrangements as appropriate". The major intellectual inputs of the UNCTAD secretariat at that time were yearly *UNCTAD Commodity Surveys* and various documents on, as well as reviews of, trends and problems concerning various commodities of importance to developing countries.[2] These documents served as background material for sessions of the Committee and made proposals for discussions and decisions by member countries.

At UNCTAD II (New Delhi, 1968) discussion on commodities was focused on a comprehensive analysis of the commodity problem presented by the UNCTAD secretariat. The Conference adopted resolutions on international actions on commodities, on general agreement on commodity arrangements, on co-ordination by UNCTAD of the activities of inter-governmental commodity bodies, on studies by international financial institutions on stabilization of commodity prices and on guaranteed minimum agricultural income (UNCTAD, 1968: 34–38).

---

[2] They included: UNCTAD, 1966a-e; 1967a, b.

The Conference agreed that the difficulties faced by 19 commodities of export interest to developing countries merited attention. These commodities were cocoa, sugar, vegetable oils (including oilseeds, oils and fats), natural rubber, hard fibres, jute and allied fibres, bananas, citrus fruits, tea, wine, iron ore, tobacco, tungsten, cotton, manganese ore, mica, pepper, shellac and phosphates (Ibid.: 34–36). It is significant to note that the Conference entrusted an important role to the World Bank for supporting price stabilization agreements in these commodities in particular by avoiding direct financing in accordance with previously accepted principles. However, the World Bank effectively did little in this direction. On the contrary, both the World Bank and the International Monetary Fund (IMF) as well as bilateral donors proceeded to encourage supply expansion of primary commodities, thus contributing to conditions of structural oversupply.

In the late 1960, the UNCTAD secretariat presented the Committee on Commodities with a series of comprehensive reviews of main problems and possible forms of international actions with respect to specific commodities as well as documents and notes on pricing policy, liberalization of trade and access to markets, disposal of surpluses and strategic reserves, diversification, marketing and distribution systems for primary commodities. Apart from that, numerous articles on commodity problems and policies were published by UNCTAD secretariat staff (de Silva, 1983). Although not all the secretariat's proposals found acceptance by all countries and were subsequently modified, their fundamental thrust reflected the functioning of the secretariat as a catalyst for ideas and a source of new and relevant proposals for specific international actions.

The next stage in the evolution of UNCTAD commodity policy was set against the background of two major developments. The first was the oil crisis of the mid 1970s and the consequent strengthening of OPEC as an oil cartel with major influence on international economic relations. The second was the adoption by the United Nations of the principles of the New International Economic Order (Maizels, 1973; Corea, 1977). At that time the secretariat's intellectual contribution in the area of commodities was not confined to a general analysis of development problems but expanded into a series of very specific proposals for changes in the existing system of international economic relations.[3] It had been already recognized at UNCTAD I that the export earnings of many developing countries depended heavily on the demand and terms of trade for their unprocessed and semi-processed primary commodity exports, and the secretariat recommended a concerted approach placing commodity export earnings at the core of economic

---

[3] Particular tribute in this respect should be paid to Gamani Corea, UNCTAD's Secretary-General (see Corea, 1980).

development. This proposal eventually led to the adoption of the Conference resolution at 93 (IV) at UNCTAD IV in 1976 on the Integrated Programme for Commodities (IPC).[4] Also important was the idea of a financial institution, the Common Fund for Commodities (CFC), becoming an integral part of the IPC. In the 1970s and the 1980s the secretariat concentrated its intellectual capacities on the formulation of the IPC and, upon its adoption, on the fulfilment of its major elements (CFC, ICAs, compensatory financing[5] and diversification).

The IPC, while recognizing the importance of dealing with the specific problems of commodities on a case-by-case basis, brought into focus similar difficulties facing many commodities where many developing countries exporting them had a common interest (Chadha, 1977). The attempt was to depart from the fragmented approach of the past by addressing current problems of international commodity trade and development within an integrated framework of principles, objectives and instruments. It was envisaged that the principal elements of the IPC would fall into two broad groups: those directed towards reducing the short-term instability of commodity markets and those aimed at dealing with longer term developmental issues related to the commodity sector. The IPC's objectives included achieving and maintaining price levels that are "remunerative for producers and equitable to consumers" by reducing excessive price fluctuations and assuring market access and reliability of supply. It also aimed at helping to expand commodity processing in developing countries, to improve marketing and distribution systems, and to support natural products in competition with synthetic substitutes. Firstly, it was agreed at UNCTAD IV to enter into negotiations for the establishment of a CFC to finance international buffer stocks or internationally coordinated national stocks, within the framework of ICAs (Corea, 1992). Secondly, negotiations were also to be launched on a wide range of commodities (though for some commodities negotiations had already begun long before, and the ICAs for some among them had already been operational) in order to establish new ICAs and strengthen existing ones. These two elements were closely interrelated since it was envisaged that the CFC, by providing an assured source of funding, would act as a catalyst in promoting the conclusion of ICAs. The third important element of the IPC was the improvement and enlargement of compensatory financing facilities for dealing with the negative impacts of shortfalls in commodity export earnings of developing countries. Conference resolution 93 (IV) also included references to other important elements of commodity policy such as

---

[4] UNCTAD IV, resolution 93 (IV) on the Integrated Programme for Commodities, 30 May 1976. http://icac.org/icac/Projects/CommonFund/Admin/english.html (original) or http://www3.jaring.my/inro/res93.html
[5] The financing of temporary shortfalls in export earnings.

the expansion of processing of primary products in developing countries and diversification of exports.

The IPC made UNCTAD a major forum for inter-governmental consultations and negotiations on commodities. Following UNCTAD IV, there was a vast expansion of commodity-related activities, including the consultations and negotiations on the CFC and on individual commodities.

The rest of this section describes the dynamics of specific elements of the IPC, namely: negotiations on individual commodities; the Common Fund for Commodities; compensatory financing and commodity diversification.

A.   Negotiations on Individual Commodities

As mentioned above, UNCTAD's activities on negotiation/renegotiation of ICAs and other international commodity arrangements surged after the launching of the IPC. In this connection, the secretariat produced numerous analytical papers and other background documents which served as the basis for discussions and decisions. Nevertheless, progress in launching agreements on the commodities listed in the IPC was extremely slow and limited. Those ICAs which had already been in existence before that time (on cocoa, coffee, sugar, tin and wheat) were successfully renegotiated under UNCTAD auspices (except on coffee, which was renegotiated by the International Coffee Council), but a new agreement was concluded only on natural rubber. For some commodities, such as jute and jute products, olive oil and table olives as well as for tropical timber commodity development, agreements with emphasis on industry and export development and promotion measures were also negotiated. These agreements did not include market regulation provisions. For the other IPC commodities, protracted discussions, consultations and, for a few commodities, even negotiations, failed to result in agreements. UNCTAD also acted as a forum for establishing the International Nickel Study Group and the International Copper Study Group, and assisted in operations of the International Lead and Zinc Study Group and the International Rubber Study Group. These are autonomous intergovernmental bodies were created to provide opportunities for regular intergovernmental consultations on production, consumption and international trade in the individual commodities.

The limited success in achieving international agreements on individual commodities resulted mostly from fundamental divergences of views between developed and developing countries on the underlying purposes and aims of ICAs. The single most fundamental factor that hindered the success of ICAs was the general opposition of the developed market-economy countries to any significant extension of regulation in commodity markets. It can also be argued that another, more technical constraint on those negotiations was the delay in establishing (and thus operationalizing) the CFC. The absence of a central financing institution increased the potential direct financial burden on countries that were otherwise much more willing to consider establishing buffer stocks. Other reasons include some periods of relatively favourable conditions in the commodity markets, which reduced the enthusiasm of some producing countries for regulating them; conflicts of interests among producing countries and between producers and consumers of particular commodities; and the failure of developing countries to present common proposals except for natural rubber (UNCTAD, 1982a).

B.   The Common Fund for Commodities

CFCs basic goals were in essence the same as proposals made by Keynes more than 30 years before. The CFC that was finally agreed on appeared to be less ambitious in many ways than originally conceived. First, contrary to UNCTAD secretariat's proposal, it would not control a central pool of funds with which to finance the buffer stock operations of International Commodity Organizations (ICOs). The consensus was that most of the CFC's financial resources would be derived from deposits made with it by the participating ICOs themselves. Consequently the CFC was endowed with only a modest amount of its own capital, although it was authorized to raise additional amounts as required by borrowing from its members, international financial institutions and private capital markets.

This final decision diminished the influence of the CFC as a new independent financial institution. Secondly, negotiators could not accept the original proposal that the CFC should itself be empowered to intervene to support prices in emergency situations on commodity markets not covered by ICAs. Third, the agreement included a new element, a "Second Account" (as opposed to a "First Account"), to finance measures other than buffer stock operations that were to be financed by the latter Account. The measures that the Second Account was to finance included: research and development, diversification programmes and productivity improvements aimed at improving the structural conditions of commodity markets and at enhancing the long-term competitiveness and prospects of particular commodities. It should also be pointed out that the Second Account was to be financed by voluntary contributions from governments.[6]

The CFC operates with a commodity focus rather than a country one, concentrating on the more general problems of particular commodities cutting across national boundaries. The CFC has developed a particular advantage in small- to medium-sized projects which are suited to demonstrative and replicable measures for, *inter alia*, transferring technology, increasing productivity, promoting investment in new end-use areas, introducing new products and disseminating research and development findings.

C.   Compensatory Financing

It has been recognized by developing countries that even if ICAs were successful in substantially reducing price instability, the commodity export earnings of countries would still be likely to suffer from fluctuations as a result of supply variations, for example in agricultural harvests. Large and unpredictable fluctuations in export earnings have been a major constraint on the ability of many developing countries to carry on their development programmes. The IPC had envisaged the improvement and enlargement of compensatory financing facilities for the stabilization of export earnings of developing countries around a growing trend. However, it was implicit that such enlarged compensatory facilities would be regarded as complementary to ICAs with stabilization mechanisms and not as substitutes for such agreements.

The role of a compensatory financing facility in stabilizing the commodity export earnings was intensively discussed at UNCTAD V (Manila, 1979). A resolution was adopted affirming the complementary nature of such a facility (UNCTAD, 1981) and requesting the UNCTAD secretariat to prepare a detailed study in consultation with the IMF on the operation of such a complementary facility (UNCTAD, 1983). The debate on the possibilities and role of compensatory financing schemes carried over to UNCTAD VI, which adopted a resolution authorizing the Secretary-General of UNCTAD to convene an expert group to consider "the need for an additional complementary facility to

---

[6] It turned out that the Second Account became CFC's only operational arm since the First Account never became operational. The CFC has therefore become an institution concentrating chiefly on commodity development projects financed from its resources by either loans or grants or a combination thereof. In 1995 the Governing Council of the CFC, in order to take advantage of the funds accumulated in the First Account, approved measures to be financed from the First Account Net Earnings that would assist developing countries and countries in transition in their transformation from regulated to liberalized market systems and in effectively participating in global commodity markets.

compensate for the export earnings shortfalls of developing countries", suggesting the possibility of a negotiating conference on such a new facility.

D.   Commodity Diversification, Processing, Marketing and Distribution

Since its establishment, UNCTAD has been in the forefront of policy analysis and advice in this field. In 1982 the Permanent Sub-Committee on Commodities discussed extensively a preliminary report by the secretariat regarding possible approaches to the frameworks of international cooperation in the areas of processing and marketing of commodities. This took into account problems identified and solutions proposed in studies on five commodities. Further research was carried out and additional information was gathered in preparing another set of five commodity studies. As a result, specific proposals were developed for a framework of international cooperation in this area (UNCTAD, 1982b).

III.   The 1980s:
Rise of Neo-liberalism and the Decline of the North–South Dialogue

The 1980s were marked by a change in the international political economy of development from regulatory towards market-oriented approaches. This change was reflected in the publications covering international negotiations in commodities (Rangarajan, 1983). When UNCTAD celebrated its twentieth anniversary in 1984 it appeared to be an appropriate time to look back at its successes and failures in all areas. In this context, it was opportune as well to highlight emerging issues for international commodity policy (Ashiabor, 1984; Maizels, 1985).

The period of the mid-1980s was also marked by a sharp decline in commodity prices and by debt problems for many developing countries. While the decline in commodity prices was an important factor in the emergence of the debt problem, the need of individual countries to service their debt by increasing their commodity exports reduced their interest in any measure that would restrict their market share, for example through production or export quotas, even if the ultimate result might have been higher export earnings by commodity exporters in general (or by each country itself). This also coincided with a critical review by the UNCTAD secretariat of prevalent international approaches to commodities. It involved questioning the usefulness of focusing almost exclusively on price issues and compensatory finance, and a move towards a more thorough analysis of commodity problems, including the impact of subsidies, as well as more emphasis on increased self-sufficiency in developing countries (*Commodity Survey, 1986*). The introductory remarks by the Officer-in-Charge of what was then the Commodities Division to the 12th session of the Committee on Commodities in February 1987 (UNCTAD, 1988) which refer to "contours of further international cooperative actions", provided a fairly detailed manifestation of the secretariat's thinking. It is noteworthy that these remarks, which emphasized the developmental aspects of the IPC, provoked strong reactions from some delegates from developing countries who interpreted this as a departure from the price stabilization spirit of the IPC.

The first half of 1980s was also characterized by a stalemate in the commodities debate, largely reflecting lack of political will to put into effect the First Account of the CFC, therefore jeopardizing the IPC's objectives. Against this background the UNCTAD secretariat put forward a pragmatic commodity policy approach emphasizing the need for a regular mechanism to enhance producer-consumer dialogue in order to tackle specific problems of individual IPC commodities, in particular metals and minerals. The rationale for establishing fora similar to International Study Groups within UNCTAD, with the involvement of experts from governments and industry from both producing and consuming countries, was that greater transparency would contribute to market stability and a more equitable distribution of the costs of instability. This proposal of the secretariat, which mainly concerned mineral commodities, was considered by many states as an innovative move in the right direction.

Through the instrument of UNCTAD Intergovernmental Groups the secretariat played a key role in providing member countries with a forum to: improve market transparency by disseminating statistics, reviews of market situations and outlooks. This helped to correct supply/demand imbalances by sharing information on capacity and investments; monitor prices along with the structure of marketing systems and stocks; and attracting the participation of major market players from industry into a concrete dialogue. Annual intergovernmental consultations on iron ore and tungsten continued within UNCTAD for more than 10 years through the Intergovernmental Group on Iron Ore and the Committee on Tungsten. Consultations on nickel, copper, tin and bauxite/alumina/aluminium, helped to advance intergovernmental cooperation on minerals and metals. The discussions on nickel and copper resulted in United Nations conferences on these two commodities leading to the creation of the International Nickel Study Group (in 1986) and of the International Copper Study Group (in 1992). It is also important to note that intergovernmental consultations helped strengthen UNCTAD's role in the provision of information on mineral and metal commodities.

The merits of policy intervention through ICAs and compensatory financing dominated the international commodity debate at UNCTAD in the 1970s and 1980s. Although the UNCTAD secretariat was of the opinion that buffer stock and export quota schemes could only be effective for short-term price stabilization and not for raising prices over a long period, such schemes had appeared to some developing countries to as an easy way to deal with the inequalities of world trade. The collapse of the International Tin Agreement in 1987 and the failure of the economic provisions of the coffee and cocoa agreements in 1988 and 1989, however, shook fundamentally the belief of many governments and development economists in these solutions. The UNCTAD secretariat stressed a wider range of policy issues for international consideration (UNCTAD, 1987). While this was not received with equanimity by many governments (who felt that the increasing sterility of debates on macro-solutions was only due to a lack of goodwill on the part of developed countries), these "new" policy issues gradually took over the policy agenda in the 1990s.

With respect to minerals, price stabilization issues lost their importance earlier than was the case for other commodities both in the international debate and in UNCTAD secretariat thinking. This was mainly due to the fact that almost no metal exhibited the clear division between producers in the South and consumers in the North that characterized most long-lived ICAs such as those for cocoa and coffee. Market-oriented developed countries are important producers of almost all minerals, a fact that weakened producer country support for intergovernmental initiatives. Finally, the privatization of State-owned mining companies that took place in most developing countries beginning in the 1980s, brought on by the need to service debt and the unsatisfactory performance of the companies in question, meant that direct government influence in the mining sector became very limited. The private sector was consistently uninterested in intergovernmental initiatives to stabilize prices.

IV. 1990 Onwards:
The Climax and Weakening of Neo-liberalism

Work done in the 1990s by the UNCTAD secretariat on international commodity issues and policies helped reform the way that others – the academic community as well as other organizations – looked at them, particularly the academic community and other organizations. In the early 1990s part of the academic debate was still on ways and means of implementing a New International Economic Order, and organizations like the European Commission had difficulty in moving away from the old and largely ineffective approach to compensatory finance through STABEX. Opponents of the "1970s" approaches advocated a barely disguised blind trust in the market: reduce the role of governments in commodity markets and the private sector will automatically fill the gaps to solve the problems. The UNCTAD secretariat argued that both were wrong, and over time its arguments have been vindicated.

In this context "A New Partnership for Development: the Cartagena Commitment", adopted by UNCTAD VIII (Cartagena, 1992) underlined the view that regarding producer-consumer cooperation in the area of commodities, market trends, occupational, health and safety matters, technology transfer and services associated with production, marketing and promotion of commodities, as well as environmental considerations should be taken into account (UNCTAD, 1993a). Although UNCTAD's intellectual contribution in the area of commodities did not lead to resolutions as strong as in earlier periods or to result in immediate action, they helped initiate complementary activities in other organizations with considerably larger resources than UNCTAD. Greater emphasis on market-based mechanisms for dealing with price instability and managing risks, sustainable development and the environmental aspects of commodity policies should be mentioned in this respect.

After UNCTAD VII the UNCTAD secretariat began to stress the importance of issues that were previously neglected. These included the importance of trade-supporting infrastructure such as commodity exchanges and commodity financing mechanisms (UNCTAD,1994d); the possibilities of using market mechanisms to enable farmers to deal with the short-term problem of price volatilities in a liberalized environment (UNCTAD, 1994c); the relevance of industry and market structures and the need to understand the functioning of the markets. This included the issue of distributing the value-added among the different actors, from producers to the retailers (a theme of the early 1970s, but thereafter mostly forgotten in the policy debate) (UNCTAD, 1993b); along with the potential for new, high value-added markets, such as organic products.

All of these issues are now high on the agenda of several international organizations and the international community at large (including NGOs), but in the early 1990s many still saw them as heretical. The UNCTAD secretariat also stressed that there was not a single commodity *problématique* appropriate for all developing countries, and consequently that there was not one unique solution: most developing countries exported some commodities and imported others and their interests concerning price levels had started to diverge. As a counterweight to those who advocated that tariff reduction alone was enough to enable developing countries to find their fair place in the world market, the secretariat showed that there were serious non-tariff barriers and other market entry problems such as private standards and important supply constraints in many countries. Moreover, the structural characteristics of markets, including the dominance by developed country firms at various stages of the chain between the producer of the raw material and the final consumer, often made it difficult for developing countries to participate successfully in commodity trade, to obtain development gains from their commodity exports and to turn the sector into an engine for development. This "market entry" argument is now widely accepted, although actions to accompany trade negotiations with concrete supply-side and market entry support are still slow in coming.

One of the areas in the early 1990s in which UNCTAD produced a pioneering work, particularly after the 1992 Earth Summit in Rio, was the relationship between commodities and the environment. While trade related environmental issues such as eco-labelling and Multilateral Environmental Agreements attracted most public attention and the interest of government representatives in Geneva, the work of UNCTAD's Commodities Division focused on topics, such as the environmental impact of commodity production and processing, the inclusion of environmental externalities in commodity prices (UNCTAD, 1995) and the promotion of trade in environmentally preferable products (UNCTAD, 1994a). While these topics were not on the agenda of international discussions at the time, the secretariat's work has been instrumental in subsequently putting them on the agenda of various international fora.

In accordance with the analysis presented by the UNCTAD secretariat on various occasions, the mandate on commodities in the Midrand Declaration, "A Partnership for Growth and Development", adopted at UNCTAD IX in 1996, and the Bangkok Plan of Action of UNCTAD X in 2000, emphasized the importance of improving the competitiveness of developing countries in the commodities area as well as of strengthening supply capacities, encouraging better participation in international supply chains along with diversification in commodity dependent developing countries (UNCTAD, 2000a). While the neoclassical approach to development, particularly as taken by the Bretton Woods institutions, argued that diversification and structural transformation of the economies of commodity dependent countries would come about as a result of correct macroeconomic policies and getting prices right, the view of the UNCTAD secretariat was that this process called for deliberate policies and actions involving concerted efforts by governments, enterprises and institutions (Fortin, 1984; UNCTAD, 1997a; 1999a). This view is now shared widely, including by those who formerly used to oppose it.

The mandate given by the Midrand Declaration in the area of market intelligence and analysis reinforced the work already carried on by the secretariat, in close cooperation with international commodity bodies, analysing recent developments in commodity markets and their prospects with particular emphasis on the implications for commodity-dependent countries. Conscious that good data are key for understanding and evaluating the commodity situation as well as for devising and implementing appropriate policies, from 1984 to 1995 the UNCTAD secretariat published the *Commodity Yearbook* (about 400 pages) covering trade values and shares of commodity aggregates, the direction of commodity exports, production, consumption and trade in agricultural commodities and minerals ores as well as metals by regions and selected countries.

From the late 1980s, and particularly in the 1990s, the secretariat turned its attention to the development implications of mining. The early focus was very much on the reasons underlying slow growth in mineral-dependent developing countries. While it was easy to describe the conditions, and while the statistical evidence showing the difference in economic performance between mining economies and others was clear, it proved very difficult to pin down any macro-economic characteristics that could predict how well a mining country would handle a mineral export boom (UNCTAD, 1994b). It was also clear, however, that governance factors played a major role in determining the growth outcome. Moreover, although the recipes for dealing with the condition were widely recognized (sterilization of export income flows, active exchange rate policy, control of government expenditure), they were often not applied in practice.

In the 1990s, the UNCTAD secretariat has promoted a wide-ranging discussion of the reasons behind the disappointing effects of minerals exports on the exporters' development. In this context a number of individual country analyses and broader research papers on the structure of the international mining industry were produced or commissioned. Since it was believed that institutional factors accounted for much of the difference in the degree of success between countries, the various factors influencing policy development were reviewed (UNCTAD, 1997b).

V. 1996–2004:
UNCTAD's Recent Research
and Development Initiatives

UNCTAD recognizes that the task of dealing with commodity problems is well beyond the capacities of a single entity. In this context it has helped the international commodity discussion move away from the old inter-governmental debates to a greater inclusion of civil society organizations and private companies. In the 1970s and 1980s, commodity trade was affected by governments' actions to a large extent, as they had a major influence on price levels and often played a major role in actual commodity trade. Towards the end of the 1980s this started changing. Inter-governmental discussions, therefore, had become much less relevant, and in order to remain effective UNCTAD had to start working with other major players in commodity trade, particularly the private sector. It has developed effective new partnerships with the private sector (in areas such as price risk management, infrastructure for commodity trade, and developmental impacts of mining) as well as with NGOs (particularly in biotrade and in recent years in work on commodity market structure issues).

In this connection UNCTAD's intellectual input was instrumental in the establishment of the Sustainable Commodity Initiative (SCI) in cooperation with the International Institute for Sustainable Development (IISD) of Canada. The principal objective of this initiative is to improve the social, environmental and economic sustainability of commodities production and trade by developing global, multi-stakeholder, market-based strategies for action on a sector-by-sector basis. The first product to be taken up, in 2003, was coffee.

In the area of mining the secretariat, having found that the absence of growth impacts from mining could not be explained by macro-economic factors alone or even institutional factors at the national level, began studying the role of mining in regions within developing countries (GOV, 1998). This approach has lately been given increased attention in the international debate, as seen for example in the project on "Mining, Metals and Sustainable Development" pursued by the world's largest mining companies from 2000 to 2002 and in the "Extractive Industries Review" initiated by the World Bank Group in 2002.

In the area of market information the *Commodity Yearbook* was revived in 2003 as a joint publication of UNCTAD/FAO/CFC. The UNCTAD secretariat also publishes the *Handbook of World Mineral Trade Statistics*, with detailed trade statistics for 32 minerals and metals as well as a market review and statistics on iron ore. The secretariat also disseminates commodity information over the Internet site, INFOCOMM (http://r0.unctad.org/infocomm/anglais/indexen.htm).

At the 1999 "Partnership for development" meeting in Lyon, UNCTAD established a cooperation arrangement with CYCLOPE, an association of academics, industry representatives and other commodity experts, and since then a joint publication has been produced (*World Commodity Survey*).[7] These Surveys discuss over 80 commodities and key industry sectors directly linked with commodities as well as the main commodity-related services; they explore recent world trends and developments that have had an impact on commodity markets and present comprehensive and practical information on the increasingly globalized markets for all commodities produced and traded internationally.

It can be said that the new international commodity policy approaches pioneered by the UNCTAD secretariat in the early1990s have largely been accepted. Some of them were not popular initially with governments, which led to major cuts in the programme after UNCTAD IX in Midrand in 1996, but these approaches now figure strongly in the work programmes not only of UNCTAD but also in those of organizations like FAO and the World Bank. For example, the UNCTAD secretariats' approach to commodities problems had always been conscious of the importance of market structures for the distribution of gains from commodities trade. Late in the 1990s market structures and the relationship between producers, traders and consumers of commodities exhibited important changes. UNCTAD was the first international organization to introduce a value chain perspective as a major element of commodity based development. This later became a mainstay of commodity-related discussions at many international organizations (UNCTAD, 1999a; 1999b; 2000a, paras. 64–68; 2002). A number of NGOs have also taken up the themes of supply chains and value chains. Private companies involved in commodity production and trade have participated at UNCTAD fora and have generated new ideas from them.

VI.   40 Years of UNCTAD and the Evolution of International Commodity Policies

A superficial look at the place that commodity issues currently occupy in the international development agenda and comparing that with the place they occupied forty years ago at the time of UNCTAD's establishment, may give the impression that the importance of commodity problems in the development process

---

[7] Thus far 3 issues: 1999-2000, 2000-2001 and 2003-2004, each about 350 pages.

has declined. This, however, is a false impression. During the period under review there have been significant changes in international economic relations and the international trading system. International market structures and the rules under which international trade is conducted have evolved. As a consequence, many new issues have emerged to demand the attention and energies of the international community, in particular the developing countries themselves. While the "old" problems associated with commodities such as price declines and instability persist, new problems have emerged such as difficulties associated with meeting increasingly stringent quality requirements and other market entry conditions. Problems associated with international commodity trade and the role of commodities in development have neither been resolved nor dwindled away but they have evolved and, more importantly, they now compete for attention with a plethora of other issues such as a very complex process of multilateral trade negotiations.

Another misleading impression arise from the observation that the share of commodity exports in total trade of developing countries has declined over the forty year period. This, however, hides the fact that the number of commodity dependent countries has not declined. The change observed in overall figures reflects the variations in the export structure of some large and relatively more developed countries in the developing countries group. The commodity sector continues to be at the heart of the development process for many countries, particularly LDCs and African countries.

Though today UNCTAD may no longer be an organization whose principal function in the international commodity arena is to try to negotiate binding new international agreements, yet its leading role in the international commodity debate is well established. Its broad and comprehensive mandate on commodities, focusing principally on the trade and development aspects of the commodity *problématique*, is not challenged. Its prevision and originality on commodity issues have been widely accepted. Even its heterodoxy has turned into accepted wisdom over time. Its central position in dealing with commodity issues, arising from its role as the focal point for work on commodities within the United Nations system, is acknowledged by all stakeholders, including governments, NGOs and the business community. Apart from the mandates emanating from UNCTAD's intergovernmental machinery, on many occasions it has been approached by these stakeholders with requests for cooperation or proposals for undertaking specific activities.

The latest such example of UNCTAD's unique role in the area of commodities, and the expectation of intellectual leadership from it, has been the request by the General Assembly of the United Nations to UNCTAD for designating "independent eminent persons to examine and report on commodity issues, including the volatility in commodity prices and declining terms of trade and the impact these have on the development efforts of commodity-dependent developing countries" (resolution 57/236). The UNCTAD secretariat report (UNCTAD, 2003), providing important elements for approaching commodity problems, was submitted to the UN General Assembly, which adopted resolution (A/RES/58/24) on the needs of commodity dependent countries based largely on this report.

Although the resources allocated for work on commodities at UNCTAD have declined considerably, and especially after UNCTAD IX in 1996, both the secretariat and the intergovernmental machinery have continued to focus on commodity issues while taking into account changes both in the realities of world trade and in the policy paradigm, particularly regarding the respective roles of government and the private sector. The secretariat has provided a balanced and realistic analysis as well as sound and innovative policy advice without being carried away by prevailing fads. As new issues arose and new modes of action were envisaged, they were brought to the attention of the international community. The proposal, in the context of UNCTAD XI, for the establishment of an International Task Force on Commodities is one such attempt to generate a forceful and effective multi-stakeholder partnership to deal with the commodity *problématique*.

References

Ashiabor A (1984). International commodity policy in the UN System: Two decades of experience. *IDS Bulletin*, 15(3): 27–32, 3 July.

Chadha I S (1977). The integrated programme for commodities: A reply to the criticism on a hearing. *Intereconomics*, (9/10): 227–230.

Corea G (1977). UNCTAD and the New International Economic Order, North–South Dialogue at the United Nations. *International Affairs*, 53(2): 180–184, April.

____ (1980). *Need for Change: Towards the New International Economic Order*. A selection from major speeches and reports. Oxford: Pergamon Press.

____ (1992). *Taming Commodity Markets: The Integrated Programme and the Common Fund*. Manchester University Press, New York.

de Silva L (1983). Commodity export policy and technical assistance. *Development Policy Review*, 1(1).

Fortin C (1984). UNCTAD and commodities: Towards a new agenda for research and action. *IDS Bulletin,* 15(3): 33–37, July.

Gordon-Ashworth F (1984). *International Commodity Control: A Contemporary History and Appraisal*. London: Croom Helm.

GOV (1998). Socio-Economic Consequences of the Restructuring and Privatization of the Alexkor Diamond Mine. Namaqualand, South Africa. Report on project SAF/97/A14 to the Department of Economic Affairs and Tourism of the Government of the Northern Cape Province, South Africa.

Keynes J M (1974) (Reprint). International control of raw materials, *Journal of International Economics*, 4, 299–315.

Megzari A (2000). La question des produits de base à la CNUCED: 36 ans d'un dialogue manqué. *Informations et Commentaires*, 113: 6, octobre-décembre (in French only).

Maizels A (1973). UNCTAD and the commodity problems of developing countries: The future of UNCTAD. *IDS Bulletin* 5(1), January.

____ (1985). Reforming the world commodity economy. In: Zammit Cutajar M, ed. *UNCTAD and the South-North dialogue. The First Twenty Years*, 101–123. Pergamon Press.

Rangarajan LN (1983). Commodity conflict revisited: From Nairobi to Belgrade. *Third World Quarterly*, 5(3): 586–609, July.

UN (1964). *Proceedings of the United Nations Conference on Trade and Development.* Vol. II: Policy Statements. E/CONF.46/141.

UNCTAD (1966a). The development of international commodity policy. TD/B/C.1/26, 26 October.

____ (1966b). Examination of measures for the expansion of commodity trade among developing countries. TD/B/C.1/27, 16 November.

____ (1966c) Problems arising from competition between natural products and synthetic materials. TD/B/C.1/28, 22 December.

____ (1966d). Programme for the liberalization and expansion of trade in commodities of interest to developing countries, TD/B/C.1/32, 8 December.

____ (1966e). Promotion of trade in primary commodities. TD/B/C.1/34, 8 December.

____ (1967a). The current international commodity situation and outlook. TD/B/C.1/30, 17 April.

____ (1967b). Role and financing of diversification programmes. TD/B/C.1/36, 9 January.

____ (1968). *Proceedings of the United Nations Conference on Trade and Development*, second session. New Delhi, Vol. I: 34–37, Agenda item 10, TD/97.

____ (1981). *Proceedings of the United Nations Conference on Trade and Development*, fifth session. Manila, Vol. III: 93–95, TD/269.

____ (1982a). Implementation of paragraph 2 of resolution 18 (IX) of the Committee on Commodities. Approach to frameworks of international co-operation on processing and marketing of primary commodities. Report by the UNCTAD secretariat. TD/B/C.1/PSC/27, 14 December.

____ (1982b). Selected issues in the negotiations of international commodity agreements: An economic analysis. Study by A. Maizels. TD/B/C.1/224, 5 January.

____ (1983). Complementary facility for commodity-related shortfalls in export earnings (paragraph 7 of the agreed conclusions of the Committees). Review of the operation of the compensatory financing facility of the International Monetary Fund. Report by UNCTAD secretariat. TD/B/C.1/243, 11 January.

____ (1987). Revitalizing Development, Growth and International Trade. Assessment and Policy Options, Report by UNCTAD secretariat to UNCTAD VII. Chapter III, Commodities. TD/328/Add.3, 27 February.

_____ (1988). Report of the Committee on Commodities on its twelfth session, TDB thirty-third session. TD/B/1132 - TD/B/C.1/292, paras. 41–62, New York.

_____ (1993a). *Proceedings of the United Nations Conference on Trade and Development*, eighth session. Cartagena de Indias, Colombia, 8–25 February 1992. Report and Annexes. TD/364/Rev.1: 31–33, New York.

_____ (1993b). Situation and prospects for commodities: Identification and analysis of factors affecting commodity markets with a view, *inter alia*, to reducing distortions. TD/B/CN.1/13, 24 September.

_____ (1994a). Reducing environmental stress of consumption without affecting consumer satisfaction. TD/B/CN.1/25.

_____ (1994b). Trade and industrial policy for sustainable resource-based development: Policy issues, achievements and prospect. UNCTAD/COM/33.

_____ (1994c). Counterpart and sovereign risk obstacles to improved access to risk management markets: Issues involved, problems and possible solutions. TD/B/CN.1/GE.1/3, August.

_____ (1994d). Risk distribution after liberalization of commodity marketing and problems of access to risk management markets for developing country entities - illustrated by the example of coffee in Africa. TD/B/CN.1/GE.1/2, August.

_____ (1995). Sustainable development and the possibilities for the reflection of environmental costs in price. TD/B/CN.1/29, August.

_____ (1997a). Diversification in commodity-dependent countries: The role of Governments, enterprises and institutions. Report by the UNCTAD secretariat. TD/B/COM.1/1, 5 September.

_____ (1997b). Management of commodity resources in the context of sustainable development: Governance issues for the mineral sector. UNCTAD/ITCD/COM/3.

_____ (1999a). The impact of changing supply-demand market structures on commodity prices and exports of major interest to developing countries, report by the UNCTAD secretariat. TD/B/COM.1/EM.10/2, 14 May.

_____ (1999b). The world commodity economy: Recent evolution, financial crises, and changing market structures, report by the UNCTAD secretariat, TD/B/COM.1/27, 16 July.

_____ (1999c). *Development Policies in Natural Resource Economies*. Cheltenham: Edward Elgar.

_____ (2000a). Plan of Action, Bangkok. TD/386, 18 February.

____ (2000b). Strategies for diversification and adding value to food exports: A value chain perspective. UNCTAD/DITC/COM/TM/1, UNCTAD/ITE/MISC.23, 14 November.

____ (2002) Export diversification, market access and competitiveness, report by the UNCTAD secretariat. TD/B/COM.1/54, 26 November.

____ (2003). Report of the Meeting on Eminent Persons on Commodities Issues. TD/B/50/11, 30 September.

Shipping

Awni Behnam and Peter Faust*

Introduction

Transport by ship is the major means of carrying world trade. This is overwhelmingly the case when trade in volume terms is considered but is also true of trade in value terms, although to a lesser extent. Thus the access to efficient and low-cost maritime transport is essential for all traders and particularly for those in developing countries where the competitiveness of their goods is more sensitive to transaction costs. During the last four decades maritime transport has experienced a technological revolution brought about by the containerization of cargo. Alongside this technological revolution, institutional and organizational changes have also occurred. The industry has been characterised by shipowners who have greater economic power than that of individual shippers on most trading routes. Thus shippers have been obliged to accept and conform to the services and conditions provided by shipowners. The decisions taken by major maritime countries on transport, together with the liner conference system, inhibited the development of developing country fleets. This lack of balance of power between shipowners and shippers has begun to change as the commercial and legal environment has evolved, influenced through the activities of UNCTAD.

Shipper/carrier relations are particularly important for developing countries, typically users of international transport services. A typical international trade transaction is often composed of an interlocking series of contracts, each of which is subject to a series of rules and regulations whether of a voluntary or mandatory nature. The success of international trade largely depends on whether the relevant rules and regulations adequately re.pond to the challenges raised by the current technological and commercial developments and succeed in creating certainty and predictability.

The UNCTAD secretariat has aimed at supporting national and international policies and at fostering the development of competitive transport markets with the

---

* Awni Behnam is the Special Adviser to the Secretary-General of UNCTAD. Peter Faust is Chief of the Trade Logistics Branch of the Division for Services Infrastructure for Development and Trade Efficiency, SITE. The authors were staff members of the former Shipping Division. They appreciate the comments and suggestions received from Gary Crook.

dual objective of helping traders obtain access to cost-effective quality transport services and of ensuring a continued participation by developing countries in maritime transport. Upgrading port and transport management standards and practices will be an important step towards the attainment of such objective, as it helps to ensure predictable and acceptable service qualities. These issues are being addressed through the secretariat's research along with intergovernmental machinery and are increasingly being supported through technical assistance activities as a means of bringing the results of UNCTAD's work to bear on the development process.

This paper describes chronologically some of the important contributions of UNCTAD to the evolution of shipping and shipping services since the mid-1960s. The work of UNCTAD has had two distinct phases. The first phase, up to the UNCTAD meeting in Cartagena in 1992, was a period when international rules for the maritime industry in the form of international conventions as well as model rules and standards were negotiated at UNCTAD based on research and analysis carried out by the secretariat. The second phase, from the meeting in Cartagena to the present, has been a period of research, consensus building and technical cooperation, with the exception of the preparation and adoption of a further two international conventions.

I.   1964–1992

UNCTAD activities in the first phase focused on the following key areas:

1.   Establishing the framework for negotiation;
2.   Addressing shipping questions;
3.   UN Code of Conduct for Liner Conferences;
4.   UN Convention on International Multimodal Transport of Goods; and
5.   Flags of Convenience or Open Registries.

A.   Establishing the Framework for Negotiations

The broad issue of shipping and development, which came to be known within the UNCTAD forum as "shipping questions", was first raised when the Third Committee of UNCTAD I (1964) decided to set up a working party to consider how shipping could best contribute to the expansion of foreign trade in developing countries and thus enhance their economic development.

The Inter-Governmental Maritime Consultative Organization (IMCO), the predecessor to the International Maritime Organization (IMO), negotiated and adopted technical standards of shipping that were universal in nature. However, the issue of developing countries' participation or the role shipping played in their economic development had never been discussed previously in the international fora. Shipping questions clearly were debated along the geopolitical lines of developing/developed, poor/rich confrontation and cooperation. Many a time delegates at the Committee of Shipping meetings raised the question: if developing countries cannot develop their shipping industry, what could they develop? Certainly in the late 1960s and 1970s it became a test case for development.

Developing countries, taking into account the importance of shipping to their economies, identified specific areas of concern in the then existing international structure of shipping, namely: the cost and structure of ocean freight rates, the equity in international distribution of labour in shipping activities, the lack or absence of national fleets of developing countries, the regulation of international shipping, the liner conference system[1] and the support services of ports and terminal facilities. The UNCTAD secretariat had a broad mandate to examine the economic and commercial activities of the shipping industry.

The mandate given to study various issues allowed the secretariat to influence the discussions, deliberations and thereafter the negotiations of governments. There were, however, two defining schools of thought that divided developing and developed countries. The developed countries claimed that shipping was a private enterprise where market forces and competition best determined the conduct of business. The developing countries were of the opinion that as shipping was a strategic industry with considerable impact on their capacity to trade, there was *a prior*, a role for governments in the development and control of international shipping. In many aspects the secretariat thinking was much closer to the latter.

An underlying current defining the philosophy of the secretariat favoured an interventionist policy by governments in developing countries to assist the development of their national fleets coupled with international support measures. It was irrefutable that the analysis the secretariat undertook had considerable influence on policy formulation and decision-making during the first six conferences of UNCTAD.

Developing countries' concerns and priorities included the reduction of transport costs and the establishment and expansion of their national merchant fleets. The debate in UNCTAD forums led to the adoption of common measures of

---

[1] Organization of a group of shipping lines operating in any particular trade where the companies agree to use a common tariff and to other arrangements.

understanding on shipping questions and to the establishment of the Committee on Shipping. The common measures of understanding related to the institutional structures in international shipping, namely the liner conference system and the conditions under which shipping could best serve international trade, particularly that of developing countries. While UNCTAD I released intensive rancour and debate on shipping that led eventually to the institutionalisation of shipping questions in an international forum, it was the initiative of the secretariat combined with forceful individual delegates from developing countries that in reality led to the establishment of the Committee on Shipping on 29 April 1965.[2]

While the first two sessions of the Committee on Shipping in the late 1960s were devoted to defining its work programme, the UNCTAD secretariat geared itself to meet a challenge in somewhat uncharted waters with wide-ranging research and preparation of studies. In fact, the secretariat became a catalyst that brought forth issues upon which governments began to act. The role of the documentation prepared by the secretariat on substantial economic matters gradually increased. It began effecting the formulation of country positions and decisions during UNCTAD II (1968) and furthermore during UNCTAD III (1972), V (1979) and VI (1983).[3] The documentation also played a very significant role during the preparations and elaboration of international conventions adopted under the auspices of UNCTAD such as the Code of Conduct for Liner Conferences (1974) and the Registration of Ships (1986).

---

[2] The terms of reference of the Committee on Shipping stipulated, *inter alia,* the need to:
- Promote understanding and cooperation in the field of shipping and to be available for the harmonization of shipping policies of governments and regional economic groupings which fall within the competence of the Trade and Development Board (TDB);
- Study and make recommendations on the ways in which and the conditions under which international shipping can most effectively contribute to the expansion of world trade, in particular of the trade of developing countries. Particular attention should be paid to economic aspects of shipping, to those shipping matters which affect the trade and balance of payments of developing countries, and to related shipping policies and legislation of governments on matters which fall within the competence of the TDB;
- Study measures to improve port operations and connected inland transport facilities, with particular reference to those ports whose trade is of economic significance to the country in which they are situated or to world trade;
- Make recommendations designed to secure, where appropriate, the participation of shipping lines of developing countries in shipping conferences on equitable terms;
- Promote cooperation between shippers and the conferences through the establishment of a well-organized consultation machinery with adequate procedures for hearing and remedying complaints by the formation of shippers' councils or other suitable bodies on a national and regional basis;
- Study and make recommendations with a view to promoting the development of merchant marines, in particular of developing countries.

[3] Shipping was not on the agenda at UNCTAD IV (1976) as the issue of the code of conduct for liner conferences was under discussion.

The secretariat was convinced, together with the overwhelming support of the developing countries, that the questions being addressed in the Committee on Shipping required international regulation in order to ensure economic equity and justice in the conduct of international shipping. The result was an evolving new economic and commercial system of international governance in shipping that previously had been left mainly to commercial practices. UNCTAD was about to influence a change in an industry that had evolved based on self-regulation. The debate in UNCTAD thus revolved around the assertion of the right of developing countries to participate in maritime transport on equal footing with the traditional shipowners of developed countries, including the right to carry national cargoes on national fleets.

The reports and studies prepared by the secretariat led to a sequence of events that had its own unique logic: it first exposed new ideas through analysis on broad subject matters, intergovernmental discussions then narrowed them down to more specific aspects, and finally the discussions led to specific decisions by governments within the context of an evolving legal framework and associated international commitments. The research, analysis and reports of the secretariat, on the basis of which developing countries structured their arguments, triggered a series of intergovernmental debates and actions that had major impacts on international shipping polices and decision-making at the national and international level.

As early as the second session in 1968, the agenda of the Committee on Shipping included such items as consultation machinery, freight rates, conference practices, expansion of merchant marines of developing countries and development of ports as well as international legislation on shipping. The secretariat benefited from an agreement (UN, 1964, Annex A.IV.22) that invited governments, shippers, shipowners, shippers' councils and liner conferences to cooperate with it by providing information for its studies on freight rates, conference practices, adequacy of shipping services, etc. As a result the secretariat was able to produce some remarkable studies that were considered at the time to be milestones due to their insights into the economic and commercial aspects of international shipping. Those reports and studies acted as a catalyst for generating a floodgate of literature from academic and professional institutions concerned with shipping.

In 1969 member States established a Working Group on International Shipping Legislation (WGISL) within UNCTAD. The mandate of this group was to review the economic and commercial aspects of international shipping legislation and practices in the field of shipping. This was to be done from the standpoint of conformity with the needs of economic development, in particular of developing countries, in order to identify areas where modifications were needed and as the basis for drafting legislation or other appropriate actions. It was through this body that international conventions, model rules, norms and standards were evolved into law or practice that influenced the functioning of international shipping.

B.   Addressing Shipping Questions

UNCTAD would address as a priority the cost of transport, in particular the structure and level of ocean freight rates. The UNCTAD secretariat produced a unique study (UNCTAD, 1968a) that became a reference point for the literature that was to follow. It demonstrated that developing countries bore the major incidence of freight costs due to, *inter alia*, the high price elasticity of both their exports and imports. It also found that developing countries tended, on average, to pay twice as much as their counterpart exporters and importers in developed countries for the same or similar services, and that conference pricing was not cost-based and reflected conference market power through cartels and monopolies to the disadvantage of developing countries.

Another study that the secretariat produced was entitled *Bills of Lading* (UNCTAD, 1971) which reviewed the economic and commercial aspects of international legislation and practices from the standpoint of their conformity with needs of economic development in particular of developing countries. The study pointed out that the rules governing the carriage of goods by sea were biased in the interest of shipowners rather than shippers. This was shown by the list of circumstances under which The Hague Rules[4] exempted shipowners from liability for loss of or damage to goods in transit.

The impact of these studies was to set a course towards creating a balance of power in the relationship between shipowners and shippers. The WGISL, in its review of The Hague Rules, set the ground for the development of the UN Convention on the Carriage of Goods by Sea (Hamburg Rules) that were adopted in 1978 and entered into force on 1 November 1992.

Consequently, the secretariat undertook a major study on the establishment and expansion of national fleets that clearly outlined the advantages and limitations of establishing or expanding national fleets by developing countries (UNCTAD, 1968b). The report listed the benefits of national fleets, such as the contribution to

---

[4] International Convention for the unification of certain rules of law relating to Bills of Lading, Brussels, 25 August 1924, known as the Hague Rules.

the balance of payments, to income generation, to economic independence, to regional and international economic integration, and to influencing the level and structure of freight rates.

While recognizing the limitations of developing countries for developing national fleets due to the absence of national shipbuilding capacities and lack of collateral for ship financing, in analysing the secretariat study, policy makers in the majority of developing countries became convinced that the benefits of having a national fleet outweighed the drawbacks. That policy of fleet development took on a greater force of commitment when developing countries proposed and negotiated two consecutive targets for the growth of national fleets of developing countries in the form of quantitative percentages. These were 10 and 20 per cent of the world fleet in the First and Second United Nations Development Decades (the 1960s and the 1970s, respectively). The importance attached by developing countries to participation in world shipping was highlighted by the fact that the International Development Strategy for the Third UN Development Decade (the 1980s) called for an increase in their participation in international seaborne trade through the appropriate structural changes where necessary, and also for a 20 per cent share of the dead-weight tonnage of the world merchant fleet for the developing countries by end of the decade.[5]

The secretariat started a number of activities to assist developing countries in achieving this target, including investigation of sources of finance and provision of technical assistance. Initially this work entailed an examination of the institutional barriers to the establishment or expansion of developing countries' fleets. The secretariat thus addressed the liner conference system, a system of cartels that had become dominant in the liner trade.

This conference system had come under the scrutiny of governments, but the cartels were allowed to continue because many governments believed that they provided a necessary stability in international shipping. The comprehensive study entitled *The Liner Conference System* (UNCTAD, 1970) provoked an outcry by developing countries for the overhaul of the system and the need to bring it under some form of international control. The secretariat soon produced a second study entitled *The Regulation of the Liner Conference System – A Code of Conduct* (UNCTAD, 1972). That study was to unleash the elaboration of the code of conduct for liner services, one of the most intensive negotiating processes in the history of UNCTAD.

---

[5] UN General Assembly resolution 35/56 of 5 December 1980.

C. UN Code of Conduct for Liner Conferences

The UN Convention on a Code of Conduct for Liner Conferences sought to give developing countries the right to carry a proportion of their own trade (the so called 40/40/20 formula – 40 per cent to be carried by ships from the exporter country, 40 per cent for the importer country and 20 per cent for third parties), to participate in the conference system and to reduce some of the adverse practices such as loyalty ties, arbitrary imposition and increase of freight rates and to institutionalise consultation and arbitration machinery in which the role of the Government was recognized.

After ten years of elaboration and negotiations the Code was adopted in 1974 and entered into force nine years later in 1983. It was the first international legal instrument to govern the economic and commercial aspects of liner shipping companies. It was a very successful convention that as of 31 August 2003 has been ratified by 78 countries. However, in the early 1990s the increasing use of containers was rapidly changing the nature and organization of the liner shipping system, resulting in a decline in the application of the convention.

D. UN Convention on International Multimodal Transport of Goods

A technological revolution was taking place in the shipping industry in the early 1970s with the use of larger vessels and the introduction of the containerization of cargo. As early as 1974 the secretariat studied the introduction of containerization and changing practices in shipping, particularly the economic and social implications of new technologies in the emerging transport system (multimodal transport) that integrated shipping and inland transport. This innovative work of the secretariat on multimodal transport motivated research activities of other international and professional institutions concerned with transport. The UNCTAD secretariat introduced the term "multimodal" into the lexicon of transport and defined it as the carriage of goods in more than one mode of transport under a single contract.

In the 1970s the Committee on Shipping addressed such issues with a view to establishing an international regulatory system that would facilitate the integration of developing countries into the new systems in the transport of goods. The secretariat argued that there was a need for a new liability and documentary regime for the benefit of all who participate in multimodal transport of goods. It was also concerned with the short lives of some investments that developing countries suffered due to the rapid introduction of new technologies in shipping.

The preparation and negotiations on the UN Convention on International Multimodal Transport of Goods took place under the auspices of UNCTAD from 1973 to 1980. The secretariat approached many of the issues in reports prepared to support the negotiations from the perspective of developing countries interests. The UN Convention on International Multimodal Transport of Goods was adopted in 1980 and so far has been ratified by 10 countries. While the Convention has not entered into force due to the lack of ratifications (it requires 30 contracting parties), its provisions have significantly influenced a number of laws and regulations governing multimodal transport adopted at the regional, sub-regional and national levels.

E.   Flags of Convenience or Open Registries

The UNCTAD secretariat was also concerned with the phenomena within the shipping industry of the increasing use of flags of convenience. The root of the problem was the ineffective exercise of jurisdiction and control over flags of convenience ships due to the absence of a "genuine link" between a vessel and its country of registration. The 1958 Convention on the High Seas stated that there must be such a genuine link but never defined what was meant by genuine link. This concept of the need for a genuine link was also recognized in the 1982 UN Convention on the Law of the Sea but again did not provide a definition.

The open registry (flags of convenience) fleet had expanded at an increasingly fast rate, reaching 28 per cent of the world shipping fleet by 1971. There was concern within governments and the industry that one-third of the world deadweight tonnage (consisting mainly of tankers and bulk carriers) was largely in the hand of "faceless men" behind a veil of corporate holdings. Furthermore, there was convincing evidence that the speculative growth of flags of convenience fleets resulted in detrimental effects upon the expansion of fleets of developing countries. Associated with these vessels was a plethora of shipwrecks, scuttling of vessels, maritime fraud and abuse of seafarers.

The first body with an official international standing to define such a genuine link was the Ad Hoc Intergovernmental Working Group on the Economic Consequences of the Existence or Lack of a Genuine Link between Vessel and Flag of Registry of UNCTAD. The deliberation of this Working Group was based on the secretariat's report on the economic consequences of the existence or lack of a genuine link (UNCTAD, 1977). The report argued that open registration enabled the traditional maritime countries to maintain their domination in world shipping despite the increasing labour costs of operating under their own flags. Based on that argument and the need to prevent abuses, the secretariat made the case for the phasing out of flags of convenience.

UNCTAD V (1979) in Manila adopted by vote resolution 120(V) – Participation of developing countries in world shipping and the development of their merchant marine – which took note of the desire of many countries to phase out open registry operations and requested further studies, including on "the repercussions of phasing out open registries, its economic and social impact on economies of developing countries, its effect on world shipping" and "the feasibility of establishing a legal mechanism for regulating the operation of open registry fleets during the phasing-out period." When the UNCTAD secretariat published another related study on beneficial ownership of open registries (UNCTAD, 1980) in 1980 it was discovered to the surprise of all that a large number of countries had little knowledge on the engagement of their nationals in the beneficial ownership of flags of convenience vessels.

However, the initial objective of phasing out open registries was not possible. The publication of a number of other studies and intensive debates at UNCTAD intergovernmental meetings failed to reach agreement on this issue. The discussion was then focused on the desirability of establishing a genuine link between a vessel and the country that accepts it on its national shipping register.

After protracted deliberations under the auspices of UNCTAD the Convention on Conditions for Registration of Ships, which established the minimum elements of the genuine link, was adopted on 7 February 1986. Meanwhile the secretariat and the organization came under great pressure from powerful lobbies to change its basic policy approach and philosophy in addressing controversial issues in international shipping. It was also the last confrontation of its kind in the area of international shipping between developed and developing countries and the beginning of a new phase of intergovernmental debate. The Convention was to enter into force when ratified by 40 countries representing 25 per cent of the world fleet. As of 1 January 2004 there were only 11 contracting parties to the Convention and it is unlikely ever to enter into force. In the meantime, open registry fleets have grown to account for almost 50 per cent of the world fleet (UNCTAD, 2003: 23, table 13).

II.   1992–Present:
The Post-Cartagena Period

Our discussion on the second period, that is the period post-Cartagena, centres on the following subjects:

1.   Assessment of changes since UNCTAD VII;
2.   International Convention on Maritime Liens and Mortgages 1993;
3.   International Organization on Arrest of Ships, 1991; and
4.   Policy reform and capacity building in the 2000s.

A.   Assessment of Changes since UNCTAD VII

During the 1980s changes in UNCTAD's mandate and in the agenda of developed countries dramatically changed shipping deliberations in UNCTAD. After UNCTAD VII (1987) where shipping was *not* placed on its agenda, the secretariat set in motion measures that were later to change the policy approaches of the work of UNCTAD in this area. This change was also due to the unprecedented changes following the demise of the socialist camp and the fall of the Berlin Wall. The combination of the unrelenting attack on UNCTAD for its policy and work in the area of shipping and the changing political and economic international environment led to the first institutional change in UNCTAD. At UNCTAD VIII (Cartagena 1992), the Committee on Shipping was dissolved and replaced by the Standing Committee on Developing Services Sector, with shipping, ports and multimodal transport included in the form of a sub-committee.

While this administrative arrangement allowed shipping to maintain its identity as a mainstream activity within UNCTAD, it became increasingly clear that this Standing Committee would be of a transitional nature only. Indeed, in the context of a general overhaul of the intergovernmental machinery of UNCTAD, UNCTAD IX (Midrand 1996) abolished the Standing Committee and reduced transport issues to one of the agenda items of the Commission on Enterprise, Business Facilitation and Development.

As the policy dialogue on shipping came to an abrupt halt in UNCTAD in 1996, no UN forum has debated the economic and commercial aspects of shipping in a coherent and comprehensive manner. However, this has not resulted in the abandonment of questions concerning maritime and related transport by UNCTAD. In fact, the removal of UNCTAD's rule-making role in the 1990s coincided with new approaches to maritime policies adopted by a large number of developing countries not only based on the changing economic environment but often also based on external pressures. There has also been an emerging tendency to tackle the question of economic and commercial regulation of shipping at the plurilateral (regional) or even unilateral level that, in turn, has produced a proliferation of conflicting rules. This has led to recurrent demands by industry sources and particularly by trading interests in developing countries for global instruments. In response to the new environment within which the developing countries' shipping industry had to operate, the secretariat prepared a new policy study (UNCTAD, 1992) which proved to be the basis for the policy work of UNCTAD in the years to come, concentrating on market access and fleet development policies with the objective of creating, improving or maintaining supply capacities. Secondly, consumer oriented policies aimed at improving service qualities gained in importance.

Despite being deprived of its rule-making authority, UNCTAD was selected to continue and conclude the work through multilateral negotiations on two related conventions, namely the UN Convention on Maritime Liens and Mortgages and the UN Convention on Arrest of Ships. The substantive work on these issues and the resulting conventions were considered necessary and beneficial for the development of the maritime industry by all stakeholders, be they the public or private sector, or from developed or developing countries. The two Conventions clearly demonstrated the positive role of UNCTAD (through its intergovernmental machinery and secretariat) played in reaching solutions to problems affecting the industry as well as the recognition by the international community of the need to bring multilateral solutions to the industry that is inherently global.

B. International Convention on Maritime Liens and Mortgages 1993

It had always been recognized within UNCTAD that the lack of finance for ship acquisition was a major difficulty for developing countries in expanding their national merchant marines. The activities of UNCTAD aiming at the alleviation of this problem included, *inter alia*, the elaboration of recommendations urging increased finance to be given to developing countries on favourable terms for the acquisition of ships, the development of a mechanism for the facilitation of requests for ship financing and the examination of ways and means of providing developing countries with information regarding the availability and terms of financial assistance for the acquisition of ships from bilateral and multilateral donors.

Member countries of UNCTAD recognized that significant differences between national regimes governing maritime securities led to complexity and uncertainty in the international enforcement of liens and mortgages and frustrated the implementation of national objectives as to the recognition and priority given to maritime claimants. It was imperative, therefore, for the international community to develop a generally acceptable legal framework governing the recognition and enforcement of maritime liens and mortgages. Also, developing countries had a particular and pressing interest in this work in view of their fleet development objectives and their need to initiate, develop or modernize national legislation on the subject consistent with those objectives.[6]

The subjects of maritime liens and mortgages and the arrest of ships had been included in the work programme of both UNCTAD and the IMO. Both the IMO Council and the UNCTAD Committee on Shipping recognized the legitimate interest of the two organizations on the subject and repeatedly called for a collaborative approach in order to avoid possible duplication of work. Thus following the resolution of WGISL, endorsed by the TDB and the IMO Council, a Joint UNCTAD/IMO Intergovernmental Group of Experts on Maritime Liens and Mortgages and Related Subjects was formed to carry out the work. The Group held six sessions (1986–1989) alternatively in Geneva and London. After reviewing the existing international instruments on maritime liens and mortgages, it prepared draft provisions for a new convention on this subject.

In May 1993 the UN/IMO Conference of Plenipotentiaries adopted, by consensus, the International Convention on Maritime Liens and Mortgages. The Convention regulates the recognition and enforcement of maritime liens and mortgages at the international level, where its main objectives are: (i) to improve conditions for ship financing and the development of national merchant fleets, and (ii) to promote international uniformity in the field of maritime liens and mortgages.[7] The Convention will enter into force in September 2004.

The Conference also recommended that: "the relevant bodies of UNCTAD and IMO, in the light of the outcome of the Conference, reconvene the Joint Intergovernmental Group with a view to examining the possible review of the International Convention for the Unification of Certain Rules Relating to the Arrest

---

[6] For detailed analysis of this subject see UNCTAD, 1984.
[7] For the text of the Convention, see UNCTAD, 1993a.

of Sea-going Ships 1952. Again, the UNCTAD secretariat was requested, together with IMO, to prepare the necessary documentation for the meetings of the Group".[8]

C.   International Convention on Arrest of Ships 1999

The arrest of a vessel is a means of enforcing maritime liens and mortgages, and thus it was considered necessary to revise the 1952 Arrest Convention to ensure that all claims giving rise to a maritime lien under the new 1993 Maritime Liens and Mortgages Convention would have the right of arrest under the Arrest Convention. Furthermore, almost half a century had passed since the adoption of the 1952 Convention; as a result some of its provisions had become out-of-date while others were considered ambiguous giving rise to conflicting interpretations, hampering uniform implementation of the Convention.

The Joint UNCTAD/IMO Intergovernmental Group was reconvened in December 1994 and devoted three sessions on the revision of the 1952 Convention on the Arrest of Ships. The Group completed the preparation of the draft articles for a new convention on the Arrests of Ships in December 1996. In March 1999, the UN/IMO Diplomatic Conference held two weeks of intensive deliberations in Geneva under the auspices of UNCTAD and finally adopted by consensus the International Convention on Arrest of Ships.[9] Around one hundred nations and over twenty intergovernmental and non-governmental organizations attended the Conference. The Convention regulates the circumstances under which ships may be arrested or released from arrest. While the interests of owners of ships and cargo lie in ensuring that legitimate trading is not interrupted by the unjustified arrest of a ship, the interest of claimants' lies in being able to obtain security for their claims. The Arrest Convention strikes a balance between these interests, bearing in mind the different approaches adopted by various legal systems.

D.   Policy Reform and Capacity Building in the 2000s

At UNCTAD X (Bangkok, 2000), governments, realizing that higher priority needed to be attributed to transport issues, initiated a work programme that was to create the foundation for a review and possible revision of the national policy framework to allow greater participation of the private sector, introduction of reform measures to make providers of transport service more responsive to user demands, streamlining of administrative procedures, promotion of the use of

---

[8] See the report of the UN/IMO Conference of Plenipotentiaries on Maritime Liens and Mortgages UNCTAD, 1993b, annex I.
[9] The text of the Convention is included in UN/IMO (1999).

information technology and strengthening of training programmes (UNCTAD, 2000, paras. 150–153). Meanwhile, the Commission on Enterprise, Business Facilitation and Development decided to establish a series of expert meetings on transport and trade facilitation. The emphasis was on the importance of a common approach to policies and regulatory regimes and the need for assistance to governments in developing countries in their endeavours to devise the necessary policy measures required to ensure that transport supply capacities would be created or strengthened, and that traders would be able to effectively take advantage of transport opportunities offered in liberalized and globalized ocean transport markets.

The Recommendations and Guidelines for Trade Efficiency adopted at the UN International Symposium on Trade Efficiency at Columbus, Ohio in October 1994 identified transport as playing a key role in international trade. It is in this context that emphasis was placed on work on e-commerce and information technology implications in trade and transport. It emerged that the transport sector was in the forefront with respect to the application of e-commerce as reflected in the endeavours to replace traditional paper transport documents by electronic alternatives. The impact of e-commerce on transport has, therefore, been one of the sectors on which UNCTAD has concentrated in ensuring the sustainability of trade and technology-based development processes.

The major thrust of the present work of UNCTAD has developed in two ways. Firstly, traditional work in the area of shipping has been incorporated in the wider context of transport and logistics. This has happened in recognition of the changes that have taken place in the industry and in the type of services potentially available to developing countries. However, even in the context of logistics, maritime transport remains the major issue as the vast majority of developing countries' external trade is carried by sea and consequently access to maritime transport services continues to constitute the major measure of connectivity and thus of integration into the world economy. Secondly, UNCTAD has strengthened its work on the improvement of supply capacities not only as a condition for developing countries to participate in an industry that is increasingly globalized but also as a prerequisite for participation in world trade. Similarly, UNCTAD's work has aimed at ensuring a meaningful involvement in trade negotiations.

The UNCTAD secretariat has developed a number of major technical cooperation programmes that have helped shape the transport sectors of beneficiary countries. Already in the mid-1980s the secretariat had studied the situation of African transport systems and identified the physical and non-physical obstacles to improving such systems. One major conclusion was that there was a need for a programme of action to monitor cargo movements. That programme of action developed into establishing a transport logistics information system called the Advance Cargo Information System (ACIS).[10] ACIS can play an important role in the development of trade relations and above all in reinforcing subregional integration because it allows all operators using the system to communicate, through modes and interfaces as well as over borders, the vital information that is required by them to improve transport efficiency. Additionally, ACIS is a powerful tool enabling national authorities or subregional organizations to rationalize and improve the quality of macro-economic transport planning to foster the optimal modal distribution patterns.

Other technical assistance activities of the secretariat aim at developing new approaches and solutions to trade and transport facilitation. A particularly successful programme to facilitate trade is the customs reform programme known as ASYCUDA (Automatic System for Customs Data) that is presently installed in over 80 developing countries. Generic solutions are being sought in the context of global projects while their application is being tested at the national/subregional level.

III. Final Remarks

The work of UNCTAD has not only focused on the preparation and negotiation of mandatory international conventions. Work on issues such as charter parties, marine insurance, standards for shipping agencies and general average have been instrumental in introducing changes in the shipping industry and its commercial practices. For example, its work on marine insurance acted as a catalyst in the reform by the London insurance market of its marine insurance clauses and policy form. The UNCTAD Minimum Standards for Shipping Agents have been widely used in over 50 countries.

Another important contribution of UNCTAD to shipping has been through the publication of its Review of Maritime Transport. In 1968 the secretariat first published the Review of Maritime Transport to provide information on the shipping industry and assist delegations in their deliberations. This report has become an annual publication of UNCTAD and is considered an authoritative

---

[10] ACIS is a generic name given to a "tool box" of computer applications designed to produce management information to address multimodal cargo transit and transport resource problems. Each application is independent of the other but is designed with a modular approach to enable all to "co-habit" and freely exchange data in an industry accepted standard form.

source of maritime information and statistics that is widely used by government, academic institutions as well as providers and users of maritime transport. The Review of 2004 will be the 37th issue and since 2003 it has been available on the UNCTAD website.

On the issue of port development there was a consensus that improvements to the operations of ports in developing countries would benefit both users and providers of transport services. Consequently, during the first two decades of UNCTAD's existence the Committee on Shipping and the secretariat addressed a large number of practical problems faced by developing countries in the area of improving ports performance and in dealing with port congestion and improving port management. The secretariat produced a number of studies, some of which are still used as reference materials (UNCTAD, 1978). Furthermore the secretariat, with extra-budgetary funding, developed and delivered a series of port management courses for managers from developing countries and over the period from 1980 to 1988 some 3000 managers received training.

Thus UNCTAD has had a significant impact on international transport over the past four decades. It continues to play an important role in supporting intergovernmental action concerning the economic and commercial aspects of international transport. Further, it seeks to enhance the capacity of developing countries to improve their competitiveness in international trade by building an efficient trade supporting services framework with particular focus on maritime and multimodal transport. This will be an essential step for the economic development of nations, in particular the LDCs and landlocked developing countries.

References

UN/IMO (1993a). United Nations/International Maritime Organization Conference of Plenipotentiaries on a Convention on Maritime Liens and Mortgages. Final Act and International Convention of Martine Liens and Mortgages. A/CONF.162/7, Geneva.

_____ (1993b). United Nations/International Maritime Organization Conference of Plenipotentiaries on a Convention on Maritime Liens and Mortgages, Report of the Conference. A/CONF.162/8, Geneva.

_____ (1999). Diplomatic Conference on Arrest of Ships. A/CONF.188/6, Geneva.

UN (1964). *Proceedings of the United Nations Conference on Trade and Development*, Geneva, 23 March – 16 June 1964. Vol. I: Final Act, Third part. Annex A.IV.22: Common Measures of Understanding on Shipping Questions, E/CONF.46/141.

UNCTAD (1968a). Establishment or expansion of merchant marines in developing countries. TD/26/Rev.1, Geneva.

_____ (1968b). Level and structure of freight rates, conferences practices and adequacy of shipping services. TD/B/C.4/38/Rev.1, Geneva.

_____ (1970). The Liner Conference System: Report by the UNCTAD secretariat. TD/B/C.4/62/Rev.1, New York.

_____ (1971). Bills of Lading. TD/B/C.4/ISL/6/Rev.1, Geneva.

_____ (1972). The Regulation of the Liner Conference System. TD/104/Rev.1, New York.

_____ (1977). Economic consequences of the existence or lack of a genuine link between vessel and flag of registry. TD/B/C.4/168, Geneva.

_____ (1978). Port Development: A handbook for planners in developing countries. TD/B/C.4/175, and TD/B/C.4/175/Rev.1 (1985), New York.

_____ (1980). Beneficial ownership of open-registry fleets. TD/B/C.4/218, Geneva.

_____ (1984). Preliminary analysis of possible reforms in the existing international regime of maritime liens and mortgages. TD/B/C.4/ISL/48, Geneva.

_____ (1992). Industry and policy developments in world shipping and their impact on developing countries. TD/B/CN.4/5, Geneva.

_____ (2000). Plan of Action, tenth session. TD/386, Bangkok, February.

_____ (2003). *Review of Maritime Transport 2003*. UNCTAD/RMT/2003, Geneva.

Technology

Assad Omer, Yehia Soubra and Victor Konde*

Introduction

The transfer and diffusion of technology in developing countries has been an integral part of UNCTAD's research and analytical work on technology during the last four decades. Member countries identified technology as one of the core elements of UNCTAD's mandate and designated it the principal forum of the United Nations for integrated treatment of trade and development and interrelated issues in the areas of finance, investment, technology and sustainable development at UNCTAD I (1964). However, it was not until UNCTAD II (New Delhi, 1968) that the issues pertaining to technology received serious attention.

There were at least three reasons why technology, which had previously been regarded mainly as a national policy concern, began to be perceived as important work for an intergovernmental and multilateral body such as UNCTAD:

- Recognition that technology and technical know-how were essential preconditions for improving productivity, promoting export growth and attaining development;
- Concern among developing countries about the growing technological gap between developed and developing countries, its implications for trade and development, and their own prospects to catch up; and
- Concern among developing countries about the excessive cost of technology and the difficulties in gaining access to advanced technologies from developed countries.

The immediate challenge (1960–1980) was to find ways in which to facilitate technology transfer in order to help developing countries acquire the technical capability needed to diversify their product range and expand their export markets. Improving developing countries' access to foreign technology was seen as

* Assad Omer was an Economic Affairs Officer in the Division of Investment, Technology and Enterprise Development (DITE), and is currently Ambassador of the Permanent Mission of Afghanistan to the United Nations in Geneva. Yehia Soubra and Victor Konde are Economic Affairs Officers, DITE. The authors appreciate the comments and suggestions received from Pedro Roffe, Khalil Hamdani, and Taffere Tesfachew.

crucial in order to bridge the technology gap and accelerate industrial growth and development, as they did not possess modern technologies of their own. In the 1980s to early 1990s UNCTAD's work focused on helping developing countries build the technological base needed to absorb, diffuse and generate technological innovations. Since the 1990s, the work on technology centred on the relationship between investment and technology transfer and diffusion, the impact of emerging technologies and the implications of emerging international arrangements on technological capacity-building in developing countries.

The objective of this paper is to trace the trajectory of UNCTAD's work programme on technology over the last four decades and to highlight some of its main intellectual contributions. The paper will also identify the main factors that influenced the focus and orientation of UNCTAD's work in the various areas of technology. The evolution of its work will be discussed under three broad themes covering three distinct periods: the late 1960s to the early 1980s; the 1980s to the early 1990s; and the 1990s to the present time.

I.   The Late 1960s – Early 1980s: The International Dimension of Technology Transfer

Technology was at the time defined as a combination of knowledge embodied in machines and equipment and the technical know-how necessary to operate them and was seen as an essential element in promoting economic growth along with socio-economic development. It was envisaged that accelerated rates of economic growth and rapid improvement in the social structure of developing countries would require, *inter alia,* a large-scale transfer of technology from developed countries. Technology transfer was also seen as critical for narrowing the initial technology gap between developed and developing countries. For these reasons the decades of the 1960s and 1980s witnessed increasing concern, both at the national and international levels, with problems related to technology transfer to developing countries.

The prospects for developing countries to accelerate their economic and industrial development would be limited without effective access to more advanced technology. Understandably, therefore, the UNCTAD secretariat's intellectual work on technology was heavily, though not exclusively, influenced by the question of technology transfer from developed to developing countries where emphasis was placed on conceptualising the technology transfer issues; identifying the constraints that developing countries face in technology acquisition; examining the channels for technology transfer from developed to developing countries, including the policies to promote such transfer; and consideration of costs as well as legal and institutional impediments that developing country firms were facing in acquiring technology (UNCTAD, 1975a; 1975b).

It is difficult to separate the intellectual contributions of the UNCTAD secretariat on these issues from the intergovernmental process that influenced their focus and direction. Indeed, soon after UNCTAD II (1968) the secretariat's intellectual work on technology was given an intergovernmental dimension. At its tenth session, (in 1970) the Trade and Development Board (TDB) decided to establish an Intergovernmental Group on Transfer of Technology (IGGTT). The TDB reached its decision on the basis of a document prepared by the secretariat which identified the specific areas related to technology transfer that required in-depth research and analysis (UNCTAD, 1970). The establishment of the IGGTT also signalled the heightened awareness among member states of the problems associated with technology transfer as deserving special attention at a multilateral level.

During this period the primary focus of UNCTAD's work in the area of technology was on issues related to the supply-side of the international dimension of technology transfer, particularly the efforts to reach an agreement on an international code of conduct on transfer of technology, and the research and analysis carried out on implications of intellectual property rights (IPRs) on technology transfer to developing countries.

Therefore, some large developing countries formulated regulations governing technology imports while others either established or significantly strengthened national science and technology institutions. This was in line with the prevailing development thinking which stressed the need for building domestic/endogenous technology capacity to adapt or modify foreign technologies to meet local needs.

A.   Code of Conduct on the International Transfer of Technology

The technology-related work of the UNCTAD secretariat in the early 1970s focused on the analysis of the cost, terms and conditions of technology transfer. It specifically addressed failure elements of the technology markets, particularly their proprietary aspects, and the need for multilateral solutions to these challenges. The terms and conditions of technology transfers were viewed as being affected by differences in economic power and access to information of the buyer and seller, leading to economic inequality and dependency. Hence the main emphasis of the secretariat's initial intellectual contribution on technology transfer was on restructuring the legal environment for international technology transfer (UNCTAD, 1975c).

The vast amount of analytical work carried out by the secretariat helped increase the awareness of member countries concerning the predicaments facing developing countries in acquiring technology, and the need for creating a multilateral system that would facilitate technology transfer at an affordable cost and in a predictable and legally protected manner. This led to an initiative to develop an international code of conduct within the UNCTAD intergovernmental machinery. To facilitate negotiations on the code, the Committee on Technology Transfer (CTT) was established in 1974, replacing the IGGTT. It was within the CTT work programmes that most of the research and analytical work on technology transfer by the UNCTAD secretariat was carried out.

Further impetus to the initiative was provided by the United Nations (UN) General Assembly at its sixth special session in 1974 on the New International Economic Order, when it approved the formulation of such a code corresponding to the needs and conditions prevalent in developing countries. Subsequently, the General Assembly decided to convene a UN Conference on an International Code of Conduct on Transfer of Technology, under the auspices of UNCTAD, to negotiate on the code elements drafted by the expert group and to take all decisions necessary for its adoption. Six sessions were held between 1978 and 1985.

UNCTAD's work on the Code of Conduct on the Transfer of Technology was groundbreaking. Although the attempt to develop the Code was later abandoned after years of negotiations, it brought to the fore of the international agenda the complexity of technology transfer issues and raised awareness among developing countries about the issues involved. Furthermore, the concepts and definitions of technology transfer and technology were clarified. For instance, it was agreed in the Code to define technology transfer as "the transfer of systematic knowledge for the manufacture of a product, for the application of a process or for the rendering of a service and does not extend to the transactions involving the mere sale or mere lease of goods" (UNCTAD, 1985). Accordingly, transactions involving technology transfer comprised each of the following cases:

- The assignment, sale and licensing of all forms of industrial property, except for trade marks, service marks and trade names when they are not part of technology transfer transactions;

- The provision of know-how and technical expertise in the form of feasibility studies, plans, diagrams, models, instructions, guides, formulae, basic or detailed engineering designs, specifications and equipment for training, services involving technical advisory and managerial personnel, and personnel training;
- The provision of technological knowledge necessary for the installation, operation and functioning of plant and equipment, and turnkey projects;
- The provision of technological knowledge necessary to acquire, install and use machinery, equipment, intermediate goods and/or raw materials which have been acquired by purchase, lease or other means; and
- The provision of technological contents of industrial and technical cooperation arrangements (UNCTAD, 1985).

In short, the Code of Conduct on the Transfer of Technology was a major attempt – mainly by developing countries and supported by the UNCTAD secretariat – to reform the international transfer of technology and to promote economic growth as well as the participation of small and medium enterprises (SMEs) in both developed and developing countries in the international technology market. The overall goals were to liberalize the technology market, improve developing countries' access to technology and promote international trade (UNCTAD, 1985).

B.   Intellectual Property Rights and Technology Transfer

The proprietary aspect of technology transfer was an issue that the UNCTAD secretariat examined in depth as part of its broader mandate on the Code of Conduct. The UNCTAD secretariat's work in this area deserves to be highlighted since it helped promote fair play in international technology transactions and enabled developing countries to protect their legitimate interests as well as better understand the legal aspects of technology transfer (UNCTAD, 1975d).

The revision of the Paris Convention on the Protection of Industrial Property, which was concluded in 1883 among 11 member countries among present developed countries, provides an excellent example of the work of UNCTAD. The call for the revision of the Convention came after intergovernmental deliberations on intellectual and industrial property rights based on research results, particularly on a report prepared by the UNCTAD secretariat in conjunction with the World Intellectual Property Organization (WIPO) secretariat (UNCTAD, 1975e). The objectives of developing countries in the revision of the

Convention focused mainly on the use of patents, i.e. on the reform of provisions dealing with compulsory licensing and preferential arrangements within the Convention for developing countries. The revision of the Paris Convention was aimed at promoting technology transfer, minimizing abuses by technology developers and encouraging industrialization.

Although the actual revision of the Convention took place at WIPO, the call for the revision was initiated and promoted by UNCTAD, particularly at UNCTAD V (Manila, 1979).

C. Reverse Transfer of Technology

During the 1970s, technology transfer was perceived mainly as the transfer of technological means of production from developed countries to developing countries. Therefore, the migration of technical skills from developing countries to developed countries, generally referred to as "brain drain", was seen as a reversal of the accepted direction of technology flows. UNCTAD referred to the process in which developing countries were 'transferring' technical skills to developed countries as "reverse transfer of technology".

To compensate for the loss of skills, developing countries relied heavily on expatriates hired from developed countries at great cost to both the public and private sectors. This led to a growing concern among several developing countries and international organizations, in particularly UNCTAD, and began to see brain drain as a potential problem that deserved as much attention at the multilateral level as other issues related to technology transfer.

The main goal was to find a favourable policy response at the international level to tackle the reverse transfer of technology. Some of the intellectual work on the economic effects of brain drain was influenced by this dilemma and the need to identify urgently policy measures, including compensation for countries that suffered from this predicament. This made brain drain part of UNCTAD's work on international transfer of technology (UNCTAD, 1975f).

A group consisting of governmental experts was set up to address the magnitude of the problem and recommend measures to mitigate the adverse impact of reverse transfer of technology. The other objectives were to develop a set of internationally agreed definitions, principles and standards on the reverse transfer of technology. These were viewed as critical elements of an international system for the collection and dissemination of quantitative and qualitative information on brain drain (UNCTAD, 1978).

The Group met five times between 1978 and 1988 and their deliberations were supported by background documents prepared by UNCTAD. Between 1975 and 1988 UNCTAD published at least 29 studies and reports on reverse transfer of technology. The work was also supported by and recognized through various United Nations General Assembly resolutions (see General Assembly resolutions 3201(S-VI), 3203 (S-VI), 3362 (XXIV) of 1974 and 35/56 of 1980, 40/1191 of 1985 and A/Res/43/184 1985, among others).

II. The 1980s – Early 1990s: Technological Capability Building

During the 1970s, UNCTAD's analytical work on technology transfer did not pay much attention to the 'learning aspects implicit in technological development. As noted above, the focus was on the legal aspects including the terms and conditions of transfer of protected technologies rather than what happens after the technology has been transferred. By the early 1980s there had been a noticeable shift from technology transfer to technological learning and capability building as well as to the policies needed to attain these objectives (UNCTAD, 1982). Building national technological and innovative capabilities dominated global thinking on technological change (UNCTAD, 1980a; 1982). It was recognized that the processes of technology transfer, adaptation and diffusion were much more complex than initially assumed. The existence of an absorptive capacity in recipient countries – including their human capital elements, as well as research and development (R&D) activities – was an important factor in determining the success of the process. It was further recognized that emerging technologies tended to be accompanied by stronger intellectual property protection regulations that provided sufficient incentives to inventors.

Considering all of these factors, rapidly emerging technologies were difficult to transfer and absorb in developing countries. Therefore, as a result of these experiences the UNCTAD secretariat's focus on technology began to change from the narrowly defined technology transfer (particularly in the light of the extremely difficult negotiations on the Code of Conduct) to all of the key issues relating to the entire process of technology transfer, diffusion, and local technological development. The secretariat carried out numerous studies that investigated the role of R&D institutions in technological change and reviewed policies and instruments for the promotion of technological innovation along with case studies of various countries. The two main aims were to help developing countries build the required capacity sufficient to absorb, diffuse and commercialize new innovations, and to demonstrate that they placed greater value on local technological learning and innovation than on simple technology transfer and production platforms from developed countries.

This evolution in thinking was reflected in Conference resolution 112 (V) adopted at UNCTAD V (Manila, 1979), which recommended specific actions to be taken to accelerate the local technological transformation. It also identified the analytical and policy-related work to be carried out by the secretariat in support of developing countries' efforts to increase their technological capacities and their ability to select and adopt suitable technologies. Some of the core areas of work under this mandate carried out in the 1980s by the secretariat included:

- Preparation of detailed case studies on technological problems in the areas of agro-industries and food-processing, pharmaceuticals, energy, design and engineering consultancy, capital goods as well as industrial machinery and electronics;
- In-depth studies focusing on development-related aspects in the transfer, development and utilization of technology and on methods to strengthen technological capacities along with studies on the effects of regulations on technology generation, the experiences and prospects of developing countries in technology extension services and the role of SMEs in local technological development;
- Creating an Advisory Service on best practices in the successful transfer and diffusion of technology; and
- Identifying the key elements of a strategy for the technological transformation of developing countries.

From UNCTAD's perspective there were two particularly noteworthy factors that influenced the shifts in its approach to technology and development. The first factor was the increasing recognition that technology transfer is a more complex process than previously assumed, where the transfer occurs not only in a one-way direction from developed to developing countries but in a multi-directional and multi-dimensional fashion involving enterprises of all sizes. The emergence of diverse sources of technology and a more open international market for technology also made the need for an international code of conduct on technology transfer less pressing.

The second factor was the emergence of newly industrializing countries in Asia. Their experiences demonstrated that what matters most in building technological dynamism is not the technology transfer *per se* but what happens to the technology once it has been transferred to them. UNCTAD was among the first international organizations to recognize the need for policy analysis on technological learning and capability building. This meant paying greater attention to the complex process of technology adaptation, assimilation and mastery rather than the simple process of technology acquisition. It also meant attaining better understanding of the process of technology development at firm, sectoral and national levels.

A.   The Capital Goods Sector

It was partly in response to these changes in the perception of the process of technology transfer that in the 1980s the work of UNCTAD – both at the secretariat and the intergovernmental levels – began to concentrate on policy-related issues with a special focus on the capital goods industry. It carried out a series of firm- and country-level case studies on capital goods which contributed greatly to increased understanding of: (a) the multi-dimensional role of the capital goods industry, particularly in the enhancement of skill formation, innovative capabilities, inter-firm linkages and capital formation; (b) the conditions and problems of entry into the capital goods sector; the process of technology transfer, adaptation and generation in the capital goods sector; (c) the constraints facing developing country firms in building capital goods capacity; and (d) the policies and institutional support systems necessary for developing and consolidating capital goods production capability (UNCTAD, 1984).

The case studies presented empirical evidence that helped strengthen the argument that the capital goods sector was an important component of an industrialized economy and an essential capability required to absorb, diffuse and commercialize new innovations (UNCTAD, 1984). The secretariat also carried out studies that investigated the role of R&D institutions in technological change and reviewed policies and instruments for promotion of technological innovation of various countries. These works contributed significantly to the understanding of the trade and development implications of technological changes and the impact of technology on competitiveness.

B.   Trade and Development Implications of Technological Change

Accelerated technological change during the 1980s gave rise to trade and development policy issues relevant to every country. Some of the prominent work was in areas that have witnessed rapid development such as information technology, materials technology and biotechnology. The increased adoption by firms in different production sectors altered the system of production, work organization and affected employment as well as international competitiveness of firms.

In this context UNCTAD kept close watch on the development and implications of technological advances in sectors as diverse as primary commodities, manufacturing and services. More specifically, UNCTAD (the secretariat and intergovernmental machinery) considered the effects of technological changes on raw-material consumption, pointing out that materials substitution and materials savings arising from technological changes contributed to the "dematerialization" of production that affected the export performance of many primary commodity producers in developing countries. In the area of manufacturing discussions within UNCTAD have centred on the diffusion of technological advances, particularly those brought about by microelectronics and their effects on trade and development. In the services sector work has concentrated on reviewing technological change and its trade, implications in different services industries including transportation, office-related activities, banking, telecommunication and computer services (UNCTAD, 1980b)

C. Impact of Technology Capability Building on Competitiveness

The UNCTAD secretariat also undertook intensive research to improve the understanding of the main factors affecting trade and industrial competitiveness. Skilled manpower was identified as one of main factors of critical importance to competitiveness, particularly to the organization and managerial ability of enterprises. Training and retraining, learning-by-doing and learning-by-interacting contributed to technological capacity-building and helped strengthen the competitive advantage of enterprises. Companies that have invested in technology training and the retention of its human capital hope to improve their ability to adapt and operate new technologies in order to create new products and services. In addition, marketing know-how, international sourcing of inputs, collaborative arrangements among enterprises – including outsourcing and subcontracting – were among other factors considered in examining the determinants of competitiveness.

III. The 1990s Onwards:
National and International Arrangements

In the 1990s UNCTAD's work on technology was driven by three important developments. First, the eighth session of UNCTAD (Cartagena, 1992) agreed to set up the Ad Hoc Working Group on the Interrelationship between Investment and Technology Transfer to guide the secretariat's work on technology and to serve as an intergovernmental discussion forum on linkages between investment and technology as well as to find ways in which technology transfer – including through foreign direct investment (FDI) – could contribute to national technological capability building.[1] Second, the restructuring of the UN secretariat in the early 1990s led to the decision to move the UN Centre for Science and Technology from New York to Geneva, which included the transfer of the responsibility of servicing the United Nations Commission on Science and Technology for Development (CSTD) that was established in 1992 to the UNCTAD secretariat. Third, various international agreements with provisions for technology transfer to developing countries were finalized during the 1990s. The UNCTAD secretariat carried out studies to identify the implications of these agreements and the implementation of the technology-related provisions enshrined in them.[2] These new institutional developments were partly influenced by the rapid global changes in technology and by the introduction of multilateral trade rules that directly impact on technology and its use and protection.

The primary objective of the Working Group was to generate greater understanding of the impacts of the new global environment on technological development and the policy options available to developing countries. Some of these issues are highlighted in a report prepared by the secretariat (UNCTAD, 1993). The report underlined how the competitiveness of firms requires the adoption of flexible production systems, higher levels of investment in R&D, the accumulation of high-level engineering and management skills, the establishment of efficient distribution networks, rapid responsiveness to customers' needs, speed of delivery and reliability of after-sales services.

The Group held three sessions within a period of 15 months (January 1993 to March 1994). One of the key components of its work was the presentation of 19 country case studies on respective national policies prepared by member countries

---

[1] For further discussions on the research of the UNCTAD secretariat on contributions of FDI, see the topical paper on FDI/TNCs contained in this volume.

[2] UNCTAD (2001) Compendium of international arrangements on the transfer of technology: selected instrument, UNCTAD/ITE/IPC/Misc.5

specifically for the consideration of the Group. The coverage and contents of the case studies included: policies to promote technology and investment flows and technological innovation; human resource development and institutional building; intellectual property protection; factors affecting competitiveness; and the role of small- and medium-sized enterprises.

It identified three sets of issues to examine in detail. The first set of issues included investment flows, technology transfer and competitiveness. The second focused on technological capability-building in developing countries, particularly the least developed countries (LDCs) and in countries undergoing the process of transition to a market economy. The third looked at the implications of the intellectual property rights on the transfer and development of technology to developing countries (UNCTAD, 1996a). It was in this context that UNCTAD revisited the question of intellectual property and technology transfer in the late 1990s. UNCTAD X (Bangkok, 2000) confirmed this orientation and provided renewed impetus for further work in these areas.

A.   Servicing the Commission on Science and Technology for Development

The Commission on Science and Technology for Development (CSTD)[3] was established in 1992 to provide high-level advice to the General Assembly and ECOSOC through analysis and appropriate policy recommendations. The UNCTAD secretariat became responsible for providing substantive servicing of CSTD, including preparing the background studies and the intellectual inputs that the Commission needed to arrive at well-informed policy advice and recommendations. Within the CSTD-related work, UNCTAD has addressed technologies for small scale economic activities, information and communication technologies for development, science and technology partnerships and networking for national development, national capacity building in biotechnology and technology development and capacity-building for competitiveness in the digital world. Case studies and background study papers addressing the issues of intellectual property rights, technology transfer and capacity building-related issues have been prepared for consideration by the CSTD. In addition, the Science and

---

[3] This subsidiary body of the Economic and Social Council (ECOSOC) was established as part of the UN reform where the General Assembly decided to abolish the Intergovernmental Committee on Science and Technology for Development (IGCSTD) and its subsidiary body, the Advisory Committee on Science and Technology for Development (ACSTD), which had been created at the time of the United Nations Conference on Science and Technology for Development in Vienna in 1979.

Technology Diplomacy Initiative (UNCTAD, 2003) was launched to provide timely advice to policy makers and diplomats in science and technology negotiations and help policy makers to participate effectively in formulation and implementation of international instruments.

In 1995 the UNCTAD secretariat was mandated by ECOSOC resolution E/RES/1995/4 to conduct science and technology policy reviews (STIPs) for developing countries. The main aim of the reviews was to help developing countries and countries with economies in transition to evaluate the effectiveness of national science and technology policies and their impact on wealth creation, industrial competitiveness and quality of life of citizens. The reviews help Governments formulate and implement science and technology policies that address their current and future national goals (UNCTAD, 2001).

B. International Arrangements for Technology Transfer

The 1990s also witnessed the evolution of international trade discussions that incorporated intellectual property as an integral part of the trading system. This created a need to improve the understanding of the development implications of the Agreement on Trade Related Aspects of Intellectual Property Rights (TRIPS) of the World Trade Organization (WTO). The objective was to strengthen the analytical and negotiating capacity of developing countries to enable their participation in negotiations from an informed position to ensure their sustainable development objectives.

Subsequently the UNCTAD secretariat initiated the assessment of the policy implications of the TRIPS Agreement for developing countries and delineated an agenda for the transitional period of implementation (UNCTAD, 1996b). The overall purpose of the work was to make developing countries – particularly LDCs – aware of the economic implications of the Agreement so that they would be able to structure their IPR systems in a way that would enhance dynamic competition, and was consistent with their development objectives. The work was also intended to support the efforts of those countries in the formulation of strategies and establishment of arrangements conducive to the implementation of IPR.

Three key points were raised by the secretariat. First, the Agreement required substantial strengthening of the protection and enforcement of IPR in many countries, which was to be phased in over varying periods of time. The strengthening of the IPR regime was expected to engender positive impacts in developing countries, including more local innovation and additional inward FDI and technology transfer. However it could also precipitate certain negative impacts, including higher prices for protected technologies and products and restricted abilities to achieve diffusion through product imitation or copyright infringement. Second, in implementing the Agreement developing countries should have aspired to strike and sustain an appropriate balance between incentives to innovate and the need for adequate diffusion of technical knowledge into their economies. Third, the impacts of the various provisions in the Agreement would differ among countries depending, *inter alia,* on the existing IPR systems, the levels of economic and technological development and the mode of implementation (UNCTAD, 1996b).

In order to respond to the continuing concerns of developing countries in the area of intellectual property, further work is being carried out in the context of the Capacity Building Project on IPRs and Sustainable Development. This project is being implemented by the UNCTAD secretariat in collaboration with the International Centre for Trade and Sustainable Development (ICTSD).[4]

Several reviews of the impact of modern technologies, such as biotechnology and information and communication technologies (ICTs), have been conducted and technological indicators have been developed to help countries gauge their performance against that of others.[5] For example the ICTs benchmarking tool, an Internet-based analytical tool, enables policy makers and policy advisers to assess the national level of connectivity in comparison with that of other nations. This work was recognized and highlighted in 2003 as a major contribution by the World Summit on Information Society and the International Telecommunication Union.[6]

IV.   Concluding Remarks

UNCTAD's work in the area of technology has evolved in response to the changing priorities of Governments and the evolution of their thinking about technology. During the 1970s the focus was mainly on issues related to technology transfer, especially the terms and conditions involved, reflecting the concerns of

---

[4] For further information, go to: http://www.iprsonline.org/unctadictsd/description.htm
[5] See http://stdev.unctad.org/ for a comprehensive list of documents on biotechnology and the information and communication technology.
[6] See the ICT benchmarking tool at http://www.tte40.net/un

developing countries lacking access to foreign technology and the ways and means for them to acquire such technology at fairer terms and conditions.

The terms and conditions of transfers were viewed as being affected by existing differences in economic power and access to information between the buyer and the seller, leading to economic inequities and dependency. Hence the emphasis in UNCTAD's initial work in this area was on issues such as the restructuring of the legal environment for the technology transfer and the international patent system. Deliberations on these issues led to the launching of a negotiating process for an international code of conduct for technology transfer that dominated the attention of Governments and the secretariat for almost two decades thereafter.

In the 1980s attitudes towards the process of technology transfer and technological change evolved significantly. First, technology transfer was no longer viewed as a one-way process, flowing from advanced to developing countries, but as a multi-directional and multi-dimensional process involving small, medium and large-scale enterprises in all countries. The emergence of the newly industrializing countries in Asia as exporters of technology had become influential in changing the traditional perception of technology flows. Second, with the emergence of alternative sources of technology transfer, the earlier preoccupation with imperfections/failures in the international technology market and the associated call for regulations on technology imported by developing countries had waned. Third, while obtaining technology from abroad remained important to most developing countries, technology transfer was seen primarily as a means of accumulating technological capacity and improving trade competitiveness rather than as an end in itself. Partly in response to the changing perception of technology transfer and technological development, the work of the secretariat began to focus on strengthening the technological capability and innovative capacity of developing countries. It also looked at trends in international technology flows, including their trade and developmental implications, and considered measures to stimulate these flows, particularly to developing countries.

In the 1990s major events had marked an important change in the scope, orientation and institutional arrangements of UNCTAD's work on technology. The first relates to the outcome of UNCTAD VIII, which suspended the CTT and created a new Ad Hoc Working Group on the Interrelationship between Investment and Technology Transfer. That body completed its work in March 1994. The second important departure was the restructuring of the UN, which included the transfer of part of the activities of the former Centre on Science and Technology for Development from New York to Geneva. This concurred with the secretariat's new responsibilities for servicing the CSTD.

These decades of work on technology capacity building and transfer process created more awareness and a better understanding of a number of key aspects involved, which in turn influenced the evolution of thinking and the policy-making process. UNCTAD has contributed greatly to the conceptualization of technology issues, clarification of the terms and conditions of the transfer process, an understanding of the capability building process, and finally identification of best practices for obtaining access to technology. Indeed, UNCTAD's influence and contribution to this work is seen in many recently concluded international agreements that have taken up many of the aspects raised earlier by UNCTAD.

References

UNCTAD (1970). Transfer of technology, including know-how and patents: Elements of a programme of work for UNCTAD, Study by the UNCTAD secretariat. TD/B/310 and Corr.1.

_____ (1975a). Major issues arising from the transfer of technology to developing countries, Report by the UNCTAD secretariat. TD/B/AC.11/10/Rev.2.

_____ (1975b). Selected principal provisions in national laws, regulations and policy guidelines; Regional regulations and other material relevant to the preparation of a draft outline of a code of conduct on the transfer of technology, compiled by the UNCTAD secretariat. TD/B/C.6/AC.1/2/Supp.I/Add.l.

_____ (1975c). Report of the Intergovernmental Group of Experts on a code of conduct on the transfer of technology on its resumed session. Geneva, 24 November to 3 December 1975. TD/B/C.6/14.

_____ (1975d). Promotion of national scientific and technological capabilities and revision of the patent system, Report by the UNCTAD secretariat. TD/B/C.6/AC.2/2.

_____ (1975e). The role of the patent system in the transfer of technology to developing countries, Report prepared jointly by the United Nations Department of Economic and Social Affairs, the UNCTAD secretariat and the International Bureau of the World Intellectual Property Organization. TD/B/AC.11/19/Rev.l.

_____ (1975f). The reverse transfer of technology: Economic effects of the outflow of trained personnel from developing countries, Study by the UNCTAD secretariat. TD/B/AC.11/25/Rev.l.

_____ (1978). The reverse transfer of technology (brain-drain): Legal and administrative aspects of compensation, taxation and related policy measures: Suggestions for an optimal policy mix. R Pomp and O Oldman, TD/B/C.6/AC.4/7.

_____ (1980a) Coordinated technological research and development in developing countries: Regional cooperation to strengthen indigenous capacity for innovation, Study prepared at the request of the UNCTAD secretariat by Mr. Jan Annerstedt and Mr. Poul Engberg-Pedersen, Roskilde University Centre, Roskilde, Denmark, TD/B/C.6/63.

_____ (1980b) The capital goods and industrial machinery sector in developing countries: Issues in the transfer and development of technology, Study by the UNCTAD secretariat. TD/B/C.6/AC.7/2.

____ (1982). Renewable energy technology: Issues in the transfer, application and development of technology in developing countries. Report by Mr. Kurt Hoffman, TD/B/C.6/AC.9/4.

____ (1984). Policies and instruments for the promotion and encouragement of technological innovation, Preliminary report by the UNCTAD secretariat. TD/B/C.6/123.

____ (1985). Draft International Code of Conduct on the Transfer of Technology, The United Nations Conference on an International Code of Conduct on the Transfer of Technology. (The Draft Code of Conduct is accessible at: http://stdev.unctad.org/compendium/frameinicial.htm.)

____ (1993). Report of the Ad Hoc Working Group on the Interrelationship between Investment and Technology Transfer on its second session. TD/B/40(2)/10.

____ (1996a). Fostering Technological Dynamism: Evolution of Thought on Technological Development Processes and Competitiveness: A Review of the Literature. TD/B/WG.5/7.

____ (1996b). The TRIPS Agreement and Developing Countries. UNCTAD/ITE/1.

____ (2001). Investment and Innovation Policy Review Ethiopia. UNCTAD/ITE/IPC/Misc.4.

____ (2003). Science and Technology Diplomacy, Concepts and Elements of a Work Programme. UNCTAD/ITE/TEB/Misc.5.

Competition Law and Policy

Philippe Brusick and Lucian Cernat[*]

Introduction

It has long been recognized that effectively addressing cross-border restrictive business practices (RBPs) – or anti-competitive practices in today's jargon – requires coordinated action at the international level.[1] Despite this recognition, most of the international efforts to deal with RBPs in the post-World War II period have failed (with the exception of the 1980 United Nations Set of Multilaterally Agreed Equitable Principles and Rules for the Control of Restrictive Business Practices, as it was originally called). The overall process of past and present attempts to adopt a multilateral framework on competition law and policy has shown that an international approach to anti-competitive practices affecting international trade has been highly contentious.

The objective of this paper is to review some of the most important attempts during the post-WWII period, focusing particularly on the achievements of UNCTAD in this area. Against this background of failed initiatives, the adoption of the above-mentioned United Nations Set of Multilaterally Agreed Equitable Principles and Rules can be considered a remarkable and decisive first step in controlling RBPs affecting international trade, particularly the trade and development prospects of developing countries (Brusick, 1983). The very fact that representatives of so many countries with different political and economic backgrounds were able to draft such a comprehensive and detailed agreement on RBPs makes the UN Set a considerable technical and diplomatic triumph. After a short description of several initiatives prior to UNCTAD's contributions, the remainder of this paper will concentrate on the adoption of the 1980 Set of Rules and Principles and the subsequent work that stemmed from it.

[*] Philippe Brusick is Head of the Competition and Consumer Policies Branch, Division on Trade in Goods and Services, and Commodities (DITC). Lucian Cernat is an Associate Economic Affairs Officer, Competition and Consumer Policies Branch, DITC. The authors would like to thank Rajan Dhanjee, Philip Marsden and François Souty for their useful comments and suggestions.
[1] The League of Nations recognized the importance of international cooperation to deal with restrictive business practices as early as 1927.

In order to understand the context in which competition policy has been brought within the ambit of UNCTAD, a cursory overview of the main attempts at international cooperation in this area is necessary. Several main driving forces can be identified in the evolution of approaches used towards competition law and policy: (i) the initial antitrust concern in 19th century North America and its subsequent influence of antitrust laws and policies adopted in other developed countries (including the various US-initiated bilateral treaties of friendship, commerce and navigation containing antitrust clauses); (ii) the post-WW II trade liberalization efforts started by the Havana Charter, the subsequent United Nations Economic and Social Council (ECOSOC) efforts during the 1951–1955 period, followed by the GATT activity on RBPs during the 1954–1960 period and its resumption in the post-Uruguay Round period in its work on trade and competition policy; (iii) the regional integration schemes, starting with the Council of Europe, the European Communities, European Free Trade Area (EFTA), and the proliferation of regional arrangements with competition rules worldwide (Andean Community, NAFTA, ASEAN, UEMOA, ANZCERTA, etc.); and (iv) the competition-development nexus initiated in UNCTAD in the early 1970s and its subsequent influence on the work of other organizations (OECD, WTO).

I.   The Pre-UNCTAD Period

Competition law and policy was born at the end of the 19th century in North America to counter large conglomerates or "trusts" that were providing steel barons with excessive economic power, linking steel with railways, mining and energy. In adopting the Sherman Antitrust Act in 1890 the US Congress recognized that competition would lead to optimal allocation of economic resources, lower prices, better quality, widest supply, enhancing social and economic structures favourable to democracy.[2]

Although the first major attempt to create a multilateral framework on trade and competition was the Havana Charter, it should be noted that the cross-border implications of antitrust issues were considered even prior to WW II, particularly in the context of inter-war international cartels and patent pools. The League of Nations expressed interest in the possibility of international antitrust regulation but the World Economic Conference (1927) held under the League's auspices concluded that differences in national antitrust policies would preclude the adoption of international rules on antitrust. Despite this conclusion it was argued

---

[2] These views are clearly reaffirmed, for example, in Northern Pacific Railway Co. v. United States, 365 U.S.,1,4 (1968).

that the League might still provide some means of supervision over international cartels and agreements with similar effects.

The United States also advocated the advantages of multilateralism and free trade versus segmentation and protectionism, citing as evidence the disastrous policies of trade protection and competitive devaluations during the Great Depression years. Consequently, in February 1946 ECOSOC unanimously approved a resolution submitted by the United States on convening a United Nations Conference on Trade and Employment. This decision eventually led to a conference in Havana from 21 November 1947 to 24 March 1948, during which the Final Act (known as the Havana Charter) was signed by 53 UN Member States. One of the purposes of the Charter was the creation of an International Trade Organization (ITO) as a UN agency. Apart from RBPs (Chapter V of the Charter), numerous objectives dealing with trade (Chapter IV), employment (Chapter II), economic development (Chapter III), investment (Chapter III), and commodities (Chapter VI) were taken up. In 1950, however, it became apparent that the United States, although instrumental in bringing about the Havana Conference, would not ratify the Charter.[3] The negative American position discouraged other countries from ratifying it and the Havana Charter never entered into force.[4]

Interesting to note is that the authors of the Havana Charter were aware that private barriers could distort trade even when governmental barriers such as tariffs and non-tariff barriers are eliminated. This was why they included provisions on RBPs in the Charter, thereby prohibiting cartels and vertical restraints by monopolies and dominant enterprises. Despite the failure to ratify the Havana Charter (and thus the ITO), the Charter has remained an important historical reference that affected the evolution of international efforts to deal with RBPs.

The idea of dealing with RBPs at a multilateral level persisted in the activities of ECOSOC. In September 1951 ECOSOC resolution 375(XIII, item 1) urged Member States to take

> "appropriate measures and cooperate with one another to prevent, on the part of private and public commercial enterprises, business practices affecting international trade which restrain competition, limit access to markets or foster monopolistic control, whenever such practices have harmful effects on the expansion or production or trade, on the economic

---

[3] This apparent paradox has been subject to many explanations. For a recent review of such theories see, for instance, Graz (1999).
[4] Chapter IV, however, was applied through a provisional protocol and formed the basis for the creation of GATT.

development of underdeveloped areas, or on standards of living".
(ECOSOC resolution 375(XIII), item 1)

The resolution also established an ECOSOC *ad hoc* Committee mandated to
submit proposals for an international agreement on RBPs in line with Chapter V of
the Havana Charter. While the draft submitted by the *ad hoc* Committee to
ECOSOC failed to reach general agreement in two instances (1953 and 1955), the
idea of setting up an international organization dealing with trade and development
subsequently received support from developing countries, particularly at the Cairo
Conference of 1962 which led to the convening of UNCTAD in 1964.

In parallel with these attempts at international cooperation, regional efforts
were also undertaken in Europe under the auspices of the Council of Europe, the
European Communities and the European Free Trade Area (EFTA). In 1949 the
Council of Europe decided to deal with international cartels in Europe. But, like
the Havana Charter and the ECOSOC draft proposal, the Council of Europe Draft
Convention for the Control of International Cartels never entered into force.
Instead it was proposed that GATT undertake further work in this field. Prompted
by this suggestion, between 1954 and 1960 GATT contracting parties discussed the
role of GATT in regulating international RBPs. Although they agreed that some
role would be desirable, there was sharp disagreement on the appropriate steps.
These efforts resulted in the 1960 GATT Decision in which GATT contracting
parties, while acknowledging potential negative impact of RBPs, decided that
under the then prevailing circumstances it would not be practicable to undertake
any form of control of such practices or to provide for investigation, although
consultations among interested parties on such practices were encouraged (GATT,
1960).

II.   1964–1974:
Work on RBPs in UNCTAD
with Emphasis on the Development Dimension

Prior to the creation of UNCTAD the numerous attempts at creating an
international architecture dealing with RBPs were influenced mainly by developed
countries, in particular the United States, although other countries (including some
developing countries) made substantive proposals or amendments to existing
proposals. The failure of these attempts shaped the perception that differences
between various countries in their national approaches towards the issue of RBPs
were considered too wide to lead to an international agreement on it. Indeed, the

perception had persisted for more than a decade prior to UNCTAD I (1964). Partly for that reason RBPs did not figure as an important discussion item during the Conference, neither for developed nor for developing countries.

However, with the adoption at UNCTAD II (1968) of resolution 25(II): Programme for the liberalization and expansion of trade in manufactures and semi-manufactures (including processed and semi-processed primary commodities) of interest to developing countries – restrictive business practices, a tentative start was made on work on RBPs. Since then RBPs have consistently remained an issue of concern for developing countries and a major area of activities for UNCTAD.

The Conference adopted the resolution by 57 votes in favour to 12 against, and 9 abstentions, with most developed countries either opposing it or abstaining from voting. Stressing the need to investigate the impact of RBPs by private enterprises in developed countries with special reference to the effects of such practices on the export interests of the developing countries, especially on the least developed among them, the resolution represented a significant landmark in the evolution of developing countries' awareness of the need for strengthened controls over RBPs, especially those affecting their exports.[5] The reasons for this significant policy shift can be found in the profound political changes that occurred in the first two post-war decades. In particular, developing countries acquired a majority at the UN General Assembly. As the political structure of the international community changed, the economic structure of the world also evolved. As many developing countries became engaged in the process of industrialization the possible use of anticompetitive practices by dominant firms, in particular transnational corporations (TNCs) originating in developed countries, became a significant concern. An UNCTAD study reported that more than 25 per cent of world trade was then estimated to take place between affiliated enterprises and that the bulk of international trade transactions on goods (whether finished, intermediate or raw materials) and services (including royalties, management and licensing fees) were controlled by TNCs (UNCTAD, 1981). The study provided greater justification for calls by developing countries for the progressive removal of RBPs.

This initial step was followed in 1970 by a more specific call, in the International Development Strategy for the Second UN Development Decade, for the identification of RBPs, particularly those affecting the trade and development, with a view to the consideration of appropriate remedial actions by the end of

---

[5] It is also worth mentioning that *prima facie*, the mandate did not include an investigation on the impact of international cartels on the imports of developing countries, a theme that subsequently became a central one to the debate on RBPs.

1972. At UNCTAD III (Santiago 1972) governments decided unanimously that the possibility should be examined of drawing up guidelines to control or eliminate RBPs adversely affecting developing countries. Following the seminal work by the first Ad Hoc Group of Experts on Restrictive Business Practices, the UNCTAD Committee on Manufactures decided in 1975 to establish a Second Ad Hoc Group of Experts to study the matter further (resolution 9(VII)).

III. 1976–1980:
Multilateral Negotiations
on the UN RBP Set

At UNCTAD IV (Nairobi 1976) governments decided in part III of resolution 96 (IV) that action should be taken by countries in a mutually reinforcing manner at the national, regional and international levels to eliminate or effectively deal with RBPs, including those of TNCs, adversely affecting international trade. Actions in this respect included, *inter alia*, negotiations with the objective of formulating a "set of mutually agreed equitable principles and rules for the control of RBPs on international trade, particularly that of developing countries, and on the economic development of these countries". The resolution launched the negotiations which resulted in the formulation of the UN Set of Principles and Rules on Restrictive Business Practices, and called for an instrument to control RBPs in the context of international trade.[6]

In 1980, after two negotiating conferences under the auspices of UNCTAD, the "UN Set of Multilaterally Agreed Equitable Principles and Rules for the Control of Restrictive Business Practices" (hereafter the Set) was approved and subsequently transmitted to the UN General Assembly which, in turn, unanimously adopted the Set in the form of a recommendation to its members (resolution 35/63). This marked the beginning of UNCTAD's active work on promoting competition law and policy at national, regional and multilateral levels, and formed part of the development dimension phase of competition law and policy.

---

[6] It should be recalled that national legislation is generally inward-looking in that while existing laws usually prohibit to a varying extent RBPs affecting the domestic market to varying extents, none prohibit such practices when their effects are felt only outside the national territory. Even United States legislation, which has a far-reaching extraterritorial application, only covers practices that affect United States commerce. Moreover, export cartels are authorized provided they are noted under the Webb-Pomerene Act. Subsequently facilities for joint ventures for exports were granted under the Export Trading Company Act 1982.

During the negotiations the following issues came to appear as the main stumbling blocks as to whether the Set would be a "binding" or "voluntary instrument"; the extent to which special or differential treatment should be accorded to developing countries; the extent to which the Set should contain "escape clauses" permitting the use of specific RBPs in particular cases; whether export cartels and international cartels should be banned; whether, and if so to what extent, intra-firm behaviour and transactions of TNCs should be covered; whether the Set should apply to private enterprises as well as state-owned enterprises (SOEs), and to international commodities agreements, including OPEC.

The binding force of the Set: During the negotiations it was realized that the international community was not ripe for the adoption of a binding agreement for the control of anti-competitive practices. The Set made it clear that there would be no dispute settlement mechanism and that the Set would not be binding.[7] Negotiators, however, accepted to opt for an interpretation of the Set as evolutionary; Section G, provision (iii) of the Set called for a "review procedure" whereby, subject to the approval of the General Assembly, five years after the adoption of the Set a UN conference would be convened by the Secretary-General of the UN under the auspices of UNCTAD for the purpose of reviewing all the aspects of the Set. Towards this end, the Intergovernmental Group will make proposals to the Conference for the improvement and further development of the Set.

Special treatment for developing countries: The question of according special or preferential treatment to developing countries, and particularly to the least-developed countries (LDCs, was dealt with in the Set. It called for States, particularly developed countries, to take into account the development, financial and trade needs of developing countries (and LDCs in particular) in their control of RBPs. Section C, provision (iii) explicitly mentioned promoting the establishment or development of domestic industries and the economic development of other sectors of the economy as well as encouraging their economic development through regional or global arrangement among developing countries, specifying that these are legitimate needs that should be taken into account. It is important to note that this provision was addressed to all countries, but particularly to developed

---

[7] "In the performance of its functions, neither the Intergovernmental Group nor its subsidiary organs shall act like a tribunal, or otherwise pass judgment on the activities or conduct of individual Governments or individual enterprises in connection with a specific business transaction. The Intergovernmental Group or its subsidiary organs should avoid becoming involved when enterprises to a specific business transaction are in dispute". (G: Provision (ii))

countries which were thereby invited to apply some sort of "comity principle"[8] in favour of firms from developing countries and LDCs if this was considered necessary for infant industry development. The latter part of the provision takes into account regional economic arrangements, such as the Andean Group, The Caribbean Common Market (CARICOM), The Association of South–East Asian Nations (ASEAN) or The Common Market for Eastern and Southern Africa (COMESA), and later The Southern Common Market (MERCOSUR), to cite just a few regional agreements among developing countries which developed or envisaged the adoption of specific rules on competition at the regional level.

Possibility of exceptions or exemptions: Under its provision 6, Section C (ii), the Set recognized that countries, while bearing in mind the need to ensure the comprehensive application of the Set, should take due account of the extent to which the conduct of enterprises, whether or not created or controlled by states, was acceptable under applicable legislation or regulations. In other words, the Set recognized that domestic laws did contain "escape clauses" and that third countries should take this into account in their controlling of RBPs. Domestic legislation prohibiting RBPs "in principle" recognized the possibility of authorizing particular agreements or arrangements on a case-by-case basis. Therefore, a first concern in this provision was to limit the extent to which such authorization should be granted under domestic legislation to ensure that the comprehensive application of the Set would not be hampered by too many exemptions or exceptions. Secondly, third countries, in controlling RBPs originating from countries where authorization had been granted, were invited to take into account the authorization but were under no obligation to accept that this prevented taking remedial action in case these practices had adverse effects in their domestic markets. For example, when an export cartel is authorized in one country there is no reason why the country where the adverse effects are felt should not take remedial action in accordance with the "effects doctrine".

---

[8] The comity principle arose out of the need to mitigate the inherent tension between cross-border economic activities and the principles of territorial exclusivity and sovereign equality. As set forth in a series of OECD recommendations concerning international cooperation on RBPs affecting international trade, "negative comity" may be described as the principle that a country should (i) notify other countries when its enforcement proceedings may have an effect on their important interests, and (ii) give full and sympathetic consideration to possible ways of fulfilling its enforcement needs without harming those interests. In the same context, "positive comity" requires that a country should (i) give full and sympathetic consideration to another country's request that it open or expand a law enforcement proceeding in order to remedy conduct in its territory that is substantially and adversely affecting another country's interests, and (2) take whatever remedial action deemed appropriate on a voluntary basis and in consideration of its legitimate interests.

A ban on export cartels and international cartels: During the negotiations there were virtually no signs that countries would agree with an absolute ban on export or international cartels. It should be noted that the Set did call upon enterprises to refrain from, *inter alia,*: "[a]greements fixing prices, including as to exports and imports" (Section D, provision 3 (a)) and calls upon States to "[s]eek appropriate remedial or preventive measures to prevent and/or control the use of RBPs within their competence when it comes to the attention of States that such practices adversely affect international trade and, particularly, the trade and development of developing countries" (Section E, para. 4)[9]. While the Set did not refer explicitly to international cartels, these may nevertheless be considered as covered by para. 3 in Section D which gave a non-exhaustive list of practices by enterprises "engaged on the market in rival or potentially rival activities".

Intra-firm behaviour: The inclusion of a provision on intra-firm behaviour and the transactions of TNC in the Set represented an important breakthrough in the area of international economic cooperation, although the coverage of relevant issues was probably the most controversial issue at the time. One specific area with potential anticompetitive effects was intra-firm trade. This is one of the areas where the UNCTAD secretariat contributed, as early as 1978, to the analytical debate with a study entitled *Dominant positions of market power of transnational corporations: Use of the transfer pricing mechanism* (UNCTAD, 1978). The study documented the extent to which manipulation of transfer prices resulted in an abuse of a dominant position in developed and developing countries and described the variety of governmental measures aimed at controlling such abuses. Furthermore, the study made a number of recommendations that were deemed necessary to making more effective the control of transfer pricing.[10] Second, intra-firm practices such as limiting access to markets or otherwise unduly restraining competition constitute an abuse and fall under the scope of this provision for an entity within an enterprise in a position of dominant market power. This provision is particularly relevant to TNCs in positions of dominant market power with subsidiaries in the markets of developing countries. The possibility of intra-firm

---

[9] Hence, for example, a country aware that one of its export cartels affected developing countries should take the action necessary to discontinue the cartel, especially if it is invited to do so by the adversely affected country. Today such action would be taken under so-called "positive" or "negative" comity action.

[10] First, intra-firm transactions of TNCs such as transfer-pricing practices should be prohibited in the case of discriminatory (i.e. unjustifiably differentiated) pricing or terms of conditions in the supply or purchase of goods or services, including by means of the use of pricing policies in transactions between affiliated enterprises which overcharge or undercharge for goods or services purchased or supplied as compared with prices for similar or comparable transactions outside the affiliated enterprises.

collusion has not been ruled out for cases where a subsidiary or affiliate is able to act independently or does so. (for further details, see UNCTAD, 1978, section D.)

Application to State-owned enterprises (SOEs): Equally important in the negotiations was the extent to which SOEs should be covered in the Set. Exempting SOEs would have meant that a large proportion of imports and exports would fall outside the scope of application of the Set. Should SOEs be treated in a different manner, for example when competing with firms from developing countries? The problem arose at the time concerning state-trading organizations of centrally-planned economies which, it was felt, needed to be covered by the Set as they, like any other private enterprise, could very well be engaged in anti-competitive practices with international implications, including in their trade with developing countries. After a laborious negotiation it was finally agreed that the Set would apply to all enterprises "irrespective of the mode of creation or control or ownership, private or State" (Section B, paragraph 3). This is a very important provision as even today countries adopting competition legislation for the first time are often tempted to exempt SOEs from the scope of the competition law.[11]

The case of international commodity agreements and the Organization of Petroleum Exporting Countries (OPEC): The negotiations of the Set took place at the time of other important negotiations at UNCTAD, such as those on the Common Fund for Commodities, as part of a price-stabilisation mechanism (see the paper on Commodities in the present volume). OPEC members were concerned that the adoption of the Set might result in a multilateral ban on its decisions to allocate production quotas and to fix oil prices. For this reason the Set exempted intergovernmental agreements, including anti-competitive practices directly caused by such agreements (Section B, provision (ii), para. 9). This provision was widely used, however, by developed countries to exempt voluntary exports restraints (VERs) and orderly marketing arrangements aimed at protecting specific domestic producers from competitive overseas exporters to their own markets.

---

[11] This should not be confused with the issue of sovereign acts of States, covered in Section B (ii), para. 9 of the Set, which states that "the Set apply to intergovernmental agreements, nor to RBPs directly caused by such agreements".

IV. 1980 and Onward:
The Application of the UN Set –
the IGE and Review Conferences

By adopting the Set in resolution 35/63 of 5 December 1980 the UN General Assembly decided to convene in 1985, under the auspices of UNCTAD, a UN Conference "to review all aspects of the Set" and requested the Trade and Development Board (TDB) to establish an intergovernmental group of experts on RBPs, operating within the framework of an UNCTAD committee, to perform the functions designated in section G (International Institutional Machinery) of the Set. Pursuant to this resolution the TDB, in its resolution 228 (XXII), established an Intergovernmental Group of Experts on Restrictive Business Practices (IGE), which held its first session in Geneva from 2 to 11 November 1981. The Group sessions met in 1983, 1984, and 1985 in the form of preparatory meetings for the Review Conference which took place in October 1985.

A.   The First 5 Years (1981–1985)

In the 5 year period which followed the adoption of the Set, negotiations of the other UN Codes of Conduct, in particular UNCTAD's Code on Transfer of Technology and the UN Commission on TNCs on the code of conduct, got bogged down in insurmountable difficulties and failed (see papers on Technology, and on FDI in this volume). Meanwhile, UNCTAD's repeated calls for financial support for technical assistance, advisory and training programmes on RBPs (as indicated in paragraphs 6 and 7 of the Set) did not materialise. The UNCTAD secretariat prepared the first Review Conference with little to show in way of implementation despite the high technical level attained in the studies prepared for the IGE and the first steps of the Model Law.[12] To address this lack of success the Group of 77 decided at the preparatory meeting in April 1985 to call for an amendment to transform the Set into a binding instrument. They felt that such transformation would force developed countries to provide more attention to the prohibition of anti-competitive practices affecting developing countries and would give an impetus at least to the provisions calling for technical assistance and exchange of

---

[12] For the early work of the secretariat on the Model Law see, for example, UNCTAD, 1984. The document revised the national experiences of both developed and developing countries with competition law, and provided a framework of "best practices" legal provisions that could serve as a useful instrument to developing countries in their drafting or amending of national competition laws.

expertise to help the developing countries adopt domestic competition legislation and strengthen their capacity for implementation.

The requests of the developing countries were rejected by the developed countries' Members of Group B, while the Review Conference once again reiterated its call to "international organisations and financing programmes, in particular the UNDP", to provide resources for the financing of technical cooperation in this field.

B.   1986–1990

It is only in 1986, with the help of the Norwegian and Swedish governments, that the first technical assistance activity in pursuance of the Set was made possible in the form of a seminar on RBPs for African countries which took place at the Kisini Centre of UNEP at Nairobi (Kenya). A series of background notes were produced by the UNCTAD secretariat in its efforts to sensitize developing countries on the adverse effects of RBPs on their trade and development.[13] This was a stepping-stone in what was going to become one of UNCTAD's important technical assistance and capacity-building activities 20 years later. Meanwhile in 1985, under the impetus of Consumer International, ECOSOC was able to negotiate and adopt the United Nations Guidelines on Consumer Protection, which was an important landmark in bringing basic principles of protection of fundamental consumer rights, including health and safety as well as consumers' economic rights, within the UN framework. Among consumers' economic rights the Guidelines made special reference to the defence of competition and the need for protection from the adverse effects of anti-competitive practices, or RBPs, as called for in the Set. Paragraph 17, Section B of the Consumer Guidelines specifically referred to the Set.

Following the failed first Review Conference, delegations held a series of consultations in Geneva which led to the adoption of a decision by the UN General Assembly in 1986 to convene a second Review Conference. During the 5 year period after the first Review Conference a phase of interest in competition policy started as a result of market-oriented reforms in many developing countries under structural adjustment programmes (SAPs) heavily inspired, or imposed

---

[13] For an early report identifying major RBPs and proposing ways to take effective actions to eliminate them, see, for example UNCTAD, 1987.

through conditionality, by the International Monetary Fund and the World Bank.[14] For a number of years the Bretton Woods institutions insisted that opening markets to foreign competition and creation of contestable markets in developing countries would be sufficient to create positive economic results once SAPs were being implemented. It is only towards the end of the 1980s that conventional wisdom turned in favour of competition policies supported by domestic competition laws and implementing authorities in developing and other countries. The interest in, and the subsequent adoption of, competition laws by a growing number of developing countries grew rapidly towards the end of the 1980s, especially in the early 1990s.

The fall of the Berlin Wall also led numerous countries in transition to embark on market-economy systems and to adopt anti-monopoly laws, basically challenging concentrations of market power and prohibiting cartel arrangements. This convergence of interest on competition legislation led to a considerable impetus in favour of implementation of the Set at the second Review Conference in 1990. The conference was a complete success, placing emphasis on technical assistance and capacity-building for developing countries and countries in transition but also on the "Model Law" aimed at helping countries engaged in the delicate exercise of drafting domestic competition legislation.

C.   1990–Present: The Rebirth of Competition Law and Policy

Recognition that market-oriented economic reforms needed to be accompanied by effective competition policies led many developing countries and economies in transition to adopt competition or antimonopoly laws in the early 1990s. Countries that had privatised SOEs while granting them long-term monopoly advantages later realized the dangers of replacing a public monopoly with a private one, especially in utilities which have an all-important bearing on the overall economy of a country. Countries that had opened their borders to imports and foreign direct investors also felt confident that domestic competition laws would enable them to avoid major pitfalls of deregulated domestic markets. In particular many countries feared that foreign firms, either through FDI or through imports, would be able to dominate and eventually monopolise domestic and

---

[14] These market-oriented reforms typically involved price liberalization and dropping of subsidies for essential necessities, devaluation and free-float of the domestic currency, opening of the markets, privatisation of state-owned firms and utilities as well as trade and FDI liberalization. All of these had one thing in common: the need for competition rules to ensure that market-oriented reforms would not be hampered by structural rigidities and existing monopolies.

markets, bringing with them international market segmentation cartel ,ments and controlling the domestic economy.

Transition economy countries were aware that price liberalisation needed to be accompanied by structural reforms if they were to avoid being blocked by vested interests in remaining pre-reform conglomerates and monopolies of the central-planning economy. Moreover, developing countries willing to engage in new North-South and East-West regional trade arrangements became very interested in adopting competition legislation as one of the pre-conditions for membership.

By the end of the 1990s, UNCTAD's activities in assisting developing countries (including LDCs) and countries in transition in their efforts to draft, adopt and implement competition law and policies had grown considerably.[15] The IGE continued to monitor annually the UNCTAD secretariat's analytical work on specific anti-competitive or RBPs[16] issues related to the implementation of the Set as well as review its technical assistance programmes in this field. Cooperation with other relevant international organisations such as the World Bank and the Organization of Economic Cooperation and Development OECD was also enhanced.

The Uruguay Round agreements have also created new trade rules which had a potential impact on competition-related issues. The UNCTAD secretariat, therefore, produced one of the first comprehensive analyses of the Uruguay Round agreements relevant to competition policy and their implications for developing and transition countries (UNCTAD, 1996). The study showed the limitations of the Uruguay Round agreements on controlling RBPs and the potential misuse of existing trade rules (e.g. on anti-dumping and subsidies, governmental regulation

---

[15] In this regard it is interesting to note one instance in which the work of UNCTAD secretariat has been highly relevant. In a merger case considered by the Pakistani Monopoly Control Authority, two UNCTAD secretariat studies are extensively cited as sources of guidance as to how to deal with such mergers. See Order in the Matter of Show-Cause Notice No. 92 of 1995-1996 issued section 11 of the Monopolies and Restrictive Trade Practices (Control and Prevention) Ordinance, 1970 to Lever Brothers (Pakistan) Ltd. By Monopoly Control Authority, Government of Pakistan, Islamabad, 1996. The studies in question were: *Restrictive business practices that have an effect in more than one country, in particular developing and other countries, with overall conclusions regarding the issues raised by these cases* (UNCTAD, 1995b) and *The role of competition policy in economic reforms in developing and other countries* (UNCTAD, 1995a.).

[16] See for instance UNCTAD, 1997, which addressed in a comprehensive manner the main issues that competition policy-makers face in the so-called "network industries". The study reviews the reasons for, and obstacles encountered in, efficient public utility regulation, particularly in the context of privatization and deregulation. See also UNCTAD, 1999, which showed that the welfare consequences and policy implications of vertical restraints depend on the specific structural conditions of the market concerned.

of the distribution sector, the use of intellectual property rights (IPRs) to facilitate international market segmentation) against consumer welfare. The study also made specific suggestions for the WTO Singapore Ministerial Conference, December 1996, where it decided to establish two new Working Groups, one on Investment and the other on the Interaction between Trade and Competition Policy, and called upon UNCTAD to ensure that the development dimension was taken fully into account. This initiated a new era of close cooperation between UNCTAD and the WTO. Furthermore, the WTO Fourth Ministerial Conference adopted the Doha Declaration in 2001 which recognised the interaction between trade and competition policy as well as acknowledging the need of developing countries and LDCs for enhanced analytical support in this area so that they may better evaluate the implications of closer multilateral cooperation in competition law and policy for their development policies and objectives along with their human and institutional development. It also acknowledged the pivotal role played by UNCTAD in this process (para 24 of the Declaration).

The Bangkok Declaration adopted at UNCTAD X in 2000 was another landmark in the field of competition law and policy, calling for "the international community as a whole ... to ensure an enabling global environment through enhanced cooperation in the fields of trade, investment, competition and finance, ... so as to make globalisation more efficient and equitable" (UNCTAD, 2000a, para. 4). In this favourable context it was decided that the UNCTAD secretariat should continue and expand its assistance to interested countries in developing their national regulatory and institutional framework in the area of competition law and policy in cooperation with UNDP, the World Bank and other relevant organizations. As part of this process the secretariat continued to explore and clarify methodologies for defining relevant markets and assessing market power and restraints in strategic sectors and their impact on developing countries and countries with economies in transition, particularly regarding their competitiveness. Other research topics covered merger control issues, including in the process of privatization, particularly as they affect the development and integration of developing countries and countries in transition into the world economy, the benefits of competition law and policy for consumers, poverty alleviation and economic development (UNCTAD, 2002a).

Finally, UNCTAD was invited to continue to provide inputs to deliberations on possible international agreements on competition, including through consensus-building activities that could clarify and further identify the goals and objectives of developing countries in competition law and policy. Other relevant policy-oriented research questions that were addressed included: the effectiveness and complementarity of cooperation at bilateral, regional, plurilateral and multilateral levels (UNCTAD, 2002b) as well as the role of possible dispute mediation mechanisms and alternative arrangements (such as voluntary peer reviews) in competition law and policy (UNCTAD, 2003). Both studies assessed critically the existing policy proposals and advanced the debates on the potential costs and benefits associated with alternative frameworks for a multilateral agreement on trade and competition.

V. Conclusion

In light of the historical background of international efforts to create a multilateral framework on competition policy, the 1980 adoption of the Set was an outstanding achievement by UNCTAD, obtained in a fairly short period (1976–1980) of intense negotiations. Presently the Set is considered a fundamental element of international cooperation on competition law and policy. As a result, UNCTAD's work covers not only the anti-competitive practices affecting domestic markets but also those affecting international trade generally. "If we accept that market economy has to promote development in the future, we must recognize the need for appropriate competition, with rules and institutions for its good functioning", said Mr. Ricupero, the Secretary-General of UNCTAD. In this connection, the Secretary-General recalled that Professor Joseph Stiglitz, in his now famous critique of the Washington Consensus, said that one of the main flaws in the consensus had been that it had devoted insufficient attention to the necessity of applying competition policy in the real economy and its rules and institutions. The Secretary-General further noted that at UNCTAD, "we have always considered that competition is indissociable from development".[17]

The fourth Review Conference unanimously reaffirmed in its resolution "the fundamental role of competition law and policy for sound economic development" and recommended the continuation and strengthening of "the important and useful work programme of the UNCTAD secretariat and the intergovernmental machinery that addresses competition law an policy issues, and proceeds with the active support and participation of competition law and policy authorities of member countries" (UNCTAD, 2000b: 3).

As a result, UNCTAD contributed to a more efficient but also more equitable world economy through globalisation based on competition rules at

---

[17] Message of Mr. Rubens Ricupero, Secretary-General of UNCTAD to the Regional post-Doha Seminar on WTO Competition Issues for Latin America and the Caribbean (São Paulo, Brazil, 23-25 April 2003).

national, regional and multilateral levels and by promoting a competition culture and consumer interests in cooperation with NGOs and consumer organisations.

Annex

The UN Set of Principles and Rules on Competition: Its Innovative Features

The Set aims to have a positive effect on international trade through the encouragement of competition. The Set should help eliminate or effectively deal with anti-competitive practices and control the concentration of economic power in international trade. Under this third objective the Set recognizes the important link between the promotion of competition and the encouragement of innovation, with a belief that controlling or eliminating anti-competitive practices should protect and promote social welfare in general and should result in lower prices, better quality and increased choice for consumers in both developed and developing countries.

The Set contains a preamble and seven main sections dealing with: A) Objectives; B) Definitions and scope of application; C) General principles for the control of RBPs; D) Provisions addressed to enterprises, including transnational corporations; E) Provisions addressed to States at national, regional and sub-regional levels; F) Provisions concerning measures to be taken at the international level; and G) Provisions concerning the setting-up of International institutional machinery.

1.   *Preamble and objectives*

The preamble clearly recognises that anti-competitive practices or RBPs can adversely affect international trade, particularly that of developing countries; these practices can therefore obstruct   economic development. Special emphasis is placed on practices observed in the increased activities of TNCs as such corporations have become major players in international trade and production. However, it notes that controlling them would be much more difficult than controlling domestic firms. For example, under domestic legislation it is often impossible to prove that a TNC has infringed the law when developing countries are unable to obtain the required information held abroad by parent companies. Clearly, in order to control practices originating in one country and affecting another, there is a need for action to be taken by countries "in a mutually reinforcing manner at the national, regional and international levels" (Section C, para. 1). It is necessary for both countries to have domestic competition legislation, and there is a need for an international instrument to enable coordinated action by both countries if such action is to be effective.

The Set was a major step in this direction. The adoption of the Set facilitated the adoption and strengthening of national competition laws, as all countries are requested to adopt and effectively implement competition legislation in accordance with it. This does not mean, however, that all laws should be identical. It has been well understood after the adoption of the Set that while convergence of competition laws and "best practices" is a long-term objective, domestic competition laws have to be tailor-made to respond to the actual needs of each country.

While recognizing the national objectives of competition policy, the Set draws attention to the trade-related effects of competition policy, particularly for developing countries. One of the primary objectives of the Set is "to ensure that restrictive business practices do not impede or negate the realization of benefits that should arise from the liberalization of tariff and non-tariff barriers affecting world trade, particularly those affecting the trade and development of developing countries". The elimination of such anti-competitive practices is expected to make possible the attainment of the second objective of the Set: "greater efficiency in international trade and development in accordance with national aims of economic and social development and existing economic structures, such as through a) the creation, encouragement and protection of competition; b) control of the concentration of capital and/or economic power; and c) encouragement of innovation".

(a)   Definitions, Scope and Principles

The definitions of "restrictive business practices", "dominant position of market power" and "enterprises" were the result of difficult negotiations and compromises. This is in contrast to a number of national competition laws which avoid defining these terms by simply providing non-exhaustive lists of anti-competitive practices and by leaving it to the control authority to decide whether an enterprise has a dominant position of market power or not.

The definition of "enterprises" was an important element, as it includes all the separate parts of TNCs and covers all undertakings "engaged in commercial activities", "irrespective of the mode of creation or control or ownership, private or State" (Section B, para 3). In addition to the provisions dealing with general principles under (ii) "Preferential or differential treatment for developing countries", Section C contains certain "General principles" calling for action by

States in a "mutually reinforcing manner" to control RBPs affecting international trade, and this includes in particular collaboration between governments at bilateral and multilateral levels; exchange and dissemination of information at the international level and the holding of multilateral consultations with regard to policy issues.

Where national legislation goes beyond the Set in proscribing the use of anti-competitive practices, the former prevails (Section C, para 5). This provision recognizes that the Set may in certain respects represent minimum standards, and aims at ensuring that it will not limit more strict prohibitions which may be adopted in domestic laws.

2.   *Provisions addressed to enterprises*

In its scope of application the Set covers all transactions in goods and services which adversely affect international trade, particularly that of developing countries and their economic development (Section B, para 5). However, as stated in the Set, neither applies to intergovernmental agreements (such as, for example, international commodity agreements) nor covers RBPs directly caused by such agreements (Section B, para 9).[18]

Section D, makes enterprises (including TNCs) operating in a country subject to the laws and "competence of the courts and relevant administrative bodies" of that country. Enterprises are enjoined to consult and cooperate with RBP control authorities of the country in which they operate and to supply information sought by competition authorities. If the information is located in another country, enterprises should provide the information to the extent that "such production or disclosure is not prevented by applicable law or established public policy" (para. 2). If the production or disclosure of information sought is prohibited by the foreign country where it is held, then the authorities of the country seeking the information can request consultations with the authorities of that country (Section F, para. 4).

The core provisions of the Set (Section D, paras. 3 and 4) enlist the main actionable anti-competitive practices or RBPs. The first provision concerns horizontal agreements or arrangements between enterprises "engaged in the market in rival or potentially rival activities". The second concerns practices engaged in by enterprises in "an abuse or acquisition and abuse of a dominant position of market

---

[18] This provision was adopted to ensure that commodity agreements arranged among sovereign states, such as OPEC, would not be covered by the prohibitions contained in the UN Set. In fact, this paragraph was later evoked by developed countries to justify voluntary export restraints (VERs) covered by their Government's policy.

power". Both provisions contain a prohibition "in principle" of the practices described. Paragraph 3, for example, calls for enterprises to refrain from the practices listed below when "they limit access to markets or otherwise unduly restrain competition". The term "unduly" implies that the rule of reason should be applied in deciding whether the practice in question should be prohibited. Without the qualification "unduly", the practices listed would have been prohibited outright or per se. Paragraph 4 of Section D also covers vertical restraints of enterprises in a dominant position of market power (i.e. restrictive practices of enterprises in a dominant position of market power over other enterprises at a different level of the production-distribution chain). Particularly worth mentioning is paragraph 4 (e), which provides for the control of abusive use of trademark rights to prevent parallel imports. Given the importance of the issue of restricted parallel imports in international trade as a means of exclusion of competitors, this provision of the Set has a considerable significance.

(a) *Provisions addressed to States*

The provisions calling for action by States at national, regional and sub-regional levels (Section E) are essential, as seen earlier, for effectively controlling anti-competitive practices "affecting international trade, particularly the trade and development of developing countries", while one of the prerequisites for dealing with such practices is the establishment of domestic legislation and control authority (Section E, para. 1). The Set does not establish a uniform pattern for such legislation. To help countries in adopting, improving and effectively enforcing appropriate legislation, continued work is called for "within UNCTAD on the elaboration of a model law or laws" (Section F, para. 5). It is thus agreed that national RBP legislation may vary according to each country's juridical system, stage of development and other considerations.

Among the provisions in Section E (calling for collaboration among States in the exchange of information and experience in the control of RBPs), the comity principle calls for countries to "seek appropriate remedial or preventive measures to prevent and/or control the use of restrictive business practices within their competence when it comes to the attention of States that such practices adversely affect international trade, and particularly, the trade and development of the developing countries" (Section E, para. 4).

(b) *Measures at the international level*

Section F refers to measures to be taken at the multilateral level, and particularly at UNCTAD. It provides for consultation procedures (Section F, para.

4), "in regard to an issue concerning control of restrictive business practices". Another important position concerns the "implementation within or facilitation by UNCTAD, and other relevant organizations of the UN system in conjunction with UNCTAD, of technical assistance, advisory and training programmes on restrictive business practices, particularly for developing countries" (Section F, para. 6).

3. Institutional machinery and review procedure

The Set establishes the IGE to provide the institutional machinery (Section G). Its functions were further described in detail in paragraph 3 (ii), mainly to provide a forum and modalities for multilateral consultations, discussion and exchange of views between States on matters related to the Set, in particular its operation and the experience arising therefrom, and to undertake and disseminate relevant studies and research. As mentioned earlier, a review procedure is envisaged in paragraph 6 (ii) of Section G, subject to the approval of the General Assembly, five years after the adoption of the Set.

References

Brusick P (1983). UN Control of Restrictive Business Practices: A Decisive First Step. *Journal of World Trade Law*, 17: 4: 337–351.

GATT (1960). Restrictive Business Practices: Arrangements for Consultations – Decision of 18 November. BISD 9S/28.

Graz J-C (1999). *Aux sources de l'OMC: La Charte de La Havane 1941–1950.* Geneva: Droz S.A.

UNCTAD (1968). Resolution 25(II). 78th plenary meeting, 27 March, Geneva. In: *Proceeding of the United Nations Conference on Trade and Development,* Vol. I: Final Act and Report. TD/97.

_____ (1978) Dominant positions of market power of transnational corporations: Use of the transfer pricing mechanism. TD/B/C.2/167.

_____ (1981). Marketing and distribution arrangements in respect of export and import transactions: Structure of international trading channels. UNCTAD/ST/MD/25, Geneva.

_____ (1984). Elements for provisions of a model law on restrictive business practices. TD/B/RBP/15/Rev.1/Corr.1, Geneva.

_____ (1987). Restrictive Business Practices Information. Issue 13, November TD/RBP/INF.19, Geneva.

_____ (1995a). The role of competition policy in economic reforms in developing and other countries. TD/RBP/CONF.4/2, 26 May.

_____ (1995b). Restrictive business practices that have an effect in more than one country, in particular developing and other countries, with overall conclusions regarding the issues raised by these cases. TD/RBP/CONF.4/6, 4 September.

_____ (1996). The scope, coverage and enforcement of competition laws and policies and analysis of the provisions of the Uruguay Round Agreements relevant to competition policy, including their implications for developing and other countries, Study by the UNCTAD secretariat. TD/B/COM.2/EM/2, Geneva.

_____ (1997). Competition and Public Utility Industries. UNCTAD/ITCD/CLP/Misc.1, Geneva.

_____ (1999). Competition Policy and Vertical Restraints, Note by the UNCTAD secretariat. UNCTAD/ITCD/CLP/Misc.8, Geneva.

_____ (2000a). Bangkok Declaration. TD/387.

_____ (2000b). Resolution of the Fourth UN Conference to Review all Aspects of the Set. In TD/RBP/CONF.5/15, Geneva.

_____ (2002a). Analysis of Market Access Issues Facing Developing Countries: Consumer Interests, Competitiveness, Competition and Development. TD/B/COM.1/L.23, Geneva.

_____ (2002b). Experiences Gained so far on International Cooperation on Competition Policy Issues and Mechanisms Used. TD/B/COM.2/CLP/21/Rev.1, Geneva.

_____ (2003). Roles of Possible Dispute Mediation Mechanisms and Alternative Arrangements, Including Voluntary Peer Reviews, in Competition Law and Policy. TD/B/COM.2/CLP/37, Geneva.

Least Developed, Landlocked and Island Developing Countries

Lev Komlev and Pierre Encontre[*]

Introduction

In his early efforts to advocate a global reform of international economic relations, Raúl Prebisch, the first Secretary-General of UNCTAD and a founder of the structuralist school of the peripheral economy, urged the international community in his report to UNCTAD I (Geneva, 1964) to recognize "differences between developing countries" in applying international support measures. He suggested, *inter alia*, that "countries at the earliest stage of economic development" should receive more preferential treatment in trade and in the allocation of international financial resources than other developing countries. He also proposed "to set special targets for national and international policy in relation to the least developed countries as well as the adoption of special measures to achieve these targets" (UN, 1964: 40 ,62) This vision was reflected in the Final Act of the first session of the Conference in 1964. It has since been a constant source of inspiration for the analytical work of the UNCTAD secretariat and in UNCTAD's advocacy for a special and differential treatment of various developing countries, in accordance with their level of development.

UNCTAD II (New Delhi, 1968) adopted resolution 24(II) "special measures to be taken in favour of the least developed among developing countries aimed at expanding their trade and improving their economic and social development". This resolution recognized "the differing characteristics and stages of development of developing countries" and requested the Secretary-General of UNCTAD to identify the least developed countries (LDCs), to review their problems and

[*] Lev Komlev is a Senior Economic Affairs Officer and Pierre Encontre is an Economic Affairs Officer in the Special Programme for the Least Developed, Land-locked and Island Developing Countries. Habib Ouane, Head of the Special Programme, undertook a detailed review of the text. Substantive comments at various stages of its preparation were received from Mussie Delelegn, Charles Gore, Ivanka Hoppenbrouwer, Shigehisa Kasahara, Massi Malmberg, Marcel Namfua and Madasamyraja Rajalingam. Stefanie West provided effective linguistic and secretarial support.

specific needs and to indicate what special measures ought to be taken in their favour.

The early debate on LDCs brought representatives from land-locked developing countries (LLDCs) to call for specific measures in their favour in order to alleviate their specific geographical handicaps. As a result, UNCTAD I adopted the Principles Relating to Transit Trade of Land-locked Countries. On the basis of these principles the United Nations Conference on Transit of Land-locked Countries adopted, in 1965, the Convention on Transit Trade of Land-locked States which entered into force in July 1967. Research work on LLDCs by the UNCTAD secretariat facilitated the adoption of UNCTAD II resolution 11(II) on the "special problems of the land-locked countries". The resolution recognized, *inter alia*, the problems faced by LLDCs in making trade an engine of economic development, in particular because of the high transport costs land-locked status entails. The Secretary-General of UNCTAD was requested to carry out a comprehensive analysis of these problems and a special study of relevant transport issues.

In turn, island developing countries (IDCs) raised their own problems at UNCTAD III (Santiago, 1972), which in resolution 65(III) recognized the particular difficulties faced by these countries as a result of their geographical disadvantages and ensuing distances from major markets, and requested the Secretary-General of UNCTAD to study their particular problems.

Through the work of the successive entities within the secretariat[1] UNCTAD has laid the foundation for identifying LDCs in light of relevant criteria and has analysed the development needs along with the national efforts of these countries and has advocated a range of international support measures for them. This work provided key inputs to three decennial programmes of action for LDCs which were adopted by the first (Paris, 1981), second (Paris, 1990) and third (Brussels, 2001) United Nations Conferences on the Least Developed Countries (UNLDC I, II, III). UNCTAD, through its work on LLDCs, was also instrumental in bringing to fruition the Global Framework for Transit Transport Cooperation between Land-locked and Transit Developing Countries and the Donor Community (1995) as well as the first international programme of action for

---

[1] UNCTAD's research and analysis work on the above-mentioned three groups of developing countries has been pursued by a special entity within the UNCTAD secretariat: first by a section of the former Research Division (late 1960s); then by the Special Programme for Least Developed, Land-locked and Island Developing Countries (1977-1992) which became the Division for Least Developed, Land-locked and Island developing countries (1992-1996), then by the Office of the Special Coordinator for Least Developed, Land-locked and Island Developing Countries (1996-2001) and finally, by the Special Programme on the Least Developed Countries, Landlocked and Island Developing Countries (2001 to present).

LLDCs (2003). Pioneering research on the particular problems and needs of IDCs gained momentum in 1994 when the United Nations (UN) adopted the programme of action for Sustainable Development of Small Island Developing States. Since its adoption, UNCTAD's work has increasingly been focusing on sustainable development among IDCs. Other agencies and programmes within the UN system as well as countries belonging to the above-mentioned three special categories and their development partners have used the results of the secretariat's research. This paper contains a presentation of the three categories of developing countries, each of which being the subject of specific thematic discussions.

I.   The Least Developed Countries

Since the denomination of LDCs was established UNCTAD has worked towards developing the conceptual, methodological and statistical frameworks to identify them. UNCTAD has also pursued a range of activities in support of national development policies in LDCs and international support measures for these countries.

A.   Contribution to the Methodology for Identifying the LDCs

In pursuance of Conference resolution 24(II), the UNCTAD secretariat prepared a report entitled *Identification of the least developed among the developing countries* (UNCTAD, 1969a), which proposed to determine the list of LDCs by ranking developing countries according to their per capita GDP and a composite index of development based on six socio-economic indicators: (i) per capita GDP at factor costs expressed in current US dollars; (ii) the percentage of manufacturing in GDP; (iii) percentage of manufactured products in total exports; (iv) per capita consumption of energy; (v) the number of medical doctors per 100,000 inhabitants; and (vi) the combined primary and secondary school enrolment ratio. The report proposed a list of the 30 LDCs situated at the bottom of the development spectrum in light of the GDP per capita as well as a composite index calculated for the year 1965 or the nearest year for which data was available (UNCTAD, 1969a: paras. 45–54).

The Committee for Development Planning (CDP) of the Economic and Social Council (ECOSOC) at its seventh session in 1971 regarded the composite index of the UNCTAD secretariat as an "interesting experimentation" but considered the construction of this index as "technically complicated and very difficult" in the absence of sufficient relevant data. The CDP accepted an alternative three-indicator proposal by the secretariat along with thresholds for inclusion into the list of LDCs: (i) per capita GDP of less than US $100 (1965); (ii) a share of manufacturing under 10 per cent of GDP; and (3) an adult literacy rate under 20 per cent. The CDP also considered that certain borderline cases should be considered eligible for inclusion in this classification (UNCTAD, 1969a: para. 60). On the basis of the agreed indicators and as suggested by the CDP, the UN General Assembly bestowed LDC status on 42 developing countries between 1971 and 1990.

A 1972 progress report by the Secretary-General of UNCTAD about the identification criteria presented some methodological and statistical suggestions such as selecting indicators that better reflected the structural characteristics of LDCs, using "dynamic indicators reflecting development potential" and "combining a number of separate indicators into a single composite indicator" (UNCTAD, 1972c: paras. 24, 25). A critical analysis of indicators and flexibility of their application for the identification of LDCs during the 1970s and beginning of the 1980s was developed in a book written by two ex-UNCTAD staff members (Weiss and Jennings, 1983: 2–19). Another book, written by an UNCTAD consultant, included a clear formulation of various common characteristics for identifying LDCs (Sottas, 1985: 4–8). These findings gave the CDP clear messages on the need to review the methodology for identifying LDCs.

In January, 1991 the Secretary-General of UNCTAD convened a meeting of experts to help the CDP for which the secretariat prepared a number of proposals for improving the methodology, including various indicators that would better capture the fundamental characteristics of LDCs. Among UNCTAD's proposals were the periodicity of the review of the list of LDCs and a mechanism for graduation from that status, with a smooth transition for graduating countries (UNCTAD, 1991). Subsequently the CDP adopted, in 1991, a new set of criteria and indicators as well as a new methodological framework with inclusion and graduation rules for the triennial review of the list of LDCs. On this basis five countries were added to the UN list of LDCs in 1991 while two others were added in 1994, the year in which Botswana graduated from LDC status. The secretariat analysed the implications of the enlarged list of LDCs in light of the aid targets that had been established in the second programme of action (1991) for LDCs and with regard to debt relief and trade concessions.[2]

---

[2] It was shown in the UNCTAD Secretary-General's Report to UNCTAD VIII (Cartagena, 1992) that the increase in the external capital requirements of LDCs, with the five new countries prior to that time, was about 18 per cent (UNCTAD, 1992a, para. 40).

Throughout the 1990s the secretariat provided qualitative and quantitative inputs to the work of the CDP regarding the methodology for reviewing the list of LDCs. In particular, UNCTAD was instrumental in persuading the CDP (renamed the "Committee for Development Policy" in 1999 while retaining the same abbreviation) and relevant intergovernmental bodies that a criterion of economic vulnerability should be introduced in the methodology for identifying LDCs. An Economic Vulnerability Index (EVI) was developed by the CDP for the 2000 review of the list. At the request of the CDP and to cast light on the situation of countries that were near inclusion or graduation thresholds, the secretariat prepared vulnerability profiles of Senegal (inclusion case) along with Cape Verde, Maldives, Samoa and Vanuatu (potential graduation cases). In the graduation cases these profiles helped the CDP understand that an immediate graduation of these countries could harm them in their development process as they were not structurally prepared to pursue their socio-economic progress without the maximum concessionary treatment their LDC status had conferred on them.

Although the CDP did not accept all suggestions made by UNCTAD on the methodological process of reviewing the list of LDCs, it had done so in most cases. In fact, many of the indicators UNCTAD proposed were used in the construction of the Augmented Physical Quality of Life Index (APQLI) and of the Economic Diversification Index (EDI), the first two composite indices introduced by the CDP in 1991, the time of the first major reformulation of the criteria. For example, two of the five indicators entering the composition of the EVI were calculated by the UNCTAD secretariat (share of modern economic activities in GDP and merchandise export concentration).

Since 2002 the UNCTAD secretariat has been advocating a reform of the graduation rule with a view that not only two but all three graduation criteria ought to be met for an LDC to be deemed able to exit the LDC category so that no country with a poor score under any criteria, i.e. the income criterion (per capita GNP), the human development criterion (Human Assets Index) or the economic structure criterion (EVI) is found eligible for graduation (UNCTAD, 2002a: 8, 12).

B. Analytical Activities in Support of National Development Policies

The capacity to formulate and implement national development policies for socio-economic transformation has always been a central need for LDCs, to which the UNCTAD secretariat has paid considerable attention. It has done so in the light of the experience of LDCs in three consecutive policy eras: first, during the early years of UNCTAD when national planning was a critical tool in economic management; second, in the context of stabilization and structural adjustment programmes (SAPs); and third, more recently, in the framework of the Poverty Reduction Strategy Paper (PRSP) process.

1. *Macroeconomic policy framework*

From the late 1960s to the beginning of the 1980s the UNCTAD secretariat made numerous recommendations to create and strengthen, with international support, the institutional capacities that were considered vital for the development of LDCs and to improve government efficiency in economic management. These proposals dealt with policy-making, national planning, mobilization of domestic resources (broadening and deepening of the tax base, rationalization of customs, etc.), export promotion, import procurement, technology transfers as well as banking and financial services. For instance, national planning was featured as a key condition for effectively implementing the Substantial New Programme of Action (SNPA) for the 1980s for LDCs at the national level.

Throughout the 1980s many LDCs undertook macroeconomic stabilization policies, via SAPs, most of which were launched with support from the International Monetary Fund (IMF) and the World Bank in response to a growing debt burden and other structural difficulties. Meanwhile the development planning was abandoned in many LDCs and public spending and investment were curtailed. While drawing the attention of policy-makers in LDCs to the risks involved in an excessive reliance on these approaches, UNCTAD continued to reiterate the importance of national institutional capacity building to enable LDCs governments to design and implement broad-based macro-economic policies (*LDCR 1989*) so as to enhance their productive capacities and human capital.

In light of the Programme of Action for LDCs for the 1990s, which had tried to reconcile stabilization policies and the long-run development objectives of LDCs, the UNCTAD secretariat's analysis highlighted the importance of macro-economic stability and the structural transformation for poverty reduction. Particular attention was given to the relationship between the objectives of macro-economic stabilization and economic diversification.

Responding to the increasing challenge of trade liberalization for LDCs, the secretariat observed how globalization intensified competition in international trade and took the view that beyond stabilisation, enhancing productive capacity in LDCs is an essential prerequisite for their development. Accordingly, UNCTAD anticipated that the focus of economic policy would shift further away from direct government intervention in markets and participation in production and trade towards the creation of an enabling environment for private entrepreneurship, with special emphasis on strengthening supply capacities, so as to enable LDCs to compete on global markets.

Globalization forces were greatly accelerated by the conclusion of the Uruguay Round in 1994 and the subsequent establishment of the World Trade Organization (WTO) in 1995. The new multilateral trading system recognized the particular situation of LDCs and maintained some scope for autonomous policy choices at the national level in these countries. However, the new multilateral trading framework has also increased the demands placed upon LDCs. UNCTAD has consistently highlighted the importance of institutional capacity building as a priority area. It has also helped in identifying LDCs' trade and development interests in the multilateral trading system, including through the establishment of an appropriate national consultative mechanism that takes into account the interests of all stakeholders within LDCs affected by various WTO agreements and disciplines in order to arrive at a broad-based national position for each LDC (*LDCR 1998*).

The widespread concern with poor economic performances in LDCs in the 1990s paved the way for rethinking the SAPs in LDCs. This resulted in the concept of the Poverty Reduction Strategy Paper (PRSP), which was introduced in 1999 by the Bretton Woods Institutions (BWIs) as a new framework for the economic policies in low-income countries supported by concessional assistance from donors. More than 30 LDCs are currently involved in various stages of the PRSP process.

Bearing this in mind, the UNCTAD secretariat analysed the current stage of the design of the PRSP and in comparing it with the SAPs identified serious design shortcomings in the context of LDC-type economies, formulating a set of proposals for its substantive improvement. The analysis showed that the design of the PRSP was founded on the hypothesis that SAPs were not working because they were not nationally owned and therefore were not property implemented. Another problem was the expectation that sustained poverty reduction is possible through the integration of a pro-poor public expenditure pattern with existing macroeconomic policies and structural reforms. In fact the analysis identified that past SAPs, even when well implemented, have not delivered growth rates sufficient to make significant impact on poverty reduction in most LDCs (*LDCR 2002*).

UNCTAD's analysis presented in the *LDCR 2002* made it evident that the SAPs in LDCs were not effective in generating economic growth and structural transformation. They not only failed to generate substantial increases in investments in LDCs and develop their potential comparative advantages in non-traditional agriculture, agro-processing and industry, but more seriously they induced "de-industrialization" in some of these countries. The new edition of the SAPs, in the form of PRSPs, could not substantively change the situation, e.g., accelerate economic growth rates and the pace of structural transformation. Such a change presupposes a reorientation of the overall national economic policy framework, with emphasis on human resource development and restructuring of the institutional, managerial and production systems so as to enhance and diversify productive capacities and improve competitiveness of LDCs. In this connection the *Report* suggested four general policy orientations, common to all LDCs implementing PRSPs, i.e. (1) the central importance of promoting rapid and sustained economic growth; (2) the establishment of a dynamic investment-export nexus; (3) the elaboration of productive development policy options; and (4) the adoption of policies to prevent marginalization of social groups and regions (*LDCR 2002*).

These orientations are consistent with the Programme of Action for LDCs for the 2001–2010. In fact they promote a development paradigm in which economic growth and development are prerequisites for the reduction of poverty (UNCTAD, 2001a) and rely on building productive capacities which are paramount for making globalization work for LDCs (UNCTAD, 2001a, paras. 42–64). This paradigm also emphasizes the need for development partners to align behind national PRSPs. Without simultaneous support from the donors and without an effort on their part to coordinate the aid planning and delivery process and target key development priorities with their aid, efforts by LDCs themselves to accelerate development through enhanced national ownership will necessarily be limited.

2. *Productive capacities and competitiveness*

During the late 1960s and 1970s the UNCTAD secretariat made substantial contributions to the assessment of productive capacities and competitiveness in LDCs, the identification of development objectives in relation to these issues and the formulation of relevant national policies. Diversification in the area of commodities received particular attention while the strengthening of the overall infrastructure for supply capacities has always been advocated as a paramount condition for enabling LDCs to integrate better with the rest of the global economy (UNCTAD, 1969b; 1971a).

Throughout the following decades the secretariat undertook various studies on issues concerning agriculture, mining and manufacturing in LDCs. In the area of agriculture, food security problems and the need to widen the export base led the secretariat to undertake more research, particularly regarding the link between agricultural development and poverty reduction in LDCs. Particular emphasis was placed on why LDC governments should give priority to the agricultural sector.[3] The causes of agricultural stagnation in LDCs were also studied.[4]

On the basis of these analyses the secretariat formulated long-term agricultural strategies together with priority actions (*LDCR 1995:* 46–47; *1997:* 45–47; *1999:* 141–142). The priorities identified included: (i) focusing on high potential areas to create the infrastructure and policy environment that would stimulate growth in productivity and increased output in commodities where most LDCs have a comparative advantage; (ii) strengthening LDCs' capabilities for technology generation and dissemination; (iii) preventing further environmental degradation; (iv) enhancing efficiency of food security systems; (v) improving agricultural statistics and food information systems; and (vi) sound policies related to domestic price stabilization schemes and international compensatory financing. UNCTAD also made policy proposals on the national mining policies of LDCs focusing both on large-scale, capital-intensive mining operations and on small-scale, artisanal mining activities (*LDCR 1995:* 46–47; *1999:* 143–148.).

Most LDCs have remained at the early stage of industrialization and many have experienced a prolonged stagnation or decline in their manufacturing output. These circumstances led the UNCTAD secretariat to study the constraints on manufacturing development in LDCs. Explaining why the SAPs have not induced more meaningful results in industrial "re-specialization", the secretariat has stressed the importance of integrating the manufacturing sector with the available domestic natural resources through the vertical diversification of agriculture, the promotion of small-sized industries, the development of export markets niche and the possible use of transnational corporations from developed and developing countries for industrial promotion in LDCs (UNCTAD, 1983b: 195–196; *1987:*

---

[3] Three main reasons were identified. First, enhancing agricultural growth increases the income of the rural population (70 per cent of LDC populations) and thus, contributes to poverty reduction and qualitative improvements in rural life. Second, increased rural incomes expand domestic markets; and Third, a dynamic agricultural sector provides the basis for agro-processing industrialization and can enhance employment opportunities. (*LDCR 1995*).

[4] Among these causes were: (a) historical factors, such as traditional production relations, rudimentary technology and the modes of access to and ownership of land; (b) government policies harmful to agricultural development, e.g. over-taxation of agricultural exports, over-valued national currencies, high level to domestic manufacturing protection, inadequate public investment in rural infrastructure; and (c) weak financial intermediation and institutional support (*LDCR 1997:* 45-47; *1999:* 141-142).

43–45; *1988:* 50–57; *1989:*. 21–30). Some of the secretariat's proposals were included in the Programme of Action for LDCs for the 1990s.

Continued stagnation in manufacturing outputs in most LDCs during the 1990s roused UNCTAD to address the constraints of manufacturing development in LDCs: structural deficiencies, market failures and limitations, paucity of endowments and inadequate policies. This analysis, presented in *The LDCR 1995*, enabled the secretariat to make policy proposals on removing the constraints on manufacturing development in LDCs in the context of globalization. The proposals included selective national interventions and specific international support measures. In the view of the secretariat, proposed national efforts should be oriented at correcting market failures and expansion, removing policy constraints in macroeconomic framework and governance along with resolving structural and endowment related constraints. International support measures for LDCs should focus on an increased external concessional financing, promotion of FDI flows, technological support as well as market access to their industrial products (Ibid *1995:* 49–69).

The secretariat has also advocated generally a simultaneous development of agricultural and manufacturing activities, including those in the informal sector of LDCs, by replicating good practices in industrial clustering rather than in individual productive sectors.[5] The focus of the analysis has been on cluster competitiveness and efficiency, particularly with regard to the dual objective of reducing transaction costs and promoting niche markets.

The development of international trade in services was also recognized by UNCTAD as an important avenue for competitive economic specialization and a possible opportunity for socio-economic prosperity. Particular emphasis was placed on tourism development in LDCs in 2001, and this was instrumental in ensuring a distinct section on the critical role of "sustainable tourism for development" in the Brussels Programme of Action for LDCs for 2001–2010 (UNCTAD, 2001a, paras. 152–155). It must be borne in mind that an important aspect of the development and poverty-reduction impact of tourism has been illustrated by the determining influence of tourism growth in the recent socio-economic progress of four LDCs (Cape Verde, Maldives, Samoa, and Vanuatu) toward eventual graduation from LDC status.

---

[5] Examples of Brazil, China and Pakistan experiences were discussed in *LDCR 1995:* 149 and 152.

3. Human resource development

The UNCTAD secretariat takes the view that development entails investing in people and that people, if strengthened in their health and skills, can in turn contribute to productivity, economic growth, structural transformation, competitiveness, and poverty reduction. Over the years the secretariat has provided LDC governments with numerous recommendations to protect health and education expenditures from the consequences of budget stringency in order to make the educational curricula and vocational training programmes consistent with the need for qualified human resources and skills (*LDCR 1999:*. 125–126). These recommendations on human capacity development substantially contributed to the formulation of the national and international commitments in the Programme of Action for LDCs for 2001–2010 (UNCTAD, 2001, paras. 30–41); they also subsequently contributed significantly to the proposed indicators for monitoring the human capacity development goals of LDCs (*LDCR 2002:* 22–23).

C. Analytical Activities regarding International Support Measures

UNCTAD has upheld the view that the limited capacities of LDCs domestically to mobilize and use financial resources has made international support measures the *sine qua non* for achieving any progress in sparing these countries further marginalization from the global economy. The continuous plea for international support measures for LDCs is consistent with UNCTAD's advocacy of special and differential treatment as a response to the intrinsic disadvantages of LDCs and the risk of their increased marginalization.

1. Development financing

FDI flows to LDCs in general have increased, but a large share of the increase has been concentrated in a few countries. Most LDCs have historically relied on official development assistance (ODA) as the main source of development financing. UNCTAD has always taken the view that ODA will continue to play a key role in enabling LDCs to extricate themselves from the poverty trap and has paid particular attention to ODA in its analytical work.

From the late 1960s to the beginning of the 1980s the UNCTAD secretariat has extensively analysed the need for external resources in LDCs. These analytical efforts highlighted: (i) the required volume of external resources for these countries;[6] (ii) the paramount importance of ODA as the main source of long-term capital flows into LDCs; (iii) the link between financial support and technical assistance geared to respond to individual LDC circumstances; (iv) the need for flexible criteria to assess the efficiency and profitability of projects;[7] and (v) the terms and sources of assistance. The secretariat recommended providing LDCs with wide access to international financial aid on concessional terms, with special emphasis on grants, as they represent the core of the International Development Association (IDA) countries. It also proposed envisaging the establishment of a link between the creation of international reserve assets and development assistance, or earmarking appropriate types of tax and tariff receipts in the developed countries for financing programmes in LDCs. Moreover, the secretariat has encouraged donors to provide long-term assurances (predictability) about future flows of financial resources and guarantee the quality of technical assistance. It also urged donors to coordinate their allocations of ODA to LDCs in order to allow for maximum effectiveness in the use of aid (UNCTAD, 1972a, paras. 55–59).

The report of the Secretary-General of UNCTAD to UNLDC I in 1981 made a number of proposals on development financing for LDCs (UNCTAD, 1983a). It proposed establishing targets for official development assistance for LDCs: 0.15 per cent of the donors' GNP by the first half of the 1980s, rising to 0.20 per cent during the second half of the 1980s. The report also recommended that an increase in the shares of total concessionary financing be allocated to LDCs, and proposed new mechanisms for increasing financial transfers to these countries. New aid modalities that would be specially suited to the particular needs of LDCs were called for: more non-project assistance, increased aid coordination among donors and LDC recipients, etc. Several of the proposals made in the report were approved by the 1981 Conference and were reflected in the SNPA.

The decade of the 1980s was marked by a slower increase in ODA. The average ODA-to-donor GNP ratio over the decade was 0.09 per cent instead of the

[6] The needs in external resources were estimated on the basis of the target rate of GDP growth and domestic saving and external trade gaps. Their volume and timing should be ascertained on the basis of national development plans and correlated with absorptive capacities of individual LDCs (UNCTAD, 1969b, paras. 36-40). For the first part of the 1970s the annual assistance flows to LDCs should be doubled and by the end of the 1970s should be increased up to five times (UNCTAD, 1972a, para. 54).
[7] The traditional rate of return criteria was considered inadequate to the socio-economic situation of LDCs. Financial aid should cover the local cost of projects in these countries (UNCTAD, 1969b, para. 10).

targeted 0.15 per cent,[8] while private flows due to a growing concern of debt underwent a dramatic fall (*LDCR 1989*: 108).[9] The composition of ODA changed, with an evolution from project-related aid to programme aid and policy-based assistance. The UNCTAD secretariat analysed the shortcomings of this evolution and recommended that structural adjustment assistance to LDCs be provided in sufficient volume, on a sufficiently long-term basis and under the terms and conditions that can be met by these countries (*LDCR 1990:* 102–111).

The slowdown trend in ODA flows in the second part of the 1980s, and the increasing understanding of the reasons for this slowdown, did not give grounds for optimistic expectations about substantive aid increase in the 1990s. However in order to stimulate ODA growth, UNCTAD recommended a differentiated increase of aid volume target for each group of donors in accordance with their previous achievements. This recommendation was accepted by UNLDC II and reflected in the Programme of Action for LDCs for the 1990s. The following ODA commitments were accordingly adopted:

- Donor countries providing more than 0.20 per cent of their GNP as ODA to LDCs continue to do so and increase their efforts;
- Other donor countries which have met the 0.15 per cent target undertake reaching 0.20 per cent by the year 2000;
- Other donor countries which have committed themselves to the 0.15 per cent target reaffirm their commitment and undertake either to achieve the target within the next five years or to make their best efforts to accelerate their endeavours to reach the target; and
- Other donor countries exercise individual best efforts to increase their ODA to LDCs with the effect that, collectively, their assistance to LDCs will significantly increase (UNCTAD, 1992b, para 23).

Contrary to the commitments reflected in the Programme of Action for LDCs, both the quantity and quality of development financing to LDCs deteriorated in the 1990s. Net ODA disbursements to LDCs in real per capita terms declined by 46 per cent over the decade, and the ODA/GNP ratio decreased to a record low of 0.05 per cent and remained at this level. Moreover, an increasing

---

[8] Over the 1980s, the ODA/GNP ratios of donors were: 0.02-0.05 per cent (the United States); 0.05-0.07 per cent (Japan); 0.08-0.14 per cent (the United Kingdom and West Germany); around 0.15 per cent (France and Italy) and about 20 per cent and more (Norway, Denmark, Sweden, the Netherlands, and Finland) (*LDCR 1991; 1992*, annex, table 19, A-29).
[9] Facing a growing indebtedness, an increased number of LDCs adopted a policy of refraining from non-commercial borrowing; *LDCR 1989; 1990.* 108.

share of total ODA flows were devoted to social infrastructure and services as well as debt reduction scheme and emergency assistance (*LDCR 2002*: 215, 268).

The UNCTAD secretariat, referring to this precarious situation, argued that the SAPs had undermined aid effectiveness and that in extreme cases the erosion observed in the quality and quantity of vital public services unravelled social cohesion in relevant countries (*LDCR 2000*: 185). It has recommended that aid delivery to LDCs be improved, in particular through a greater involvement of government and civil society organisations in the preparation and implementation of economic policies and poverty reduction strategies (Ibid.: 202). These proposals and the secretariat's estimates of aid requirements in relation to the UN Millennium Development Goals constituted important inputs to the Programme of Action for LDCs for 2001–2010 which urged the donor community to implement the commitments made for the previous decade.

The secretariat showed that the previously mentioned PRSP process had the potential to increase aid effectiveness and underlined the need for several policy shifts to that end. The need to break the donor-driven aid/debt spiral in LDCs and untie aid to these countries is of particular importance. In the run-up to the UNLDC III (May 2001), the OECD finally agreed to take steps to untie ODA to LDCs. The secretariat also advocated the concentration of aid flows to LDCs in development areas of highest importance such as productive sectors and economic infrastructure (*LDCR 2002*: 217–223).

2. *Debt relief*

The debt problem in many LDCs has frustrated their efforts to achieve sustained economic development as debt service payments have reduced import capacities and drawn on resources that could have been used for public investment in human and physical capital in LDCs. During the 1970s UNCTAD highlighted the need for debt alleviation and proposed to start with writing off ODA debt to LDCs and extending new external financing on grant terms. TDB resolution 165 (S-IX, adopted in 1978) and SNPA (paras. 70–71) took these proposals into account. During the 1980s, the secretariat has maintained the view that debt relief measures have generally been insufficient to solve their debt overhang and called for a more effective international debt relief strategy (*LDCR 1989:* 113–120). Such a strategy should not only be comprehensive and integrated but coupled with an aid strategy. The secretariat has recommended possible elements of this strategy, including differentiation in the creditors' approach to debt reduction according to the individual requirements of relevant indebted countries.

The idea of an international debt strategy for LDCs was taken into account in the Programme of Action for LDCs in the 1990s. Later, the UNCTAD secretariat took the view that an agreement on a comprehensive strategy of debt reduction for LDCs "would be a major contribution towards improving their chances of economic progress" (*LDCR 1995:* 112).

In 1996, a debt relief strategy was initiated by the BWIs with the highly indebted poor countries (HIPC) initiative. In 1999 the HIPC initiative was revised so as to enhance its effectiveness. This initiative was targeted at "poor countries", but almost three quarters of the recognized HIPCs were LDCs. The UNCTAD secretariat analysed the strengths and weaknesses of the HIPC initiative.

While the Programme of Action for LDCs for 2001–2010 called for a "full, speedy, and effective implementation of the enhanced HIPC initiative...", (UNCTAD, 2001a, para. 86) the UNCTAD secretariat argued that the initiative was not designed to create the national and international conditions for sustained economic growth, the *sine qua non* for an LDC to rise above unsustainable indebtedness (*LDCR 2000* and *LDCR 2002*). Consequently it took the view that the international community should provide deeper, faster and broader debt relief based on lower thresholds of sustainability and more realistic forecasts of export earnings especially for primary commodity-dependent LDCs. Moreover, the analysis carried out on the "poverty trap" in the LDCs has identified unsustainable debt burden as one of the causes of this problem (*LDCR 2002*).

3. Trade policy

The UNCTAD secretariat's analytical work on the trade policy issues relevant to LDCs has mainly focused on market access, international commodity policies and supply capacities. Since the end of the Uruguay Round in 1994, issues relevant to the multilateral trading system have also been given prominent attention.

(a) Market access

During the late 1960s to 1980s analytical work of the secretariat resulted in the recommendation of the two groups of measures for inclusion in preferential schemes of preference-giving countries: (1) to extend the range of products of particular interest to LDCs in the framework of preferences granted to all developing countries; and (2) to grant LDCs special concessions not available for other preference-receiving developing countries, i.e. greater tariff reduction, exemption from the operation of safeguard measures, provision of more liberal treatment, with respect to rules of origin and removing tariff and non-tariff protectionism (UNCTAD, 1969b, paras. 24–32; 1972a, paras. 40–46; 1983a, paras. 430–464).

Over the period of 1981 to the mid 1990s the new economic environment, characterized by increasing liberalization and resulting from the SAPs and the Uruguay Round negotiations, influenced the market access *problématique* for LDCs. As a result of reforms under SAPs, LDCs increasingly adopted export-oriented strategies and thus became more dependent on preferential access to external markets. With the Generalized System of Preferences (GSP), preference-giving countries adopted special concessions for LDCs. However, the UNCTAD secretariat's analysis showed that the impact of the concessions on their exports was small and that its stimulus to their economic diversification was modest. The Global System of Trade Preferences among Developing Countries (GSTP), which also provides special treatment, only entered into force in 1989.

In 1994 the UNCTAD Special Committee on Preferences, at its twenty-first session, concluded that a priority task of the international community was to assist LDCs in maximizing the utilization of GSP schemes, improving the schemes by extending their product coverage, duty and quota-free treatment and more flexible rules of origin requirements in favour of LDCs. These improvements should be complemented by broader liberalization of non-tariff barriers affecting products of particular export interest to LDCs and by international support measures to increase the capacity of LDCs to design, produce and market products. The last suggestion was of particular importance, given the changes in the international trading system arising from the Uruguay Round Agreement whereby LDC exporters needed to compete more than before on the basis of economic factors such as productivity and quality of production rather than on the basis of special and more favourable treatment (*LDCR 1988:* 119–123; *1989:* 86–91; *1995:* 128–134).

Since the agreements of the Uruguay Round were concluded, particularly during the preparation of and soon after UNLDC III, a number of initiatives were adopted by the international community to improve market access for LDC products. The UNCTAD secretariat analysed the Quad group's initiatives: the European Union's (EU) "Everything But Arms" initiative (EBA); the United States' "African Growth and Opportunity Act" (AGOA); and the improvement in favour of LDCs in Canada's and Japan's preferential schemes. The analysis showed some substantive progress in these schemes and illustrated their positive effects on trade, investment, job creation and poverty reduction in some LDCs. However, the analysis pointed out that these schemes had not dismantled all duties and quotas on the products from LDCs and that further removal of trade restrictions could generate benefits for LDCs with competitive manufacturing capacities, especially in the area of textiles and apparel. The secretariat also identified the main factors that have hindered the effective utilization of market access preferences by LDCs: relative unpredictability of preferences; stringent and complicated rules of origin; various non-tariff barriers, especially product standards and sanitary and phytosanitary measures; cumbersome administrative procedures; and the lack of technical knowledge, human resources and institutional capacity to take advantage of preferential arrangements. Nevertheless, the ultimate constraint on realizing the benefits of trade preferences was weak productive and supply capabilities. In order to remedy this situation the secretariat recommended that beyond further improvements in preferential schemes adequate technical assistance should be provided to build the capacity required in LDCs, as well as increased aid flows to promote investment in productive sectors. These analyses, suggestions, proposals and recommendations were extensively documented (*LDCR 2002:* 22–23; UNCTAD, 2001b: XVII and 38 ; 2001c: 6–17; 2003b: 3–14).

Finally, through its technical assistance the secretariat provided intellectual support to LDCs in their pursuit of effective duty-free and quota-free treatment. This support helped LDCs prepare for multilateral trade negotiations (in particular, for the Seattle and Doha WTO Ministerial Conferences). In the ongoing Doha negotiation, the LDCs negotiating objectives include, *inter alia*, the following elements: (1) long term security and predictability of preferential market access for LDCs, ensured through a binding commitment on duty-free and quota-free treatment for all products from LDCs; (2) realistic, flexible and simplified rules of origin which take into account the productive capacity of LDCs, in order to increase their market share in world trade; (3) a moratorium on anti-dumping measures, safeguard measures and the imposition of other contingency measures on products from LDCs in order to ensure that duty-free and quota-free market access is not nullified by non-tariff measures; (4) restraint in applying TBT and SPS measures to products from LDCs; where such measures are necessary, comprehensive technical and financial assistance should be provided to LDCs for compliance with TBT and SBS requirements to expand exports from these countries; (5) establishing compensatory and other appropriate mechanisms to fully address the impact of erosion of preferences, including measures that promote exports of LDCs; and (6) providing targeted technical and financial assistance to LDCs to address supply-side constraints through enhancing and diversifying their productive capacities (WTO, 2003: 4–6). On this basis, LDCs submitted a number of proposals in the Doha negotiations related to the improvement of S&D treatment reflecting the above elements.

(b)   Commodities

From the late 1960s to 1980 research work mainly focused on the elaboration of the proposals related to special conditions for LDCs' participation in the international commodity agreements (ICAs), in the envisaged Common Fund for Commodities (CFC) as well as compensatory financing facilities for exports earning shortfalls in LDCs (UNCTAD, 1969b, paras. 11–23; 1972a, paras. 30–32; 1983a, paras. 430–464). These proposals were reflected in the commitments of SNPA adopted in 1981 (UNCTAD, 1983a, paras. 74–83).

From 1981 to the mid 1990s the secretariat recommended the exemption of small producers among LDCs from quota restrictions and from the obligation to share the financial costs in all price-stabilization ICAs and argued that priority should be given to commodities of interest to LDCs in the utilization of the second account of the CFC. Regarding compensatory financing, UNCTAD proposed a broadening of the EU compensatory financing facilities for African, Caribbean, and Pacific LDCs. When Compex, a new facility similar to Stabex was created, the secretariat suggested that the non-EU developed countries consider the possibility of setting up a similar institution (*LDCR 1985:* 244–245; *1987:* 81; *1989:* 91). These suggestions were reflected in the Programme of Action for LDCs for the 1990s and in the Mid-Term Global Review on the implementation of this programme (*LDCR 1996:* 109–113; *1986*).

Since the late 1990s the secretariat has undertaken continued revisions in its commodity policy proposals. In its analytical reports for the second part of the 1990s, attention was refocused on supporting capacity building, diversification programmes and taking advantage of niche markets. The Programme of Action for LDCs for 2001–2010 reflects those changes (UNCTAD, 2001c, paras. 68(t)–(bb). The secretariat also provided some ideas about a framework for action by primary commodity exporters and importers that would aim to enhance the potential of commodity production and exports for development and poverty reduction in LDCs.[10]

---

[10] This framework would address three issues complementary to WTO negotiations: (i) the availability in primary commodity producing countries of exportable products in sufficient volumes and quality; (ii) the need to enter supply chains for these products at points where high degrees of value added are generated; and (iii) the need to mitigate excessive instability in primary commodity prices and address the problem of a continual downward trend of these prices. It also highlighted the importance of cooperation among the three pillars of the international commodity policy (international organizations within the UN system, providers of bilateral assistance and NGO, and international commodity bodies, including the CFC) in dealing with these three issues. (*LDCR 2002:* 230-236).

The report also proposed to create high risk management instruments and urged the creation of appropriate compensatory financing facilities for LDCs, as well as mechanisms for voluntary supply management schemes, while stimulating the increasing consumption of commodities through generic promotion and new and innovative uses. It underlined the link between the ability of more advanced developing countries to move up the ladder of development and the chances for LDCs to expand commodity exports. Finally, it proposed that the WTO negotiations support the design and implementation of international commodity policy supportive of commodity promotion and the diversification efforts of LDCs (*LDCR 2002:* 230–236).

(c)   The Integrated Framework

The 1997 agreement on the Integrated Framework for Trade-Related Technical Assistance, including Human and Institutional Capacity-Building to Support Least Developed Countries in their Trade and Trade-Related Activities, was a response to the Uruguay Round decision on measures in favour of LDCs. The objective of the Integrated Framework (IF) was to maximize the benefits from trade-related technical assistance being provided by six core international agencies including UNCTAD.[11]

The secretariat provided a number of suggestions in *LDCR 2002* that could help enhance and improve the implementation of the IF. This analysis confirmed the importance of integrating trade into PRSPs through an examination of how trade can be better fitted into the strategies. It emphasized that the trade integration process should be seen in integration studies as a means to promote trade reforms in a way that supports development and poverty reduction rather than to strengthen the environment for trade liberalization as an end in itself. It also underscored the particular importance of the full respect of the principle of the national ownership in the trade integration studies for strengthening national ownership of PRSPs, as a whole. As envisaged in the report, "ideally, the trade integration studies will themselves be a process through which national capacities are strengthened" (*LDCR 2002*: 30).

The process of mainstreaming trade into national development and poverty reduction strategies involved the introduction of Diagnostic Trade Integration

---

[11] The IF was adopted by the High-Level Meeting on Integrated Initiatives for LDCs Trade and Development which was organized under the auspices of the WTO with the collaboration of International Trade Centre (ITC), IMF, UNCTAD, United Nations Development Programme (UNDP) and the World Bank in accordance with the Programme of Action to improve the export capacities of LDCs which had been adopted during the first WTO Ministerial Conference in December 1996.

Studies. The UNCTAD secretariat's contributions to them include the analysis of the linkages between trade and poverty, recommendations on trade facilitation, and the business environment. It also identified and recommended pre-DTIS activities which enhance LDCs capacities for IF ownership.[12]

(d)   LDCs and the multilateral trading system

The coming into force of the Uruguay Round Agreements and the establishment of the WTO motivated UNCTAD to discuss the impact of these changes on LDCs. The analysis was widely reflected in recent *LDC Reports* (*1995–1998*) which dealt, *inter alia*, with three issues. First, as for the potential of the agreements to accommodate LDCs' interests, the reports stated that the special and differential treatment provisions in favour of LDCs in various agreements would be of little value. With the exception of a few provisions in the Agreements of agriculture, subsidies, textiles and GATS they simply grant longer time periods for LDCs to undertake their obligations, e.g. sanitary and phytosanitary measures (SPS), trade-related investment measures (TRIMs) and trade-related aspects of intellectual property rights (TRIPS). The reports reviewed the agreements on agriculture, textiles, TRIMS, subsidies and anti-dumping, and identified those aspects that may have an adverse impact on LDCs. They, nevertheless, may derive significant benefits from basic improvements in the Agreements on dispute settlement, the balance of payments and others. The analysis also gave an impetus for taking into account LDCs' interests in discussions on new issues such as the environment, investment, competition policy and government procurement. Second, the UNCTAD secretariat considered that the need for quicker, more lenient and easier accession of LDCs to the WTO should be met with favourable terms and conditions of accession. Third, the need for international assistance aimed at improving LDCs' human and institutional capacities to cope with the agreements and demands of WTO membership was discussed. It was recommended that this assistance be directed at: (a) removing legislative, institutional, personnel and other obstacles that could frustrate LDCs' compliance with the Uruguay Round Agreements and participation in WTO activities; and (b) identifying new trading opportunities based on existing export facilities for LDCs,

---

[12] The activities could include providing institutional arrangements for the IF process and ensuring a functional link with PRSP committees or other similar bodies; IF sensitisation and awareness, including on trade and poverty reduction link, targeting policymakers (trade, finance, planning, agriculture, tourism, etc.), private sector, civil society and policy research institutions; human resource strengthening at national IF focal points, particularly at the Trade Ministry, to improve policy formulation, analysis, coordination and support for the IF process; and building partnerships with existing policy research institutions to secure greater involvement of nationals in carrying out the DTIS.

e.g. to increase the level of utilization of preferential market access schemes (*LDCR 1996*: 66–67; *1998:* 73–80).

The secretariat has always stressed that special and differential treatment measures are merely interim measures. The eventual challenge for LDCs posed by the multilateral trading system and WTO is the enhancement of their international competitiveness. The problems confronting LDCs in meeting such competitiveness goals are of a long-term structural nature and their resolution lies beyond the ambit of the WTO. Therefore, the secretariat has called for using available momentum and substantively strengthening the international support measures in all areas in favour of LDCs in order to transform them from relief tools into effective instruments needed to reduce supply-side constraints. Several of these measures, such as market access, made possible the creation of the IF as well as achieving progress in dealing with debt relief (enhanced HPIC), enjoying some degree of improvement during the end of the last and beginning of the current decade. These changes were analysed in the more recent UNCTAD documents and publications on LDCs (*LDCR 1999:*119–167; *2002*: 207–236).

4. *South–South cooperation*

Various proposals made by the UNCTAD secretariat in its analysis of South-South cooperation are based on the principle of non-reciprocity and the special and differential treatment approach. Some of these proposals have been incorporated into the objectives and strategies of different trading arrangements among developing countries (UNCTAD, 1969b, paras. 45–58; 1971, paras. 41–44; 1983a, para. 464).

At the inter-regional level the previously mentioned GSTP, which entered into force in 1989, provides LDCs (article 17) with more liberal rules of origin, a longer list of products eligible for preferences than the rules and lists applying to other signatories. At the regional level the African Economic Community (article 79) includes special provisions for LDCs. Sub-regional groupings (e.g. Economic Community of West African States (ECOWAS) and Common Market for Eastern and Southern Africa (COMESA), or the Bangkok Agreement) do not formally grant special provisions de jure to LDCs. Nevertheless, they agreed *de facto* on a differential approach to their member countries that means non-reciprocal special and differential treatment in favour of LDCs (UNCTAD, 1990a: 7).

LDCR 1996 included a study that identified the potential benefits, issues and possible concerns of regional trading arrangements (RTAs) for LDCs. Among the potential benefits it indicated: (i) larger regional markets for LDC firms; (ii) more attractiveness because of larger markets for both domestic investment and FDI; and (iii) enhanced access of LDC firms to technology, entrepreneurship and market information. Among the concerns it indicated: (i) the risk of de-industrialization and loss of employment for those LDCs whose firms cannot compete with the more industrially advanced members of RTAs; (ii) the risk that the location of new economic activities could skew in favour of the more advanced members of RTAs; and (iii) a possible loss of tariff revenue if regional tariff rates are reduced. Finally the report concluded that under the right conditions RTAs might facilitate LDCs' access to export markets, technology and FDI. One of these conditions is international assistance to LDCs to adjust and take advantage of trading and investment opportunities in RTAs (*LDCR 1996:* 74–82).

While the importance of enhanced South–South cooperation for LDCs was recognized in all decennial programmes of action, the last one (2001–2010) specifically encouraged developing countries to make "the best use of the possibilities provided by the triangular mechanisms, through which successful South-South cooperation may be attained using financial contributions from one or more donors, and taking advantage of economic complementarity among developing countries" (UNCTAD, 2001a, para. 19). *The LDCR 2002* identified possible areas for the application of these triangular mechanisms in light of the programme of action and stressed a complementarity and synergy between North–South cooperation and South-South cooperation as the *sine qua non* for structural transformation and trade expansion of LDCs. In this context the report concluded that "it will be difficult for LDCs to get on and move the ladder of development if the more advanced developing countries face a "glass ceiling", which blocks their development". Therefore it insisted that policies that counter the increasing polarization in the global economy are necessary for economic development and poverty reduction in LDCs (*LDCR 2002:* XVII and 235).

D.   New Areas of Research Activities

The overarching goal of the Programme of Action for LDCs for 2001–2010 is "to make substantial progress towards halving the proportion of people living in extreme poverty" (UNCTAD, 2001a, para. 6). The UNCTAD secretariat has strengthened its intellectual contributions towards this goal through the expansion of its research activities. The main purpose of *The LDCR 2002* was to provide a solid analytical basis for national and international policies designed to promote poverty reduction in LDCs. The main purpose of UNCTAD's other studies (see below) on the effective benefits derived from LDC status and the question of smooth transition for graduation is to further strengthen this analytical basis and ensure a more effective design and implementation of such policies.

1. Designing national and international policies to promote poverty reduction

The LDC Report 2002 provided a detailed account of poverty in LDCs and analysed the pattern of trade integration. It paid particular attention to the relationship between commodity dependence and poverty while taking into account the implications of implementing effective poverty reduction strategies. Its strategic recommendation, which reflected a shift from "adjustment-oriented" poverty reduction strategies to "development-oriented" poverty reduction strategies, consisted of the following general policy orientations: (i) promoting rapid and sustained growth; (ii) establishing a dynamic investment-export nexus; (iii) elaborating the productive development policy options; and (iv) adopting policies to prevent social exclusion and marginalization within LDCs. These national strategies should be supported by international support measures: increasing levels of aid and aid effectiveness, re-enhanced debt-relief, improved market access and its effectiveness and international commodity policy supportive to LDCs' diversification efforts complemented by North–South and South–South cooperation in favour of LDCs (*LDCR 2002*: I–XVII).

2. Making LDC status an effective instrument to promote graduation

The studies undertaken in this area (UNCTAD, 2001c; 2002a; 2002b; 2003a) identified, *inter alia*, that LDC status is a determinant of special treatment in three main areas: (a) in the preferential access of LDC products to the markets of trading partners that offer an LDC-specific treatment; (b) in several WTO agreements; and (c) in terms of the access of LDCs to special measures of technical assistance offered by the aforementioned six core agencies: the World Bank, IMF, UNCTAD, ITC, UNDP, and WTO that sponsor the Integrated Framework for trade-related technical assistance to LDCs. In contrast, most ODA inflows and debt reduction-related operations have been determined on the basis of other criteria, most of which were low income-related criteria. The studies indicated that large gaps exist between: (a) the announced international support measures and the ones delivered; (b) the delivered international support measures and those effectively used by LDCs; and (c) all the international support measures effectively used along with those that actually involved a genuine structural impact. In order to reduce these gaps, in the context of shared responsibility between LDCs and their development partners, the studies advocate ways to transform LDC status into an efficient instrument for promoting LDCs' graduation. The UNCTAD secretariat examined the position of each LDC under the graduation thresholds which allowed a distinction to be made between LDCs that are clearly off the graduation route and those few for whom graduation can eventually be anticipated. It proposed elements of smooth exit strategies for graduating countries. These ideas contributed to UNCTAD's endeavours to formulate technical assistance projects on the effective benefits derived from LDC status and on the assistance to the countries eligible for graduation, particularly through formulating individual "exit strategies" towards eventual graduation.

II. Developing Countries
with Geographical Handicaps

The specific geographical constraints and problems of landlocked and island LDCs have been deserving of special attention in UNCTAD. Many UNCTAD studies and documents have discussed their specific needs in light of national, regional and international measures in their favour. All three decennial programmes of action for LDCs have dealt with obstacles arising from land-locked status and remoteness of many LDCs. In addition, UNCTAD ensures within its mandate analytical coverage of all LLDCs and SIDS whether they are LDCs or not.

A.   Land-locked Developing Countries

In pursuance of resolution 11(II), adopted by UNCTAD II (New Delhi, 1968 – see introduction), in 1970 a group of experts prepared a report on the special problems involved in the trade and economic development of LLDCs (UNCTAD, 1970). On the basis of this report the UNCTAD secretariat carried out an Action Programme in favour of LLDCs which was submitted to UNCTAD III (Santiago, 1972). This Programme identified specific economic difficulties arising from land-locked status and formulated needs in specific efforts at the national, sub-regional and international levels to alleviate them. At the national level, the Programme recommended, *inter alia*, the elaboration by LLDCs of economic development strategies, which would reduce the difficulties created by land-locked status through: (a) the intensive development of exportable products, which can bear the relatively high transport costs; (b) the possibilities for indigenous production of low value bulk products which they were importing; and (c) increased economic cooperation with their neighbouring countries, including serving LLDCs local markets as well as adjacent areas of neighbouring countries (UNCTAD, 1972d, 4: 74–82, paras. 15–18). At the sub-regional level the Programme highlighted the importance of transit transport cooperation between LLDCs and their transit neighbours to improve the effectiveness and economical use of existing transit transport infrastructure and to establish economically viable alternative routes. At the international level the Programme requested LLDCs' development partners fully to take into account the critical nature of transport investment for LLDCs in their aid policies (UNCTAD, 1972d 4: 74–82, paras. 6, 8).

A year later a second expert group produced a broad conceptual framework for an integrated planning approach to transit problems of LLDCs, which mainly aimed at promoting and consolidating cooperative arrangements between LLDCs and their transit neighbours (UNCTAD, 1974a). In 1975 the UNCTAD secretariat prepared a study on the establishment of a fund in favour of LLDCs. This study was submitted to the UN General Assembly, which, in turn, adopted resolution 3504 (XXX) in 1976 establishing the special fund for LLDCs. However, this fund received only very limited resources and never became operational; therefore, the UNCTAD activities were limited to exploring the relevance of the integrated planning approach in the field, including numerous technical studies within the framework of regional transit transport projects in Asia and Africa. These studies analysed the adequacy of existing legislation, conventions and working agreements that governed international transit transport regulation and transit rate structures of transit corridors. With a special emphasis on the existing capacity and quality of transit routes, the studies also explored various ways and means to improve their institutional and physical infrastructure, as well as possibilities for creating new transit corridors. On the basis of the recommendations of these studies, UNCTAD IV (Nairobi, 1975), UNCTAD V (Manila, 1979) and UNCTAD VI (Belgrade, 1983) adopted resolutions 98 (IV), 123 (V), and 137 (VI) respectively, in favour of LLDCs. Since the late 1980s the secretariat has prepared annual reports on the progress of the implementation of specific actions related to the particular needs and problems of LLDCs and has submitted them annually to the General Assembly. These reports have developed the concept of an integrated planning approach to the transit problems of LLDCs, together with a comprehensive framework for regular collection of information on the transit transport system.

In the early 1990s the secretariat expanded its research activities to include nine "newly" independent LLDCs.[13] Its studies analysed the changing trade directions of new LLDCs; the changing structure of their transport charges; their existing rail, road and inland waterways; and the main alternative transit transport routes.

The increased number of LLDCs further stimulated the secretariat's efforts in the search for an effective international strategy for mitigating the difficulties of these geographically handicapped countries and created the conditions for its comprehensive consideration by the international community. Thus, in 1995, the secretariat prepared guidelines for such a strategy.[14]

Since the late 1990s, the UNCTAD secretariat has carried out numerous studies on different transit transport corridors for LLDCs in Asia, Africa and Latin America. Implementing some of the recommendations contained in these studies have provided LLDCs and transit States, *inter alia,* with an opportunity to substantively reduce the time and cost of transit transportation. This, in turn, increased the international recognition of the problems of land-locked status and the necessity to deal with these at the global level.

In 2001 the UN General Assembly, in its resolution 56/180, decided to convene the first International Ministerial Conference on Landlocked and Transit Developing Countries and Donor Countries and International and Financial Development Institutions on Transit Transport Cooperation. This resolution also requested UNCTAD to provide substantive support to the Conference. In response, the secretariat carried out several studies on the improvement of transit systems in

---

[13] They were: Armenia, Azerbaijan, Kazakhstan, Kyrgyzstan, Macedonia, Moldova, Tajikistan, Turkmenistan, and Uzbekistan. For results of the new research activities, see, for example UNCTAD, 1994a and UNDP/UNCTAD, 1995.

[14] The guidelines consisted of two parts: fundamental transit transport policy issues and selected issues. The first included general recommendations for LLDCs and transit countries' policies covering the areas of balance between immediate necessity and the commercial viability of the transit transport sector as well as the interests of LLDCs and coastal States in maintaining the existing routes and creating alternative ones. It also made suggestions concerning: the improvement of mechanisms to monitor and promote the implementation of coordination agreements and arrangements; enhancing efforts to adhere to these conventions by other LLDCs and transit countries; reducing the dependency on overseas markets; balanced and managed use of both rail and road; training; and the environmental protection and mobilization of adequate resources for effectively carrying out the transit transport infrastructure programme. The second part, selected issues, addressed the policy aspects, projects, programmes and operational issues of transit sub-sectors (railways, roads, port facilities and services, inland waterways, air freight and communication). It also recommended a set of international support measures in financing and technical cooperation of transit transport programmes, as well as implementation and follow-up mechanisms (UNCTAD, 1995).

different parts of the world.[15] On the basis of these studies it prepared its Secretary-General's report to the Almaty Conference in 2003, entitled *Challenges and Opportunities for Further Improving the Transit Systems and Economic Development of Landlocked and Transit Developing Countries*. The report reviewed the current situation of transit systems, including the implementation of the 1995 Global Framework, and recommended, *inter alia*, that LLDCs and transit developing countries should strengthen their efforts in three main areas: (1) the improvement of transit systems in order to reduce transit costs and enhance LLDCs' competitive position; (2) the promotion of regional trade and integration to attract FDI; and (3) the specific measures to attract FDI to industries and activities, particularly in the production of high-value and low-weight products which are less sensitive to distance. The report also suggested taking into account the differences among LLDCs (distances, economic context, historical ties, etc.) in policy formulation. It stressed the necessity of enhancing international support measures to landlocked countries and developing countries of transit through new modalities of financing (e.g. regional venture funds, equity participation in local financial institutions, co-financing, bank-to-bank loans, etc.), ensuring priority to these countries in technical cooperation programmes, attracting FDI that would foster non-distance sensitive activities, strengthening assistance to regional integration groupings with LLDCs participation, etc.[16]

The Conference, which took place in Almaty, Kazakhstan, 25–29 August 2003, adopted "The Almaty Programme of Action: Addressing the Special Needs of Landlocked Developing Countries within a New Global Framework for Transit Transport Cooperation with Landlocked and Transit Developing Countries". The Almaty Programme of Action echoed the UNCTAD Secretary General's report calling for technical assistance beyond the traditional boundaries in the transit transport and extended its coverage to pipelines. UNCTAD was requested to implement specific sub-programmes for LLDCs in the areas of trade facilitation, electronic commerce and accession to the WTO. The secretariat will also provide substantive and technical support to the Office of High Representative on the Least Developed, Land-locked and Small Island Developing Countries (OHRLLS) in reviewing the implementation of this Programme of Action.

---

[15] For details on specific regions see UNCTAD, 2003 c-h.
[16] Including UNCTAD technical cooperation programmes such as ASYCUDA, ACIS as well as programmes in the areas of competition, trade and environment (UNCTAD, 2003i: 20-31).

B.   Small Island Developing States (SIDS)

In response to resolution 65(III), adopted by UNCTAD III (Santiago, 1972), a panel of experts identified and studied the particular needs of IDCs and the findings of this panel were subsequently published in 1974 (UNCTAD, 1974b). On the basis of this report the secretariat made a number of policy proposals on special and differential treatment in favour of IDCs. Many of them were incorporated in resolution 98(IV) (UNCTAD IV, Nairobi, 1976). In 1977, in line with the request of this resolution, a Group of Experts on Feeder and Inter-island Services by Air or Sea for Developing Island Countries was convened. The Report of this group, published in 1978 (UNCTAD, 1978), complemented the secretariat's approach to the particular problems of these countries and strengthened its proposals, which resulted in resolution 111 (V) (UNCTAD V – Manila, 1979). As a result of these two reports the major difficulties hampering the economic development of many IDCs were identified[17] and international support measures were proposed to alleviate them.

The secretariat proposed three types of international support measures based on its concept of special and differential treatment. The first type consisted of specific measures to cope with the geographical disadvantages faced by IDCs. These measures were aimed at resolving the specific problems of these countries in the areas of shipping, air services, telecommunications, commercial policy, import cooperation, ecology of small islands, natural disaster prevention and mitigation,

---

[17] Difficulties resulted from the unfavourable geographical situation of the islands: the remoteness from markets centres and often from world traffic routes, especially in archipelagos; frequent natural disasters, etc. In addition the countries were deemed handicapped by the smallness of their internal markets, high costs of transport and communications as well as their heavy dependence on a few products/services for their foreign exchange earnings (UNCTAD, 1974b, paras. 2-6, 9-14, and 19-23).

and adequate participation of IDCs in international conferences.[18] The second type of international support consisted of special measures to enhance the economic development of IDCs. These measures included special assistance to IDCs in the areas of economic diversification, access to market, investment promotion, institutional capacity-building, negotiating capacities, etc. The third type of measures comprised action to promote potential comparative advantages of IDCs such as marine and sub-marine resources, tourism resources and favourable geographical locations for international shipping, air transit, refuelling services, etc.[19]

The analysis undertaken by the UNCTAD secretariat on IDC-related issues contributed significantly to a better understanding of these countries' development and challenges and was a determining factor in the growing international recognition of their specific development problems. This recognition was reflected in five resolutions on IDCs in the UN General Assembly between the mid-1970s and early 1980s. The outcome of the secretariat's work was also the basis for proposals contained in resolution 111 on "concrete specific action, taking into account, *inter alia*, the traditional island life and institutions, the physical environment, development priorities and the problems of island countries in the international economy".

From the early 1980s to the beginning of the 1990s the UNCTAD secretariat carried out in-depth studies on the main problems facing these countries with a view to proposing specific action to minimize the constraints resulting from

---

[18] In shipping the measures included the facilitation of transhipment to prevent discrimination against island ships; promotional freight rates; special research and development efforts to evolve appropriate types of ship and shore facilities for archipelagic countries; better cooperation with shipping conferences on freight rates and port surcharges; training for ship repairs and maintenance; and assistance in the establishment of shipping services to promote regional cooperation in the improvements of ports. In air services these measures could include advice on appropriate types of aircraft and ground facilities; establishment of consultation machinery between IDC and airlines on the matter of freight rates and fares; and assistance (from UNCTAD) in promoting sub-regional cooperation with participation of IDCs and in promoting the establishment of international air transport companies to develop IDC trade with the countries of the same sub-region. In the area of telecommunications the measures could include the creation and improvement of inter-island telecommunication links with the rest of the world. In the area of commercial policy specific measures to encourage IDC in their exports were recommended, taking into account their specific difficulties and peculiarities. Technical and financial assistance should be extended to groups of IDCs on the basis of collective import operations which could represent substantial savings, in terms of cost, insurance, freight and handling charges as well as storage charges (UNCTAD,1974b, paras, 57-70; 1978, paras. 32-111; resolution 98 (UNCTAD IV), paras. 38-66; resolution 111 (UNCTAD V), paras. 1-10.
[19] See UNCTAD, 1974b, paras. 76, 77; resolution 98 (UNCTAD IV), para. 62; resolution 111 (UNCTAD V), para. 2.

their geographical situations which inhibit their development efforts. These studies took into account various limitations on the viability of small island developing economies, their development priorities, problems and issues of economic vulnerability, and capacity-building.[20] This work provided inputs for the UN Secretary-General's annual reports on IDCs, with recommendations on different types of special international support measures for this group of countries. Maintaining economic viability, reducing vulnerability to natural disasters and external economic shocks as well as integrating the resources of large exclusive economic zones in national development strategies, were three core elements of UNCTAD's supportive action in favour of IDCs.

After the Global Conference on Sustainable Development of Small Island Developing States (Barbados, 1994), UNCTAD concentrated its island-related action on supporting the implementation of the economic aspects of the Barbados Programme of Action for the Sustainable Development of Small Island Developing States (SIDS). The relevant analytical work has been concentrated on these IDCs' responses to challenges arising from trade liberalization and globalization (UNCTAD, 1994b; 1996). This work has involved: (1) analysis of economic vulnerability through the preparation of vulnerability profiles and (2) research on: (i) substantive support to SIDS in their efforts to seek differential modalities of special treatment in the main multilateral arenas; (ii) research and analysis on a range of issues of immediate relevance to SIDS, in particular, on economic vulnerability; and (iii) technical assistance at the national or regional levels. In the context of preparation for the international meeting to review the implementation of the Barbados Programme of Action (Mauritius, 2004), the UNCTAD secretariat has been pursuing efforts to enhance the credibility of the SIDS denomination in order to support these countries in their efforts to gain more differential and favourable responses to their problems from the international community. This research work provides analytical inputs to SIDS in their preparations for the 10-year review of the implementation of the Barbados Programme of Action and the Mauritius Conference on SIDS (August–September 2004).

---

[20] Contained in Sevele, 1982; Dommen and Hein eds., 1985; Dolman, 1986; UNCTAD, 1983c; 1983d; 1988; 1990b.

References

Dommen E and Hein P, eds. (1985). *States, Microstates, and Islands*. London: Croom Helm, Ltd.

Dolman AJ (1986). Small Island Developing Countries and the Development Potential of Exclusive Economic Zones. UNCTAD/ST/LDC/7, 27 March.

Sevele F (1982). The Benefits of the Integrated Programme for Commodities for Island Developing Countries. TD/B/1891, 3 August.

Sottas E (1985). *The least developed countries: Introduction to the LDCs and to the substantial new programme of action for them*: 4–8. UNCTAD, TAD/INF/PUB/84.2, United Nations, New York.

UN (1964). *Proceedings of the United Nations Conference on Trade and Development*. Vol. II: Policy Statements, Geneva, 23 March – 16 June 1964, E.CONF.46/141.

UNCTAD (1969a). Identification of the least developed among the developing countries. TD/B/269, 11 July.

_____ (1969b). Special measures in favour of the least developed countries among developing countries. TD/B/288, 18 December.

_____ (1970). Special Problems of Land-locked Countries. TD/B/308, Geneva, 11 June.

_____ (1971). Special Measures in Favour of the Least Developed Countries Among the Developing Countries. Report of the Ad Hoc Group of Experts on Special Measures in Favour of the Least Developed Countries Among the Developing Countries. TD/B/349 and Rev.1, New York and Geneva.

_____ (1972a). Special Measures for the Least Developed Among the Developing Countries: Action programme submitted by the Secretary-General of UNCTAD. TD/135, Geneva, 9 March.

_____ (1972b). Other Special Measures Related to the Particular Needs of the Land-locked Developing Countries: Action Programme submitted by the Secretary-General of UNCTAD. TD/136, Geneva, 9 March.

_____ (1972c). Special Measures in Favour of the Least Developed Among the Developing Countries: Progress Report on Identification Criteria by the Secretary-General of UNCTAD. TD/137, Geneva, 9 March.

_____ (1972d). *Proceedings of the United Nations Conference on Trade and Development*. Volume IV, Third session, Santiago de Chile, 13 April – 21 May 1972, TD/180.

____ (1974a). A transport strategy for landlocked developing countries. TD/B/453/Add.1/Rev.1, New York.

____ (1974b). Developing Island Countries, Report of the Panel of Experts. TD/B/443/Rev.1, Geneva and New York.

____ (1978). Report of the Group of Experts on Feeder and Inter-island Services by Air or Sea for Island Developing Countries. TD/B/687, Geneva, 2 May.

____ (1983a). The least developed countries in the 1980s: Report by the Secretary-General of the United Nations Conference on the least developed countries; The least developed countries and action in their favour by the international community. A/CONF.104/2/Rev.1: 25–104.

____ (1983b). Progress in the Implementation of the Substantial New Programme of Action for the 1980s for Least Developed Countries, Report by the UNCTAD secretariat, sixth session. TD/276, Belgrade, Yugoslavia, 6 June.

____ (1983c). Viability of Small Island States: A descriptive study by F. Doumenge. TD/B/950, Geneva, 22 July.

____ (1983d). The Incidence of Natural Disasters in Island Developing Countries, study by the UNCTAD secretariat in collaboration with UNDRO. TD/B/961, Geneva, 23 September.

____ (1984–2004). *The Least Developed Countries Reports.* (Due to the frequent references in the text this report was specially designated as *LDCR 1984...LDCR 2004*).

____ (1988). Specific Problems of Island Developing Countries: Report of the Meeting of the Group of Experts on Island Developing Countries, Malta, 24–25 May 1988. UNCTAD/ST/LDC, 5 July.

____ (1990a). Economic Integration Among Developing Countries: Trade Cooperation, Monetary and Financial Cooperation and Review of Recent Developments in Major Economic Cooperation and Integration Groupings of Developing Countries, Report by the UNCTAD secretariat. TD/B/C.7/AC.3/10, 12 December.

____ (1990b). Report of the Meeting of Governmental Experts of Island Developing Countries and Donor Countries and Organizations. TD/B/AC/4, 8 August.

____ (1991). Review of Criteria for Identifying the Least Developed Among the Developing Countries. UNCTAD/RDP/LDC/Misc.17, January.

____ (1992a). The Programme of Action for the Least Developed Countries for the 1990s: Report by the Secretary-General of UNCTAD, eighth session, Cartagena de Indias, 8 February 1992. TD/359, 24 January.

____(1992b). Paris Declaration and Programme of Action for Least Developed Countries for the 1990s. UNCTAD/RBP/LDC/58, Geneva.

____(1994a). Transit transport system of the newly independent and developing landlocked states in central Asia and their developing neighbours: Current situation and proposals of future action, Report of the Secretary-General. A/49/277, Geneva, 25 July.

____(1994b). A Development Strategy for Island Developing Countries: New Challenges, Prospects, and Opportunities for Cooperative Action, Report of the Secretary-General. A/49/227, Geneva, 18 July.

____(1995). Global Framework for Transit Transport Cooperation between Landlocked and Transport Developing Countries and Donor Community. TD/B/LDC/AC.1/6, Geneva, 4 July.

____(1996). Development Challenges Facing Island Developing Countries: Basic Issues and Prospects in the Context of Trade Liberalization and Globalization, Report by UNCTAD secretariat. UNCTAD/LLDC/IDC/2, Geneva, 9 February.

____(2001a). Report of the Third United Nations Conference on the Least Developed Countries. A/CONF.191/13, Geneva, September.

____(2001b). Duty and Quota-free Market Access to LDCs: An analysis of quad Initiatives. UNCTAD and Commonwealth Secretariat joint study. UNCTAD/DITC/TAB/Misc.7, London and Geneva.

____(2001c). The benefits associated with the least developed country status and the question of graduation, Note by the Secretary-General prepared by the secretariat of UNCTAD. E/2001/CRP.5 and Add.1, July.

____(2002a). Least developed country status: Effective benefits and the perspectives of graduation, Report of the UNCTAD secretariat. TD/B/49/7, Geneva, 1 August.

____(2002b). Graduation from the least developed country status: Where do the LDCs stand? UNCTAD/LDC/Misc.83, Geneva, April.

____(2003a). Smooth transition for countries graduating from LDC status. CDP 2003/PLEN/21, April.

____(2003b). Main recent initiatives in favour of least developed countries in the area of preferential market access. TD/B/50/5, 7 August.

____(2003c). Improvement of Transit Systems in West Africa. UNCTAD/LDC/2003/2.

____ (2003d). Improvement of Transit Systems in Southern and Eastern Africa. UNCTAD/LDC/2003/3.

____ (2003e). Improvement of Transit Systems in the Horn of Africa. UNCTAD/LDC/2003/4.

____ (2003f). Improvement of Transit Systems in Central Asia. UNCTAD/LDC/2003/5.

____ (2003g). Improvements of Transit Systems in Latin America. UNCTAD/LDC/2003/6.

____ (2003h). Improvement of Transit Systems in Central Africa. UNCTAD/LDC/2003/7.

____ (2003i). Challenges and opportunities for further improving the transit systems and economic development of landlocked and transit developing countries. UNCTAD/LDC/2003/8.

UNDP/UNCTAD (1995). Central Asia's Trade Links with the World. Silken Past, Troubled Present, Promising Future. Expanding Trading Through Regional Transit Transport Cooperation. UNDP/UNCTAD Project RER/95/001, New York and Geneva.

Weiss TG and Jennings A (1983). *More for the Least? Prospects for Poorest Countries in the Eighties.* Toronto: Lexington Books.

WTO (2003). Dhaka Declaration, Part II, LDC-II/2003/5, 13 June.

Services in Development[*]

Shigehisa Kasahara[**]

Introduction

There are contending views on what activities should constitute the service sector. The narrowest definition includes all private economic activities with intangible outcomes, which means that the sector excludes construction, utilities and public administration and defence in addition to agriculture, mining and manufacturing. In a broad definition, the list of activities could be expanded to include utilities, or utilities and public administration, or utilities, public administration and construction.[1] We are concerned in this paper with the service sector fairly broadly defined.

While the entirety of the United Nations (UN) system as an institutionalized network of public administration belongs to the service sector under a very broad definition, its numerous organs and specialized agencies have been dealing with specific activities that are included in narrower definitions.[2] For its part, UNCTAD has a long history of involvement in some trade-related service activities, very notably: shipping, insurance, and financing related to trade, as well as issues

---

[*] *Note*: This short topical paper supplements two topical papers on specific service activities: Shipping and Technology. In functional terms, it is also related to the topical papers of Trade; Money, Finance and Debt; Development Strategies, and FDI/TNCs, as the latter papers contain activities involving the service sector (i.e. trade in services; international financial services; public administration; and FDI/TNCs in the service sector, respectively). This paper presents an historical presentation depicting how the UNCTAD secretariat's conceptual and analytical work on the service sector as whole began and developed.
[**] The author is an Economic Affairs Officer in the Macroeconomic and Development Policies Branch, Division of Globalization and Development Strategies (GDS).
[1] For further discussions on the alternative definitions, see UNCTAD, 1983: 18-22.
[2] For instance, the International Telecommunication Union (ITU) and the Universal Postal Union (UPU) have been active in setting norms of conduct and promulgating standards for adoption by Governments in the area of communications since long before the establishment of the UN. While many specialized agencies, such as the International Civil Aviation Organization (ICAO) and the International Maritime Organization (IMO) have a responsibility for certain services, others, such as the World Intellectual Property Organization (WIPO) and the United Nations Educational, Scientific and Cultural Organization (UNESCO), deal with issues pertinent to a variety of services. Furthermore, issues related to particular services, such as transport and banking, in a specific regional and sub-regional context have also been dealt with by the Regional Commissions of the UN.

related to technology.[3] This involvement was partly due to the concern that these activities chronically induced external deficits in most of the developing countries. Indeed, a growing number of developing countries have attempted to develop export capacity in a wide range of service activities. Some have been dependent on the export of services (e.g. by offering offshore financial services) for their foreign exchange earnings. For others, strengthening their service sector, perhaps most notably shipping, has become crucial to enhancing their position in international trade in goods (particularly for bulky commodities). But the issue of concern still remains largely intact; i.e. that most of the developing countries have continued to be net service importers.

Under a broad definition of the service sector, one important and controversial element is how to include public administration. One contentious issue here is the appropriateness of including specific principal providers of public service activities (goods or services): whether public or private providers should be included as well as whether domestic or foreign. Many service activities are closely linked to infrastructure-related public investments, thus under relatively tighter public regulations. In the early post-war period of the 1950s and 1960s many newly independent countries held the perception that the administrative system inherited from the colonial period were not providing the public services necessary to create the impetus for "genuine" economic development.[4] This prompted an extensive range of interventionist policies by the new administration, in the manufacturing sector as well as the service sector.

From the early 1970s onward, the UNCTAD secretariat undertook detailed studies on specific service activities with greater intensity, for instance shipping, tourism, insurance, etc. along with their impacts on national economies, particularly on trade and development in developing countries. The question of priority assigned to public investment in these activities – due to their importance in national employment policies and in export strategies – formed an important subject for research and analysis. During the 1980s many developing countries

---

[3] Technology enters into the discussion of services in two ways. One is as an output of the service sector, which constitutes the transactions on a contractual basis of proprietary and non-proprietary technology as well as technological services related to investment and production. The other way is through technology used for the generation and supply of new services (UNCTAD, 1984: 1).

[4] In particular, the financial systems that had emerged during the colonial period were not well developed and were dominated by foreign-owned commercial banks concentrating on the provision of trade finance and /or lending to expatriate business. Discontents with the role of foreign banks centred around the failure to extend credit to indigenous businesses and farmers, to provide long-term capital for the development of industry and to extend banking services to the rural areas (UNCTAD, 1996: 87-88).

undertook liberalization and privatization measures of their service sector, most notably the financial sub-sector, usually as part of Structural Adjustment Programmes prescribed by the Bretton Woods institutions. However, the lingering problems of many developing countries that had implemented the service sector liberalization drew critical attention from an increasing number of observers.

At the 1982 Ministerial Meeting of the General Agreement on Tariffs and Trade (GATT), developing countries were under pressure to undertake joint negotiations for liberalization of trade in services. At that time developing countries were well united, and stoutly opposed these movements, consequently succeeding in preventing the introduction of services into multilateral trade negotiations. This opposition of developing countries was due to their perception that their service activities, generally underdeveloped and narrow, would not have good prospects (in terms of the improvement of their share in international trade) under a more liberalized regime. However, by the time when the Uruguay Round was launched with the Punta del Este Ministerial Declaration in 1986, the subject of trade in services had been included firmly among the items of negotiations.[5]

This paper attempts to depict the evolution in the methodological approach underlying UNCTAD's intellectual activities in the service sector. It is argued that during the 1980s there was a rapid build-up of interest in research on services, where the UNCTAD secretariat began to treat the service sector as a whole rather than to concentrating on specific sub-sectors, while transforming the framework of analysis from the services-trade to the services-development nexus. The holistic approach toward the service sector was relatively short-lived, however. After UNCTAD VIII (1992), and despite the decision therein to create the Commission on "Developing service sectors", the holistic approach was rapidly taken over by a specialized functional approach, where the framework of analysis shifted back again to treating its specific selected sub-sectors, while again focusing functionally on relations between services and trade (and to a lesser extent FDI) rather than on those between services and development. (While this does not mean that the development approach was given up altogether, the concern over the effects of individual service sub-sectors on development appeared to be less explicit.)

---

[5] According to Gibbs and Mashayekhi (1991: 6), the developing countries agreed to participate in the negotiations on services to pre-empt unfavourable unilateral actions as well as discriminatory bilateral and regional arrangements against them. These countries were successful in establishing a legally distinct negotiating process on trade in services so that actual negotiations would be conducted in an *ad hoc* judicial frame of reference outside GATT, which reportedly meant that formal trade-off and linkages between goods and services were excluded from the outset of the negotiations.

I.   1964–1982:
Gradual Build-Up of Interest in Services

There was a tendency in the earlier days (up to the end of the 1970s) to downplay the importance of services as a whole in the development process. The conventional theory of the role of services in the national economy tended to suggest that growth in the services sector was a result of the development process. The shift of employment from the manufacturing to the services sector was seen as attributable to a loss in productivity growth for the economy as a whole.[6] Services were considered importance only in so far as they were essential to overall social welfare (water, electricity, waste disposal, roads, etc), supportive of trade in goods and strategic from a national security viewpoint. Over this period, however, the conventional theory was increasingly questioned. This was because growth of employment in services in many developing countries continued despite the slow (stagnant) growth of their overall economies. In other words, the percentage employed in the primary sector continued to drop, while that in the secondary and tertiary sectors both increased, and more so in the latter sector.

For its part, UNCTAD dealt with some specific service sub-sector activities in the hope that assisting poor countries in developing these activities would reduce foreign exchange outflows (shipping, insurance and technology) or augment foreign exchange inflows (tourism). Thus the selected service activities were mostly trade-related. A full understanding of the role of the service sector as whole in development was yet to be developed, as economic policies in UNCTAD forums did not take adequate account of the potential effect various service activities might have on economic development.

In the early 1980s, some countries initiated placing the international debates on various issues pertaining to services in a more general developmental context. Subsequently, UNCTAD's involvement in service activities came to include, more explicitly than before, concerns about their linkages with the overall process of economic development of developing countries. It was also technological advances that served to change the way services were provided as well as changing the perception of the service sector as whole. Services came to be seen as key

---

[6] The implication of this conventional theory was that (a) growth in the services sectors (in employment and value-added) would occur automatically, as a result of the process of post-industrial development; (b) there was no need for a services policy; in fact, such expansion might even be undesirable as it could reduce productivity and slow down the development process; and (c) a logical international division of labour would emerge, with developed countries specializing in the producing of services and developing countries in the export of goods.

economic activities, which were undertaken in their own right (known as "consumer services") or as a component of some product or another service (known as "producer services"). Technological advances began to have a revolutionary impact on the production and trade of both goods and services and on world patterns of trade and development, thus justifying their examination in a universal and interdisciplinary forum where the overall trade and development aspects could be taken into account. A closer examination of the role of services in the development process, it was thought, would seem to constitute an essential component of this general reassessment of development strategies at the national, regional and multilateral levels.

While technological advancements, particularly in the transport and communications filed, have expanded the degree of "transportability", and thus "tradability" of services, they have also complicated the trade/FDI distinction. More specifically, there have been "grey" areas where activities might seem to come under the guise of trade but in fact involve FDI and should be dealt with accordingly.

A major outcome of the Uruguay Round was to devise new multilateral disciplines in the areas of "trade-related investment measures" (TRIMS) as well as in "trade in services", and to link them to the GATT rights and obligations through the institutional "umbrella" of the World Trade Organization (WTO) and its integrated dispute settlement mechanism. Since the UNCTAD secretariat absorbed the UN Department on Transnational Corporations (formerly the UN Centre on Transnational Corporations (UNCTC)) from New York in 1993, and particularly since the inclusion of TRIM in the WTO disciplines, the UNCTAD secretariat's work on FDI (including in the service sector) has rapidly drawn attention.[7] (See the topical paper on FDI/TNC in this volume.) At any rate, the secretariat has been increasingly involved in various issues of services concerning investment and trade as well as in development, particularly in developing countries.

---

[7] The UNCTAD secretariat's research on FDI in the service sector has been very limited. In the 1990s, the *WIR 1997* dealt with FDI in services in the context of the FDI-trade relationship, showing how FDI in services differ from FDI in other areas with respect to the impacts on trade. Most recently, the secretariat prepared a full analysis on FDI in services in *WIR 2004*. As of this writing, the content of the report, however, cannot be revealed.

II. 1982–1996:
The Period of Holistic Approach to Services

UNCTAD's holistic approach to services began in 1982 as a result of the Trade and Development Board (TDB) Decision 250 (XXIV) initiated by developing countries and accepted by developed countries. It was agreed that, when dealing with factors of relevance to the issues of protectionism and structural adjustment as well as policies influencing structural adjustment and trade, commensurate attention should be paid to services. The first study undertaken in this context was presented to the 26th session of the TDB in 1983, namely, *Production and trade in service, policies and other underlying factors bearing upon international service transactions* (UNCTAD, 1983). While subsequent works of the secretariat on services had more polished analyses and policy suggestions, this pioneering work set the overall tone of argument.

Developing countries sought to focus the attention of the international community on collective efforts to strengthen their service sector and to devise mechanisms for increasing their participation in international transactions (i.e. trade and investment) in services. In this regard the single most important event was the Fifth Ministerial Meeting of the Group of 77 (28 March – 9 April 1983, Buenos Aires, Argentina) – held just before UNCTAD VI (1983, Belgrade). The final document of the Ministerial Meeting, among other things, sought to set up a major study programme in UNCTAD to identify and establish priorities regarding services of particular importance to developing countries and to devise programmes that would enable the developing countries to have greater participation in international service transactions. It proposed setting up mechanisms for multilateral cooperation to this end.[8]

Subsequently, Conference resolution 159 (VI),[9] gave the UNCTAD secretariat a broad mandate to study the role of the service sector in the development process, keeping in view the special problems of the least developed

---

[8] The final document entitled *The Buenos Aires Platform* was reissued as the attachment to a note of the Secretary-General of UNCTAD to UNCTAD VI. For details see UNCTAD (1983), particularly Section IV. C: resolution on International Trade in Goods and Services, of the Platform.

[9] Conference resolution 159 (VI) entitled, "International Trade in Goods and Services: Protectionism, Structural Adjustment and the International Trading System", consists of four parts: I. Protectionism and structural change (A: protectionism, B: structural adjustment); II. International trading system; III. Generalized System of Preferences; and IV. Services. The provisions discussed in the text can be found in Part IV.

countries (LDCs).[10] This was followed by Board decision 309 (XXX) of 1985 that provided further direction for future work by UNCTAD on services.

The secretariat subsequently embarked on one major study, *Services and the development process* (UNCTAD, 1985b), an initial effort to establish a basis for considering services within both a general and framework. The study identified definitional and statistical problems confronting further analyses and considered possible methods for overcoming such problems. It concentrated on some of the most pertinent questions raised, selecting (a) the rise of enhanced producer services and their effect on trade and development, (b) the opportunities presented to developing countries by the process of trans-nationalization of service production, and (c) possible objectives and policy measures aimed at strengthening the contribution of services to development along with the implications for these objectives of current proposal for international cooperation on services. This study directly challenged the conventional view of the growth of the service sector (for example, in terms of sectoral share of national output) as a consequence of the development process, and argued that the former could be one of the preconditions for the latter.

A shorter follow-up study (UNCTAD, 1986) focused on selected priority issues. The study made a series of recommendations aimed at establishing a development-oriented framework for further work on services. This was accompanied by a series of sectoral and other special studies. Studies on individual service activities (maritime transport, banking, insurance, engineering and consultancy services and trans-border data flows) examined the various issues identified in the general study as well as the special importance of services to LDCs. The document was only able to touch upon these activities in a preliminary fashion but clearly indicated the need for, and areas of, future work.

At the Group of 77 level, the Guatemala Expert Group Meeting on Services related to Trade, held in January 1984, identified transportation, insurance and reinsurance, and communication as priority areas, as well as banking, engineering, and consultancy services, computer services and computer data flows, and communication media and advertisement.

The Final Act, adopted by the Conference VII (1987, Geneva), contained specific reference to UNCTAD's role in services which stated: "UNCTAD should

---

[10] In parallel to this exercise of preparing for the Twenty-ninth session of the TDB it was envisaged that individual countries would be conducting national studies of the role of services in their own economies. A questionnaire circulated by the secretariat in the late 1983 had the dual objective of collecting information and of stimulating governments' interest in services (especially those of developing countries).

continue its useful work in the field of services under its mandate, as contained in Conference resolution 159 (VI) and Board decision 309 (XXX) of 29 March 1985". From the point view of developing countries and in the context of its overall development objective, the Secretary-General of UNCTAD was also requested "to analyse the implications of the issues raised in the context of trade in services"; and "to explore appropriate *problématiques* for trade in services, keeping in mind the technological changes in the field of services" (para.19). Another paragraph stated that: "UNCTAD is requested to continue its programmes of technical assistance to developing countries in the fields of services. UNCTAD is invited to consider favourably the requests for the provision of financial resources for this purpose." (para.20).

During the period between UNCTAD VII (1987) and VIII (1992), the most dramatic changes occurred in the way the secretariat handled services. The secretariat came to emphasize services in the developmental context in addition to the trade context. The subject of services was taken up for the first time in the secretariat's Report to the Conference (UNCTAD, 1987, paras. 839–863), although it was discussed largely in the context of international trade during the Conference itself.

In the secretariat's Report (UNCTAD, 1992, paras. 625–678) to UNCTAD VIII the subject of "services" was presented more extensively than before, in an independent chapter of its own, and trade and development-related implications (together with case studies of specific service sub-sectors, namely financial services and telecommunications) were there discussed. UNCTAD VIII was also a historical conference in terms of the implications of the subject of services to its inter-governmental machinery, as it decided to establish a standing committee on "Developing service sectors" in the context of the structural reforms.[11]

During this inter-Conference period, the secretariat presented a most comprehensive and polished analysis on services (in a broad sense) in the development context in *The Trade and Development Report 1988* (*TDR 1988*). It examined services in the developed market economies, the then-socialist countries of Eastern Europe and the developing countries. It analysed trade in services in the

---

[11] UNCTAD VIII decided to "suspend" virtually all of the existing intergovernmental bodies and to replace them with standing committees on the following topics: Commodities; Poverty alleviation; Economic cooperation among developing countries; and Developing service sectors. The Conference additionally agreed to establish five *ad hoc* working groups to deal with: (I) Investment and financial flows; non-debt-creating finance for development; new mechanisms to increasing investment and financial flows; (II) Trade efficiency; (III) Comparative experiences with privatization; (IV) Expanding trading opportunities for developing countries; and (V) Interrelationship between investment and technology transfers.

world economy along with the strategic role of services, and suggested a set of service strategies for development. Among the most innovative ideas emerging from the analysis concerned the importance of "externalization of service production" (*TDB 1988*: 144), which meant that the significance of producer-services (particularly knowledge-intensive kinds) was seen to be from economic development.[12] One of the most important contributions of the UNCTAD secretariat here was the proposal of the concept of "mode of delivery" (later termed the "modes of supply") by identifying what actually crosses national borders when trade in service occurs. Some observers argue that the Report set out much of the intellectual basis for negotiations on trade in services. (For further discussions, see the topical paper of International Trade.)

By the time of UNCTAD IX (1996, Midrand) however, the overall enthusiasm towards the holistic approach to services seemed to have dissipated. Furthermore, the above-mentioned structural reform of the UNCTAD intergovernmental machinery, including the standing committee on "Developing service sectors", proved to be short-lived and was again replaced by another reform agreed at UNCTAD IX. Now the TDB had three principal subsidiary bodies: the Commission on Trade in Goods and Services; the Commission on Investment, Technology and Related Financial Issues; and the Commission on Enterprise, Business Facilitation and Development. Service-related issues were distributed among three groups, or clusters, which are related to trade, investment (basically FDI) and enterprise development, respectively. This fragmentation reflected the strengthened (applied) microeconomic, rather than macroeconomic, orientation of the secretariat toward services. Thus for the subject on services, the holistic (and development-oriented) approach was abandoned.

One exception to the functional fragmentation in the secretariat's handling of services is *the Least Developed Countries Reports* (*LDCRs*). Virtually every issue of the *LDCR* during the 1990s contained some discussions (of varying lengths) about specific services activities in the context of promoting economic development. Many service sub-sectors, such as education and public health, which have received little attention from the other UNCTAD flagship publications (*TDRs* and *WIRs*) have been extensively analysed. One major reason for this is that the contributions of trade and FDI to the LDCs' economic performances have been

---

[12] In conceptual terms the externalization of service production is largely seen "as a manifestation of the transformation in how production take place and more specifically of a shift in emphasis within firms toward such functions as finance, advertising, research, product development (Ibid.)." In practical terms, externalization takes place in two ways: in-house services being increasingly replaced by the purchase of specialized services from other firms, or in-house services being sold to outside clients.

generally very limited, and much of services are provided as part of public administration (the largest service provider in society).

In retrospect, at the height of its holistic (developmental) approach to the services, the secretariat dealt with typical strategic questions such as:

- To what extent should the public (rather than the private) sector provide service products and welfare purposes?
- To what extent should domestic (rather than foreign) producers provide particular service products for security reasons?
- What service sub-sectors should be given priority in order to ensure balanced growth and development?
- To what extent should particular service sub-sectors be supported for production and export of goods?
- To what extent should each service sub-sector contribute to the attainment of employment and balance-of-payments goals?
- To what extent can regional cooperation among developing countries be a means to overcome various constraints that may construe the establishment and efficient running of services organizations in developing countries.

III. 1996–Present: Trade in Services[13]

During the Tokyo Round in the 1970s, the term, "trade in service" did not appear in the language of multilateral commercial diplomacy. Around the end of the decade, however, some developed countries intensified their campaign to create a consensus in favour of international negotiations on trade in services with the view to establishing a multilateral framework for services. The United States was the single most prominent proponent of including trade in services in the Uruguay Round Agreement. The proposal met with resistance from the developing countries, who were concerned that the discussion of services in a GATT context could create a basic assumption that GATT principles, such as national treatment, should apply to services and that they would be open to retaliation on trade in goods if they did not apply such principles. As explained earlier, they ultimately

---

[13] Trade in services had been defined previously as "invisible transactions" in GATT. The definition of what would constitute such trade (which included factor movements) had to be worked out during the negotiations of the Uruguay Round. This led to certain incongruities between the definition of trade in goods and that of trade in services. Trade in service has been defined to include "four modes of supply": supply through cross-border movement, the movement of consumers, commercial presence, and the presence of natural persons.

agreed to conduct negotiations on trade in services once it was settled that such negotiations would be conducted within an ad hoc juridical framework of reference outside GATT, and that the promotion of economic growth of all trading partners and the development of the developing countries through the expansion of trade in services under the conditions of transparency and progressive liberalization would be their main aim.

The General Agreement on Trade in Services (GATS) was the first ever agreement of legally enforceable rules – indeed, it was an entirely new contractual framework – to govern trade in services. It drew upon GATT principles such as national treatment, but placed them in a different context. The Agreement consists of (i) a general framework; (ii) sectoral annexes; and (iii) national schedules containing commitments on market access and national treatment and additional commitments in specific service sub-sectors. The most notable feature of the Agreement is not so much the degree of liberalization that it has achieved but rather the extension of the scope of multilateral trade rights and obligations to cover measures affecting such diverse aspects as FDI flows, professional qualifications as well as the movements of persons and electronic data across national boundaries, thus making them legitimate subject-matter in the future negotiations.

GATS establishes a series of general obligations, including unconditional MFN treatment for all measures affecting trade in services, with the exception of specific derogations that have to be notified by countries wishing to claim them when accepting the Agreement. National treatment and market access commitments, however, are confined to those relating to the sectors, sub-sectors and modes of supply specifically included in the individual Schedules of Commitments of each member. The promotion of development is an inherent objective of the Agreement and is not stated in terms of "special" treatment.

IV. 1995–Present:
FDI in Services

One of the earliest studies of the UNCTAD secretariat in FDI in the service sector is found in *TDR 1988*, which, as already discussed, included an extensive research on services. The report pointed out a recent tendency for some manufacturing TNCs to divest themselves of these lesser value-added components in the production process and have ended up no longer producing any physical goods, but only providing various high value-added services. (Ibid.: 178). The movement of capital abroad to establish a "presence" in foreign markets is a common means of delivering services to foreign markets. The report also pointed out the unclear demarcation between "trade in service" and "investment" (Ibid.: 180).

As a result of the absorption of the Commission on Transnational Corporations in 1993, the UNCTAD secretariat's involvement in FDI-related research has rapidly developed. Particularly, the annual publication of the *World Development Report* (*WIR*) has drawn increasing attention to a wide range of FDI-related issues. The inclusion of FDI in the Uruguay Round agreement (TRIMS) was likewise another important factor underscoring the importance of FDI-related issues.

As the service sector has grown to occupy a larger and larger share of national economies, the sector has drawn attention as a principal destination for FDI. The ascendance of services in FDI in host countries took place in developed countries (which have also always been dominant home countries for service FDI), with developing host countries joining the process in the second half of the 1980s (when they began to open service sub-sectors to FDI), and transition economies becoming involved in the early 1990s. With the liberalization of FDI during the 1990s, a new industry pattern of service FDI began to emerge. While trading and financial services remained large industries for service FDI, they were no longer the most dynamic ones. Opening of utilities to FDI through privatization programmes triggered unprecedented increases in FDI in telecommunications and power generation/distribution.[14] However, purchases of State-owned enterprises (SOEs) in many service sub-sectors reached a peak around 1997–1998 before falling subsequently.

WIR 1996 presented a comprehensive analysis of the relationship of FDI with trade. However, the report was basically concerned with the "overall" relationship. The sector specific analysis of the relationship – particularly that of service FDI with trade – was a marginal component in the presentation. The report nevertheless explained that while the service TNCs often exhibit the typical motive of "following customer", this does not always have to be the case; some operate by exploiting ownership-specific advantages. In the cases of service sub-sectors such as banking, advertising, airlines, insurance, hotel and the like, firms may decide they had to follow others expanding abroad to protect their position in the oligopoly. While admitting that little had been known about the trade impact of

---

[14] Between 1990 to 2001, inward FDI stock in telecommunications and power generation/distribution increased worldwide, respectively, 16 times (9 times in developing countries) and 13 times (16 times in developing countries) (UNCTAD, 2003: 6).

FDI in service, it concluded that it should be much smaller that of FDI in manufacturing.

WIR 1996 also offered the three types of general relationships between FDI and trade, depending on whether FDI is made in manufacturing, natural resources or services.

"In natural resources, trade often lead to FDI, and FDI is necessarily trade-supporting and/or trade-creating. In manufacturing, in which market-seeking FDI could either replace or complement trade in a particular product, empirical studies suggest that, on balance, FDI and trade at the industry and country levels are positively related to each other. In tradable services, the situation is similar to that in manufacturing. In non-tradable services, the only thing that matters is trade associated with FDI which is, by definition, positively related to FDI (Ibid.: 91)."

While *WIRs* have analysed the FDI–development nexus, the focus on service FDI has not been strong. In this regard, let us report that the most recent and very extensive research in FDI in services is to be presented in *WIR 2004*, a report which carries the subtitle of "the shift in FDI towards services". The report analyses the principal factors underlying the recent trend of sectoral concentration of FDI in the services sector. The report included intensive research covering wide ranges of services activities. However, as of this writing the report is under embargo, and its contents cannot be revealed further.

References

Das, Bhagirath Lal (1998), *The WTO Agreements: Deficiencies, Imbalances and Required Changes.* London and New York: Zed Books Ltd.

Dunkley G (1997), *The Free Trade Adventure: The WTO, the Uruguay Round and Globalism – A Critique.* London and New York: Zed Books Ltd.

Gibbs M and Mashayekhi M (1991). Development in the Uruguay Round Negotiations on Trade in Services, In: UNCTAD, ed., *Services in Asia and Pacific: Selected Papers, Vol. Two.* UNCTAD/UNDP technical assistance project for support to Asia-pacific developing countries in multilateral trade negotiations. UNCTAD/ITP/51.

UN (1994). Role of transnational corporation in services – Expansion of foreign direct investment and trade in services, Report by the UNCTAD secretariat. E/C.10/1994/4.

UNCTAD (1983). Production and trade in services, policies and their underlying factors bearing upon international services transaction, Report by the UNCTAD secretariat. TD/B/941 and Corr.1.

_____ (1984). Technology in the Context of Services and the Development Process. TD/B/102.

_____ (1985a). *The History of UNCTAD 1964-1984.* UNCTAD/OSG/286, New York.

_____ (1985b). Services and the development process, Study by the UNCTAD secretariat. TD/B/1008/Rev.1.

_____ (1986). Services and the development process: Further studies pursuant to Conference resolution 159 (VI) and Board decision 309 (XXX). TD/B/1100 and Corr.1.

_____ (1987). Revitalizing Development, Growth, and International Trade: Assessment and Policy Options, Report to UNCTAD VII. TD/328/Rev.1.

_____ (1988). *Trade and Development Report 1988.* New York.

_____ (1991). Accelerating the development process: Challenge for national and international policies in the 1990s, Report by the Secretary-General of the United Nations Conference on Trade and Development to the eighth session of the Conference. TD/354/Rev.1.

_____ (1992). UNCTAD VIII: Analytical report by the UNCTAD secretariat to the Conference. TD/358, New York.

_____ (1993). *The Least Developed Countries Report 1992*. TD/B/39(2)/10.

_____ (1994a). The Outcome of the Uruguay Round: An initial assessment – Supporting papers to the *Trade and Development Report. 1994*. New York.

_____ (1994b). *Trade and Development Report 1994*. New York.

_____ (1996). *World Investment Report 1996*. New York and Geneva.

_____ (2003). FDI and development: The case of privatization–related services FDI: Trends impacts and policy issues, Note by the UNCTAD secretariat. E/C.10/1994/4.

_____ (2004). *World Investment Report 2004 – Part II: Shift toward Services*. New York and Geneva.

Foreign Direct Investment
and Transnational Corporations

Torbjörn Fredriksson and Zbigniew Zimny *

Introduction

The thinking and development-oriented work of UNCTAD on foreign direct investment (FDI) and transnational corporations (TNCs) has moved from a marginal position on UNCTAD's agenda to a key area of work in which the Organization has earned a strong reputation for contributing to mainstream thinking on the subject. UNCTAD's approach to FDI and development reflects changes in the outside world, in particular evolving attitudes of countries towards FDI and TNCs – from perceiving TNCs as being part of the problem to being part of the solution. The changing attitudes took the form of widespread opening up to FDI – since the mid-1980s in developing countries and since the early 1990s in transition economies – and further FDI liberalization in developed countries. Liberalization has led to intense competition among countries to attract FDI.

TNCs, helped by technology and under competitive pressure, responded to liberalization. As a result FDI has grown fast –faster than world output or exports – with its inward stock increasing worldwide from $1 trillion in 1985 to over $7 trillion in 2002. TNCs have also increased vastly in numbers,[1] including those from developing countries, and have become more important in the globalizing world economy, with implications for both developed and developing countries. The number of parent firms worldwide is now over 60,000, controlling some 870,000 foreign affiliates and forming with them a system of international

*Mr. Zimny was Head of the Investment Issues Analysis Branch, Division on Investment, Technology and Enterprise Development (DITE). Mr. Fredriksson is Officer-in-Charge, Policy Issues Section, Investment Issues Analysis Branch, DITE. The authors have benefited greatly from useful comments by John H. Dunning, Persephone Economou, Fulvia Farinelli, Masataka Fujita, Charles Gore, Shigehisa Kasahara, Padma Mallampally, Peter Mihalyi, Anne Miroux, Lorraine Ruffing, Satwinder Singh, Anh-Nga Tran-Ngyuen, and Jörg Weber. Special thanks for comprehensive comments go to Karl P. Sauvant, Director of the Division on Investment, Technologies and Enterprises (DITE), responsible for the analytical work of the TNC programme since the time of the United Nations Centre on Transnational Corporation (UNCTC) in New York.
[1] For example, the number of 7,000 TNCs from 14 OECD countries in the late 1960s had grown to 24,000 by 1990.

production, a key driving force of globalization. They account for some two thirds of world trade, an even greater share of research and development (R&D) and employ directly more than 53 million workers in their foreign affiliates around the world (*World Investment Report (WIR) 2003*). Global sales of foreign affiliates are about two and a half times higher than global exports (compared to almost parity two decades ago) and the global gross product attributed to foreign affiliates is about one-tenth of global GDP (compared to 5 per cent in 1982). TNCs are principal agents of globalization, for better or worse.

Over the years the activities of TNCs and their principal form, FDI, which are embedded increasingly deeply not only in the economic but also the political, social and cultural fabric of host societies, have been subject to heated debate both outside and within UNCTAD. The tone of the debate has changed, with attitudes of countries towards TNCs changing from hostile or cautious to positive. Today few question the *potential* benefits FDI can bring to host countries (in terms of capital, technology, employment, access to markets, competition, etc.), but many also draw attention to the possible negative consequences an increased level of foreign ownership can imply or to the fact that expected benefits have not materialized or simply that a large number of developing countries remains marginalized in the global economy, not receiving enough FDI. Yet the debate is still full of misunderstandings or oversimplifications and is often guided by human and political emotions rather than economic analysis. Understanding TNCs' activities and their full implications is still a challenge since they involve a vast number of areas (ranging from finance, through trade, employment and environment to technology), take a variety of forms (FDI is but one of them – others are non-equity forms such as partnerships, alliances, franchising, licensing, etc.) and have many non-economic implications. Moreover, poor data on both FDI and TNCs do not make the task of better understanding easy.

UNCTAD – an economic development agency – has participated in and contributed to this debate since its inception both through its intergovernmental machinery and through the secretariat, although with differing intensity. UNCTAD's role increased in the early 1990s, when it became the focal point within the UN system for all matters related to FDI and TNCs, the time that the Programme on TNCs (implemented since the mid-1970s by the UN Centre on Transnational Corporations) was transferred from New York. The purpose of this paper is to review how UNCTAD's intellectual contribution in the area of FDI has evolved over time within the United Nations (UN) system and place UNCTAD's work in a relevant political and economic context. It reflects discussions with some of those who have been involved either as contributors to the work or as readers of the works of UNCTAD. An important source of guidance has been the reviews of *WIRs*, highlighting the merits and weaknesses of individual *WIRs* over the years.[2] The discussion is organized chronologically, marking the evolution of attitudes towards TNCs and FDI: the 1960s and 1970s, the 1980s and the 1990s up to the present.

I.   The 1960s and 1970s:
From Interest in Capital Inflows
to Criticism of TNCs

UNCTAD as an organisation was established with its main interest and focus on trade. FDI was not seen at that time as mattering much for development. Still, the importance of private investment capital was noted in UNCTAD's documents although it was not much reflected in its work programme. This mirrored the spirit of that time which was characterised *inter alia* by the end of colonialism and the example of centrally planned economies (many of which were still growing rapidly). Many developing countries relied on planning and state ownership of enterprises in sectors crucial to development such as financial services (commanding heights of the economy), infrastructure (strategic industries) and large manufacturing enterprises. Import-substitution strategies were in fashion in many countries, especially in Latin America and Africa and in most Asian countries, except for a few East Asian tigers. All this meant a rather limited role for FDI (and in centrally planned economies no role) in development strategies. Many foreign enterprises were nationalized in the post-colonial era. A number of countries, notably in Latin America, attracted FDI to manufacturing as part of their industrialization effort under import substitution strategies. Indeed, at that time Latin America was the largest host region for FDI among developing countries.

Early UNCTAD documents emphasized the capital flow aspect of FDI.[3] At the first UNCTAD Conference in 1964 some recommendations called upon member countries to "adopt measures which will stimulate the flow of private investment capital for the economic development of the developing countries, on terms that are satisfactory both to the capital-exporting countries and the capital-

---

[2] For reviews of various *WIRs*, see www.unctad.org/wir.
[3] Even before UNCTAD the UN had addressed the role of foreign investment. In the Havana Charter (1948) the investment provisions were among the most controversial, contributing to the failure of establishing the International Trade Organisation (ITC) in the late 1940s (see United Nations Conference on Trade and Employment, 1948).

importing countries", noting the responsibilities of home countries, host countries, investors and the international community (UN, 1964: 49–50).

UNCTAD I recommended that Governments of *capital-exporting* developed countries avoid measures "preventing or limiting the flow of capital from such countries to developing countries, and ... take all appropriate steps to encourage the flow of private investments to developing countries, such as tax exemption or reductions, giving investment guarantees to private investors, and by facilitating the training of managerial and technical staff." With regard to *private-capital-importing* countries, the Conference recommended that they take "all appropriate steps to provide favourable conditions for direct private investment". Developing countries were encouraged to "set up investment bureaux and investment advisory services ... establish and strengthen credit institutions and development banks and ... determine and publicize the areas of investment, manner of investment and investment policy." The Conference furthermore recommended developing countries "to establish information centres in capital markets and adopt other suitable means to supply all the necessary information about investment conditions, regulations and opportunities in the developing countries" (UN, 1964: 49). Moreover, UN bodies and developed country Governments were requested to assist developing countries in these endeavours.

As regards the role of foreign private investment, UNCTAD I concluded that "based upon respect for the sovereignty of the host country, [it] should co-operate with local initiative and capital, rely as far as possible on existing resources in developing countries, and ... work within the framework and objectives of the development plans with a view to supplying domestic markets and, in particular, expanding exports". The Conference expressed its expectation that foreign private investment would "...recognize the desirability of re-investment of profits in the developing countries concerned ... availability of "know-how" ... employment opportunities...and other corresponding measures". Finally, the UN Secretary General was encouraged to arrange for studies on all aspects of foreign private investment and the World Bank was requested to "expedite its studies on investment insurance".

The general perception in 1964 was that FDI could contribute to greater capital formation, thus economic development, with little recognition yet of its importance as a package of resources whose potential benefits to development go much beyond supplementing domestic savings. Indeed, the general message was to make all parties concerned assume responsibility for facilitating more such capital flows to developing nations.

During the 1970s the focus shifted for the first time from private capital flows to the activities of TNCs, and not in a positive direction. The shift was triggered by events in both developed and developing countries. In the United States allegations concerning the malpractices of a number of large United States TNCs caught the attention of the Securities and Exchange Commission. There were also allegations concerning the interference of TNCs in political matters in developing countries. In a speech at UNCTAD III, in Santiago, President Allende, in his capacity as Head of the host country for the Conference, made a passionate speech at the opening session accusing United States TNCs of intervening in Chile's internal affairs.[4]

Resolution 56 (III) of UNCTAD III, convened in May 1972 on the eve of these events in Santiago, Chile, indicated changing sentiments about TNCs. It emphasized the right of developing countries to regulate TNCs in line with national development needs and to avoid possible adverse effects, highlighting the negative impact outflows of private capital had had on the balance of payments. The Conference affirmed "the sovereign right of developing countries to take the necessary measures to ensure that foreign capital operates in accordance with the national development needs of the countries concerned". It also expressed "its concern [about certain aspects of private foreign investment] that disrupt competition in the domestic markets, and their possible effects on the economic development of the developing countries". Furthermore, the Conference recognized "that private foreign investment, subject to national decisions and priorities, *must* facilitate the mobilization of internal resources, generate inflows and avoid outflows of foreign exchange reserves, incorporate adequate technology, and enhance savings and national investment". Finally, it urged "developed countries to take the necessary steps to reverse the tendency for an outflow of capital from developing countries" (UNCTAD, 1973a: 89). Meanwhile, a report prepared for the Committee on Invisibles and Financing related to Trade (CIFT) added a nuance by stating that it was impossible to draw general conclusions on the effect of private foreign investment on the economies of developing countries and that the outcome would vary from case to case (UNCTAD, 1973b).

The oil crisis of 1973, which was a result of the success of the Organisation of Petroleum Exporting Countries (OPEC) in raising and controlling prices, and the concerns related to the perceived growing political and economic power of TNCs, contributed to a wave of nationalizations which peaked in the first half of the 1970s. Political sentiments vis-à-vis TNC activities had drawn public attention to

---

[4] In a subsequent speech at the UN General Assembly in November 1972, President Allende singled out the International Telephone and Telegraph Corporation (ITT).

ways and means through which governments could gain more control over their activities. By the mid-1970s TNCs were seen in many quarters as agglomerations of too much political and economic power and as necessary evils at best. Their activities in developing countries were perceived as a threat to sovereignty. If not controlled they could be detrimental to host countries, carrying the risk of neo-colonialism and environmental and social degradation as possible outcomes. Against this background the policy response was to seek ways for national and international bodies to monitor, restrict and regulate TNCs.

The objectives set by the New International Economic Order (NIEO) through UN resolutions on the Code of Conduct reflected the change of general perceptions, triggered by political and economic events. The focus became the problem of controlling the political and economic activities of TNCs out of developing countries' genuine concerns about their sovereignty, considered an important prerequisite for economic development at that time. But the work of the Commission on TNCs, including that on the Code of Conduct, was affected by Cold War confrontations characteristic of the work of the UN. Cases in point were the endless discussions on what constitutes a TNC. Were State-owned enterprises, originating from centrally planned economies with activities in more than one country (e.g. Aeroflot), to be regarded as TNCs? If so, should they be covered by the Code of Conduct in the same way as private enterprises driven by "capitalist" motives? With major state-owned enterprises (SOEs) on both sides of the "Iron Curtain" the issue was never resolved. But on a number of substantive issues the Code negotiations achieved surprisingly good compromises which were reflected in international investment agreements concluded later.

In the Cold War context, attitudes towards TNCs became more cautious or even hostile. Apart from the events of the early 1970s there was not much economic necessity for change: Western banks were swamped with petrodollars and international credit was easy to obtain, even for centrally planned economies. This reinforced the reliance on SOEs: even if in trouble they could count on financial support from governments.

As regards UNCTAD, UNCTAD IV (1976) adopted resolution 97 (IV) on TNCs recommending, in the spirit of the NIEO, action at the national, regional and international levels to achieve a reorientation in the activities of TNCs and thus to safeguard the interests of developing countries. The resolution also recommended that measures be designed and implemented to strengthen the participation of developing countries' national enterprises in TNC activities. The content of this resolution reflected the overall critical sentiment of many developing countries pushing for the formulation of an international code of conduct for TNCs.[5]

During the second half of the 1970s the intergovernmental machinery of UNCTAD was also engaged in discussions concerning the possible impact of restrictive business practices of TNCs.[6] This work eventually resulted in the Set of Multilaterally Agreed Equitable Principles and Rules on Restrictive Business Practices which was adopted by the UN General Assembly in 1980 (see also the topical paper on Competition, Law and Policy in this volume).

II.   The 1980s:
The Pendulum Swings Back

In the 1980s the pendulum started to swing back: for several reasons the focus of attention increasingly turned towards the possible positive impacts of FDI on development. The decennium started with recession and stagflation in the main markets. Meanwhile, a large number of developing countries ran into a severe debt crisis as a result of which many sources of financing dried up.[7] Thus developing countries became more interested in non-debt creating sources of external private finance, and FDI was viewed as such a source. The lingering debt crisis in many developing countries, however, continued to stifle FDI flows to them by feeding the general perception of high risk, diminished profitability and poor growth prospects. In fact, the share of net FDI inflows to developing countries in total FDI fell from more than one-quarter in the early 1980s to less than one-fifth in the late 1980s.[8] Moreover, as indebted countries had to turn to international financial institutions for additional support or debt rescheduling, these institutions were given greater say in what these countries should do to get help. Structural adjustment programmes entered the standard policy prescriptions, and the "Washington Consensus" ideology was an important basis for many of these prescriptions. In this context a part of the recommendations was to open up not only to trade but also to FDI (including through privatization) and to assign in

---

[5] Meanwhile, the same resolution also included a request that UNCTAD extend "full co-operation to the Commission on Transnational Corporations and the Information and Research Centre on Transnational Corporations" in selected area (para. 3).
[6] See for example Conference resolution 73(VI) of UNCTAD II, paragraphs 4a and 4b; Conference resolution 96(IV) of UNCTAD IV (1976), part III; and the document entitled *Dominant position of market power of transnational corporations: Use of the transfer pricing mechanism* (TD/B/C.2/167) of 1978.
[7] Even though the Cold War continued, the Soviet Union ran into economic difficulties and was not so eager any longer to provide financial rescue to indebted developing countries.
[8] In absolute terms, however, the inflows of FDI to developing countries did increase.

general a greater role to market forces while limiting the role of the State, especially as an owner of assets.

Three other key developments initially remained unnoticed but would to have a profound impact on the way FDI was viewed in the development process: (i) the technological revolution and its impact on many industries and economic activities; (ii) the economic success of a few East Asian countries shifted attention to an export-led development strategy, some of them relying on FDI (notably Malaysia, Singapore and Thailand) while other economies (such as Taiwan Province of China and the Republic of Korea) leveraged non-equity forms like original equipment manufacturing contracts; and (iii) the deregulation and liberalization of the services sectors, including FDI, starting in the United States but also affecting Europe, especially through the Single Market programme of the European Union.

These factors pushed towards greater reliance on market forces and a bigger role for FDI. Nationalizations subsided, giving way to a rising wave of privatizations more and more frequently with FDI. This trend gained momentum when Latin American countries, which years before had manifested their shift towards a State-based economic paradigm by nationalizing their infrastructure services, started to re-privatize them. Although some may argue that these steps were mainly a result of pressure from the International Monetary Fund (IMF), with time more and more governments found this to be the desired way to go. Forces that were unleashed by the initial impetus started working on their own, fuelling one another and soon giving rise to fierce competition for FDI. Countries in Central and Eastern Europe were not forced by the IMF to move to a market economy but still took similar steps towards the end of the century, reinforcing the overall shift. Neither was China. Nor were the EU countries which, with the single market programme, addressed for the first time in their history internal barriers to trade and FDI in services. With greater competitive pressure, state-owned enterprises became not only a drain on government budgets but also reduced the international competitiveness of countries. Widespread unilateral FDI liberalization led developed countries to introduce investment issues into the Uruguay Round in an attempt to unify rules. This resulted more modestly in a multilateral framework for trade in services (GATS), which also covers most of FDI in services, and in the Agreement on Trade-related Investment Measures (TRIMs).

This changing attitude towards FDI contributed to a stalling of the Code negotiations in the Commission on TNCs, although UNCTAD VII (1987) in Geneva supported this endeavour (UNCTAD, 1989: 13). As far as the UNCTC was concerned, reflecting the changing times, questions addressed became more focused on the potential positive rather than the possible negative effects of FDI. UNCTC thus continued its work to address the needs of developing countries, but now in a context in which they were increasingly and unilaterally opening up to FDI. This involved addressing the issue of how FDI could affect development and trying to help developing countries negotiate FDI in services within the Uruguay Round without any statistical and analytical support. The former was first reflected in the UNCTC (1988) (the fourth and last voluminous issue of the series, *Transnational Corporations in World Development* of the UNCTC) and in the first few issues in the series of *WIRs* which commenced in 1991. The latter was reflected in a series of publications on FDI and TNCs in services, highly valued by developing country negotiators in the Round. But in spite of that the UNCTC shared the fate of its governing body, the Commission on TNCs, and was dissolved in the early 1990s with its work programme being transferred to UNCTAD.

III. The 1990s into the 21st century: Increased Competition for FDI and Search for More Benefits

The work of UNCTAD – of both the secretariat and the intergovernmental machinery – reflected the change in perception towards FDI and its role in the development process. From the critical stance of the early 1970s the overall emphasis was placed increasingly on the question of *attracting* FDI. Initially, not much attention was paid to the fact that each FDI dollar is not necessarily equal in terms of its developmental impact.

At UNCTAD VIII (1992) in Cartagena this tendency was already clearly visible. In an analytical paper for the conference the Secretariat concluded that the complexity of the interrelationships between FDI and trade, finance, technology and services "and the role of FDI as an engine of growth and development have become crucial issues of the 1990s" (UNCTAD, 1992a:35). In the Final report of UNCTAD VIII the problems of developing countries in relying on domestic savings and external private lending were highlighted. More specifically, the conference in its final document – a new partnership for development: the Cartagena Commitment – argued that countries should create a "favourable environment" for FDI and all member countries were encouraged to consider "ways and means to encourage beneficial flows of [FDI] to the developing world". In this context, reference was made to the use of MIGA's insurance schemes, bilateral investment treaties (BITs), double taxation treaties (DTTs) and incentives to attract FDI (UNCTAD, 1992b: 20).

After Cartagena UNCTAD became the focal point within the UN secretariat for all matters related to FDI and TNCs when the UNCTC's work programme was transferred to Geneva in 1993.[9] UNCTAD was thereby assigned the responsibility for furthering the understanding of the nature of TNCs and their contribution to development, and for creating an enabling environment for international investment and enterprise development through research, policy analysis, technical assistance and consensus building.[10] Consequently the UNCTAD secretariat expanded its activities in this field and, among other things, overtook the responsibility of producing the *WIR*,[11] which has since emerged as one of UNCTAD's flagship reports and is today commonly used as a source of data and analysis related to FDI and development.[12] Contributions by the secretariat since the early 1990s can be summarized within three main areas:

- *Data development to measure the expansion of TNC activities*. Given that the FDI area is relatively new to both researchers and policy makers, development of data and their presentation in user-friendly ways have contributed to a better measurement and understanding of FDI-related phenomena (see annex).

- *Conceptual development and economic analysis*. Various issues of the *WIR* as well as other UNCTAD publications have contributed to the development of new concepts and new approaches to analysing ideas, facts, scholarly research etc. to form a more coherent picture of TNC activities.[13] This work has involved a critical assessment of TNC activities and formed a basis for policy analysis and international consensus building.

- *Policy analysis, technical assistance and consensus building*. Based on the above, the secretariat has been in a position to provide policy advice to governments and/or intergovernmental entities – and indeed to the international community as a whole – as to what actions and policy measures might be taken to increase the contribution of FDI and TNCs to development in not only efficient but also socially acceptable ways and to ensure stakeholder confidence through increased transparency and accountability.

---

[9] Before the transfer the UNCTC had first been subsumed under an economic division at UN headquarters.

[10] The Division on Transnational Corporations and Investment - the initial name of the relevant division within the UNCTAD secretariat - has been changed to the Division on Investment, Technology and Enterprise Development.

[11] As mentioned in the text, the annual *WIRs* replaced the previous quinquennial surveys produced by the UNCTC, the last of which was published in 1988 (UNCTC, 1988).

[12] The more than one million downloads as of February 2004 of *WIR 2003* (or parts of it) from the UNCTAD website after its launch in September 2003 can be seen as a rough indicator of interest in the Report.

[13] For a listing of the sales publications of the UNCTC and UNCTAD as they relate to FDI, see UNCTAD (2004b).

During the period leading to UNCTAD IX (1996) in Midrand, countries intensified efforts to welcome FDI. The Cold War was history, the Single European Market's 1992 programme was implemented and regional integration efforts gained momentum in other parts of the world, including among developing countries. Within the OECD plans were prepared to conclude a multilateral agreement on investment – an attempt that would eventually share the same fate of similar earlier endeavours. Nationally the emphasis was squarely on FDI liberalization and improved standards of treatment and protection of foreign investors in developed, developing and transition economies: during the period 1990–2002, 1,551 (95 per cent) out of the 1,641 changes introduced by 165 countries in their FDI laws were in the direction of greater liberalization (*WIR 2003*: 20). By the mid 1990s virtually all countries welcomed –and increasingly competed for – inward FDI: the vast majority of countries had established investment promotion agencies at the national and sub-national levels to attract inflows of FDI as was once proposed in 1964 at UNCTAD I. The World Association of Investment Promotion Agencies (WAIPA) was established in 1995, with UNCTAD as its secretariat.[14]

The work of the secretariat provided new policy analysis and insights into the evolving international organization of TNC activities. *WIR 1993* conceptualized international production, documented its emergence over three decades and its growing role in the integration of national production systems. It noted the shift in international production towards systems of *integrated international production*. The changing organizational structures of international production raised a number of issues, including that of the "nationality" of TNCs and their affiliates, criteria for taxation of multi-country activities and the responsibilities of TNCs for generating and supporting sustainable production in the countries in which they operate.

When UNCTAD took over the work programme of the UNCTC it also inherited the Intergovernmental Working Group of Experts on International Standards of Accounting and Reporting (ISAR), established in 1982 by a UN Economic and Social Council (ECOSOC) resolution (number 1982/67) in response to the desire to increase the knowledge of what went on inside companies. The Group, which held its 20th session in 2003, offers guidance to policy makers, standard setters and the profession in the areas of accounting and reporting; it remains the only forum open to all developing countries and economies of transition on issues related to accounting and auditing. Since its transfer to UNCTAD, the Group has produced three guidelines: on integrating environmental

---

[14] Currently, there are over 160 national IPAs and well over 250 sub-national ones.

costs and liabilities into financial statements (UNCTAD, 1999b);[15] on the qualifications necessary for professional accountants (UNCTAD, 1999c); and on accounting by SMEs, which is due to be published in 2004.[16]

At Midrand the member countries agreed on a text that reflected optimism with regard to the positive potential role TNCs could play. Paragraph 36 of the Final document – entitled *A Partnership for Growth and Development* – from the Conference conveys the message clearly (UNCTAD, 1996b):

> "Foreign direct investment (FDI) can play a key role in the economic growth and development process. The importance of FDI for development has dramatically increased in recent years. FDI is now considered to be an instrument through which economies are being integrated at the level of production into the globalizing world economy by bringing a package of assets, including capital, technology, managerial capacities and skills, and access to foreign markets. It also stimulates technological capacity-building for production, innovation and entrepreneurship within the larger domestic economy through catalysing backward and forward linkages."

As regards policy responses, the focus was on ways to *attract* more FDI capital. To do so, (para. 37):

> "it is essential to have in place a stable, supportive, effective and transparent legal framework. Intellectual property protection is an essential component of an environment conducive to the creation and international transfer of technology. Investment agreements which signal that investment is valued and that all investors will be treated fairly also promote investment."

In the subsequent paragraph the Partnership document underlined the potential benefits from privatization while acknowledging the need to take possible social aspects into account. Furthermore, the Conference recognized that there had been "very few investment flows to the least developed countries, and in particular into Africa" (para. 40) and it noted that there was "no comprehensive, multilateral framework [for investment] that covers a great majority of countries" but that the "desirability, nature, issues and scope of such a multilateral framework, and especially its development dimensions, are increasingly being analysed and discussed" (para. 41).

---

[15] In 2004, a manual for preparers and users of eco-efficiency indicators was also published (UNCTAD, 2004a).
[16] The Group is currently working on corporate governance and corporate social responsibility within the context of improving the transparency of information provided by enterprises and making them more accountable for their performance and impacts on society.

Although the OECD's attempt to conclude the MAI failed, there was heightened interest in international investment agreements (IIAs) which proliferated rapidly at bilateral and regional levels, increasingly interacting with national FDI policy-making. Yet in distinction to the long tradition of trade negotiations, investment negotiations were uncharted territory, especially to negotiators from developing countries. Issues such as standards of treatment of foreign investors (national treatment, most-favoured-nation treatment and fair and equitable treatment), transfer pricing or investment protection and dispute settlement were new.

In response to this, *WIR 1996 Investment, Trade and International Policy Arrangements,* initiated a work programme on IIAs aimed at helping developing countries negotiators familiarize themselves in depth with complex investment policy concepts and their development implications. A series of nearly 30 "issues papers", known as "pink papers", followed, addressing key concepts and issues relevant to IIAs.[17] In addition, the volume *Bilateral Investment Treaties in the Mid-1990s* (UNCTAD, 1998b) included a comprehensive analysis of the scope, nature and role of BITs in a globalizing world economy. The programme generated various conceptual innovations such as investment-related trade measures (IRTMs), "flexibility" and "national policy space" in the area of FDI policy. In the inter-governmental machinery, based on the Partnership document of UNCTAD IX (paragraph 89(b)), the development dimension of IIAs was reviewed starting in 1997 with an Expert Meeting on "Existing agreements on investment and their development dimension" (UNCTAD, 1997c: question 7:11; 1997d, para. 8), continuing with a meeting on "Existing regional and multilateral investment agreements and their development dimensions" (UNCTAD, 1997e, para. 5; 1998c, para. 4), and culminating in the Expert Meeting on "International investment agreements: concepts allowing for a certain flexibility in the interest of promoting growth and development" (UNCTAD, 1999d; 1999e). UNCTAD also introduced the idea that the concept of "transparency" – central to IIAs – should not only be seen in reference to host countries but also in reference to home countries and TNCs.

---

[17] The series covers the following topics: admission and establishment; competition; dispute settlement (investor-State); dispute settlement (State-State); employment; environment; fair and equitable treatment; FDI and development; home country measures; illicit payments; incentives; IIAs: flexibility for development; investment-related trade measures; lessons from the failed MAI; most-favoured-nation treatment; national treatment; scope and definition; social responsibility; state contracts; taking of property; taxation; transfer of funds; transfer of technology; transfer pricing; transparency; and trends in IIAs - an overview.

IIAs continue to set parameters for national policy making (*WIR, 2003*). At the *bilateral* level the most important instruments are BITs and double taxation treaties (DTTs), with 2,181 BITs and 2,256 DTTs by the end of 2002.[18] At the *regional* level few agreements deal exclusively with investment issues: the trend has been to address such issues in trade agreements. In effect, free trade agreements today are often also free investment agreements. At the *multilateral* level, finally, the General Agreement on Trade in Services (GATS) covers investment issues in the services sector in a comprehensive way and a few other agreements deal with specific issues (such as trade-related investment measures, insurance, dispute settlement, social policy matters).

UNCTAD's normative work and consensus building in the area of IIAs has been recognized internationally. For example, the WTO Ministerial Declaration in Singapore (para. 20) noted that two new WTO working groups on trade and investment and on trade and competition would:

"...draw upon and be without prejudice to the work in UNCTAD and other appropriate intergovernmental fora. As regards UNCTAD, we welcome the work under way as provided for in the Midrand Declaration and the contribution it can make to the understanding of issues. In the conduct of the work of the working groups, we encourage cooperation with the above organizations to make the best use of available resources and to ensure that the development dimension is taken fully into account."

In this context *WIR 2003* examined interactions between international rule-making and national policies. It stressed the importance of sufficient policy space to pursue national policies to promote development benefits from FDI. It also highlighted the need to strengthen home country measures as well as the potential treatment of good corporate citizenship in the context of IIAs – all with a view towards enhancing the development dimension of such agreements.[19] For example, as regards the former it was noted that encouraging outward FDI to developing countries has seldom taken the form of international commitments. Weak links between the needs of developing countries and the design and execution of home country measures, as well as the often uncertain duration of assistance, limit the

---

[18] *WIR 2003* concluded that, as of 2002, BITs covered an estimated 7 per cent of the world stock of FDI and 22 per cent of the FDI stock in developing countries and economies in transition, respectively. DTTs, meanwhile, covered some 87 per cent of world FDI and 57 per cent of FDI in developing countries and transition economies. In addition, more and more bilateral free trade agreements include investment provisions.

[19] In terms of the role of home countries in stimulating FDI flows to developing countries and economies in transition, various areas of intervention have been identified including liberalizing FDI outflows, providing information and incentives, encouraging technology transfers and mitigating risk.

development impact of these measures. Consequently, a key message was that future IIAs "should contain commitments for home country measures" (*WIR, 2003*:163).

The social responsibility of TNCs has also received renewed attention in international discussions. The topic was examined in *WIR 1999* and *WIR 2003*. *WIR 1999* offered an update of developments including the challenge by the Secretary-General Kofi Annan to TNCs to form a "Global Compact" with society, adhering to a set of principles that would protect especially the environment, human and labour rights. Recently a question has been raised of whether an additional aspect of corporate social responsibility should be for TNCs to contribute directly to the advancement of development, e.g. through the creation and upgrading of linkages between foreign affiliates and local enterprises, thereby creating additional employment opportunities, raising skills levels and transferring technology.

Throughout the 1990s the secretariat paid increased attention to the relationship between FDI and development.[20] One important contribution was an analysis of the links between market structure, competition policy and FDI.[21] This is a very pertinent policy area since TNCs tend to be best represented in industries with a high level of market concentration. *WIR 1997* explored the balance between liberalization and competition policy, merger laws conducive to development along with the need for, and obstacles to, international cooperation. In *WIR 1998* the secretariat underlined the role of government policy in attracting desired kinds of FDI. In particular, the volume showed that the importance of traditional FDI determinants (e.g. natural resources, low-cost labour, national market size) was declining while access to "created assets" (such as skills and technology) and to regional markets (such as the European Community and the North American Free Trade Agreement (NAFTA)) had become more important. But the key contribution to nuancing the debate on the role of FDI on development was the *WIR 1999* with the subtitle *FDI and the Challenge of Development* – prepared as an input to UNCTAD X (2000). It provided a comprehensive examination of the role of FDI

---

[20] Three *WIR*s have undertaken comprehensive assessments of the impact of FDI on growth, competitiveness and development. *WIR 1992* with the subtitle *Transnational Corporations as Engines of Growth* contained the secretariat's first full-scale assessment of the links between FDI and growth.

[21] As noted above, however, UNCTAD has worked actively on issues related to competition and to the control of restrictive business practices by TNCs For a long period of time. UNCTAD was, *inter alia*, responsible for the negotiations on and conclusion of the United Nations Set of Multilaterally Agreed Equitable Principles and Rules for the Control of Restrictive Business Practices which was approved by the UN General Assembly on 5 December 1980 in its resolution 35/63. (See also the topical paper on Competition Law and Policy in this volume.)

in economic development through structural transformation and growth, focusing on five areas in which TNCs can complement domestic efforts to meet development objectives.[22] One chapter addressed the role of FDI in increasing financial resources and investment giving special attention to the question of whether FDI "crowds in or out" domestic investment.

It is probably fair to say that the expectations concerning FDI were at their peak at the time of UNCTAD X (2000) in Bangkok. The Conference coincided with the last year of the strongest FDI boom in history, due to a dramatic increase in cross-border mergers and acquisitions (M&As) mainly among developed countries but also involving developing countries: in East and South-East Asia as a result of the Asian financial crisis; and in Latin America and Central and Eastern Europe as a result of privatization programmes. This led to concerns that FDI in the form of foreign takeovers of domestic firms represent merely a change in ownership but contribute little to development. *WIR 2000* helped clarify the impact of cross-border M&As on development, distinguishing between "normal" and "exceptional" situations (such as during systemic change to market economies and during financial crisis) in which foreign acquisitions take place on the one hand, and between short-term and long-term impacts on host countries on the other.

The Bangkok Declaration placed the emphasis on the need of countries to *attract* FDI (paragraphs 47 and 48), emphasizing that many countries, notably LDCs, are hardly receiving any FDI:

> "The mobilization of external resources for development in the 1990s has been characterized by an increasing privatization of resource flows to developing countries. International investment flows have increased at a faster pace than world output and world trade since the early 1980s. As a result, international investment and in particular FDI has emerged as one of the driving forces in the world economy, contributing not only to the integration of markets, but also, increasingly to the integration of national production systems. Countries that do not attract sufficient FDI flows are also deprived of other tangible and intangible resources which are central to development."

> "To attract such resources, developing countries strive to create a favourable and enabling investment climate to attract international investment flows. In addition, national efforts at liberalization are increasingly complemented by facilitation and protection efforts at the

---

[22] The five areas are: increasing financial resources and investment; enhancing technological capabilities; boosting export competitiveness, generating employment and strengthening the skills base; and protecting the environment.

international level. However, while FDI flows to developing countries have increased, the LDCs' share in total FDI flows stood at less than one-half of one per cent in 1998. To remedy this situation, policies need to be developed by developing countries to attract and benefit from FDI. The international community should support developing countries in their efforts to devise FDI strategies and appropriate proactive policy frameworks and institutions which would impose the least possible burden on fiscal resources. Some countries have introduced home country measures to promote FDI flows to developing countries, and such measures deserve to be encouraged. A favourable and enabling investment climate which mobilizes FDI and domestic savings and channels them into productive investments also requires that the suppliers of capital have reliable, transparent and comparable financial information."

After the end of the FDI boom of the latter half of the 1990s high expectations on FDI continued to prevail, but they were also increasingly qualified. Countries have actively sought to attract FDI, sometimes giving rise to excessive incentives-based competition between (or within) countries.[23]

But disappointments and disillusionment also grew in the light of unmet expectations resulting from simply opening up to FDI. After the Asian financial crisis (1997–1998)[24] and the end of the major privatization programmes in many Latin American countries, as well as the continuously low levels of FDI to Africa, it has become generally recognized that FDI is only a complement to domestic investment – the bedrock of economic development. Moreover, sustainable development benefits to host countries depend to a high degree on the absorptive capacity of the local enterprise sector. This has led to more focus on policies that could help overcome disappointments and also to a search for ways to benefit more from FDI as well as address various concerns related to such investment. As noted above, there has been resumed interest in the possible role of both host and home country policies.

Responding to this interest, *WIR 2001* and *WIR 2002* went beyond policy recommendations at a fairly general level, formulating policies aimed at achieving two widely expected benefits from FDI: linkages between FDI and domestic enterprises and export promotion involving foreign affiliates.[25] The former showed

---

[23] The expanded use of incentives to attract FDI was documented in UNCTAD (1996a), which offered a comprehensive survey of their use and types, drawing attention to their limited effectiveness for attracting FDI.
[24] The secretariat helped clarify the role and impact of FDI in the crisis and the subsequent recovery (UNCTAD, 1998a).
[25] The role of FDI in the area of services will be reviewed in *WIR 2004.*

that where linkage creation takes place, production and exports by foreign affiliates are not only likely to be more sustainable and broadly beneficial for host countries, they are also likely to involve higher domestic value added and contribute more to strengthening the competitiveness of the domestic enterprise sector. The question of how best to promote linkages between foreign affiliates and domestic firms was also addressed.[26]

In *WIR 2002* the analysis showed that the role of foreign affiliates in the export performance of many developing and transition economies is pervasive and has led to significant shifts in the geographical composition of world exports.[27] It also noted that export-oriented foreign affiliates often rely considerably on imported inputs, implying a low level of local value-added in the exported products. Thus addressing various ways to augment the interaction between foreign affiliates and the local economy has become more important.[28]

During the 1990s, complementing its policy analysis and normative work, UNCTAD expanded its technical assistance programme in the area of investment. In particular it launched a series of *Investment Policy Reviews* (first advocated in *WIR 1993)*,[29] *Investment Guides for LDCs*,[30] investment promotion and linkage promotion activities. In addition it initiated a broad-based technical assistance programme on matters related to IIAs, including BITs among developing countries. Jointly with the WTO, UNCTAD contributed to a significant post-Doha technical assistance programme on investment (UNCTAD, 2002b; 2003).

The broader work was based on the experience of three generations of investment promotion: from general liberalization and opening up to FDI (first generation), to setting up investment promotion agencies and related activities

---

[26] The work has been translated into concrete actions in the field in the form of an UNCTAD linkage promotion programme within EMPRETEC (short for Empresas Technologicas), a technical cooperation programme initiated in 1988 by UNCTC to help developing countries establish the institutional structures for the promotion of entrepreneurship along with small and medium-sized enterprise (SME) development.

[27] Just 20 economies together account for over three-quarters of the value of world trade, with the developed countries being the largest traders. However, during the period 1985-2000 it was mainly developing economies such as China, Mexico, the Republic of Korea, Singapore, Taiwan Province of China and Thailand, along with economies in transition such as the Czech Republic, Hungary and Poland, who accounted for the largest *gains* in market share. The growth of exports from many of these countries was directly linked to the expansion of international production systems, especially in the electronics and automotive industries.

[28] The analysis has been carried forward into the area of policy analysis and technical assistance especially as regards possible instruments to ensure that a location is conducive to export-oriented FDI, and in terms of the organization of targeted investment promotion, an area in which UNCTAD has developed a specific technical assistance programme.

[29] For more information, see http://r0.unctad.org/ipr/.

[30] For more information, see http://r0.unctad.org/en/pub/investguide.en.htm.

(second generation), moving to the proactive marketing of investment opportunities in a targeted way (third generation). The message conveyed underlined the importance of domestic enterprise development, the need to "work with the market" and create the necessary conditions for investment, coupled with proactive government intervention to induce TNCs to forge local linkages and establish export platforms with a high local value added.[31]

At UNCTAD XI, member States reaffirmed the importance of attracting investment and benefiting from it. They encouraged an integrated policy approach to the issues of investment, technology and enterprise development. The South-South dimension and the issue of policy space were identified as areas in need of careful attention. The Conference encouraged UNCTAD to continue its research and policy analysis, technical assistance and consensus building, as part of UNCTAD's system wide lead role in the area of investment. The São Paulo Consensus reaffirmed the mandate of the Bangkok Plan of Action and highlighted the role of UNCTAD in the area of corporate responsibility. UNCTAD was furthermore called upon to expand its activities in the area of home country measures, investment policy reviews and related follow-up activities, linkages between TNCs and local firms, South–South cooperation and the interrelationship between ODA and FDI.

IV. Concluding Remarks

During the past 40 years the relative emphasis on the pros and cons of development strategies relying on inward FDI has oscillated in response to events in the world. However it is now widely recognized that FDI, as a complement to domestic investment, can bring important development benefits for both host and home economies. It is also clear that policy makers should not rely on passive liberalization and market forces alone. The secretariat's research and policy analysis has underscored the crucial role of active government policies to help ensure that FDI brings development gains: "policy matters" has become a consistent message. On the other hand, FDI is no panacea for breaking out of underdevelopment. The scope for benefiting from inward FDI is closely linked to a country's ability to foster its domestic capabilities, and under the right circumstances FDI can act as a catalyst for economic growth and development. The challenge is to identify the best approaches to leveraging such investment.

---

[31] During the 1990s the secretariat offered three important contributions by the secretariat in the area of enterprise development and cluster policies: see publications (UNCTAD, 1997a) and (UNCTAD, 1998d).

Moreover, international agreements at various levels should recognize the need for governments to be able to design and implement national policies that can help advance development objectives.

At both national and international levels the growth of FDI and the international production systems of TNCs are regarded as critical factors for the formulation of policy responses to the challenge of globalization. Throughout its work the secretariat has documented how important these phenomena are, addressed key themes at early stages as well as developed new concepts and kept following them over time. In this way UNCTAD has helped to bring out the subject of FDI and TNC activities from a fairly small corner in the study of, and policy formulation related to, international economic relations and has contributed to according it a more central place as a factor in those relations. Moreover, the research and policy work has interacted with technical assistance work in the field as well as with national Governments through its intergovernmental machinery.

In the area of FDI and development there are no clear-cut answers or one-size-fits-all solutions. The secretariat has played its role in advancing the intellectual comprehension of the phenomenon of FDI and has developed policies to deal with it. According to John H. Dunning, perhaps the most prominent scholar of FDI and TNC activities,

> "Successive *WIRs* have helped governments, in a way no other publication has done, to know about TNCs – their nature, strategies and likely impact; and to guide them in their information gathering, policy formulation, institution building, and implementation devices."[32]

The expansion of international production, production under the common governance of TNC, underlines the importance of the objectives that were once set for the UNCTC: to improve the understanding of the nature of TNCs and to analyse their effects on home and host countries, including economic relationships between the two. The work of the UNCTAD secretariat (and earlier of the UNCTC) has provided important inputs to policy makers. By collecting, disseminating and analysing data, developing knowledge and applying it to FDI with a focus on developing countries and assessing policy options, it has contributed to placing the relationship between FDI and economic development on the international economic and political agenda. While 40 years of research and policy analysis have brought new insights and knowledge as regards the impacts of TNC activities, the same challenges that faced policymakers in 1964 are still largely relevant today: as once underlined in the UNCTAD I recommendation, in

---

[32] Communication by John H. Dunning to UNCTAD, 19 December 2002.

order to address them in a satisfactory way and to maximize the developmental impact, all parties concerned – host countries, home countries, investors and the international community at large – need to assume their respective roles and responsibilities.

Annex

Measuring the expansion of TNC activities

Without reliable and comprehensive data it is impossible to measure and analyse any economic phenomenon. Given that FDI is relatively new to both researchers and policy makers, the development of data and their presentation in a user-friendly way have been a key pre-requisite to a better understanding of FDI. The development of a database on FDI and other TNC-related activities represents a key contribution by the secretariat.

First, UNCTAD's database (www.unctad.org/fdistatistics) contains different types of data for more than 190 economies on inward and outward flows and stocks of FDI as well as ratios comparing FDI with GDP and gross fixed capital formation. A recent addition is information on cross-border mergers and acquisitions (M&As). These statistics are featured regularly in the statistical annex of the *WIR* and, where relevant, in other publications on FDI and TNCs. They form the basis for the analysis of global and regional trends of FDI and nature of TNC activity in Part One of the *WIR.*.

This overall picture is complemented by national data on up to 88 specific variables (if available) on inward and outward FDI flows and stocks such as their composition by sectors, industries and regions and countries. Variables also refer to operations of foreign affiliates located in individual countries and TNCs based in these countries as well as legal FDI framework. Such information has been published in UNCTAD's *World Investment Directories* (*WID*) and since 2003 in the *WID Country Profiles* available on-line. Finally, depending on the needs of various publications and the special theme selected for the *WIR,* each year a wealth of data is collected and presented on an *ad-hoc* basis.

Second, in addition to FDI-related data the secretariat has developed information on the world's largest TNCs, including several variables on the top 100 TNCs,[33] the top 50 TNCs based in the developing world and recently, the top 25 TNCs based in Central and Eastern Europe. These statistics have allowed for the documentation of TNCs from developing countries. The first list of the world's top 100 TNCs was introduced in *WIR 1993* with data for 1990. At that time all top

---

[33] The largest TNCs are ranked according to the size of their foreign assets.

TNCs were based in developed countries. Only in 1995 (*WIR 1997*) did the first developing country TNCs enter the list.[34]

A third category of statistics relates to the evolving policy framework governing FDI. At the *national* level the tracking of changes in FDI laws and regulations has shown the significant shift that has taken place in the attitude of countries vis-à-vis FDI. For example between 1991 and 2002, out of the more than 1,640 changes that were made in national laws that were observed by UNCTAD, 95 per cent intended to create a more favourable investment climate for inward FDI. At the international level the secretariat monitors bilateral investment treaties, double taxation treaties and other international instruments related to FDI.[35] As part of these efforts (starting in 1996) it has published a total of twelve volumes of *International Investment Instruments: A Compendium.*[36]

While the data compiled by the secretariat on FDI and other international production activities are far from perfect, mirroring the state of national data collection, they constitute the most comprehensive statistical yearbook on the role of TNCs in the global economy. A comparison of the length of the statistical annexes of the first few *WIRs* (25 pages) with that of the most recent one (80 pages) depicts the progress that has been made in this area during the past decade. A massive data-collection effort takes place on a continuing basis in cooperation with national data collecting agencies to ensure that the data presented are as reliable, up to date and comprehensive as possible. In order to facilitate availability, more and more data are being made available online (see http://stats.unctad.org/fdi).

Based on the wealth of statistics, a number of novel analytical and statistical tools have been developed, the better to measure globalization and its implications for developing countries. For example, the data have been used to map the evolving geography of FDI. The very first issue of the *WIR* published in 1991 applied the Triad (the United States, the European Community and Japan) concept to the geographical distribution of FDI and noted that these economies accounted for the bulk of both inward and outward FDI. With regard to FDI between

---

[34] The firms were Daewoo Corporation (Republic of Korea) and Petróleos de Venezuela (Venezuela).
[35] The full listing of bilateral investment treaties is available on-line at http://stats.unctad.org/fdi/eng/ReportFolders/Rfview/explorerp.asp. The actual texts of BITs will be available on-line as of early 2004.
[36] They contain a comprehensive collection of relevant instruments on international investment law, conventions, treaties, declarations, codes and resolutions. The first three volumes start with the Havana Charter of 1948 and end with the 1994 Energy Charter Treaty and the Marrakech Agreement of the World Trade Organization (WTO). In the subsequent volumes, more recent developments at the bilateral, regional and multilateral levels are captured.

developed and developing countries, *WIR 1991* found that TNC networks often have a strong regional dimension with significant links between individual Triad members and associated host countries. This finding was re-confirmed 12 years later in *WIR 2003*.[37] Moreover, the geography of international production featured prominently in *WIR 2001*, in which an effort was made to map various geographical dimensions of TNC activities.

In *WIR 1995* the "transnationality index for the largest TNCs" in the world was introduced. This index captures the average of three ratios: the shares of foreign to total assets; foreign employment to total employment; and foreign sales to total sales. Another innovation, the "transnationality index of host countries" (introduced in *WIR 1999*), measures the degree of transnationalization of economic activities in host economies. Recent additions include the FDI performance and potential indices (see *WIR 2001* to *WIR 2003*). Moreover, the database has allowed the secretariat to undertake and publish analytical work on topical or new issues, e.g. on the Asian financial crisis and FDI (UNCTAD, 1998a), the performance and potential of FDI in Africa (*WIR 1995;* UNCTAD 1999a) and FDI in least developed countries (LDCs) (UNCTAD, 2002a). The database is of major importance not only to the secretariat but also to policy-makers, researchers and journalists around the world.

---

[37] For example, TNCs from the United States played a dominant role in Latin American countries such as Argentina, Chile, Mexico, Panama and Venezuela as well as in the Philippines and Saudi Arabia; the European Community's firms dominated FDI in many countries in Central and Eastern Europe, and in Brazil, Ghana and Indonesia; whereas Japanese firms accounted for more than 50 per cent of total FDI into Hong Kong (China), the Republic of Korea and Thailand. As of 2002 this picture had not changed much, which draws attention to the underlying geographical structure of FDI and international production (*WIR, 2003*).

References

UN (1964). *Proceedings of the United Nations Conference on Trade and Development*, (I), Final Act and Report, E/CONF.46/141 (I), New York.

_____ (1973). Multinational Corporations in World Development, ST/ECA/190, New York.

_____ (1974). Summary of The Hearings Before the Group of Eminent Persons to Study the Impact of Multinational Corporations on Development and on International Relations, ST/ESA/15, New York.

UNCTAD (1973a). Proceedings of the United Nations Conference on Trade and Development, TD/180 (I).

_____ (1973b). Main findings of a study of private foreign investment in selected developing countries: Report of the UNCTAD Secretariat, TD/B/C.3/111.

_____ (1978). Dominant position of market power of transnational corporations: Use of the transfer pricing mechanism, TD/B/C.2/167.

_____ (1985). *The History of UNCTAD 1964–1984*, UNCTAD/OSG/286.

_____ (1989). Final Act of UNCTAD VII, In: *Proceedings of the United Nations Conference on Trade and Development*, seventh session, Geneva, 9 July–3 August 1987, Report and Annexes (1), TD/352.

_____ (1991–2003). *World Investment Report* (Due to the frequent references in the text this report was specially designated as WIR, 1991…WIR 2003).

_____ (1992a). UNCTAD VIII: Analytical report by the UNCTAD secretariat to the Conference, TD/358.

_____ (1992b). Proceedings of the United Nations Conference on Trade and Development, eighth session, Report and Annexes, Part I, Section A, TD/364/Rev.1.

_____ (1994). Technological Dynamism in Industrial Districts: An Alternative Approach to Industrialization in Developing Countries, UNCTAD/ITD/TEC/11.

_____ (1996a). Incentives and Foreign Direct Investment, UNCTAD/DTCI/28.

_____ (1996b). Midrand Declaration and A Partnership For Growth And Development, TD/377.

_____ (1997a). An overview of activities in the area of inter-firm cooperation: A progress report, UNCTAD/ITE/EDS/2.

_____ (1997b). Survey of Best Practices in Investment Promotion, UNCTAD/ITE/IIP/1.

_____ (1997c). Bilateral investment treaties and their relevance to a possible multilateral framework on investment: Issues and questions, TD/B/COM.2/EM.1/2, 21 March.

_____ (1997d). Report of the Expert Meeting on existing agreements on investment and their development dimensions, TD/B/COM.2/5 - TD/B/COM.2/EM.1/3, 18 August.

_____ (1997e). Investment promotion and development: Issues and questions, TD/B/COM.2/EM.2/2, 1 July.

_____ (1998a). The Financial Crisis in Asia and Foreign Direct Investment: An Assessment, TD/UNCTAD/PUBL/98/26.

_____ (1998b). Bilateral Investment Treaties in the Mid-1990s, UNCTAD/ITE/IIT/7.

_____ (1998c). Report of the Expert Meeting on existing regional and multilateral investment agreements and their development dimensions, TD/B/COM.2/11 - TD/B/COM.2/EM.3/3, 22 April.

_____ (1998d). Promoting and sustaining SMEs clusters and networks for development, TD/B/COM.3/EM.5/2.

_____ (1999a). Foreign Direct Investment in Africa: Performance and Potential, UNCTAD/ITE/IIT/MISC.15.

_____ (1999b). Accounting and Financial Reporting for Environmental Costs and Liabilities, UNCTAD/ITE/EDS/4.

_____ (1999c). Guideline for National Requirements for the Qualification of Professional Accountants, UNCTAD/ITE/EDS/9.

_____ (1999d). International investment agreements: Concepts allowing for a certain flexibility in the interest of promoting growth and development, TD/B/COM.2/EM.5/2, 5 February.

_____ (1999e). Report of the Expert Meeting on international investment agreements: Concepts allowing for a certain flexibility in the interest of promoting growth and development, TD/B/COM.2/17–TD/B/COM.2/EM.5/3, 6 May.

_____ (2000a). Tax Incentives and Foreign Direct Investment: A Global Survey, UNCTAD/ITE/IPC/Misc.3.

_____ (2000b). FDI Determinants and TNC Strategies: The Case of Brazil, UNCTAD/ITE/IIT/114.

_____ (2001a). The World of Investment Promotion at a Glance, UNCTAD/ITE/IPC/3.

_____ (2001b). Social Responsibility. UNCTAD Series on Issues in International Investment Agreement, UNCTAD/ITE/IPC/2003/7.

_____ (2002a). FDI in Least Developed Countries at a Glance: 2002, UNCTAD/ITE/IIA/6.

_____ (2002b). Progress report. Work undertaken within UNCTAD's work programme on international investment agreements between the 10th Conference of UNCTAD, Bangkok, February 2000, and July 2002. UNCTAD/ITE/Misc.58.

_____ (2003). Progress Report: Implementation of post-Doha technical assistance work in the area of investment UNCTAD/ITE/IIT/2003/3.

_____ (2004a) A Manual for the Preparers and Users of Eco-Efficiency Indicators.

_____ (2004b), List of publications on foreign direct investment and transnational corporations (1973–2003), UNCTAD/ITE/2004/1.

UNCTC (1988). Transnational Corporations in World Development: Trends and Prospects, United Nations Centre on Transnational Corporations, ST/CTC/89, New York.

United Nations Conference on Trade and Employment (1948). Final Act and Related Documents, E/CONF.2/78.

Part Three

List of Official Documents

UNCTAD/UN Documents[*]

Secretary-General's reports, secretariat reports and *inter alia*

Title	Document No.
International Trade	
Statement by Mr. R. Figueredo, Director of the Manufacturing Division at the Fourth Meeting of Sessional Committee I on 1 October 1981.	TD/B(XXIII)/SC.I/MISC.1
Multilateral trade negotiations: Background note by the UNCTAD secretariat. (1982)	TD/913
Protectionism, trade relations and structural adjustment: Report by UNCTAD secretariat. (1983)	TD/274
Services and the development process: Study by the UNCTAD secretariat. (1985)	TD/B/1008/Rev.1
Trade and Development Report, 1988, Part II, Chapter 3, The strategic role of services	UNCTAD/TDR/8 (Offprint)
Trade in services: Sectoral issues: Studies by the UNCTAD secretariat. Forward and overview:1–48. (1989)	UNCTAD/ITP/26
Uruguay Round Papers on Selected Issues. Section on services: Elements of a multilateral framework of principles and rules for trade in services; Section on developing countries and TRIPs: Developing countries and trade-related aspects of intellectual property rights; Section on tropical products: Tropical products in the Uruguay Round. (1989)	UNCTAD/ITP/10
Uruguay Round: Further papers on selected issues, Part I, Chapters: "Anti-competitive practices in the services sector" and "Notes on a possible multilateral framework for international trade in banking services". (1990)	UNCTAD/ITP/42
Strengthening international organizations in the area of multilateral trade: Note by the Secretary-General of the United Nations. (1991)	A/46/565

---

[*] Kanako Ishiyama compiled this list of historically significant official documents.

287

Title	Document No.
Multilateral trade organization: A preliminary analysis. (1993)	UNCTAD/MTN/INT/CB.27
Supporting papers on the Outcome of the Uruguay Round: An initial assessment, Introduction, Chapter 1: Agreement establishing the world trade organization and Chapter 5: Future issues. (1994)	UNCTAD/TDR/14(Supplement)
Trade and Development Report,1994, Part III: The Uruguay Round: An initial assessment	UNCTAD/TDR/14
New and emerging issues on the international trade agenda: Note by the UNCTAD secretariat. (1995)	TD/B/EX(10)/CRP.1
Report of the Secretary-General of UNCTAD to UNCTAD IX. Chapter 2: Promoting international trade as an instrument for development in the post-Uruguay Round. (1995)	TD/366
Strengthening the participation of developing countries in world trade and the multilateral trading system. (1996)	TD/375/Rev.1
Midrand Declaration and a partnership for growth and development. Chapter 1 A.2: International trade in goods and services, and commodity issues; and Chapter 2 C: International trade in goods and services, and commodity issues (1996)	TD/377
Report of the Secretary-General of UNCTAD to UNCTAD X (2000)	TD/380
Bangkok Plan of Action, Chapter II: UNCTAD's Engagement: C. International Trade. (2000)	TD/390
Positive agenda and future trade negotiations: Studies by the UNCTAD secretariat, Chapter I: Positive agenda for developing countries; Special and differentiated treatment in the context of globalization; and Notes on the implementation of the agreement on agriculture.(2000)	UNCTAD/ITCD/10

Title	Document No.
Trade agreement, petroleum and energy policies. Executive summary and Chapter 1: Implications of the WTO agreements for petroleum policy and trade in petroleum products: 1–59. (2000)	UNCTAD/ITCD/TSB/9
Systems and national experiences for protecting traditional knowledge, innovation and practices: Background note by the UNCTAD secretariat. (2000)	TD/B/COM.1/EM.13/2
WTO accession and development policies, Forward and Introduction: xi–xxiii; and Chapter 2: General Issues in WTO accessions: 159–264 (2002)	UNCTAD/DITC/TBCD/11
Energy and environmental services: Negotiating objectives and development priorities. Forward and Chapter 1: Energy services: vi–69. (2003)	UNCTAD/DITC/TNCD/2003/3
Environmental goods and services in trade and sustainable development: Note by the UNCTAD secretariat. (2003)	TD/B/COM.1/EM21/2
Environmental goods: Trade statistics of developing countries. (2003)	TD/B/COM.1/EM21/CRP.1
Preparation for UNCTAD XI: Submission by the Secretary-General of UNCTAD, Part II, Chapter 3: Assuring development gains from the international trading system and trade negotiation: 37–47. (2003)	TD(XI)/PC/1
Report of the expert meeting on definitions and dimensions of environmental goods and services in trade and development. (2003)	TD/B/COM.1/EM.21/3
Review of developments and issues in the post-Doha work programme of particular concern to developing countries: the outcome of the fifth WTO ministerial conference: Note by the UNCTAD secretariat. Chapter 3: Development benchmarks and Chapter 4: UNCTAD's role: 18–22. (2003)	TD/B/50/8
Trade and Environment Review. (2003)	UNCTAD/DITC/TED/2003/4
Environmental requirements and market access for developing countries: Note by the UNCTAD secretariat. (2004)	TD/(XI)/BP/1

Title	Document No.

Money, Finance and Debt

The case for an international commodity reserve currency. In: Proceeding of United Nations Conference on Trade and Development, Geneva, 23 March – 16 June 1964 (III) Commodity and Trade. AG Hart, N Kaldor and J Tinbergen (1964)	E/CONF.46/141
International monetary issues and the developing countries: Report of the Group of Experts. (1965)	TD/B/32 - TD/B/C.3/6
International monetary reform and cooperation for development: Report of the Expert Group on international monetary issues. (1969)	TD/B/285/Rev.1
International monetary system – Issues relating to development financing and trade of developing countries: Study by the UNCTAD secretariat. (1969)	TD/B/198/Rev.1
The Link: Report prepared by the UNCTAD secretariat. (1971)	TD/118/Supp.4 (A revised version of TD/B/356)
The international monetary situation - impacts on world trade and development: Report by the UNCTAD secretariat. (1972)	TD/140/Rev.1
Debt problems in the context of development: Report by the UNCTAD secretariat. (1974)	TD/B/C.3/109/Rev.1
Report of the Ad Hoc Group of Government Experts on the debt problems of developing countries on its third session (1975)	TD/B/545
Ways and means of accelerating the transfer of real resources to developing countries on a predictable, assured and continuous basis: report by the Secretary-General (1976)	A/31/186
Compensatory financing for export fluctuations: Note by the UNCTAD secretariat. (1979)	TD/B/C.3/152/Rev.1
International financial cooperation for development: Current policy issues: Report by the UNCTAD secretariat. (1979)	TD/234 (Prepared for UNCTAD V)
International monetary issues: Report by the UNCTAD secretariat. (1979)	TD/233

Title	Document No.
Trade and Development Report 1985. Part II: *Debt, development and the world economy*: 62–148.	UNCTAD/TDR/5
Revitalizing development, growth and international trade: assessment and policy options. Chapter 2: Resources for development, including financial and related monetary questions: 47–80. (1987)	TD/328/Rev.1
Trade and Development Report 1999. Part II: Trade, external financing and economic growth in developing countries: 72–146	UNCTAD/TDR/1999
Capital flows and growth in Africa. (2000)	UNCTAD/GDS/MDPB/7
Recent developments in the debt situation of developing countries: Report of the Secretary-General. (2000)	A/55/422
Trade and Development Report, 2001. Part II: Reform of the international financial architecture: 61–153.	UNCTAD/WIR/2001

Global Interdependence and National Development Strategies

Towards a New Trade Policy for Development, *Report of the Secretary-General to UNCTAD I* (1964)	E/CONF.46/141
Towards a Global Strategy of Development, *Report of the Secretary-General to UNCTAD II. (1968)*	TD/3/Rev.1
The Balance of Payments Adjustment Process in Developing Countries: Report to the Group of Twenty-four, Summary and Recommendations; Chapter 3: Evaluation of Issues; Annex A: Origins of the Principle of Conditionality. (1979)	UNDP/UNCTAD Project INT/75/015
TDR 1981, Part III, Chapter 1: The Internationalization of output and trade; Chapter 3: Structural changes in manufacturing output and trade; Chapter 4: International money markets.	TD/B/863/Rev.1
TDR 1982, Part III, Chapter 1: The meaning and relevance of structural change; Chapter 4: Structural change in manufacturing industries; Chapter 5: Structural change and trade in manufactures.	UNCTAD/TDR/2/Rev.1

Title	*Document No.*
TDR 1984, Part II, Chapter 1: Introduction: The trend towards international economic integration; Chapter 4: The growth of international bank lending to developing countries. Part III, Chapter 2: Systems performance and growth; Chapter 3: Towards reform of the trade and payments system.	UNCTAD/TDR/4/Rev.1
TDR 1985, Part Two, Chapter II: Debt and the development crisis.	UNCTAD/TDR/5
TDR 1987, Part Two, Chapter II: Trends in the international flow of technology.	UNCTAD/TDR/7
TDR 1988, Part One, Chapter IV: Debt and development	UNCTAD/TDR/8
TDR 1989, Part One, Chapter IV: Macroeconomic disorder in developing countries; Chapter V: Trade policy reform and export performance in developing countries in the 1980s. Part Two, Chapter II: Structural adjustment programmes in the LDCs; Chapter III: Overview: Experience of Eight Least Developed Countries.	UNCTAD/TDR/9
TDR 1991, Part Two, Chapter III: Financial reform and the development process.	UNCTAD/TDR/11
TDR 1992, Part Three, Chapter I: Reforming trade policies; Chapter II: Reforming public enterprises.	UNCTAD/TDR/12
TDR 1993, Part Two, Chapter II: Adjustment and stagnation in sub-Saharan Africa; Chapter III: Recovery and uncertainty in Latin America; Chapter V: Collapse and transition in Central and Eastern Europe.	UNCTAD/TDR/13
TDR 1994, Part Two, Chapter I: The visible hand and industrialization in East Asia.	UNCTAD/TDR/14
TDR 1995, Part Two, Chapter II: The invisible hand, capital flows and stalled recovery in Latin America; Part Three, Chapter II: Trade, technology and unemployment.	UNCTAD/TDR/15
TDR 1996, Part Two: Rethinking Development Strategies: Some Lessons from East Asian Experience.	UNCTAD/TDR/16

List of Official Documents

Title	Document No.
TDR 1997, Part Two: Globalization, Distribution and Growth.	UNCTAD/TDR/17
TDR 1998, Part One, Chapter 3: International financial instability and the East Asian crisis; Part Two, Chapter 1: Growth and development in Africa: Trends and prospects; Chapter 3: Agricultural policies, prices and production; Chapter 5: Policy challenges and institutional reforms.	UNCTAD/TDR/18
TDR 1999, Part Two: Trade, External Financing and Economic Growth in Developing Countries.	UNCTAD/TDR/19
TDR 2000, Chapter 4, Crisis and recovery in East Asia.	UNCTAD/TDR/20
TDR 2001, Part Two, Chapter 5: Exchange rate regimes and the scope for regional cooperation.	UNCTAD/TDR/21
TDR 2002, Part Two: Chapter 3: Export dynamism and industrialization in developing countries (including annexes); Chapter 4: Competition and the Fallacy of Composition.	UNCTAD/TDR/22
TDR 2003, Part Two: Capital Accumulation, Growth and Structural Change.	UNCTAD/TDR/23
LDCR 2000. Part Two: Chapter 4, Structural adjustment, economic growth and the aid-debt service system; Chapter 5: Debt relief, the new policy conditionality and poverty reduction strategies.	UNCTAD/LDC/2000
LDCR 2002. Part Two: Chapter 2, Generalized poverty, domestic resource availability and economic growth; Chapter 3: Patterns of trade integration and poverty; Chapter 4: Commodity export dependence, the international poverty trap and new vulnerabilities; Chapter 5: National development strategies, the PRSP process and effective poverty reduction.	UNCTAD/LDC/2002
LDCR 2004. Part Two, Chapter 5: Trade liberalization and poverty reduction in the LDCs; Chapter 7: Improving the trade-poverty relationship through national development strategies.	UNCTAD/LDC/2004

Title	Document No.
Development strategies in a globalizing world. (2003)	UNCTAD/GDS/MDPB/Misc.15

Commodities

Towards a new trade policy for development: Report by the Secretary-General of the Conference. Part I, Chapter 2: Primary commodity exports and the deterioration in the terms of trade: 9–13. (1964)	E/CONF.46/141
Approach to frameworks of international cooperation on processing and marketing of primary commodities: Report by the UNCTAD secretariat. (1982)	TD/B/C.1/PSC/27
Selected issues in the negotiation of international commodity agreements – An economic analysis: Study by A. Maizels. (1982)	TD/B/C.1/224
Review of the operation of the compensatory financing facility of the International Monetary Fund: report by the UNCTAD secretariat. (1983)	TD/B/C.1/243
Revitalizing Development, Growth and International trade: A report by the UNCTAD secretariat to UNCTAD VII, Chapter III: Commodities: 81–121. (1987)	TD/328/Add.3
The impact of changing supply-and-demand market structures on commodity prices and exports of major interest to developing countries: Report by the UNCTAD secretariat. (1999)	TD/B/COM.1/EM.10/2
The world commodity economy: recent evolution, financial crises, and changing market structures: Report by the UNCTAD secretariat. (1999)	TD/B/COM.1/27
Strategies for diversification and adding value to food exports: A value chain perspective. (2000)	UNCTAD/DITC/COM/TM/1 UNCTAD/ITE/MISC.23
Export diversification, market access and competitiveness: Report by the UNCTAD secretariat. (2002)	TD/B/COM.1/54

Title	Document No.

Shipping

Establishment or expansion of merchant marines in developing countries. (1968)	TD/26/Rev.1
Level and structure of freight rates, conference practices and adequacy of shipping services. (1968)	TD/B/C.4/38/Rev.1
Bills of Lading. (1972)	TD/B/C.4/ISL/6/Rev.1
The Regulation of Liner Conferences. (1972)	TD/104/Rev.1
Economic consequences of the existence or lack of a genuine link between vessel and flag of registry. (1977)	TD/B/C.4/168 and Add.1
Beneficial ownership of open-registry fleets. (1980)	TD/B/C.4/218
Industry and policy developments in world shipping and their impact on developing countries. (1992)	TD/B/CN.4/5

Technology

Transfer of technology, including know-how and patents: Study by the UNCTAD secretariat. Elements of a programme of work for UNCTAD. (1970)	TD/B/310 and Corr1.
An international code of conduct on transfer of technology. Introduction: 1–4. (1975)	TD/B/C.6/AC.1/2/Supp.1/Rev.1
Major issues arising from the transfer of technology to developing countries: Report by the UNCTAD secretariat. (1975)	TD/B/AC.11/10.Rev.2
Promotion of national scientific and technological capabilities and revision of the patent system: Report by the UNCTAD secretariat. (1975)	TD/B/C.6/AC.2/2
Report of the intergovernmental group of experts on a code of conduct on transfer of technology on its resumed session. (1975)	TD/B/C.6/14
Selected Principal Provisions in National Laws, Regulations and Policy Guidelines. (1975)	TD/B/C.6/AC.1/2/Supp.1/Add.1

Title	Document No.
The reverse transfer of technology: Economic effects of the outflow of trained personnel from developing countries: Study by the UNCTAD secretariat. (1975)	TD/B/AC.11/25/Rev.1
The role of the patent system in the transfer of technology to developing countries: Report prepared jointly by the United Nations Department of Economic and Social Affairs, the UNCTAD secretariat and the International Bureau of the World Intellectual Property Organization. (1975)	TD/B/AC.11/19/Rev.1
Legal and administrative aspects of compensation, taxation and related policy measures: Suggestions for an optimal policy mix. Study by R Pomp and O Oldman (1978)	TD/B/C.6/AC.4/7
Coordinated technological research and development in developing countries: Regional cooperation to strengthen indigenous capacities for innovation: Study prepared at the request of the UNCTAD secretariat by Jan Annersted and Poul Engberg-Pederson, Roskilde University Centre, Roskilde, Denmark. (1980)	TD/B/C.6/63
Renewable energy technology: Issues in the transfer, application and development of technology in developing countries: Report by Mr. Kurt Hoffman. (1982)	TD/B/C.6/AC.9/4
Policies and instruments for the promotion and encouragement of technological innovation: Preliminary report by the UNCTAD secretariat. (1984)	TD/B/C.6/123
Draft International Code of Conduct on the Transfer of Technology. The United Nations Conference on an International Code of Conduct on the Transfer of Technology. (1985)	
The Rio Declaration on Environment and Development: Report of the United Nations Conference on Environment and Development. (1992)	A/CONF.151/26(I)
Report of the Ad Hoc Working Group on the interrelationship between investment and technology transfer on its second session, Geneva. (1993)	TD/B/40(2)/10

List of Official Documents

Title	Document No.
Investment, research and development and interaction among economic agents in technological capacity-building. Country case study submitted by the Arab Republic of Egypt: Prepared by M.B.E. Fayez (1994)	TD/B/WG.5/MISC.20
Compendium of documents and reports relating to the work of the UNCTAD ad hoc working group on the interrelationship between investment and technology transfer: Report by the UNCTAD secretariat. (1995)	UNCTAD/DST/3
Fostering technological dynamism: Evolution of thought on technological capacity-building and competitiveness. (1996)	TD/B/WG.5/7
The TRIPS Agreement and Developing Countries. (1996)	UNCTAD/ITE/1
World Investment Report 2000: Cross-border mergers and acquisition and development: 172–180.	UNCTAD/WIR/2000
Investment and Innovation Policy Review: Ethiopia. (2002)	UNCTAD/ITE/IPC/MISC.4
Report of the Commission on Investment, Technology and Related Financial Issues on its fifth session. (2001)	TD/B/COM.2/31
Science and technology diplomacy, concepts and elements of a work programme. (2003)	UNCTAD/ITE/TEB/MISC.5

Competition Law and Policy

Dominant positions of market power of transnational corporations: Use of the transfer pricing mechanism. (1978)	TD/B/C.2/167
Marketing and distribution arrangements in respect of export and import transactions: Structure of international trading channels. (1981)	UNCTAD/ST/MD/25
Restrictive Business Practices Information, Issue on 13 (1987)	TD/RBP/INF.19
Competition Policy and Vertical restraints: Note by the UNCTAD secretariat (1999)	UNCTAD/ITCD/CLP/MISC.8

Title	Document No.
The UN Guidelines on Consumer Protection (1999)	UNCTAD/DITC/CLP/MISC.21
The scope, coverage and enforcement of competition laws and policies and analysis of the provisions of the Uruguay Round Agreements relevant to competition policy, including their implications for developing and other countries: Study by the UNCTAD secretariat. (1996)	TD/B/COM.2/EM.2
The Set. (2000)	TD/RBP/CONF/10/Rev.2
Analysis of market access issues facing developing countries: consumer interests, competitiveness, competition and development. (2002)	TD/B/COM.2/CLP/21/Rev.1
Experiences gained so far on international cooperation on competition policy issues and mechanisms used. (2002)	TD/B/COM.2/CLP/37
The Revised Model Law. (2002)	TD/RBP/CONF.5/7
Roles of possible dispute mediation mechanisms and alternative arrangements, including voluntary peer reviews, in competition law and policy. (2003)	TD/COM.2/CLP/37

LDCs

Least Developed Countries

Proceeding of the United Nations Conference on Trade and Development (II), Report by the Secretary-General of the Conference: 39, 40 and 62. (1964)	E/CONF.46/141
Special measures in favour of the least developed among the developing countries, identification of the least developed among the developing countries: Report by the UNCTAD secretariat. (1969)	TD/B/269
Special measures in favour of the least developed among the developing countries, report of the group of experts on special measures in favour of the least developed among the developing countries: 1–31. (1969)	TD/B/288

List of Official Documents

Title	Document No.
Proceeding of the United Nations Conference on Trade and Development (IV). Special measures in favours of the least developed among the developing countries, action programme submitted by the Secretary-General of UNCTAD: 227–240. (1972)	TD/135
Proceeding of the United Nations Conference on Trade and Development (IV), Special measures in favour of the least developed among the developing countries, Progress report on identification criteria by the Secretary-General of UNCTAD: 261–265. (1972)	TD/137
The Least Developed Countries and Action in their favour by the International Community. (1983)	A/CONF.104/2/Rev.1
The Least Developed Countries Report 1987: 19–26, 29–45 and 77–85.	TD/B/1153
The Least Developed Countries Report 1989: 15–45 and 113–121.	TD/B/1248
Paris Declaration and Programme of Action for the Least Developed Countries for the 1990s. (1992)	UNCTAD/RDP/LDC/58
The impact of trade liberalization on export and GDP growth in Least Developed Countries: 1–16. Mehdi Shafaeddin (1995)	
The Least Developed Countries Report 1995: 33–70 and 128–134.	TD/B/41(2)/4 UNCTAD/LDC/1995
The Least Developed Country Report 1997: 27–36, 101–119 and 125–147.	TD/B/44/6 UNCTAD/LDC/1997
The Least Developed Countries Report 1998: 63–135 and 157–166.	UNCTAD/LDC/1998
The Least Developed Countries Report 1999:. 21–52 and 109–169.	UNCTAD/LDC/1999
The Least Developed Countries Report 2000	UNCTAD/LDC/2000
Report of the Third United Nations Conference on the Least Developed Countries, Brussels Declaration and Programme of Action for the Least Developed Countries for the Decade. 2001–2010: 1–69. (2000)	A/CONF.191/13

Title	Document No.
Duty- and quota-free market access for LDCs: An analysis of Quad initiatives: XV–XIX and 127–129. (2001)	UNCTAD/DITC/TAB/MISC.7
The Least Developed Countries Report 2002: I–XVII, 17–36 and 137–236.	UNCTAD/LDC/2002
Least developed country status: effective benefits and the perspective of graduation: 1–17. (2002)	TD/B/49/7
Main recent initiatives in favour of least developed countries in the area of preferential market access: Preliminary impact assessment: 1–17. (2003)	TD/B/50/5

Landlocked Developing Countries

Principles relating to transit trade of land-locked countries; preparation of a convention relating to the transit trade of land-locked countries: 25–26, 62–63 and 317–320. (1964)	TD/97
Report of the Group of Experts on the special problems involved in the trade and economic development of the landlocked developing countries: 1–12. (1970)	TD/B/308
Specific action related to the particular needs and problems of landlocked and island developing countries: Report by the UNCTAD secretariat, Part I: Land-locked developing countries. (1983)	TD/279(Part I)
Transit transport systems of the newly independent and developing landlocked states in Central Asia and their developing neighbours: Current situation and proposals for future action: Report of Secretary-General: 1–19. (1994)	A/49/277
Central Asia's trade links with the world, Silken past, troubled present, promising future, Expanding trading through regional transit transport cooperation: 1–21. (1995)	UNDP/UNCTAD Project RER/95/001
Global framework for transit transport cooperation between landlocked and transit developing countries and the donor community: 1–21. (1995)	TD/B/LDC/AC.1/6

Title	Document No.
Challenges and opportunities for further improving the transit systems and economic development of landlocked and transit developing countries: 1–42. (2003)	UNCTAD/LDC/2003/8
The Almaty Programme of Action: Addressing the special needs of landlocked developing countries within a new global framework for transit transport cooperation for landlocked and transit developing countries and donor countries, and international financial and development institutions on transit transport cooperation: 10–27. (2003)	A/CONF.202/3
Small Island Developing States *Developing island countries, Report of the Panel Experts:* 1–23. (1974)	TD/B/443/Rev.1
Report for the group of experts on feeder and inter-island services by air or sea for island developing countries: 1–45 (1978)	TD/B/687
Specific action related to the particular needs and problems of landlocked and island developing countries: Report by the UNCTAD secretariat, Part II: *Island developing countries.* (1983)	TD/279(Part II)
Viability of small island states, A descriptive study by F. Doumenge: 1–37. (1983)	TD/B/950
Small island developing countries and the development potential of exclusive economic zones: 34–69 (1986)	UNCTAD/ST/LDC/7
Development challenges facing island developing countries: basic issues and prospects in the context of trade liberalization and globalization: Report by UNCTAD secretariat: 1–23 (1996)	UNCTAD/LLDC/IDC/2

Services in Development

Trade and Development Report, 1988. Part II: Services in the World Economy: 135–219.	UNCTAD/TDR/8

Title	*Document No.*

Foreign Direct Investment and Transnational Corporations

World Investment Report 1991: The Triad in Foreign Direct Investment, Chapter II: Patterns of Foreign Direct Investment in the Triad: 31–65	ST/CTC/118
World Investment Report 1993: Transnational Corporations and Integrated International Production. Chapter V: Strategies of transnational corporations: 115–132	ST/TCT/156
World Investment Report 1996: Investment, Trade and International Policy Arrangements, Chapter VI: Policy approaches, key issues and fora:161–200	UNCTAD/DTCI/32
Paper on Inter-firm Cooperation. An overview of activities in the area of inter-firm cooperation: A progress report: 83–102 (1997)	UNCTAD/ITE/EDS/2
World Investment Report 1997: Transnational Corporations, Market Structure and Competition Policy, Chapter V: Policy implications: 183–238	UNCTAD/ITE/IIT/5
Bilateral Investment Treaties in the Mid-1990s. Chapter I: Introduction: 1–19 and Chapter V: Conclusions: 138–146 (1998)	UNCTAD/ITE/IIT/7
World Investment Report 1998: Trends and Determinants, Chapter IV: Host country determinants of Foreign Direct Investment: 89–140	UNCTAD/WIR/1998
ISAR Guidelines I. *Accounting and Financial Reporting for Environmental Costs and Liabilities*: 5–27. (1999)	UNCTAD/ITE/EDS/4
ISAR Guidelines II. *Guideline for National Requirements for the Qualification of Professional Accountants*: 1–12. (1999)	UNCTAD/ITE/EDS/9
World Investment Report 1999: Foreign Direct Investment and the Challenge of Development. Chapter VI: Increasing financial resources and investment: 157–193.	UNCTAD/WIR/1999

Title	*Document No.*
World Investment Report 2000:Cross-border Mergers and Acquisitions and Development, Chapter IV: Trends in cross-border M&As: 99–136 and Chapter VI: FDI and development: Does mode of entry matter?: 159–209.	UNCTAD/WIR/2000
World Investment Report 2001: Promoting Linkages, Chapter VI: Key elements of a linkage promotion programme: 209–215 and Chapter V: Policies to strengthen linkage: 163–208	UNCTAD/WIR/2001
World Investment Report 2002: Transnational Corporations and Export Competitiveness, Chapter VI: Patterns of export competitiveness: 143–184 and Chapter VII: Policy measures: 197–220.	UNCTAD/WIR/2002
World Investment Report 2003: *FDI Policies for Development: National and International Perspectives*, Chapter VI, Section A and B: Home countries and investors: 155–170.	UNCTAD/WIR/2003

Decisions, Recommendations, Resolutions

UNCTAD Intergovernmental Machinery

Title	Document
International Trade	
The Final Act of UNCTAD I. (1964)	In: *Proceeding of the United Nations Conference on Trade and Development.* Geneva, 23 March – 16 June, United Nations: New York.
Resolution 21 (II) of UNCTAD II (1968)	In: *Proceedings of the United Nations Conference on Trade and Development. Second session.* (I) Report and Annexes. United Nations: New York.
Decision 75-IV of the TDB introducing the agreed conclusions of the special committee on preferences. (1970)	A/8015/Rev.1
Resolution 159 (VI) of UNCTAD VI on International trade in goods and services: Protectionism, structural adjustment and the international trading system	In: TD/326 (I)
UN General Assembly resolution 49/99. International trade and development. (1995)	In: A/RES/49/99
Money, Finance and Debt	
Resolution 222 (XXI) Section B: Report of the UNCTAD secretariat. Review of the implementation of trade and development board. (1983)	
Commodities	
Annex I. Resolutions, Declarations and other Decisions. Commodities problems and policies: Agenda item 10. (1968)	In: TD/97. *Proceeding in United Nations Conference on Trade and Development. Second session.* New Delhi (I): 34–38

Title	Document
Resolution 93 (IV) on the integrated programme for commodities. (1976) UNCTAD VI.	In http://icac.org/icac/ Projects/CommonFund/Admin/ resolution/pdf (original) or http:www.3.jaring.my/inro/res93.html

Competition Law and Policy

Resolution 25(II). 78th plenary meeting (1968). Programme for the liberalization and expansion of trade in manufactures and semi-manufactures (including processed and semi-processed primary commodities) of interest to developing countries' restrictive business practices	

LDCs

Resolution 24 (II) Special measures to be taken in favour of the least developed among the developing countries aimed at expanding their trade and improving their economic and social development.	In: *Proceeding of United Nations Conference on Trade and Development.* Second session, New Delhi, 1 February to 29 March 1968, (I) Report and Annexes.
Resolution 11 (II) Special problems of the land locked countries.	In: *Proceeding of United Nations Conference on Trade and Development.* Second session, New Delhi, 1 February to 29 March 1968, (I) Report and Annexes: 30–32.
Resolution 65 (III) Developing island countries	In: *Proceeding of the United Nations Conference on Trade and Development.* Third session, Santiago de Chile, 13 April to 21 May 1972, (I) Report and Annexes: 74

UN Shipping Conventions

with heavy involvement of UNCTAD

Title	Document Number
United Nations Convention on a Code of Conduct for Liner Conferences. (1974)	TD/CODE/13/Add.1
United Nations Convention on the Carriage of Goods by Sea, known as the Hamburg Rules, Annex I. (1978)	A/CONF.89/13
United Nations Convention on International Multimodal Transport of Goods. (1980)	TD/MT/CONF/17
United Nations Convention on Conditions for Registration of Ships. (1986)	UNCTAD/RS/CONF/23
International Convention on Maritime Liens and Mortgages. (1993)	A/CONF.162/7
International Convention on Arrest of Ships. (1999)	A/CONF.188/6